I0891135

Influences of Social Media on Consumer Decision-Making Processes in the Food and Grocery Industry

Theodore Tarnanidis
International Hellenic University, Greece

Maro Vlachopoulou
University of Macedonia, Greece

Jason Papathanasiou
University of Macedonia, Greece

IGI Global
PUBLISHER of TIMELY KNOWLEDGE

A volume in the Advances in Marketing, Customer Relationship Management, and E-Services (AMCRMES) Book Series

Published in the United States of America by
IGI Global
Business Science Reference (an imprint of IGI Global)
701 E. Chocolate Avenue
Hershey PA, USA 17033
Tel: 717-533-8845
Fax: 717-533-8661
E-mail: cust@igi-global.com
Web site: http://www.igi-global.com

Library of Congress Cataloging-in-Publication Data

Names: Tarnanidis, Theodore, 1977- editor. | Vlachopoulou, Maro, 1956- editor. | Papathanasiou, Jason, editor.
Title: Influences of social media on consumer decision-making processes in the food and grocery industry / edited by: Theodore Tarnanidis, Maro Vlachopoulou, and Jason Papathanasiou.
Description: Hershey, PA : Business Science Reference, [2023] | Includes bibliographical references and index. | Summary: "This comprehensive book explores the tireless efforts of grocery and food entrepreneurs to evaluate the farreaching effects of social media on the consumer decision-making process. It investigates various web-based social media platforms and tools, delves into the impact of social media and mobile apps, and examines the utilization of cutting-edge Information & Communication Technologies (RFID, QR codes, NFC, cloud, SaaS, mobile devices, robots, and more) within the grocery and food sector. The book also explores the interplay between digital marketing, online decision-making processes, and the intricacies of the grocery and food industry. Furthermore, it provides in-depth coverage of Multicriteria Decision Analysis (MCDA) techniques employed in the grocery and food industry, including the application of PROMETHEE methods"-- Provided by publisher.
Identifiers: LCCN 2023025886 (print) | LCCN 2023025887 (ebook) | ISBN 9781668488683 (hardcover) | ISBN 9781668488720 (paperback) | ISBN 9781668488690 (ebook)
Subjects: LCSH: Food industry and trade--Internet marketing. | Consumer behavior. | Social media--Influence. | Food industry and trade--Marketing--Technological innovations.
Classification: LCC HD9000.5 .I543 2023 (print) | LCC HD9000.5 (ebook) | DDC 338.19068/8--dc23/eng/20230626
LC record available at https://lccn.loc.gov/2023025886
LC ebook record available at https://lccn.loc.gov/2023025887

This book is published in the IGI Global book series Advances in Marketing, Customer Relationship Management, and E-Services (AMCRMES) (ISSN: 2327-5502; eISSN: 2327-5529)

British Cataloguing in Publication Data
A Cataloguing in Publication record for this book is available from the British Library.

Advances in Marketing, Customer Relationship Management, and E-Services (AMCRMES) Book Series

ISSN:2327-5502
EISSN:2327-5529

Editor-in-Chief: Eldon Y. Li, National Chengchi University, Taiwan & California Polytechnic State University, USA

MISSION

Business processes, services, and communications are important factors in the management of good customer relationship, which is the foundation of any well organized business. Technology continues to play a vital role in the organization and automation of business processes for marketing, sales, and customer service. These features aid in the attraction of new clients and maintaining existing relationships.

The Advances in Marketing, Customer Relationship Management, and E-Services (AMCRMES) Book Series addresses success factors for customer relationship management, marketing, and electronic services and its performance outcomes. This collection of reference source covers aspects of consumer behavior and marketing business strategies aiming towards researchers, scholars, and practitioners in the fields of marketing management.

COVERAGE

- Legal Considerations in E-Marketing
- Mobile CRM
- B2B marketing
- Social Networking and Marketing
- Web Mining and Marketing
- Telemarketing
- Online Community Management and Behavior
- Cases on Electronic Services
- Text Mining and Marketing
- Data mining and marketing

The Advances in Marketing, Customer Relationship Management, and E-Services (AMCRMES) Book Series (ISSN 2327-5502) is published by IGI Global, 701 E. Chocolate Avenue, Hershey, PA 17033-1240, USA, www.igi-global.com. This series is composed of titles available for purchase individually; each title is edited to be contextually exclusive from any other title within the series. For pricing and ordering information please visit http://www.igi-global.com/book-series/advances-marketing-customer-relationship-management/37150. Postmaster: Send all address changes to above address.

Titles in this Series

For a list of additional titles in this series, please visit:
http://www.igi-global.com/book-series/advances-marketing-customer-relationship-management/37150

Contemporary Approaches of Digital Marketing and the Role of Machine Intelligence
Afzal Sayed Munna (University of Sunderland in London, UK) Md Sadeque Imam Shaikh (University of Wales Trinity Saint David, UK) and Baha Uddin Kazi (Humber Institute of Technology and Advanced Learning, Canada)
Business Science Reference • copyright 2023 • 260pp • H/C (ISBN: 9781668477359) • US $250.00 (our price)

Social Media and Online Consumer Decision Making in the Fashion Industry
Theodore Tarnanidis (International Hellenic University, Greece) Eyridiki Papachristou (International Hellenic University, Greece) Michail Karypidis (International Hellenic University, Greece) and Vasileios Ismyrlis (Hellenic Open University, Greece & Hellenic Statistical Authority, Greece)
Business Science Reference • copyright 2023 • 393pp • H/C (ISBN: 9781668487532) • US $250.00 (our price)

Management and Marketing for Improved Retail Competitiveness and Performance
José Duarte Santos (Accounting and Business School, Polytechnic of Porto, Portugal) Inês Veiga Pereira (Accounting and Business School, Polytechnic of Porto, Portugal) and Paulo Botelho Pires (Centre for Organizational and Social Studies, Polytechnic of Porto, Portugal)
Business Science Reference • copyright 2023 • 457pp • H/C (ISBN: 9781668485743) • US $325.00 (our price)

Global Developments in Nation Branding and Promotion Theoretical and Practical Approaches
Andreas Masouras (Neapolis University, Cyprus) Sofia Daskou (Neapolis University, Cyprus) Victoria Pistikou (Democritus University of Thrace, Greece) Dimitrios Dimitriou (Democritus University of Thrace, Greece) and Tim Friesner (University of Winchester, UK)
Information Science Reference • copyright 2023 • 324pp • H/C (ISBN: 9781668459027) • US $240.00 (our price)

For an entire list of titles in this series, please visit:
http://www.igi-global.com/book-series/advances-marketing-customer-relationship-management/37150

IGI Global
PUBLISHER of TIMELY KNOWLEDGE

701 East Chocolate Avenue, Hershey, PA 17033, USA
Tel: 717-533-8845 x100 • Fax: 717-533-8661
E-Mail: cust@igi-global.com • www.igi-global.com

Editorial Advisory Board

Table of Contents

Preface xv

Chapter 1
The Influence of Social Media on Food Choices: A Bibliometric Approach 1
Şirin Gizem Köse, MEF University, Turkey
Ece Özer Çizer, Yıldız Technical University, Turkey

Chapter 2
Impact of Social Media on Consumer Decisiveness in the Food and Grocery Sector 24
Dharshini Karthikeyan, CHRIST University (Deemed), India
Ramya Barathi Manoharan, Annamalai University, India
Pavithra Karthikeyan, Meritto, India
S. Pradeep, Freshworks, India

Chapter 3
Greek Consumers' Perceptions on Sponsored Food Advertisement Through Social Media and Its Effects on Their Purchasing Behavior 56
Nikolaos Sklavounos, International Hellenic University, Greece & Perrotis College, American Farm School of Thessaloniki, Greece
George Kartsiotis, Perrotis College, American Farm School of Thessaloniki, Greece
Konstantinos Rebholz, Perrotis College, American Farm School of Thessaloniki, Greece

Chapter 4
Moderating Effects of Likelihood to Use In-Store Technology in Grocery Stores: Perceived Value of Retailtainment 86
Adesegun Oyedele, University of the Incarnate Word, USA
Fuat Firat, The University of Texas-Rio Grande Valley, USA
Monica Hernandez, Texas Lutheran University, USA
Emily Goenner Munson, St. Cloud State University, USA

Chapter 5
Exploring Mexican Attitudes Toward the Front Labeling System for Food and Beverages: A Twitter Analysis 111
Monica D. Hernandez, Texas Lutheran University, USA
Edith Galy, The University of Texas-Rio Grande Valley, USA

Chapter 6
Impact of Social Media Platforms on the Consumer Decision-Making Process in the Food and Grocery Industry 119
Tanu Gupta, KR Mangalam University, India
Pallavi Pandey, KR Mangalam University, India
Yogita Yashveer Raghav, KR Mangalam University, India

Chapter 7
How Customer Rating on Digital Restaurant Guides Influence Consumer Satisfaction: The Zomato Platform Experience 140
Alexandre Duarte, ICNOVA, FCSH, Universidade Nova de Lisboa, Portugal
Joana Fernandes, Catholic University of Portugal, Portugal
Claudia Pernencar, ICNOVA, FCSH, Universidade Nova de Lisboa, Portugal

Chapter 8
Grocery E-Commerce Transformation 173
Maria Kalyvaki, Minnesota State University, Mankato, USA

Chapter 9
Review and the Use of PROMETHEE Methods in Marketing (Problems) 196
Theodore K. Tarnanidis, University of Macedonia, Greece
Jason Papathanasiou, University of Macedonia, Greece
Maro Vlachopoulou, University of Macedonia, Greece
Bertrand Mareschal, Université Libre de Bruxelles, Belgium

Chapter 10
Social Media Adoption by the Greek Dairy Industry 213
Sotiris Karetsos, Agricultural University of Athens, Greece
Nikolaos Zafeirakopoulos, Agricultural University of Athens, Greece
Evi Papadopoulou, Agricultural University of Athens, Greece
Constantina Costopoulou, Agricultural University of Athens, Greece

Compilation of References 242

Related References 276

About the Contributors 307

Index 315

Detailed Table of Contents

Preface...xv

Chapter 1
The Influence of Social Media on Food Choices: A Bibliometric Approach........1
Şirin Gizem Köse, MEF University, Turkey
Ece Özer Çizer, Yıldız Technical University, Turkey

Social media channels are increasing day by day and the time spent on social media channels has become a significant part of the day. Social media, which is one of the facts that cannot be ignored, affects food choices to a great extent, as it does in every field. Being aware of the power of social media, food companies, and groceries also develop strategies for this medium and heavily use social media as a communication tool. In line with these developments and facts, this study aims to highlight the influence of social media on food. A bibliometric study has been conducted to enlighten the literature development on social media and food subjects. The results are expected to be helpful for both literature and practice as well as social media managers and food brand managers.

Chapter 2
Impact of Social Media on Consumer Decisiveness in the Food and Grocery Sector...24
Dharshini Karthikeyan, CHRIST University (Deemed), India
Ramya Barathi Manoharan, Annamalai University, India
Pavithra Karthikeyan, Meritto, India
S. Pradeep, Freshworks, India

Consumers are currently inclined to acknowledge online information but purchase food and grocery products offline. Also, the buyer's decision is coherent with the factors like income, age, social media influences, cost of products, etc. The chapter studies the Influence of Social Media on Consumer Decision-making in the food and Grocery Sector. As per the findings, the effectiveness of marketing tools and techniques has a homogeneous effect on all GenX, GenY, GenZ. Contrary to expectation, Gen X was most influenced by offers. Social media equally influenced all generations to make purchases, irrespective of their incomes. Post Covid there is a shift in consumption habits disregarding generations and income brackets of all the participants.

Chapter 3
Greek Consumers' Perceptions on Sponsored Food Advertisement Through Social Media and Its Effects on Their Purchasing Behavior................................56
Nikolaos Sklavounos, International Hellenic University, Greece & Perrotis College, American Farm School of Thessaloniki, Greece
George Kartsiotis, Perrotis College, American Farm School of Thessaloniki, Greece
Konstantinos Rebholz, Perrotis College, American Farm School of Thessaloniki, Greece

As the usage of social media becomes more and more infused in the daily life of billions of individuals, paid advertisement via them offers companies an enormous degree of visibility and exposure. This research investigates the perceptions, attitudes and behavioral responses of young Greek consumers regarding sponsored food products in order to determine the impact of this advertising method on their purchasing behavior. This study applies quantitative research methods to collect primary data besides the review of secondary sources from the existing literature. The collected data are analysed with the appropriate statistical tools and the research findings are discussed thoroughly. The results of the study reveal indicators and information about how food brands and sponsored food advertisement on social media are perceived by young social media users and how users respond and behave when in contact with sponsored advertisements while browsing on social media platforms. Finally, recommendations for future research are also presented.

Chapter 4
Moderating Effects of Likelihood to Use In-Store Technology in Grocery Stores: Perceived Value of Retailtainment...86
Adesegun Oyedele, University of the Incarnate Word, USA
Fuat Firat, The University of Texas-Rio Grande Valley, USA
Monica Hernandez, Texas Lutheran University, USA
Emily Goenner Munson, St. Cloud State University, USA

The purpose of this study is the assessment of the moderating effects of consumers' likelihood to use instore technologies on the relationship between retailtainment value and satisfaction with retailtainment in physical grocery stores. A questionnaire designed to test our model was administered to 332 undergraduate students. The data were analyzed using AMOS-SEM. The results show that perceived benefit, enjoyment, and unique values of retailtainment were significant in explicating satisfaction with retailtainment. Regarding the interaction effects of likelihood to use instore technology, the results reveal the positive relationship between human interactivity-instore, benefits, and unique values, and the dependent variable satisfaction with retailtaiment are stronger for individuals with low likelihood to use instore technologies. Results confirmed that retailtainment, which provides enjoyment and perceived informative benefits in terms of experience with the consumption of products, is likely to increase satisfaction and improve loyalty as well as propensity to return to the store.

Chapter 5
Exploring Mexican Attitudes Toward the Front Labeling System for Food and Beverages: A Twitter Analysis 111
Monica D. Hernandez, Texas Lutheran University, USA
Edith Galy, The University of Texas-Rio Grande Valley, USA

Recently, the Mexican government implemented a simple labeling system that would apply to 85% of the food products. The aim of the system is to report high amounts of calories, sugars, sodium, fats and trans fats. Labels are displayed on the front of the package individually or in groups. No studies have been conducted to analyze public attitudes toward the labeling system. In order to fill this gap, the purpose of the study is to conduct an exploratory analysis of the Mexican attitudes toward the new labeling system on Twitter. The Twitter API was used to collect tweets published between January 01, 2020 to June 30, 2021. QSR NVivo 12 software was used to conduct thematic content analysis. The emerged themes were related to consumer education, impact on the industry and businesses, and support or rejection to the labeling system. A category emerged as reflection of the unique cultural traditions.

Chapter 6
Impact of Social Media Platforms on the Consumer Decision-Making Process in the Food and Grocery Industry 119
Tanu Gupta, KR Mangalam University, India
Pallavi Pandey, KR Mangalam University, India
Yogita Yashveer Raghav, KR Mangalam University, India

The rise of online social networking platforms has created a network around the globe among people for communicating and interacting with each other. Customer's view of an organization's contributions and brand are probably going to impact a buy choice. This idea is the focus of an investigation into trends, entertainment, customization, electronic word-of-mouth, and interactivity, additionally, fadedness, risk, interactivity, and personalization were perceived; keywords were also examined in order to test social media marketing in the insurance industry. Moreover, few additional metrics are used to evaluate the success of social media marketing, such as immediacy, accessibility, responses, information, interactivity, entertainment, perceived risk, trendiness, and customizability are all important factors. Also due to sudden hit of covid-19, the change in trend of customer purchase behaviour and interest is also discussed.

Chapter 7
How Customer Rating on Digital Restaurant Guides Influence Consumer Satisfaction: The Zomato Platform Experience 140
Alexandre Duarte, ICNOVA, FCSH, Universidade Nova de Lisboa, Portugal
Joana Fernandes, Catholic University of Portugal, Portugal
Claudia Pernencar, ICNOVA, FCSH, Universidade Nova de Lisboa, Portugal

Nowadays, anybody is a potential food critic, only requiring a smartphone to write an opinion and evaluate a restaurant through a digital app. As people trust other people's opinions - even strangers - more than the service provider's own marketing strategies, restaurant recommendation apps are great tools to analyze and improve performance. This keeps up with a recent consumer behaviour: gathering opinions that have impact on both ends of the consumer-organization relationship. This research aims to identify the relevant factors when classifying a restaurant and understand if Zomato app influences a restaurant choice, by identifying the features that lead a consumer to choose restaurant X over Y, whether it's a workday lunch, family lunches, dinners with friends or a romantic dinner. The chapter analyzes Zomato's case study: competition along catering industry dimension and the competitive position. Results point to how consumers perceive restaurant experience and how they influence others' decisions with online evaluating.

Chapter 8
Grocery E-Commerce Transformation 173
Maria Kalyvaki, Minnesota State University, Mankato, USA

This chapter traces the evolution of grocery shopping, spotlighting the rise of e-commerce in the sector, particularly since 2020 due to COVID-19. The pandemic accelerated digital sales growth, condensing a decade's progress into mere months. This shift towards convenient, time-saving shopping methods was instrumental in integrating e-commerce into the food industry, including the fresh fruit and vegetable market. Amid COVID-19 restrictions, e-commerce became a vital food distribution tool, bolstering supply chain resilience. The chapter reviews the status of online grocery shopping, discussing customer hesitations and strategies to boost market share. Urging retailers to modernize business models, restructure supply chains, and develop efficient, eco-friendly local food delivery systems. Policy suggestions and vital investment areas for sustainable e-commerce development are presented. It advocates for urban governments to foster a supportive environment that capitalizes on e-commerce while minimizing its adverse impacts on traditional retail, traffic, and greenhouse gas emissions.

Chapter 9
Review and the Use of PROMETHEE Methods in Marketing (Problems) 196
Theodore K. Tarnanidis, University of Macedonia, Greece
Jason Papathanasiou, University of Macedonia, Greece
Maro Vlachopoulou, University of Macedonia, Greece
Bertrand Mareschal, Université Libre de Bruxelles, Belgium

The method of PROMETHEE belongs to Multiple Criteria Decision Making (MCDM) techniques, which helps decision-makers to examine problems where there are multiple and conflicting criteria calculated in different parameters and units. Furthermore, they help people in assessing all the information included in a problem from a realistic and pragmatic viewpoint (Vincke, 1992).The next table shows a classification of the most widely used MCDM methods. According to relevant scholars (Triantaphyllou et al., 1998; Georgiadis et al., 2013) the general format of a PROMETHEE task involves the construction of the measurement analysis of the problem with the identification of relevant criteria and alternatives, the estimation of the relative importance and impact of the weights (i.e. statistical measures), and the final stage involves the decision of the best evaluations that comes from the ranking/assessment of each alternative.

Chapter 10
Social Media Adoption by the Greek Dairy Industry 213
Sotiris Karetsos, Agricultural University of Athens, Greece
Nikolaos Zafeirakopoulos, Agricultural University of Athens, Greece
Evi Papadopoulou, Agricultural University of Athens, Greece
Constantina Costopoulou, Agricultural University of Athens, Greece

Social media have become an important part of modern everyday life and are used for various purposes such as communication and interaction, content sharing, brand awareness, customer engagement, and market research. Numerous businesses employ them as marketing tools, adopting various strategies to achieve their goals. The objective of this chapter is to investigate the social media adoption by the dairy industry in Greece since the last years it has been hit hard by the COVID-19 pandemic and the energy crisis. More specifically, this chapter provides a literature review of social media in dairy industry and examines the digital presence of Greek dairy companies. Next, it analyses data from social media usage of 55 dairy companies in correspondence to their annual turnover for 2022. The results indicate that dairy companies can enhance their business outcomes by leveraging social media more effectively to harness their positive influence.

Compilation of References 242

Related References 276

About the Contributors 307

Index 315

Preface

Entrepreneurs in the grocery retail industry face many difficulties in transforming their digital operations and services. Therefore, the current book aims to examine how businesses use online communication strategies through the digital marketing techniques for social media, in order to influence consumers' purchase decision-making processes.

We can argue that the grocery sector includes supermarkets, food shops, convenience stores, kiosks, mini markets, as well as other street markets. The specific sector shows an increasing number of specialized food stores all over the globe. For example, policy makers are trying to offer competitive and branded products that have better quality, taste and environmentally friendly ingredients. Additionally, they are trying to find new ways to influence consumer purchase decisions through the crafting of digital strategies with the use of social media metrics and analytics in marketing.

In recent years, social media are powerful communication platforms that are used for marketing, promotion and customer service. This radical change in marketing processes has brought a new aspect to monitor customer behavior and preferences. With the use of social media communications, sellers are trying to successfully reach the target audience by positioning and categorizing the data. What is more, MCDM has been used at all levels of agricultural- and environmental-related decision making problems, ranging from farm-level decisions through to agricultural policy decision making. As such, MCDM methods are used in the area of marketing, regarding the selection of different grocery and food products, where multiple criteria exist.

The main objective of the book is to analyze how companies in the current sector take advantage of the use of social media communication technologies and influence the decision-making process of consumers. Web-based social media tools are pertinent for businesses to energize their core competencies and capabilities. The book consists of nine chapters (9) representing all issues the use of social media in the current sector.

Chapter 1, *The Influence of Social Media on Food Choices: A Bibliometric Approach* investigates the influence of sociamedia on food choices. A bibliometrics tudy has been conducted to enlighten the literature development on social media and food subjects. The results are expected to be helpful for both literature and practice as well as social media managers and food brand managers. Results of the bibliometric analysis show that "marketing", "social marketing", "food", "food marketing", and "advertising" are the most repetitive words in the articles. The findings also underline the strong relationship of food marketing with social marketing. Among the reasons for these, as mentioned in the literature review, marketing communication messages especially targeted at children and adolescents are focal points and the marketing of unhealthy food products is highly criticized in terms of social marketing. Furthermore, the most repetitive words are found as "social media", "sustainability", "social media marketing", "children", "covid-19", "nutrition" "adolescents", "digital marketing" and "food industry". From the most repeated words, it is deduced that the results of the relationship between Covid-19 and nutrition are still being investigated, and sustainability maintains its impact and importance in the food sector, as it is in every field.

Chapter 2, *Impact of Social Media on Consumer Decisiveness in the Food and Grocery Sector*, shows that consumers are currently inclined to acknowledge online information but purchase food and grocery products offline. Also, the buyer's decision is coherent with the factors like income, age, social media influences, cost of products, etc. The chapter investigates the influence of social Media on consumer decision-making in the food and grocery sector. As per the findings, the effectiveness of marketing tools and techniques has a homogeneous effect on all GenX, GenY, GenZ. Contrary to expectation, Gen X was most influenced by offers. Social media equally influenced all generations to make purchases, irrespective of their incomes. Post Covid there is a shift in consumption habits disregarding generations and income brackets of all the participants.

Chapter 3, *Greek Consumers' Perceptions on Sponsored Food Advertisement Through Social Media and Its Effects on Their Purchasing Behavior*, provides an examination of the usage of social media becomes more and more infused in the daily life of billions of individuals, paid advertisement via them offers companies an enormous degree of visibility and exposure. This research investigates the perceptions, attitudes and behavioral responses of young Greek consumers regarding sponsored food products in order to determine the impact of this advertising method on their purchasing behavior. This study applies quantitative research methods to collect primary data besides the review of secondary sources from the existing literature. The collected data are analysed with the appropriate statistical tools and the research findings are discussed thoroughly. The results of the study reveal indicators and information about how food brands and sponsored food advertisement on social media are perceived by young social media users and how users respond and behave when in contact with sponsored advertisements while browsing on social media platforms. Finally, recommendations for future research are also presented.

Chapter 4, *Moderating Effects of Likelihood to Use In-Store Technology in Grocery Stores: Perceived Value of Retailtainment*, assesses the moderating effects of consumers' likelihood to use instore technologies on the relationship between retailtainment value and satisfaction with retailtainment in physical grocery stores. A questionnaire designed to test our model was administered to 332 undergraduate students. The data were analyzed using AMOS-SEM. The results show that perceived benefit, enjoyment, and unique values of retailtainment were significant in explicating satisfaction with retailtainment. Regarding the interaction effect of likelihood to use instore technology, the results reveal A positive relationship between human interactivity-instore, benefits, and unique values, and the dependent variable satisfaction with retailtaiment IS stronger for individuals with low likelihood to use instore technologies. Results confirmed that retailtainment technologies, which provide enjoyment and perceived informative benefits in terms of experience with the consumption of products, are likely to increase satisfaction and improve loyalty, and propensity to return to the store.

Chapter 5, *Exploring Mexican Attitudes Toward the Front Labeling System for Food and Beverages: A Twitter Analysis*, provides an explanation and further analysis of the Mexican government labeling system of the food products'). The aim of the system was initially crafted in order to report high amounts of calories, sugars, sodium, fats and trans fats. Labels are displayed on the front of the package individually or in groups. No studies have been conducted to analyze public attitudes toward the labeling system. In order to fill this gap, the purpose of the study is to conduct an exploratory analysis of the Mexican attitudes toward the new labeling system on Twitter. The Twitter API was used to collect tweets, published from January 2020 to June 30, 2021. QSR NVivo 12 software was used to conduct thematic content analysis. The emerged themes were related to consumer education, impact on the industry and businesses, and support or rejection to the labeling system. A category emerged as reflection of the unique cultural traditions.

Chapter 6, *Impact of Social Media Platforms on the Consumer Decision-Making Process in the Food and Grocery Industry,* proposes that the rise of online social networking platforms has created a network around the globe among people for communicating and interacting with each other. Customer's view of an organization's contributions and brand are probably going to impact a buy choice. This idea is the focus of an investigation into trends, entertainment, customization, electronic word-of-mouth, and interactivity, additionally, fadedness, risk, interactivity, and personalization were perceived; keywords were also examined in order to test social media marketing in the insurance industry. Moreover, few additional metrics are used to evaluate the success of social media marketing, such as immediacy, accessibility, responses, information, interactivity, entertainment, perceived risk, trendiness, and customizability are all important factors. As such, due to sudden hit of covid-19, the change in trend of customer purchase behaviour and interest is also discussed.

Chapter 7, *How Customer Rating on Digital Restaurant Guides Influence Consumer Satisfaction: The Zomato Platform Experience*, explores how the internet, companies have relinquished control over information that is shared and have become dependent on others' opinions. This means that consumer behaviour has also changed, as individuals presently wish to feel satisfaction when sharing experiences of all kinds on social networks. As people trust other people's opinions - even strangers - more than the service provider's own marketing strategies, restaurant recommendation apps are great tools to analyze and improve performance. Hence, this research identifies the relevant factors when classifying a restaurant and understand if Zomato app influences a restaurant choice, by identifying the features that lead a consumer to choose restaurant X over Y, whether it's a workday lunch, family lunches, dinners with friends or a romantic dinner. The chapter analyzes Zomato's case study: competition along catering industry dimension and the competitive position. Results point to how consumers perceive restaurant experience and how they influence others' decisions with online evaluating.

Chapter 8, *Grocery E-Commerce Transformation*, explores the evolution of grocery shopping, spotlighting the rise of e-commerce in the sector, particularly since 2020 due to COVID-19. The pandemic accelerated digital sales growth, condensing a decade's progress into mere months. This shift towards convenient, time-saving shopping methods was instrumental in integrating e-commerce into the food industry, including the fresh fruit and vegetable market. Amid COVID-19 restrictions, e-commerce became a vital food distribution tool, bolstering supply chain resilience. The chapter reviews the status of online grocery shopping, discussing customer hesitations and strategies to boost market share. Urging retailers to modernize business models, restructure supply chains, and develop efficient, eco-friendly local food delivery systems. Policy suggestions and vital investment areas for sustainable e-commerce development are presented. It advocates for urban governments to foster a supportive environment that capitalizes on e-commerce while minimizing its adverse impacts on traditional retail, traffic, and greenhouse gas emissions.

Chapter 9, *Review and the Use of PROMETHEE Methods in Marketing (Problems)*, provides an analysis and a review of PROMETHEE methods to the examination of marketing problems for which are appropriate. We, therefore refer to the classic work of Brans (1982), which later developed further by Brans and Vicke (1985), Brans and Mareschal (1985), Mareschal and Brans (1988) and Brans and Mareschal (2005). As such in this research we offer a treatment of PROMETHEE methods (mathematical, computational software-Visual PROMETHEE) to marketing problems. The collection of reference papers included in the use PROMETHEE can serve to guide researchers, and PhD students interested in evaluaring marketing decisions for promoting the use of social media technologies by the ranging of best to the worst option.

Chapter 10, *Social Media Adoption by the Greek Dairy Industry*, describes the importance of the use of social media as an important part of modern everyday life, which are used for various purposes such as communication and interaction, content sharing, brand awareness, customer engagement, and market research.Numerous businesses employ them as marketing tools, adopting various strategies to achieve their goals. This chapter investigates the social media adoption by the dairy industry in Greece since the last years it has been hit hard by the COVID-19 pandemic and the energy crisis. More specifically, this chapter provides a literature review of social media in dairy industry andexamines the digital presence of Greek dairy companies. Next, it analyses data from social media usage of 55 dairy companies in correspondence to their annual turnover for 2022. The results indicate that dairy companies can enhance their business outcomes by leveraging social media more effectively to harness their positive influence.

Further the proposed book would benefit advanced students and researchers. The collection of reference papers in the book may serve to inspire future researchers, and PhD students, as well in promoting the use of social media technologies in analyzing consumer decision-making processes of the food sector. Finally, we believe, the book will bring together scholars of different research backgrounds.

Thanks are also given to the editorial board for supporting it, and particularly those who contributed with research work and reviewing of submitted papers. We hope the published book *Influences of Social Media on Consumer Decision-Making Processes in the Food and Grocery Industry* to be a major catalyst within representing ideas and research work in the specific field.

Theodore Tarnanidis
International Hellenic University, Greece

Maro Vlachopoulou
University of Macedonia, Greece

Jason Papathanasiou
University of Macedonia, Greece

Chapter 1
The Influence of Social Media on Food Choices:
A Bibliometric Approach

Şirin Gizem Köse
https://orcid.org/0000-0003-4075-7166
MEF University, Turkey

Ece Özer Çizer
https://orcid.org/0000-0002-8597-2073
Yıldız Technical University, Turkey

ABSTRACT

Social media channels are increasing day by day and the time spent on social media channels has become a significant part of the day. Social media, which is one of the facts that cannot be ignored, affects food choices to a great extent, as it does in every field. Being aware of the power of social media, food companies, and groceries also develop strategies for this medium and heavily use social media as a communication tool. In line with these developments and facts, this study aims to highlight the influence of social media on food. A bibliometric study has been conducted to enlighten the literature development on social media and food subjects. The results are expected to be helpful for both literature and practice as well as social media managers and food brand managers.

DOI: 10.4018/978-1-6684-8868-3.ch001

INTRODUCTION

Increasing usage of social media, which is one of the most important realities of today, is one of the most discussed topics. Social media is far from just being a fad and becoming mainstream (Quesenberry, 2019). Internet and Web 2.0 technologies in today's society have triggered the growth of social media platforms and significantly altered the environment in which customers interact (Nash, 2019). Due to the convenience and opportunities it provides to both businesses and consumers, the use of social media by both companies and consumers and the number of users are increasing rapidly. The numbers show that social media has experienced an astounding growth in use; as of January 2023, the number of worldwide internet users was 5.16 billion, which is 64.4 percent of the global population. In addition, there were 4.76 billion social media users in the world, which is 59.4 percent of the world's population. On the other hand, Facebook is still the market leader of all social media platforms. Four of the biggest social media platforms, namely Facebook, WhatsApp, Facebook Messenger, and Instagram belonging to Meta Platform (Statista, 2023).

Today social media affects practically every aspect of the human experience. The fact that social media makes people able to share ideas, personal traits, and daily activities with social networks has inevitably altered how people perceive themselves and their social worlds (Bayer et al, 2020). Social media is defined as an internet-based channel that helps users to communicate with each other as well as present themselves. This interaction could be real-time and also not synchronous (Carr & Hayes, 2015). Social media has inevitably become the reality of today as a phenomenon that affects both our daily lives and our social relations. Social media tools, which have an impact on every aspect of life, are also used by brand managers as effective marketing tools. Social media, which is a very useful way for the message they want to convey to reach the target audience, is also preferred in terms of fast feedback and measurability.

Social media has brought three critical changes to the markets. First, social media facilitates the connection between businesses and customers in ways that weren't possible before. Second, social media have changed how businesses and customers communicate with and affect one another. Third, companies are increasingly becoming better at managing customer interactions and improving corporate decision-making because of social media data (Li et al., 2021). Since brands have a high interest in social media, social media has also become a channel for commercial activity. Brands are striving to be influential on social media platforms and strengthen their relationships with their consumers by generating high engagement (Kırcova et al., 2018). Everyday, more and more companies are recognizing the value of social media as a strategic tool for user engagement, brand and product promotion, and relationship building (Shiau et al.,2018). When a company wants to increase media coverage of the brand or affect the consumers in their decisions, social media marketing is highly relevant (Tuten, 2021). Companies use a variety of social media sites, including Facebook, Snapchat, Twitter, and others, for social media marketing. Social media platform selection is chosen by considering marketing strategy and target audiences (Dwivedi et al.,2021). Food brands also benefit from users' social networks and increase the reach and personal relevance of their marketing messages by utilizing the interactive and social aspects of social media to market products (Freeman et al., 2014).

Researchers from several areas have turned their attention to social media use in recent years, particularly because of the widespread use of social media programs by smartphone users of all ages. Changes have taken place across numerous industries as a result of social media's strong presence in our lives. Individuals' behaviors have altered in many sectors, including education, marketing, business, health, and sports, which has affected how we communicate and conduct business (Ünal, 2020). The food industry is also one of the leading sectors affected by the increasing use of social media. People make food choices based on individual and environmental elements (Shipman, 2022). Social media is one of the tools that people get suggestions. Social media is also used to learn new recipes and increase the number of food choices (Simeone & Scarpato, 2020). The choice of food and the choice of materials in the preparation of food is affected by social media trends, and it has begun to be seen as a socially accepted activity for people to share their food on social media. In this regard, it would be fruitful to explore the literature development on the effect of social media on food choices.

Therefore, the aim of this study is to understand the influence of social media on food choices by making a bibliometric analysis. In this direction, this book chapter is framed as follows: in the first part, the literature on the subject is explained, and then bibliometric analysis is applied to the subject. Finally, the conclusion part is presented.

LITERATURE REVIEW

Social Media

The digital revolution has made the biggest influence on consumer behavior, and as more and more people regularly log on to the internet, its influence will grow significantly (Solomon, 2020). The production and distribution of information have been faster and easier with the internet. In parallel with the proliferation of the internet, social media platforms like blogs, social networking sites, and online communities have opened new ways to receive and, more importantly, provide information (Rutsaerd et al., 2013; Krupa-Kotara et al.2023). Social media is considered one of the largest information sources; consumers utilize the internet and social media to learn more about goods or services (Dedeoğlu, 2019). Social media offers individuals a free and interactive environment. The users of social media share their feelings and thoughts through various platforms, and they might be supported by other users. Information and ideas are spreading faster than ever before in any media environment, and the ideas can even turn into actions by being transferred from the virtual environment to the real world (Ayan et al., 2019).

Social media comprises online tools, media, and platforms which are used to foster collaboration, communication, and content sharing (Erkan & Evans, 2016; Pilar et al.,2021). Social media can be viewed as a technology-centered ecosystem where a wide range of complex and varied behaviors, interactions, and exchanges that involve multiple interrelated actors such as individuals, companies and governmental agencies can take place (Appel et al.,2019). Social media is now more than a communication tool; it is a medium that affects how people live and consume by changing socialization and communication methods (Dedeoğlu & Kabasakal, 2019). Social media has become a communication platform that is used by many people of all ages for different reasons such as communicating, gaining information, sharing their experiences and spending free time. This new communication tool has opened a brand new era in the communication age. It is seen that many people in society, especially young individuals, have started to use social media tools for very different purposes in all areas of life as social networking sites have become a part of daily life. The high amount of time spent on social media has affected not only our social life but also our consumption habits (Engin & İbiş 2016).

Nowadays, social media is considered as a main tool for brands to market themselves. Social media platforms are greatly used for marketing, promotion, lead generation, market research and also for commercial purposes. The fact that social media helps to engage and interact with potential customers in real time also increases customer satisfaction (Pallas, 2019). Recent studies found that social media marketing enhances brand equity (Sağtaş, 2022) and purchase intention (Sağtaş, 2022, Alkış & Karakan, 2021). Traditional marketing, advertising, and public relations initiatives are also more successful when using social media. Integration is vital in the process and running a marketing, advertising, or public relations campaign together with social media brings fruitful results (Quesenberry, 2019) such as consumer engagement (Dwivedi et al., 2021) Social media consumers differ from other consumer types because they are more engaged and they react quickly to anything. Companies active on social media can promote products and connect with consumers more rapidly, and receive instant feedback (Basev, 2022). They also utilize social media for new product introductions since social media eases social interaction and is useful for harnessing the power of word of mouth (WOM). Those features can increase the number of customers reached and speed up the dissemination of information about the new products (Baum et al., 2019). When companies noticed that having favorable reviews had a great impact on the consumer decision-making process as a result of eWom, they moved towards social media marketing (Nash, 2019).

Social Media and Food Choice

Marketing in general affects food preferences, choices, and consumption (Cairns et al., 2013). Social media is one of the tools that altered consumers' consumption patterns to affect purchasing decisions and came to the forefront as a new method of competing with other enterprises (Acar et al., 2021). The digital revolution and the widespread use of social media have altered eating patterns and food perception. Social media users post pictures of their meals eating experiences frequently (Çaycı, 2019). The expansion of social media brings customers more food alternatives they might not otherwise be aware of. Both horizontal information exchange within social networks and vertical communication from producers are information sources for food choices (Teerakapibal & Melanthiou, 2020). The visual and performance quality of food has significance for the restaurant and food business. The dishes that get the most popular on social media are often those that look the best rather than those that taste the best. The look of the food has more chance to be viral when compared to the taste. Therefore, having a strong social media presence in the first place and then making food that goes viral would provide fruitful marketing strategy solutions (Turner, 2022).

Social media is frequently used by consumers to share and seek out food information either actively or passively. Consumers might passively look for information about food or food-related behavior or actively share food related information (Hamshaw et al., 2018). There are some prominent reasons to explain food-sharing behavior on social media. Being proud of what we have made ourselves, recording a special event or occasion to remember later, documenting what we have eaten and keeping a food diary. In addition, sharing food tells something about us that we want to reinforce and sometimes we share food on social media just because the food looks nice or different (Turner, 2022). Social media also offers recipes that increase food choices and help people to arrange meals (Vaterlaus et al., 2015). In addition, social media is also used as a tool for self-presentation (Dedeoğlu & Kabasakal, 2019). Photos, videos and written content with food content are frequently shared on social media and accordingly, food blogs, food forums and food-related travel groups in online social networks have increased. Users share photos of their eating experiences with various popular tags. The content they share shapes the virtual identity and social identity of the individual (Çaycı, 2019). Social media enables consumers to share their eating and drinking experiences. They can influence the preferences of others by commenting, or they pursue new experiences with the influence of other individuals and want to try different foods (Seçer & Boğa, 2017).

Studies show the effect of social media on eating behaviors. A recent study underlines the importance of social media concerning adolescent eating; according to the study, self-reported exposure to food marketing and overall food messages on social media has positive relationships with eating attitudes, behaviors, perceived norms and food literacy among adolescents (Qutteina et al., 2022). Sharing or following experiences on social media is particularly important for food and beverage businesses since consumers can not try the products or services beforehand. In order to satisfy their eating and drinking needs, as well as other needs, potential customers can determine their choices through the use of social media (Pekerşen & Kaplan, 2020; Acar, 2021). There are also studies highlighting the importance of social media marketing on food choice. Hanaysha's (2016) research shows that social media advertising affects all dimensions of brand equity which are brand image, brand loyalty, brand preference, and brand leadership for fast-food restaurants. The findings of this study underline the importance of social media advertisements in improving the brand image of food and restaurant brands and building brand loyalty. A recent study revealed that the information dimension of social media marketing activities of food and beverage companies positively influences brand loyalty and customer inspiration. Oh the other hand, it was found that the entertainment dimension of social media marketing activities affects brand loyalty positively in the food and beverage business (Rahimi, & Kırkbir, 2022). Another research aimed to understand how Youtube food channels influence the tasting behavioral intent. Results show that the dimensions of presenting experience, forming empathy and cyber community positively affects behavioral intention of the tasting (Uçan et al., 2021). Aktaş et al., (2022) also found that gastronomy blogs affect tasting behavior and Açar et al. (2021) revealed that shares in social media influence the choices and decisions made about the food and beverage companies. According to Engin & İbiş's (2016) research, students utilize social media to get information about products and services and especially they follow the campaigns on social media. Furthermore, they use social media reviews as a selection criterion when deciding about food and beverage they consume. Cankul et al. (2018) found that food and beverage companies actively utilize social media tools, take advantage of social media to conduct advertising and marketing campaigns, and engage with their target market's clients using social media more quickly, easily, affordably, and effectively. The study also points out that food and beverage businesses respond to customer requests more quickly in an interactive virtual environment.

There is lots of food-related content on social media. Ventura et al. (2021) made a systematic review on food and social media. According to the review, studies can be divided into two categories based on the direction of communication flow: from (customer as message sender) and to consumers (consumer as a receiver). User-generated content, information measures and risk communication, digital marketing and exposure were found as fundamental categories.

Sometimes social media might have negative effects; especially in the food industry. Social media is criticized because of the possibility that regular social media exposure to marketing messaging from food and drink companies may promote or strengthen unhealthy eating habits (Klassen et al., 2018). Unhealthy food marketing is a major risk factor for childhood obesity (Tan et al., 2018). A study examined YouTube video blogs of influencers well-known among kids in order to ascertain the quantity and type of food and drink cues featured. According to the study, "less healthy" cues were repeated more than "healthy" ones and they were characterized positively (Coates et al., 2019). Lately, research proved that even if the food is unhealthy, adolescents may favor the product marketed by their favorite influencer (Kucharczuk et al., 2022). Another important issue to be addressed is misinformation disseminated by social media, which is even more important for the food industry since the products are directly related to the health of the consumers. As Diekman et al. (2022) point, the widespread use of social media has given trained or credentialed professionals in the scientific community additional chances to interact with customers and the general public. Self-proclaimed experts or health gurus use social media tools to have more followers, affect ideas, and draw attention by disseminating (often false) advice on food and nutrition.

Vaterlaus et al. (2015) underlined that although social media increased food choices by paving the way to reach more food recipes, it might also prevent teenagers and young adults from making healthy food decisions. In addition, the fact that you can target a specific audience via social media blurred the line between enjoyment and advertising (Greene et al., 2021). Ventura et al. (2021) found that social media may have a virtuous effect, it may increase knowledge and information but on the other side, it can also have a bad effect on individuals' behavior such as increasing unhealthy food consumption. While profiling consumers and targeting advertising makes social media the "enemy", disseminating health and research content to the right people makes it "friend" (Vassallo et al., 2021). These dual effects of social media have made it more important than ever to examine this subject.

Social media influencers are another essential issue that needs to be addressed when it comes to the effects of social media. Both influencers and consumers have the power in the novel sector that was created by social media tools. In today's world, consumers also create new content on social media rather than just consuming it (Erdoğmuş & Karakaya, 2022). Influencers create and publish content to followers that they have built on social media platforms (Grau, 2022). Because they can access many people and create engagement with their followers, influencers have become a central part of social media marketing (Tuten, 2021). Influencers are defined as people who consistently express their opinions on their preferred social media channels and actively create content such as words, photos, and videos. Influencers are followed by large social media audiences (Sun et al., 2022). Social media influencers also establish and maintain connections with followers and they can inform, and entertain the followers and maybe affect their opinions, attitudes, and actions via personal branding (Dhanesh & Duthler, 2019). According to Jiménez-Castillo and Sánchez-Fernández's (2019) study, followers' perceived influence is positively related to followers' positive word-of-mouth (WOM) about the brands influencer recommendation and purchase intention.

The rise of social media has made this channel stand out as a business area, and many content producers and influencers have been included in this system. Some of the research on social media and food choices has also focused on influencer marketing. The food environment that influencers create with their content is very important. The fact that the majority of Influencer marketing is done on low-nutrient foods and beverages should be taken into account in the regulations made on this subject.The use of platforms like TikTok, YouTube, and Instagram among kids calls for the creation of effective policies, as well as measures to ensure that they are followed (Winzer et al., 2022). Another study found that influencer marketing raises children's immediate consumption of the promoted snack compared to other brands (Coates et al., 2019). Influencers using social media also help consumers to shape food-related decisions. For example, Satı & Kazançoğlu (2020) found that the perceived usefulness of food influencers' advice positively affects the intention to purchase food products and services.

RESEARCH METHOD

In the study, a bibliometric analysis was made of the studies in the literature from the past to the present regarding the concept of social media on food choices. Bibliometric analysis is useful for examining and probing vast amounts of scientific data. The analysis helps to explore a particular field's evolutionary history and also clarifies emerging areas in that specific area (Donthu et al.,2021). For analysis, articles containing the keywords "social media", "food or grocery" and "marketing" were searched from the Web of Science database. A total of 1010 articles were reached. Bibliometric analysis was applied to the articles with the R Studio analysis program.

Figure 1. Word cloud

FINDINGS AND DISCUSSION

Figure 1 includes the 50 most repeated words in the data set. Among these words, it is seen that words such as "marketing", "social marketing", "food", "food marketing", "advertising" and "obesity" are frequently used in articles.

In Figure 2, the word tree of the keywords in the data set is given. The word tree shows the frequency distributions of the keywords in order. In addition to the most prominent words in the word cloud in Figure 1, the most recurring keyword in the dataset is "social media". In addition, the keywords "sustainability ", "social media marketing", "children", "covid-19", "nutrition" "adolescents", "digital marketing" and "food industry" in the word tree are frequently used keywords in studies the concept of social media on food choice in the literature.

In Figure 3, the distribution of the trending topics from 2010 to the present in the studies carried out within the scope of social media on food choice the literature by years is given. The prominent word in the trend topics graph in 2010 is "food safety". The concepts of "public health" and "diet", on the other hand, are among the topics that were frequently studied in 2011 and 2012, respectively. In 2018, there was an increase in the number of studies focusing on social media-oriented

Figure 2. Word tree

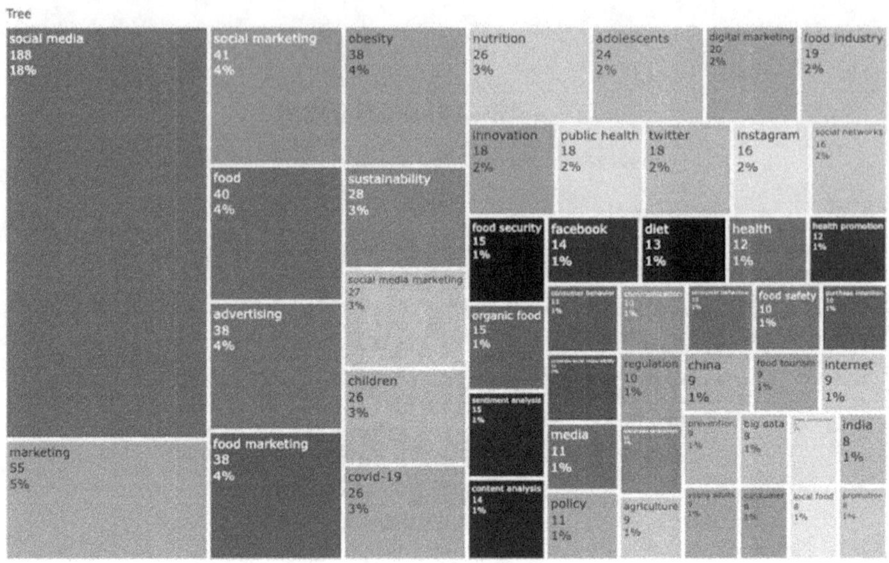

Figure 3. Trend topics

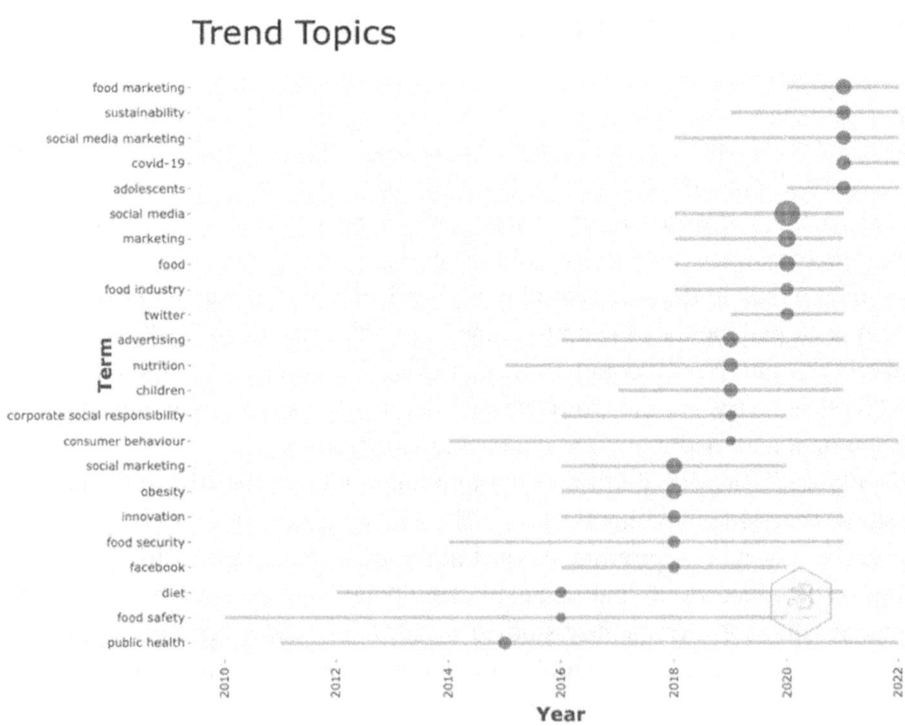

concepts such as "social marketing", "innovation" and "facebook". In addition to these concepts, studies on the concepts of "obesity" and "food security" were also frequently studied in 2018. The studies carried out between 2018-2020 focused on "consumer behavior", "corporate social responsibility", "children", "nutrition" and "advertising". It is seen that the studies carried out in the period from 2020 to the present are focused on the effect of Covid-19. In general, the concepts of "sustainability" and "social media" have gained importance in the studies carried out in the last period.

In Figure 4, the thematic map regarding the prominent themes in studies on the scope of social media on food choice is given. The themes in the upper right corner of a thematic map are called motor themes. Motor themes show the most important and developed main areas of study for that period. It is seen that the studies in the motor themes section within the scope of social media on food choice take place in one cluster. This cluster, "sustainability", "food industry" and "innovation" topics are frequently discussed and studied together.

The section in the upper left part of the thematic map is called niche themes. The subjects in this section have strong ties among themselves and differ from other subjects. In the first cluster of niche themes, it is seen that "consumer", "promotion"

Figure 4. Thematic map

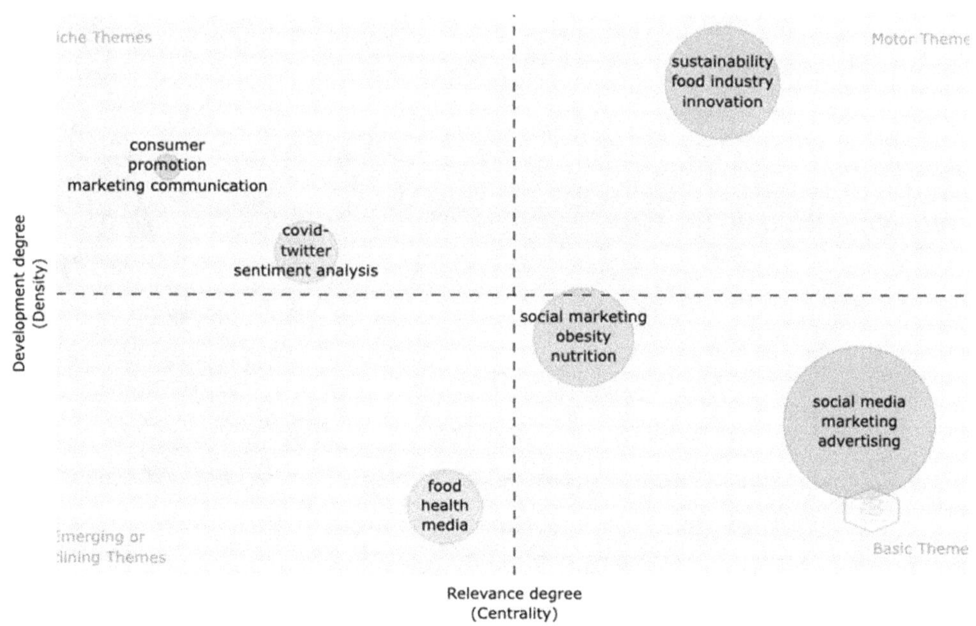

Figure 5. Most cited countries

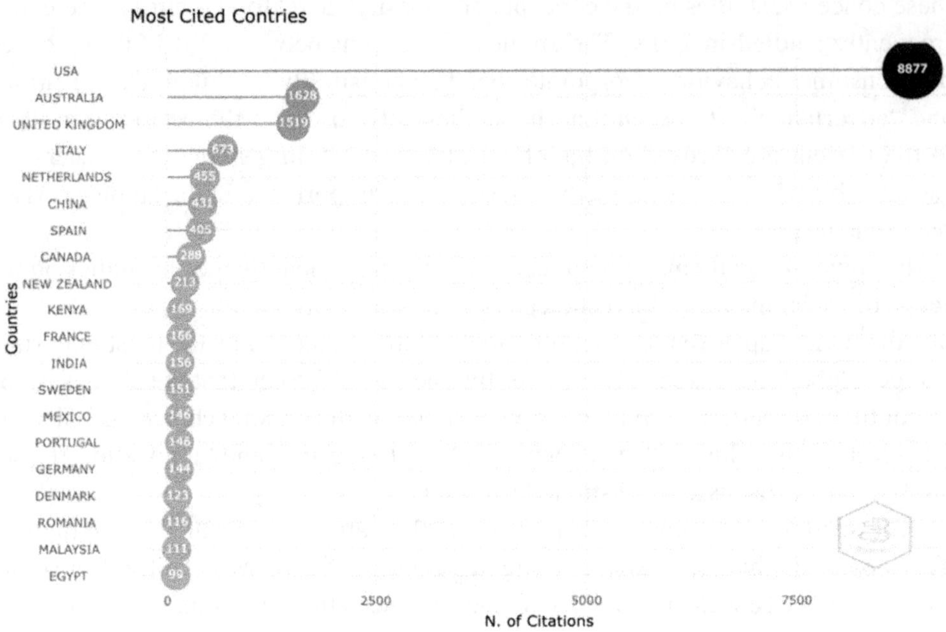

Figure 6. Annual scientific production

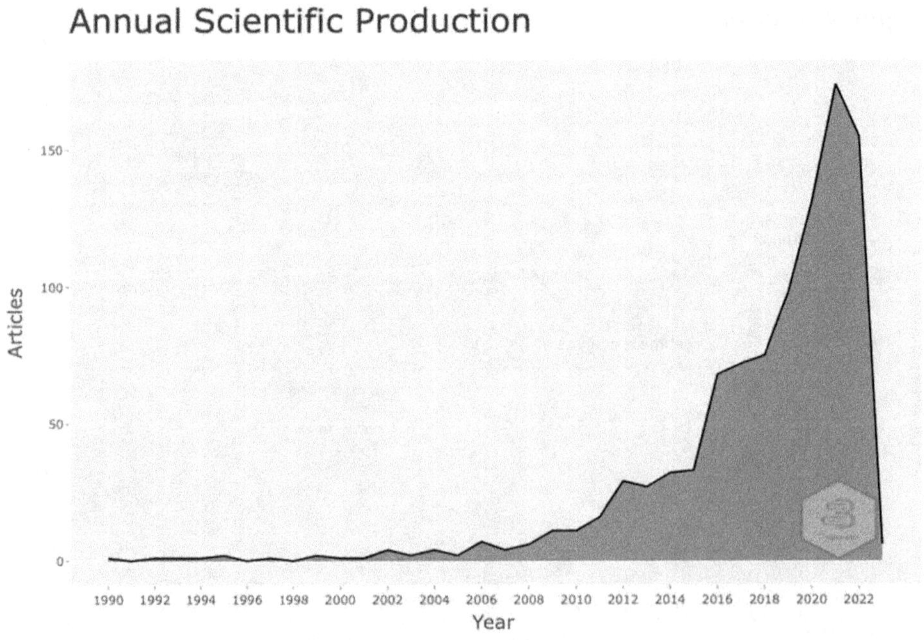

and "marketing communication" are studied together. In another cluster, it was determined that the subjects are "covid", "twitter" and "sentiment analysis".

The section in the lower left part of the thematic map is called emerging and declining themes. The subjects in this section are the subjects where the studies on the subjects have decreased or the subjects that have only just begun to be studied. There is a cluster in this section. "food", "health" and "media" subjects took place in this cluster.

The section at the bottom right of the thematic map is called basic themes. The topics in this section highlight the importance of further work in this area. The largest and most intense cluster of this section includes "social media", "marketing" and "advertising". The second cluster contains more general topics such as "social marketing", "obesity" and "nutrition".

According to Figure 5, it is seen that the most cited publications in studies on social media and food are presented by authors from USA, Australia, United Kingdom, Italy and Netherlands, respectively.

In Figure 6, it is seen that the first studies on social media and food were put forward in 1990. In addition, the number of studies increased rapidly starting from 2012. In the graph, sudden increases are observed in the number of studies on social

Figure 7. Corresponding author's country

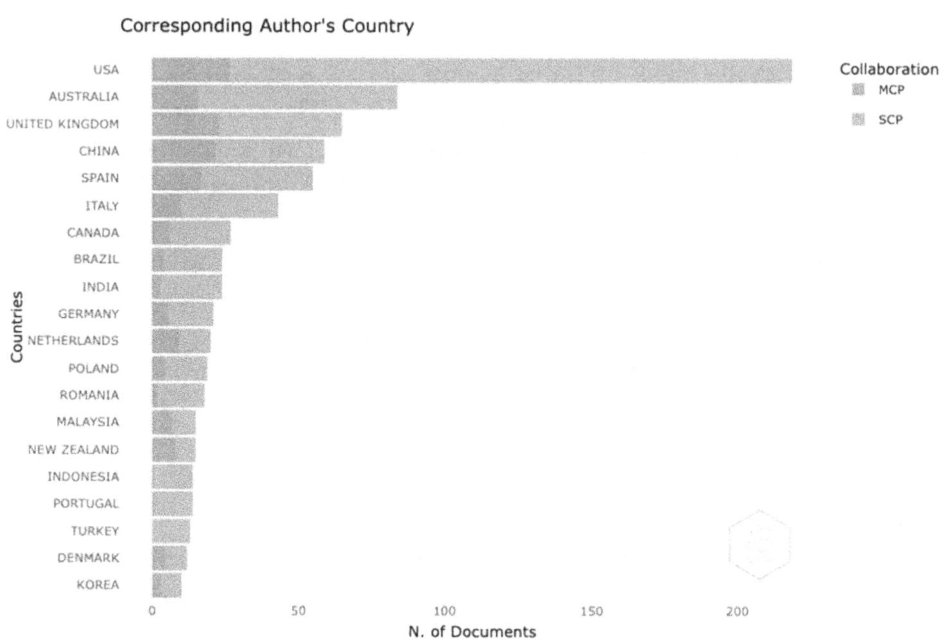

Figure 8. Most relevant sources

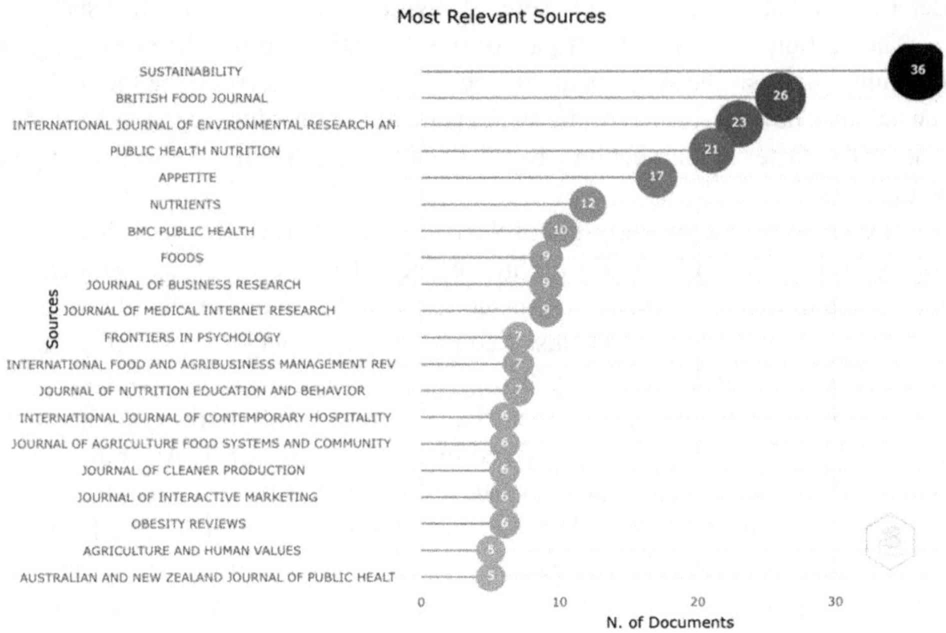

media on food choice in 2012, 2016, 2018. The year in which the most studies on food and social media were published is 2021.

The countries of the corresponding authors whose studies were included in the data set were examined and shown in Figure 7. According to Figure 7, it is seen that the country with the highest number of publications is USA. USA is followed by Australia, United Kingdom and China, respectively. The green colors in the table show that the broadcasts were made in a single country, while the orange parts show the number of broadcasts from more than one country. Authors from Turkey worked as sole authors in their publications.

The most preferred journals were searched to publish studies on the scope of social media on food choice. According to the most relevant sources graph in Figure 8, "Sustainability", "British Food Journal" and "International Journal of Environmental Research and Public Health" are the most popular scientific journals, respectively.

MANAGERIAL IMPLICATIONS

The results of the study may lead to a number of implications for marketing professionals. Understanding the motivations of food choice will help design and deliver appropriate marketing strategies and products suitable for each target group. In this way, consumers will be able to find foods suitable for their characteristics, preferences and values, while brands will transfer their resources to the right places. Considering that social media is one of the leading factors that shape consumers' preferences, understanding the interaction of social media and food consumers' preferences will guide brands for superior strategies.

Social media also provides a lot of data that can create insights for brands. The digital footprints left by users contain many clues about consumption practices. Food brands can make significant gains from this data by closely following and analyzing their consumers on social media. How consumers would react to targeted marketing communication messages are still one of the most important questions in developing marketing strategy.

FUTURE RESEARCH DIRECTIONS

Social media and its effect on food choices is an issue that draws attention in the literature as well as in practice. The bibliometric analysis shows that some subjects are really promising and have lots of potential. In the thematic map, the prominent themes in studies on the scope of social media on food choice are demonstrated. The thematic map shows that "sustainability", "food industry" and "innovation" are full of opportunities to do academic research. Although these subjects are developed, they are essential subjects for conducting research. Future studies related to the food industry can focus on sustainability and innovation in the food since they are promising areas. In addition, the thematic map also points out that covid-19 studies are still relevant for the food industry and have great potential. Future research might be conducted on Covid-19 and its effect on the food industry and what kind of implementations can be done in order to recover from negative aspects of post-covid. Twitter, sentimental analysis and tracing down consumer data on social media also carries potential. Marketing communication and promotion in the food industry are also promising areas for future studies.

CONCLUSION

Modern social media tools have transformed how individuals communicate, create and share content. The changing structure of communication enabled by the internet paves the way for using social media in choosing products and services. The aim of this study is to shed light on the development of academic publishing on social media and food choices. Social media has huge influential power and therefore can be useful in social areas such as healthy food consumption, and encouraging activities for not creating waste food. Therefore, it is essential to understand how social media affects food choices and also how the literature is growing in this particular area.

Results of the bibliometric analysis show that "marketing", "social marketing", "food", "food marketing", and "advertising" are the most repetitive words in the articles. The findings also underline the strong relationship of food marketing with social marketing. Among the reasons for these, as mentioned in the literature review, marketing communication messages especially targeted at children and adolescents are focal points and the marketing of unhealthy food products is highly criticized in terms of social marketing. Furthermore, the most repetitive words are found as "social media", "sustainability", "social media marketing", "children", "covid-19", "nutrition" "adolescents", "digital marketing" and "food industry". From the most repeated words, it is deduced that the results of the relationship between Covid-19 and nutrition are still being investigated, and sustainability maintains its impact and importance in the food sector, as it is in every field.

Trend topics that changed over time in the literature are also examined in the chapter. It is seen that the trend topics change according to the conditions of the time and the topics of interest. While the popular topic was "food safety" in 2010, the prominent words of the year 2011 and 2012 were "public health" and "diet", respectively. This reveals the rise of health concerns and shows its effect in literature. The spread of the internet and the increase in its use in business and social life made issues related to social media and the internet more important. As of 2018, "Facebook" and "innovation" topics have become prominent along with other topics. In addition, it is underlined that the issue of "obesity" increased its importance together with social issues. Between 2018 and 2020, it is seen that social issues maintain their importance and the issues of consumer behavior", "corporate social responsibility", "children", "nutrition" and "advertising" come to the fore. Food marketing for children received great attention in the literature.

The other part of the study focused on most cited countries, annual scientific production, corresponding author's country and most relevant sources. Authors from the USA, Australia, United Kingdom, Italy and Netherlands have the most cited sources in social media and food choice research. China, Spain and Canada follow them, respectively. When annual scientific production is examined, it can be seen that studies on food and social media emerged in 1990. Starting in 2012, the number of studies expanded quickly parallel with social media expansion. There has been a sharp rise in publications on social media and food since 2012. 2021 was the year in which the most research on food and social media was published. It can also be inferred that these dates are closely related to the development of the internet. "Sustainability", "British Food Journal" and "International Journal of Environmental Research" stand out as the most popular scientific journals when publishing in the area of social media and food choice. It can be concluded that journals related to health and business also publish studies on food choices.

In conclusion, it is seen that the food sector and food preferences are closely related to the health and nutrition sector. The strong relationship between social media and food preference has also been demonstrated by studies in the literature. With the increase in the number of social media tools and users, it is predicted that studies on food selection and social media use will increase both in practice and in the literature.

REFERENCES

Acar, N., Çizmeci, B., & Turan, A. (2021). A research on consumer perceptions of food and beverage marketing on social media. *OPUS International Journal of Society Researches*, *17*(34), 813–830.

Aktaş, F., Çetiner, H., & Keskin, E. (2022). Gastronomi blogları ve tatma davranışı arasındaki ilişkilerin analizi. *Abant Sosyal Bilimler Dergisi*, *22*(2), 873–886. doi:10.11616/asbi.1102562

Alkış, H., & Karakan, A. (2019). Algılanan sosyal medyanın tüketici davranışı ve satın alma niyetine etkisi üzerine bir araştırma. *Sosyal. Beşeri ve İdari Bilimler Dergisi*, *2*(10), 702–718.

Appel, G., Grewal, L., Hadi, R., & Stephen, A. T. (2020). The future of social media in marketing. *Journal of the Academy of Marketing Science*, *48*(1), 79–95. doi:10.100711747-019-00695-1 PMID:32431463

Ayan, B., Can, M., & Gürsoy, U. T. (2019). Sosyal Medya Madenciliği İle Firmaların Twitter Verilerinin İncelenmesi. *Uluslararası İktisadi ve İdari İncelemeler Dergisi*, (23), 237–256.

Aypar, S., & Kazancioğlu, İ. (2020). The Effect Of Food Influencers On Consumers' Intention To Purchase Food Products/Services. *Journal of Gastronomy Hospitality and Travel*, *3*(2), 150–163. doi:10.33083/joghat.2020.40

Basev, S. E. (2022). The impact of social media on children's consumption: Instagram example. *OPUS Journal of Society Research*, *19*(47), 462–476.

Baum, D., Spann, M., Füller, J., & Thürridl, C. (2019). The impact of social media campaigns on the success of new product introductions. *Journal of Retailing and Consumer Services*, *50*, 289–297. doi:10.1016/j.jretconser.2018.07.003

Cairns, G., Angus, K., Hastings, G., & Caraher, M. (2013). Systematic reviews of the evidence on the nature, extent and effects of food marketing to children. A retrospective summary. *Appetite*, *62*, 209–215. doi:10.1016/j.appet.2012.04.017 PMID:22561190

Cankul, D., Metin, M., & Özvatan, D. (2018). Food and Beverage Business and Social Media Usage. *Journal of Gastronomy Hospitality and Travel*, *1*(1), 29–37. doi:10.33083/joghat.2018.4

Carr, C. T., & Hayes, R. A. (2015). Social media: Defining, developing, and divining. *Atlantic Journal of Communication*, *23*(1), 46–65. doi:10.1080/15456870.2015.972282

Çaycı, A. E. (2019). Sosyal medya'da dijital yemek kültürü. [UKSAD]. *Uluslararası Kültürel ve Sosyal Araştırmalar Dergisi*, *5*(1), 120–136.

Coates, A. E., Hardman, C. A., Halford, J. C., Christiansen, P., & Boyland, E. J. (2019). Food and beverage cues featured in YouTube videos of social media influencers popular with children: An exploratory study. *Frontiers in Psychology*, *10*, 2142. doi:10.3389/fpsyg.2019.02142 PMID:31616344

Coates, A. E., Hardman, C. A., Halford, J. C. G., Christiansen, P., & Boyland, E. J. (2019). The effect of influencer marketing of food and a "protective" advertising disclosure on children's food intake. *Pediatric Obesity*, *14*(10), e12540. doi:10.1111/ijpo.12540 PMID:31168959

Dedeoğlu, A. Ö., & Kabasakal, E. (2019). Consumer anxiety, well-being and social media use: The Case Of# HealthyNutrition. *Ege Academic Review*, *19*(3), 341–357. doi:10.21121/eab.536840

Dedeoglu, B. B. (2019). Are information quality and source credibility really important for shared content on social media? The moderating role of gender. *International Journal of Contemporary Hospitality Management*, *31*(1), 513–534. doi:10.1108/IJCHM-10-2017-0691

Dhanesh, G. S., & Duthler, G. (2019). Relationship management through social media influencers: Effects of followers' awareness of paid endorsement. *Public Relations Review*, *45*(3), 101765. doi:10.1016/j.pubrev.2019.03.002

Diekman, C., Ryan, C. D., & Oliver, T. L. (2022). Misinformation and Disinformation in Food Science and Nutrition: Impact on Practice. *The Journal of Nutrition*. PMID:36913465

Donthu, N., Kumar, S., Mukherjee, D., Pandey, N., & Lim, W. M. (2021). How to conduct a bibliometric analysis: An overview and guidelines. *Journal of Business Research, 133*, 285–296. doi:10.1016/j.jbusres.2021.04.070

Dwivedi, Y. K., Ismagilova, E., Hughes, D. L., Carlson, J., Filieri, R., Jacobson, J., Jain, V., Karjaluoto, H., Kefi, H., Krishen, A. S., Kumar, V., Rahman, M. M., Raman, R., Rauschnabel, P. A., Rowley, J., Salo, J., Tran, G. A., & Wang, Y. (2021). Setting the future of digital and social media marketing research: Perspectives and research propositions. *International Journal of Information Management, 59*, 102168. doi:10.1016/j.ijinfomgt.2020.102168

Engin, Y., & İbiş, S. (2016). Öğrencilerin Yiyecek Ve İçecek İşletmesi Seçiminde Sosyal Medyanın Rolünün Belirlenmesi Determining The Role of Social Media Use For The Selection of Food and Beverage Enterprise. *Mehmet Akif Ersoy Üniversitesi Sosyal Bilimler Enstitüsü Dergisi, 8*(17), 322–336.

Erdoğmuş, Z. İ., & Karakaya, M. (2022). Engaging with Social Media Influencers on Youtube: A Cluster Analysis. *Istanbul Business Research, 51*(1), 359–373. doi:10.26650/ibr.2022.51.842750

Erkan, I., & Evans, C. (2016). The influence of eWOM in social media on consumers' purchase intentions: An extended approach to information adoption. *Computers in Human Behavior, 61*, 47–55. doi:10.1016/j.chb.2016.03.003

Freeman, B., Kelly, B., Baur, L., Chapman, K., Chapman, S., Gill, T., & King, L. (2014). Digital junk: Food and beverage marketing on Facebook. *American Journal of Public Health, 104*(12), e56–e64. doi:10.2105/AJPH.2014.302167 PMID:25322294

Giumetti, G. W., & Kowalski, R. M. (2022). Cyberbullying via social media and well-being. *Current Opinion in Psychology, 45*, 101314. doi:10.1016/j.copsyc.2022.101314 PMID:35313180

Grau, S. L. (2022). *Celebrity 2.0: The Role of Social Media Influencer Marketing in Building Brands*. Business Expert Press, LLC.

Greene, T., Seet, C., Barrio, A. R., McIntyre, D., Kelly, B., & Bragg, M. A. (2022). Brands with personalities–good for businesses, but bad for public health? A content analysis of how food and beverage brands personify themselves on Twitter. *Public Health Nutrition, 25*(1), 51–60. doi:10.1017/S1368980021001439 PMID:33820575

Hamshaw, R. J., Barnett, J., & Lucas, J. S. (2018). Tweeting and eating: The effect of links and likes on food-hypersensitive consumers' perceptions of tweets. *Frontiers in Public Health, 6*, 118. doi:10.3389/fpubh.2018.00118 PMID:29740573

Hanaysha, J. (2016). The importance of social media advertisements in enhancing brand equity: A study on fast food restaurant industry in Malaysia. *International Journal of Innovation, Management and Technology*, *7*(2), 46–51. doi:10.18178/ijimt.2016.7.2.643

Kırcova, İ., Yaman, Y., & Köse, Ş. G. (2021). Instagram, Facebook or Twitter: which engages best? A comparative study of consumer brand engagement and social commerce purchase intention.

Klassen, K. M., Borleis, E. S., Brennan, L., Reid, M., McCaffrey, T. A., & Lim, M. S. (2018). What people "like": Analysis of social media strategies used by food industry brands, lifestyle brands, and health promotion organizations on Facebook and Instagram. *Journal of Medical Internet Research*, *20*(6), e10227. doi:10.2196/10227 PMID:29903694

Krupa-Kotara, K., Grajek, M., Rozmiarek, M., Malchrowicz-Mośko, E., Staśkiewicz, W., León-Guereño, P., & Castañeda-Babarro, A. (2023). The Role of Social Media in Internalizing Body Knowledge—A Cross-Sectional Study among Women with Different Food Preferences. *International Journal of Environmental Research and Public Health*, *20*(3), 2069. doi:10.3390/ijerph20032069 PMID:36767433

Kucharczuk, A. J., Oliver, T. L., & Dowdell, E. B. (2022). Social media's influence on adolescents′ food choices: A mixed studies systematic literature review. *Appetite*, *168*, 105765. doi:10.1016/j.appet.2021.105765 PMID:34687823

Nash, J. (2019). Exploring how social media platforms influence fashion consumer decisions in the UK retail sector. *Journal of Fashion Marketing and Management*, *23*(1), 82–103. doi:10.1108/JFMM-01-2018-0012

Pallas, D. (2019). *Mastering Social Media Marketing 2019: How to Dominate Social Media for The Next Decade*. Independently Published.

Pekerşen, Y., & Kaplan, M. (2020). Tüketicilerin yeme içme alışkanlıkları ve yiyecek-içecek işletmesi tercihlerinde sosyal medya kullanımının rolü: Muğla örneği. *İşletme Araştırmaları Dergisi, 12*(3), 2362-2381.

Pilař, L., Stanislavská, L. K., Kvasnička, R., Hartman, R., & Tichá, I. (2021). Healthy food on instagram social network: Vegan, homemade and clean eating. *Nutrients*, *13*(6), 1991. doi:10.3390/nu13061991 PMID:34207910

Quesenberry, K. A. (2019). *Social Media Strategy: Marketing, Advertising, and Public Relations in the Consumer Revolution*. Rowman & Littlefield Publishers.

Qutteina, Y., Hallez, L., Raedschelders, M., De Backer, C., & Smits, T. (2022). Food for teens: How social media is associated with adolescent eating outcomes. *Public Health Nutrition*, *25*(2), 290–302. PMID:34325764

Rahımı, Z., & Kırkbir, F. (2022). Sosyal Medya Pazarlama Faaliyetlerinin Yeme-İçme İşletmeleri Müşterilerinin İlhamı Ve Marka Bağlılığı Üzerindeki Etkisi: Karadeniz Teknik Üniversitesi Öğrencileri Üzerinde Bir Çalışma. *Uluslararası İktisadi Ve İdari İncelemeler Dergisi*, (36), 111–130.

Rutsaert, P., Regan, Á., Pieniak, Z., McConnon, Á., Moss, A., Wall, P., & Verbeke, W. (2013). The use of social media in food risk and benefit communication. *Trends in Food Science & Technology*, *30*(1), 84–91. doi:10.1016/j.tifs.2012.10.006

Sağtaş, S. (2022). The effect of social media marketing on brand equity and consumer purchasing intention. *Journal of Life Economics*, *9*(1), 21–31. doi:10.15637/jlecon.9.1.02

Sánchez-Fernández, R., & Jiménez-Castillo, D. (2021). How social media influencers affect behavioural intentions towards recommended brands: The role of emotional attachment and information value. *Journal of Marketing Management*, *37*(11-12), 1123–1147. doi:10.1080/0267257X.2020.1866648

Seçer, A., & Boğa, M. (2017). Sosyal medyanın tüketicilerin gıda ürünleri satın alma davranışına etkisi. *KSÜ Doğa Bilimleri Dergisi*, *20*(4), 312–319.

Shiau, W. L., Dwivedi, Y. K., & Lai, H. H. (2018). Examining the core knowledge on facebook. *International Journal of Information Management*, *43*, 52–63. doi:10.1016/j.ijinfomgt.2018.06.006

Shipman, Z. D. (2020). Factors Affecting Food Choices of Millennials: How they Decide What to Eat? *Journal of Tourismology*, *6*(1), 49–62. doi:10.26650/jot.2020.6.1.0036

Simeone, M., & Scarpato, D. (2020). Sustainable consumption: How does social media affect food choices? *Journal of Cleaner Production*, *277*, 124036. doi:10.1016/j.jclepro.2020.124036

Solomon, M. R. (2020). *Consumer Behaviour: Buying, Having and Being* (13th ed.). Pearson Education.

Statista (2023). https://www.statista.com/statistics/272014/global-social-networks-ranked-by-number-of-users/

Statista (2023). Number of internet and social media users worldwide as of January 2023. https://www.statista.com/statistics/617136/digital-population-worldwide/

Sun, Y., Wang, R., Cao, D., & Lee, R. (2022). Who are social media influencers for luxury fashion consumption of the Chinese Gen Z? Categorisation and empirical examination. *Journal of Fashion Marketing and Management*, *26*(4), 603–621. doi:10.1108/JFMM-07-2020-0132

Teerakapibal, S., & Melanthiou, Y. (2020). The new helping the old: Social media as a facilitator for variety seeking in food choices of the grey population. *British Food Journal*, *122*(1), 272–290. doi:10.1108/BFJ-08-2018-0559

Turner, P. (2022). "The Insta-Food Diet". Head of Zeus: London.

Tuten, T. L. (2021). *Social Media Marketing*. Sage Publishing.

Uçan, B. Z., Girgin, G. K., & Karaman, N. (2021). Youtube Yemek Kanallarının Tatma Davranışsal Niyeti Üzerine Etkisi. *Kırklareli Üniversitesi Sosyal Bilimler Dergisi*, *5*(1), 1–28. doi:10.47140/kusbder.887291

Ünal, A. T. (2020). A comparative study of social media addiction among Turkish and Korean university students. *Journal of Economy Culture and Society*, (62), 307–322. doi:10.26650/JECS2020-0064

Vassallo, A., Jones, A., & Freeman, B. (2022). Social media: Frenemy of public health? *Public Health Nutrition*, *25*(1), 61–64. doi:10.1017/S136898002100269X PMID:34165062

Vaterlaus, J. M., Patten, E. V., Roche, C., & Young, J. A. (2015). # Gettinghealthy: The perceived influence of social media on young adult health behaviors. *Computers in Human Behavior*, *45*, 151–157. doi:10.1016/j.chb.2014.12.013

Ventura, V., Cavaliere, A., & Ianno, B. (2021). # Socialfood: Virtuous or vicious? A systematic review. *Trends in Food Science & Technology*, *110*, 674–686. doi:10.1016/j.tifs.2021.02.018

Winzer, E., Naderer, B., Klein, S., Lercher, L., & Wakolbinger, M. (2022). Promotion of Food and Beverages by German-Speaking Influencers Popular with Adolescents on TikTok, YouTube and Instagram. *International Journal of Environmental Research and Public Health*, *19*(17), 10911. doi:10.3390/ijerph191710911 PMID:36078625

KEY TERMS AND DEFINITIONS

Social Media: a tool by which individuals engage in virtual networks to create and share content and/or exchange information as well as ideas.

Social Media Marketing: using digital technologies and social media channels to create and deliver valuable content.

Bibliometric Analysis: a scientific computer-assisted review process that is carried out to find key authors or pieces of research as well as their relationships by analyzing publications relevant to a particular subject.

Food Choice: people's preference of food they consume.

Influencer Marketing: a kind of social media marketing that is done by influencers who have a social impact.

Influencer: a person who has the power to influence followers by showing or recommending products on his/her social media accounts.

Food Brand: a branded product operating in the food industry.

Chapter 2
Impact of Social Media on Consumer Decisiveness in the Food and Grocery Sector

Dharshini Karthikeyan
CHRIST University (Deemed), India

Ramya Barathi Manoharan
Annamalai University, India

Pavithra Karthikeyan
Meritto, India

S. Pradeep
Freshworks, India

ABSTRACT

Consumers are currently inclined to acknowledge online information but purchase food and grocery products offline. Also, the buyer's decision is coherent with the factors like income, age, social media influences, cost of products, etc. The chapter studies the Influence of Social Media on Consumer Decision-making in the food and Grocery Sector. As per the findings, the effectiveness of marketing tools and techniques has a homogeneous effect on all GenX, GenY, GenZ. Contrary to expectation, Gen X was most influenced by offers. Social media equally influenced all generations to make purchases, irrespective of their incomes. Post Covid there is a shift in consumption habits disregarding generations and income brackets of all the participants.

DOI: 10.4018/978-1-6684-8868-3.ch002

INTRODUCTION

Food and Grocery Industries

Food and Groceries are necessities that are required every day. With rapid industrialization and Urbanization, there is a visibly increased demand for groceries. (*Food and Grocery Retail Market Size, Share, Opportunities & Forecast*, 2022) The result of the improved standard of living led to the requirement for higher-food quality. The main factors that influence the purchase are the price of the products and the convenience of purchase. Apart from these, the factors like promotional activities, offers, ads, attractive packaging, supply chains, consumer's lifestyle and marketing strategies influence a product to be purchased.

Future of Grocery Shopping

The words Supermarkets and Grocery stores are used interchangeably (Momin, 2023). However, in reality, supermarkets are enormous and provide a wide variety of products. The grocery stores are customized according to the destined/situated area, and small retail stores specifically hold goods that are locally needed and bought. Retail shops are basically the goods sold to the public. They are able to gain experience by looking at and using samples of the products. This makes the products more appealing. This tempts consumers to understand more about the product and purchase more. The elevated usage led to an increase in the number of grocery stores and foods. We do find Food and Grocery Industry Analysis to help the shopkeeper in track the product sold and that to be replenished. Consumer awareness through social media promotions has become a significant source in achieving high sales.

DIGITAL GROCERY SHOPPING

The lifestyle of adapting to the use of digital applications to buy groceries and food are being accepted. There is a need for prior knowledge of technologies to have a smooth shopping experience.

Some people emphasize the advantages of multichannel purchasing, ie. both online and in-store purchases.

Mrs.A can check out the product in person in a nearby local shop and buy it online after using the samples.

Price parity is always one of the deciding factors to determine sales and purchases.

The Smart Retail technology models are customized as per the needs of the local people. It brings out the easy flow of the shopping experience. Digital shopping may not be as interactive and interconnective as the traditional shopping experience. Nevertheless, it is filled with a rational and logical approach.

EVOLUTION OF MARKETING

Marketing as a concept has changed over the centuries, decades, and years. From being a production-oriented concept to the present era of relationship marketing, constant evolution is happening. The production-oriented marketing practice before the twentieth century was conservative and hidebound by rules of thumb and lack of information. Science & technology developments, and especially the development of information technology, have now changed how people live, do business, and sell and purchase.

As users increased, the landscape evolved from email to search engines like Yahoo! (1994) and Google (1997) and e-commerce sites like Amazon (1994) and eBay (1995). For marketing, this was a goldmine. Now, there is a massive set of the population that has wholly involved itself in the swirl of cyberspace. Eventually, Digital Marketing became the new norm of the era, with a 30% growth rate.

In simple terms, Digital Marketing promotes products over the Internet or any form of electronic media. The Digital Marketing Institute states, "Digital Marketing is the use of digital channels to promote or market products and services to targeted consumers and businesses." With advances in ideas and strategies, the wings of Digital marketing expanded extensively. Two of them will be studied in this paper: Viral Marketing and Social Media Marketing.

SOCIAL MEDIA AND FOOD & GROCERY SECTOR

The social media platforms and their role in product awareness create a dramatic effect on the customer's purchase decision. (Ramanathan et al., 2017) examine the customer's acceptance and satisfaction of buying a product with social media reviews, and its promotions acting as influencers. Surprisingly social media reviews and product promotions are interrelated. Even some customers are willing to buy offline after reading the reviews.

(Knezevic et al., n.d.) explain how social media is an active platform in customer engagement and social networking. With the help of Facebook, the localities could contribute much to the Social Supermarkets. The Social Supermarkets are basically for donating and offering products at discounted prices to the low-income population. The possibility of a wide network and communications paved the way through social media, and supported the concept of "SOCIAL SUPERMARKETS". From this, we can understand that not only the promotional activities and eye-catching attractive posters go viral, but also the non-profitable information spreads fast.

Social media marketing is a new trend and a rapidly growing way for businesses to target customers quickly. *Social media marketing* uses social media channels to promote a company and its products (Barefoot & Szabo, 2010). By encouraging users to spread messages to personal contacts, social media marketing has injected a new term of exponential dissemination and trust into mass communication and mass marketing (Hafele, 2011). With this new approach of outreach and marketing, new tools are being developed and increased in turn for businesses. Social media marketers are gaining more practical insight by introducing analytic applications on official social network site platforms (Hafele, 2011).

Social media technology has modified the ways of managing the relationship between brands and customers. The success of social media lies in the fact that it has provided the medium through which people interact. They have maintained connections with one another (Pauwels, 2004). Marketers are using social media sites to foster brands. They employ social media to understand customer expectations and develop appropriate strategies to promote their offerings to achieve the marketing goal (Donath, 2004).

There are numerous social media sites that take many different forms and contain different features. A few of them that have been analyzed in the paper are Facebook, Instagram, and Youtube.

INSTAGRAM

Instagram is renowned as one of the most engaging social media platforms available. A study on the 25 most successfully engaging global brands revealed that the average Instagram post gained an engagement rate of 3.31%. 80% of Instagram users follow at least one business account, and at least 30% of users have purchased a product they discovered via an advert on their feed. Instagram stories receive 250 million daily visitors. 65% of top-performing Instagram posts feature products. Effective hashtagging system – posts with hashtags receive around 12.6% more engagement. One in five minutes people spend on a mobile device is on Facebook or Instagram.

FACEBOOK

Facebook remains the reigning champ of social media sites, the number one spot where friends connect and share online. Beyond just a meeting place for friends, Facebook has become a venue for businesses to market themselves through customer interaction and self-promotion. Facebook has global coverage of Over 1.5 billion users visiting daily and about 2.3 billion monthly. More than 7 million active companies create ads for this massive audience.

YOUTUBE

YouTube is the go-to destination for video content, and the second-most visited site after Google. There are now 2 billion unique YouTube users every month–a 5% increase from the previously reported numbers in 2018. These stats make it one of the biggest social media platforms. The platform also accounts for 27.1% of digital video ad spending, with 62% of marketers planning to increase their spending on YouTube.

BACKGROUND

Review of Literature

A. Analysis of Generation

Generation X make decisions while purchasing with prior knowledge from the past combined with future predictions - this brings another point to our understanding that the Xers use their social media with a restricted approach as they have used both traditional and modern lifestyles. In comparison, Gen Y is people who have constantly been witnessing social media and technology; hence, their decisions are technology intended. They are also avid social media users, where all their decisions are based on the comments and posts put on social media. They even go to the extent of sharing social media content just by viewing the content's title. So their decisions are entirely influenced by social media and technology. This study is conducted for both generations separately on the influence of decisions by social media in the food sector.

(Andreani et al., 2021) studies about how social media and influencers play a huge role in influencing Generation Z. Generation Z is immersed and influenced highly by social media in finding cafes and restaurants for food and groceries. Hence the study attempts to evaluate how the reach, relevance, and resonance of SMI (Social media influencers) creates a more profound impact in the decision making capacity of Generation Z. Gen Z can relate themselves with the celebrities of cyberspace and hence they are influenced highly to visit the cafe or restaurant. The research clearly states that relevance and the resonance of the social media influencer significantly impacted decisions made by Gen Z. Consumers who have to make decisions for visiting cafes and restaurants can relate to the relevance involved in the videos shared by the SMI. The SMI is to be selected in a way that they are on par with the mindsets of the targeted consumers.

(Zhang et al. 2017) examine how Generation Y has the power of social media and mobile technology to instantly record their intentions about the services of the restaurants/ cafes of the food industry. These advanced features combined with technology help Gen Y to post their mind about the positive and negative services provided in any of the places they visit. Electronic Word of mouth is a vital aspect amongst people, and it acts as a review for future other customers. Once a customer receives best-in-class service or even a satisfactory service after a service failure, Gen Y will start sharing positive EWOM about the services offered. Positive EWOM and satisfactory comments post the food will expand the reach of the cafe/ restaurant. While if there is a service failure, negative EWOM flashes across all the social media platforms. Negative EWOM will cost the reputation of any service. These results are from Gen Y's closeness to their devices and technology. It has given them the space and room to comment on all the services offered at the cafe/ restaurant without any constraints.

(Bolton et al., 2013) probes Generation Y's behavior as it is unique from the other cohorts. They have grown up witnessing technology and digital transformation; hence, they are collectively called the digital natives, while the prior Gen belongs to the digital immigrants' category. Gen Y uses social media to create, share, and consume content. This article also tried to understand the frequency and intensity of the use of social media among Gen Y. The impact of social media has more significant consequences on individual, societal, and firm levels.

(Abdul et al., 2022) tries to find how social media positively correlates between EWORM and ESAT. This article also explores the three-way interaction between EWOM, risk, and trust to influence the ESAT of consumers.

(Sashi, 2012) attempts to understand the advent of Web 2.0 which has created a closer relationship between social media and consumers. This study implies that a mix of digital techniques along with traditional ones have paved the way for four types of relationships to emerge. The relationships each generation through the cycle are transactional customers, delighted customers, loyal customers, and fans.

(Balakrishnan et al., 2014) grills down and analyzes that the online marketing communications, specifically, E-WOM, online communities and online advertisement are effective in promoting brand loyalty and product purchase intention through company website and social media platforms. This study also implies that Boomerang Kids have higher usage of social media This research is intended to provide a base for future marketers to get used to online marketing techniques for increasing their sales volumes.

B. Pre and Post Covid shifts in buying food and grocery products based on social media influence:

(Campo & Breugelmans, 2015) The experience of buying Online is examined. The reinforcing change is required in the old marketing mix. They are multi-channel grocery shoppers who check out the product online and offline. Sometimes, promotional activities and offers do not attract customers a lot without having prior experience with the product. People try to combine the online shopping experience by visiting in-person stores before buying the products.

During the pandemic situation, the usage of social media has increased than the normal times. People were connected virtually despite social distancing. (Sulthana and Shanmugam, 2021)

The Covid-19 situation exemplifies the need for unprecedented details, which in turn provides symmetric information to everyone. (Naeem, 2021) concurs that insecurities, product unavailability, expert opinions, and political announcements lead to stockpiling/ panic buying of products. The influence of social media platforms makes people more engaged and generates collective response for similar products. This is developed as social proof to demonstrate the importance of social media during the pandemic in deciding consumers' buying behavior. The paper also highlights the fact of crowd behavior. The suggestions and shared messages by their friends connected via social media are also taken into consideration by the consumers.

Further (Zhang & Du, 2020) compares the utilization and effective use of the social media message strategy between the B2C and B2B companies. The adaptation of social media messaging strategies has more rational appeals over emotional appeals in terms of B2B, where constant interactions & interactivities are found. Customer engagement and perceived value have become readily measurable by employing social media marketing strategies.

(Zolfaghari et al., 2022) examine the acceptance and adoption of technology by shoppers. The consumers' prior-to-use knowledge of technology helps to use social media platforms while adapting to Digital Grocery Shopping (DGS). The online grocery appeal impacts directly or indirectly the adoption of new methods of grocery e-shopping. The results emphasize that the consumer's digital trust, digital readiness and digital convenience play a vital role in purchasing via smart retail technology.

(Ananda et al., 2023) compares online food and grocery shopping in comparison with in-store grocery shopping. This is done to understand the food waste generated by spending higher on groceries when bought online. There is straightforward coherence found, ie. Online shoppers buy a more significant portion of food comparatively. However, people who buy at discounted prices and promotional offers did not tend to waste food. We find that online shoppers continue to purchase more when their income increases.

With the support of the sustainability messaging on TWITTER, the authors (Garner & Mady, 2023) identify the different dimensions of sustainability in their relationship with the people, profit, and the planet. The sustainability messaging in the Food Industry in Business and Business to Companies are determined. Using Twitter as a social media Platform, the B2B companies are more people or employees oriented sustainable. In contrast, B2C emphasizes more on the economic sustainability of profit.

C. Income and Social Media:

(Akbarov, 2020) says that the income of the consumer decides between brand conscious and value-conscious with respect to SMM(Social Media Messaging). The lower income group tends to be more brand loyal and the higher income population has a direct effect on the value-consciousness.

D. Influence of social media while purchasing - online and offline

(Pütter, Michael. (2017)) Social media has become vital for companies to market their offerings and reach their target customers. Companies worldwide are constantly seeking new ways to get consumers with the likes of social media influence. Social media's openness to the end users is crucial as it decides the consumer's purchase behavior. Based on the earlier studies, through the free flow of information in social media, consumers could make more accessible and faster decisions towards their purchases.

(Timothy, Dotsey. (2019)) The study by the scholars states that out of 100% of the people among whom the survey was conducted, 30% are only being influenced by social media when they purchase, while the rest, 70%, are not. 70% of them use social media tools to have social engagement than to allow them to decide on purchasing online or offline. The study also states that among the 100% of social media users who determine their buying decisions based on social media influence, around 53.3% purchase based on social media recommendations, while 47.6% don't.

Thoumrungroje, A. (2014). A vast majority of people around the globe are spending their time on social media sites for digital consumption. It is undeniable that social media tools play a vital role in people's daily lives. Companies are aligned to evolving consumer behavior through innovative marketing tools to capitalize and adapt to the new lifestyle. Data were collected from Thai consumers, showing direct and indirect influences (i.e., via EWOM) of social media intensity on conspicuous consumption.

Khaleeli, Majdi. (2020) The study was intended to find the effect of Social Media Advertising, Sales Promotion on consumers" online purchase intention. The findings indicate that social media sales promotions influence consumers and their purchase decision significantly. The discovery of this research draws the attention of companies. Hence, they need to focus mainly on sales promotion and are advised to minimize the pure advertisements of their products and services through Social Media and focus more on promotional campaigns that carry direct and explicit benefits for customers, such as offers coupons and discounts as these sales promotional methods found to be positively and significantly associated with Online Purchase Intention.

E. Impact of social media while purchasing online

In their study, Barysevich (2020b) states that social media significantly influence people's purchase decisions as the time spent on social media has increased since the 2020 lockdown. As more users spend time on social media, companies continuously develop their marketing strategies through the widely available social media marketing options to be specific with their target audience about their offerings. In their study, Barysevich (2020b) also stated that 54% of social media users use social media to research products, and 71% are more likely to purchase products and services based on social media referrals.

Asgari et al. (2023) The study was conducted in May 2020 to understand the underlying factors influencing people's online shopping decisions. The results indicated that those with more experience using online grocery shopping platforms were likelier to continue purchasing their groceries online. The results also indicated that those who showed a higher frequency of online grocery shopping during the pandemic would also be more likely to shop more frequently for groceries online after the pandemic.

The online grocery e-commerce sector is witnessing exponential growth and will continue to see the same in the future. The pandemic catalyzed grocery e-commerce adoption and change. The extensive research conducted by the Mckinsey & Company shows that consumers will continue to favor e-commerce in the coming days. The study suggests continued support for e-commerce from consumers who intend to buy more groceries online. The research also states that the primary driver of online shopping during COVID-19 was consumers preferred moving with convenience and safety.

F. Push Notification and Influence on audience

The article pivots around how Facebook has been used as a platform to communicate with the audience in real time. (Peeroo et al., 2017) illustrates that the stores believe that both positive and negative comments are registered on the Facebook platform.

Positive comments will be like a WOM/ Referal for the stores. Hence social media is considered as influencer for the store's marketing and promotional activities.

The article revolved around how push notifications on mobile apps have an influence. It analysis if there is a relationship between push notifications and customer purchases in the Portuguese grocery market. Then it proceeds to analyze the RFM variables. As per the record, these push notifications have increased the count in the number of transactions. (*The Effect of Promotional Push Notifications From Supermarket Branded Apps on Purchase Behavior - ProQuest*, **n.d.**)

THEORIES:

Symbolic interactionism, the theory, explains how individuals react during different situations. Their reactions are based on their everyday interaction with the social community they are Aquitaine with. This theory has been dynamic and evolved but stands on the basis that different mediums may be used for communication between individuals and social communities. Post the contacts; only the individuals think and process the associations.

Sociological Model of Consumer Behavior This theory walks us through how societal groups influence the people they are part of. The behavior of being with their peer groups forces all the peer members to follow the same buying patterns. This is a peer group mentality of the consumers which is influenced by the social groups formed on all mediums, whether offline or online.

Maslow's "Hierarchy Of Needs", this theory helps us to understand the different factors that constitute the hierarchy of needs. One among them is the pressure of belonging to peer groups. Belongingness has evolved over the period. Today we stand in an era where social media posts and being part of social media groups are terms of belongingness. We might get influenced and share the same need being part of these groups.

Pragmatic theory: This theory talks about how humans are inclined to believe in shallow information even if the understanding is basic. They become instantly satisfied with the readily available information. The audience sees a piece of information, and eventually, they purchase the product. They start to view other people's perspectives and believe that is the truth or facts. Hence the influence of other people matters and is considered as validation in society.

The Psychology of Discounts: The theory revolves around how pricing influences the buyers to instantly purchase an item. People believe that shopping is smarter and cheaper when they buy via offers and discounts. This makes them feel very proud of themselves. Hence there is a statistic that says 70% of millennials view offers or discounts before they make any purchase. This also creates a sense of urgency and makes the buying process spontaneous and rapid as this reduces the room space to think twice before making the purchase decision. Discounts and offers are high influencers in the buying process.

The Social Learning Theory: The theory talks about our behaviors are influenced by the people and society we live. This theory is taking us through 4 major aspects: Attention, Retention, Reproduction, and Motivation. This theory explains how the behaviour of any other person is grasped, remember and imitated.This is a mixed influence of both cognitive and societal factors that are involved.

RESEARCH METHODOLOGY:

The research plan is developed followed by the formation of the questionnaire, determining sample size, collection of data and analysis according to the need identified by the research questions.

The research design used for the project is **Descriptive design** and **Exploratory Design.** Descriptive research is a type of research that describes a population, situation, or phenomenon that is being studied. It focuses on answering the how, what, when, and where questions. It observes and describes a research subject or problem without influencing or manipulating the variables. It is closely associated with observational studies. Exploratory research, as the name implies, intends merely to explore the research questions and not to offer final and conclusive solutions to existing problems. This type of research is usually conducted to study a problem that has yet to be clearly defined. It is conducted to understand the existing problem better but will need more conclusive results. It is often referred to as the grounded theory approach or interpretive research as it is used to answer questions like what, why, and how.

PRIMARY OBJECTIVE

To study the influence of social media on consumer decision-making in the food and grocery sector

SECONDARY OBJECTIVE

1)to understand the marketing tools & techniques and their effectiveness in affecting the consumer's perception and

2)to determine the impact of income and generation on the purchase decision

3)to know the shifts in food purchase habits post covid experienced by gen x, y, z.

PURPOSE OF THE STUDY

This study aims to demonstrate the correlation between social media influences and their impact on the consumer's decisiveness in the food and grocery industry. It explains the significance of technological usage in marketing food and grocery items through the review of relevant literature. It outlines the benefits of digitalization during the epidemic phase.

It also discusses digital-compelling and how it benefits the food industry by providing a variety of options for consumers to choose from. This calls for effective influence and decision-making processes.

Furthermore, it emphasizes tools and techniques used, the E-Commerce & Grocery Transformation of its impacts on GenX, and GenZ, with this topic.

SAMPLE SIZE

The sample size is 116 respondents from Tamil Nadu across various demographic profiles.

SAMPLING TECHNIQUE

The sampling technique for this study is random and convenience sampling.

STATISTICAL TOOLS

Percentage analysis: It was used for analysis of the most popular social media platforms among the participants, checking the fact that most influenced generations basis the current perception is valid or not

Correlation: Correlation was used to ascertain whether the people who are influenced by social media do actually purchase or not.

ANOVA: It was used for finding out the differences between the generations' susceptibility to be influenced by social media, effectiveness of social media notifications, offers/discounts on consumer behaviour in purchasing online/offline

Pie chart and Mean plots: These were used to illustrate the findings in a more easily digestible way.

DATA INTERPRETATION

RESEARCH QUESTION 1: Do participants consider themselves to be influenced by social media?

50.9% of participants said that they were influenced by social media. 26.7% of participants said that they did not know. 22.4% of participants said that they were not influenced by social media. This is illustrated in the pie chart given in Fig 1 given above.

RESEARCH QUESTION 2: Did the participants actually make purchases due to influences from social media?

Contrary to the above question, only 36% of participants were actually influenced by social media to make a lot of purchases. 32% of participants made a few purchases. And the rest 32% of participants did not make any purchases. This is illustrated in the pie chart given in Fig 2 given above.

RESEARCH QUESTION 3: Do people who consider themselves to be influenced actually make more purchases? Is there a relation between the two?

H0: $\rho=0$; the correlation coefficient is 0; There is no association

H1: $\rho>0$; the correlation coefficient is greater than zero. There is an association. a positive correlation could exist

Figure 1. Opinion of the participants regarding influence of social media on their decision making

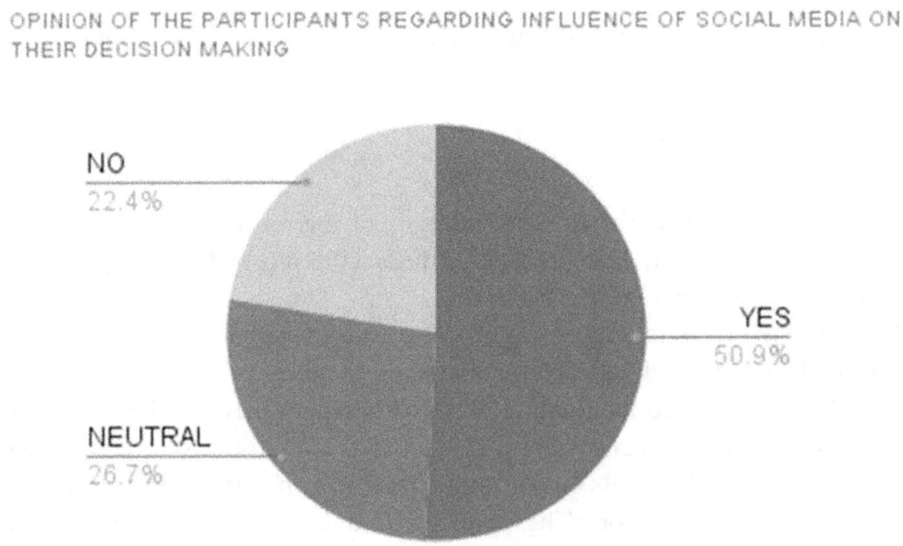

Figure 2. Participants actually influence by social media to make a purchase

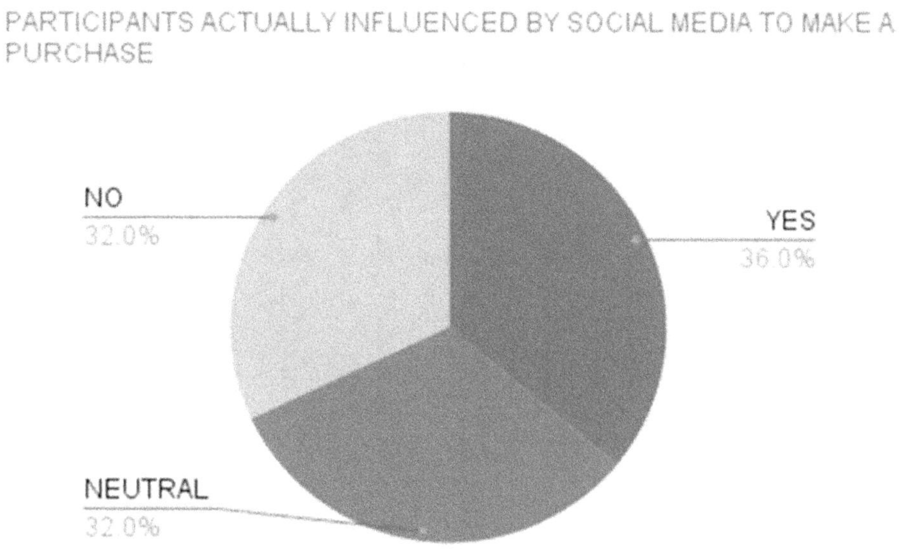

Table 1. Table showing correlation coefficient between consumers' perception of the influence of social media and the actual purchases made due to the influence of social media

CORRELATION	0.1031436332	LOW POSITIVE CORRELATION

Interpretation: $\rho > 0$, the null hypothesis is rejected, the alternate hypothesis is accepted. Therefore, there can be a positive correlation between the perception of the consumer and the actual effect in Food and Grocery purchase decisions being influenced by social media. The ρ value is 0.103 (before excluding outliers) as shown in Table 1, which indicates that **there is a weak positive association.**

All participants are equally affected in their food and grocery purchase decisions irrespective of their perceptions/belief. Those who perceived themselves to be influenced to make purchases due to social media did not necessarily make more purchases than those who perceived themselves to not be influenced by social media. The same is also illustrated by Fig 3 shown below:

RESEARCH QUESTION 4: Is there a difference in the generations' susceptibility to be influenced by social media?

Figure 3. Correlation between perception of influence of social media vs actual purchases made due to it

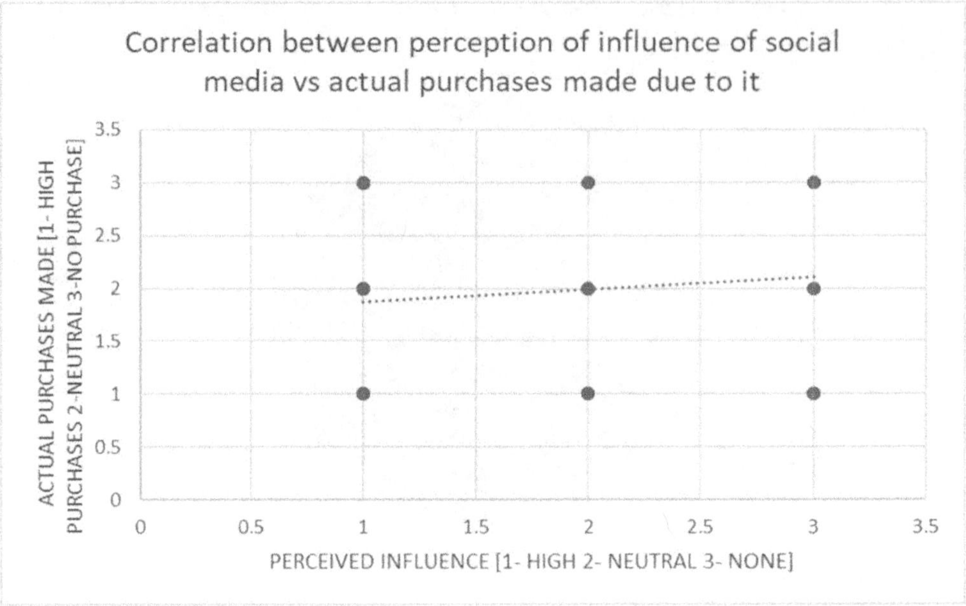

Table 2. Table Showing Anova For Differences In The Three Generations' Tendency To Be Influenced By Social Media

Anova: Single Factor						
SUMMARY						
Groups	*Count*	*Sum*	*Average*	*Variance*		
X	31	99	3.193548	2.427957		
Y	40	129	3.225	1.76859		
Z	45	117	2.6	1.609091		
ANOVA						
Source of Variation	*SS*	*df*	*MS*	*F*	*P-value*	*F crit*
Between Groups	10.3087	2	5.154352	2.739437	0.0689	3.076574
Within Groups	212.6137	113	1.881537			
Total	222.9224	115				

NULL HYPOTHESIS (H0): There is no significant difference in the generation's susceptibility to be influenced by social media.

ALTERATIVE HYPOTHESIS (H1): There is a significant difference in the generation's susceptibility to be influenced by social media.

Interpretation: There was no statistically significant difference in the generation's susceptibility to be influenced by social media as demonstrated by the one-way ANOVA ($F(2,113)=2.73$, $p = 0.0689>0.05$. This is shown in Table 2 given above.

Since the p value is higher than 0.05, we accept the null hypothesis (H0).

As can be seen in the descriptives table, there is no significant difference between the generations' tendency to be influenced by social media to make a purchase. All generations are equally susceptible to being influenced by social media. No one generation is more affected than the others.

RESEARCH QUESTION 5: Are the current perceptions of the most influenced generation, correct?

Fig 4 above shows the perception of the participants regarding the most influenced Generation. With 64% of participants choosing Gen Z, perceptions are largely skewed towards GEN Z being the most easily influenced by social media but results of this study (as denoted in the previous section) show that there is no difference between the generations. Gen X and Y are equally likely to be influenced by social media as Gen Z. However, as shown in Fig 4, there is a big difference in perception with

Figure 4. Most influenced generation according to the perception of participants

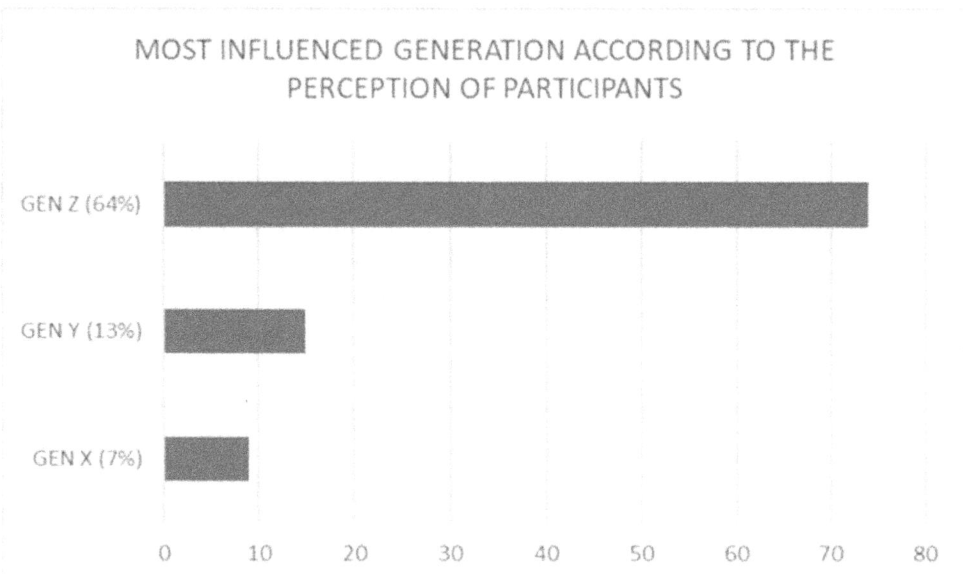

Figure 5. Most popular social media platforms

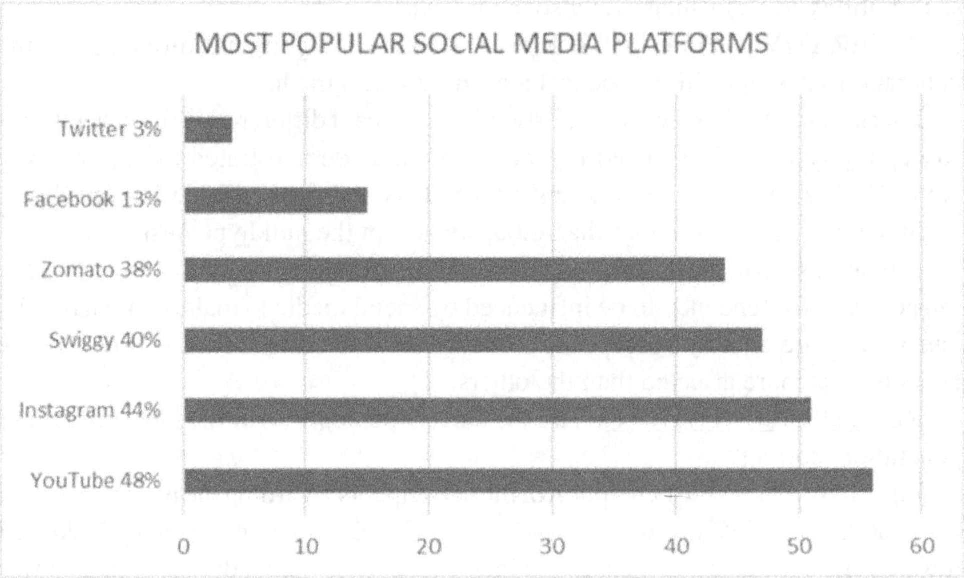

only 13% and 7% of participants considering Gen Y and Gen X to also be influenced by social media.

RESEARCH QUESTION 6: What are the most popular social media platforms among the participants?

YouTube followed by Instagram, Swiggy and Zomato are the most popular platforms which influence consumers in India to make their food and grocery purchase decisions. A bar chart showing the popularity of social media platforms is given above in Fig 5.

RESEARCH QUESTION 7: How effective were notifications for influencing participants to make a purchase?

As shown in the above bar chart given in Fig 6, Notifications are widely ineffective for influencing consumers to make a purchase with a whopping 58% saying that notifications do not influence them to make a purchase (D- Disagree and SD- Strongly Disagree in Fig 6). 16% say that they don't know (N- Neutral in Fig 6) and only 26% agree that notifications influence them to make purchases (A- Agree and SA- Strongly Agree in Fig 6)

RESEARCH QUESTION 8: How effective are notifications for influencing different generations?

NULL HYPOTHESIS (H0): There is no significant difference in the generations' tendency to be influenced by notifications

Figure 6. Effectiveness of notifications or influencing consumers' purchase decisions

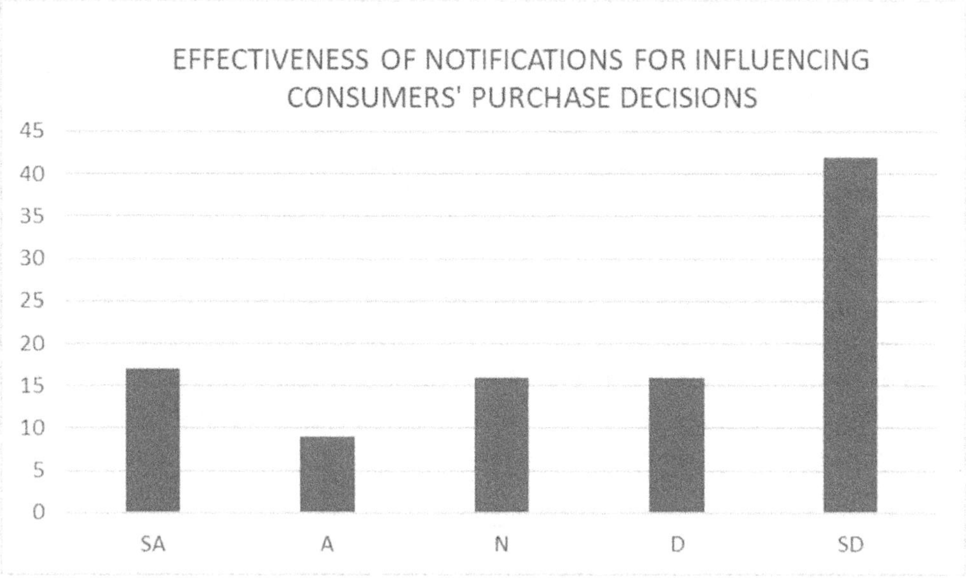

ALTERATIVE HYPOTHESIS (H1): There is a significant difference in the generations' tendency to be influenced by notifications

Table 3. Table Showing Anova For Differences In The Three Generations' Tendency To Be Influenced By Notifications

Anova: Single Factor						
SUMMARY						
Groups	*Count*	*Sum*	*Average*	*Variance*		
X	31	101	3.258065	3.197849		
Y	40	164	4.1	1.476923		
Z	45	149	3.311111	2.173737		
ANOVA						
Source of Variation	*SS*	*df*	*MS*	*F*	*P-value*	*F crit*
Between Groups	17.26835	2	8.634174	3.91549	0.022691	3.076574
Within Groups	249.1799	113	2.205132			
Total	266.4483	115				

Interpretation: There is a significant difference in the influence of notifications on generations as demonstrated by the one-way ANOVA ($F(2,113)=3.92$, $p=0.0226 < 0.05$. This is shown in the above Table 3.

Since the p value is lower than 0.05, so we accept the alternative hypothesis (H1)

There is a significant difference in the generations' tendency to be influenced by notifications.

As can be seen in the descriptives table, there is a difference between the mean influence values of the generations. An influence value of 1 denotes most influenced and a 5 indicates least influenced. Though the effectiveness of notifications in influencing purchases is low, Generation X is said to be influenced the most with the lowest mean influence value of 3.2 in comparison, followed by Gen Z and Gen X respectively. This is shown under the Average column in Table 3.

RESEARCH QUESTION 9: How effective are offers/ discounts for influencing the participants to make a purchase decision?

As shown in the above bar chart given in Fig 7, Offers and discounts are a better way to influence consumers to make purchase decisions compared to notifications. With 40% saying offers influence them to make purchases (A- Agree in Fig 7), offers are the most effective way to influence consumers to make a purchase. 36% said that they don't know (N- Neutral in Fig 7) and only 24% said that it does not influence them to make a purchase (D- Disagree in Fig 7).

Figure 7. Effectiveness of offers/discount for influencing consumers' purchase decisions

Table 4. table showing anova for the differences in the three generations' tendency to be influenced by offers and discounts.

Anova: Single Factor						
SUMMARY						
Groups	*Count*	*Sum*	*Average*	*Variance*		
X	31	79	2.548387	2.322581		
Y	40	114	2.85	2.951282		
Z	45	115	2.555556	2.161616		
ANOVA						
Source of Variation	*SS*	*df*	*MS*	*F*	*P-value*	*F crit*
Between Groups	2.318366	2	1.159183	0.467999	0.627462	3.076574
Within Groups	279.8885	113	2.47689			
Total	282.2069	115				

RESEARCH QUESTION 10: How effective are offers/ discounts for influencing different generations?

NULL HYPOTHESIS (H0): There is no significant difference in the generations' tendency to be influenced by offers/ discounts

ALTERATIVE HYPOTHESIS (H1): There is a significant difference in the generations' tendency to be influenced by offers/ discounts

Interpretation: There is no significant difference by the influence of offers and discounts on various generations as demonstrated by the one-way ANOVA ($F(2,113)=0.47$, $p = 0.627 > 0.05$. This is shown in the above Table 4.

Since the p value is higher than 0.05, we accept the null hypothesis (H0).

There is no significant difference in the generations' tendency to be influenced by offers/ discounts. All generations are equally affected by offers/ discounts. No one generation is more easily influenced than the others.

RESEARCH QUESTION 11: Does cost influence purchase decision irrespective of influence of social media or does influence of social media take precedence?

The pie chart given in the above Fig 8 shows that 38% of participants said that they would not purchase if the cost exceeds their budget. Whereas only 25% of participants said that they would purchase even if the cost exceeds their budget when they find a social media post of a food establishment they liked. 37% considered both cost and social media equally saying that they would save up to purchase from a food establishment they found on social media.

Figure 8. Priority to cost constraint or social media influence in decision making process

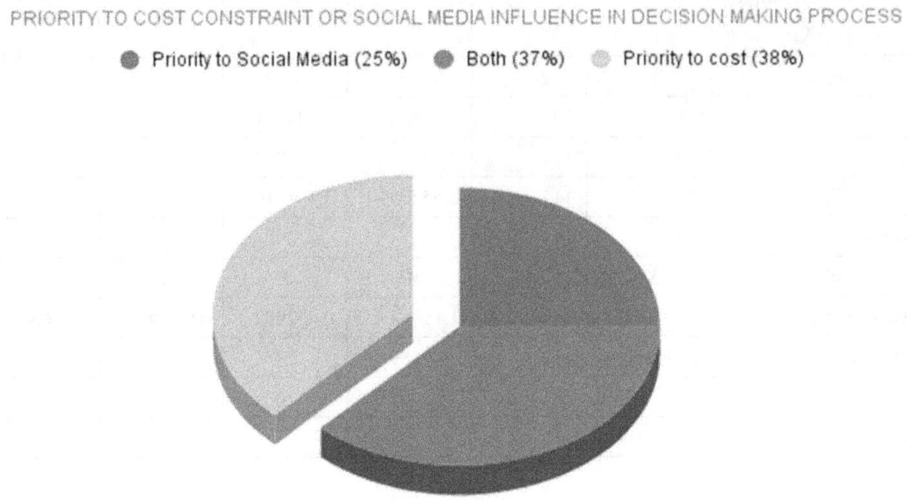

Table 5. Table showing frequency (mode) of ordering online by each generation

FREQUENCY OF ORDERING ONLINE BY EACH GENERATION			
	GEN X	GEN Y	GEN Z
0 to 10 times a month	29	34	38
11 to 25 times a month	2	5	4
More than 25 times	0	1	3
MODE	0 to 10 times a month	0 to 10 times a month	0 to 10 times a month

Thus about 62% of participants would purchase at some point if they found a food establishment they liked on social media, either by exceeding their budget or by saving up.

<u>RESEARCH QUESTION 12</u>: How often do different generations order online?

All generations prefer ordering online 0 to 10 times a month as given in Table 5

<u>RESEARCH QUESTION 13</u>: How often do people from different income brackets order online?

Table 6. Table showing frequency (mode) of ordering online by income groups

FREQUENCY OF ORDERING ONLINE IN EACH INCOME BRACKET			
	HIGH [Rs. 0 to Rs. 2.5 lacs]	**MID [Rs. 2.5 lacs to Rs. 7.5 lacs]**	**LOW [Above Rs. 7.5 lacs]**
0 to 10 times a month	29	30	42
11 to 25 times a month	6	1	4
More than 25 times	1	2	1
MODE	0 to 10 times a month	0 to 10 times a month	0 to 10 times a month

Table 7. Table showing frequency (mode) of going to restaurants by generations

FREQUENCY OF GOING TO RESTAURANTS BY EACH GENERATION			
	GEN X	**GEN Y**	**GEN Z**
0 to 4 times a month	30	25	28
5 to 15 times a month	1	14	15
More than 15 times	0	1	2
MODE	0 to 4 times a month	0 to 4 times a month	0 to 4 times a month

Participants from all income brackets prefer ordering online 0 to 10 times a month as shown in Table 6

RESEARCH QUESTION 14: How often do different generations go to restaurants?

Table 8. Table showing frequency (mode) of going to restaurants by income groups

FREQUENCY OF GOING TO RESTAURANTS IN EACH INCOME BRACKET			
	HIGH [Rs. 0 to Rs. 2.5 lacs]	**MID [Rs. 2.5 lacs to Rs. 7.5 lacs]**	**LOW [Above Rs. 7.5 lacs]**
0 to 4 times a month	22	22	39
5 to 15 times a month	13	9	8
More than 15 times	1	2	0
MODE	0 to 4 times a month	0 to 4 times a month	0 to 4 times a month

Figure 9. Shift in food habits due to COVID

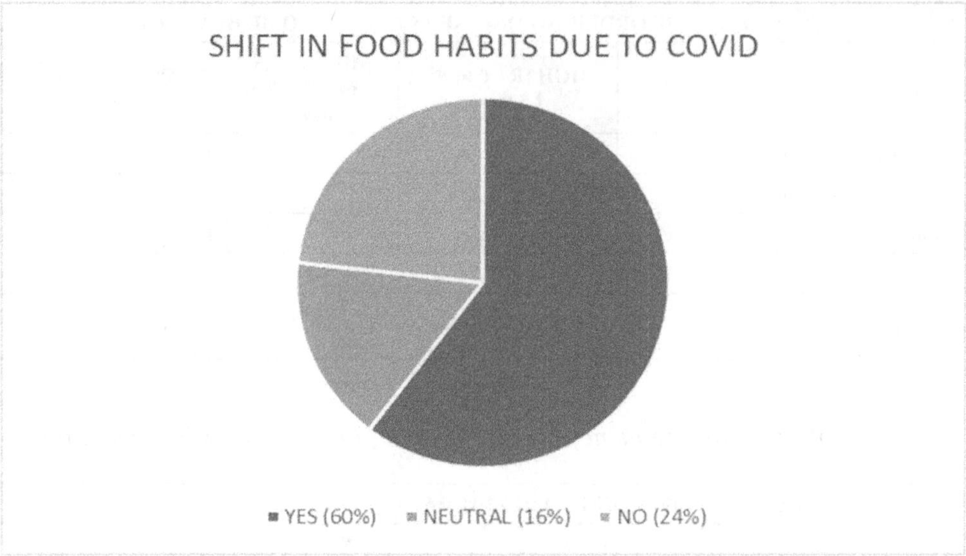

All generations prefer going to restaurants 0 to 4 times a month as shown in Table 7

RESEARCH QUESTION 15: How often do people from different income brackets go to restaurants?

Participants from all income brackets prefer going to restaurants 0 to 4 times a month as shown in Table 8

RESEARCH QUESTION 16: Did COVID shift consumption habits?

As shown in the pie chart given in Fig 9, 60% of participants said that their food habits shifted due to covid. 16% of participants said that they don't know. 24% of participants said that their food habits did not shift due to covid.

FUTURE RECOMMENDATIONS.

The study shows that social media can influence consumers' purchase decisions across all generations. The future of online and offline consumer purchase behavior is expected to continue evolving with advancements in technology, changing consumer preferences, and external factors. Here are a few key trends and possibilities that may shape consumer purchase behavior in the future:

a) **Rise of E-commerce:** The growth of online shopping is expected to continue as more consumers embrace the convenience, variety, and competitive pricing offered by e-commerce platforms with the rise in smartphone and internet penetration.

b) **Omnichannel Experiences:** Consumers increasingly seek seamless shopping experiences that integrate online and offline channels. This involves strategies like ONDC, click-and-collect services, in-store pickup, and personalized recommendations across various touchpoints. The future will likely see more integration and synchronization between online and offline retail experiences.

c) **Mobile and Voice Commerce:** With the increasing adoption of smartphones and voice-activated assistants, mobile and voice commerce will likely become more prevalent. Consumers can make purchases using their mobile devices or simply by voice commands, streamlining the buying process further.

d) **Personalization and Customization:** Consumers are seeking personalized and tailored experiences. Future consumer purchase behavior will likely involve increased personalization in marketing messages, product recommendations, and customized offerings that align with individual preferences and needs.

e) **Social Commerce:** Social media platforms are already influencing consumer purchase behavior, which is expected to continue. The integration of shopping features within social media platforms, such as "buy" buttons or direct checkout options, will likely increase, allowing consumers to make purchases without leaving the platform.

f) **Augmented Reality (AR) and Virtual Reality (VR):** AR and VR technologies can potentially transform how consumers experience and interact with products online. Virtual try-on, virtual showrooms, and immersive shopping experiences can enhance consumer engagement and confidence in online purchases.

It's important to note that these trends are not exhaustive, and consumer behavior is subject to various external factors, cultural influences, and technological advancements. The future of consumer purchase behavior will likely be a dynamic landscape shaped by ongoing technological developments, changing consumer expectations, and market dynamics.

FINDINGS AND CONCLUSION:

Social Media platforms stand part and parcel of our life, and it is inevitable to live without them. Digital Acceptance supported the digital supermarket concept. This gave power to the buyers to decide their mode of purchase (either online or offline). When food and grocery products are considered, there is a homogenous effect viewed in all the generations, who are influenced by marketing tools and techniques. The study finds that 50.9% of participants said social media influenced them. 26.7% of participants said that they did not know. 22.4% of participants said that social media did not influence them. Contrary to the above, only 36% of participants were actually influenced by social media to make a lot of purchases. 32% of participants made a few purchases. And the remaining 32% of participants did not make any purchases.

Correlation analysis between perceived influence of social media on self and actual purchases made by the participants showed that all participants are equally affected in their food and grocery purchase decisions irrespective of their perceptions/belief. Those who perceived themselves to be influenced to make purchases due to social media did not necessarily make more purchases than those who perceived themselves to not be influenced by social media. There were not any generational differences as well. Perceptions are largely skewed towards Gen Z being the most influenced by social media but results of this study show that there is no such significant difference. Gen X and Y are equally likely to be influenced by social media as Gen Z. 60% of participants said that their food habits shifted due to covid. 16% of participants said that they don't know. 24% of participants said that their food habits did not shift due to covid. Notifications are widely ineffective for influencing consumers to make a purchase with a whopping 58% saying that notifications do not influence them to make a purchase. While only 26% said they were influenced. Further, Offers and discounts are a better way to influence consumers to make purchase decisions compared to notifications. With 40% saying that offers influence them to make purchases and only 24% saying that it does not have an effect. 38% of participants said that they prioritize cost constraints over the influence of social media while making purchase decisions. 25% said they would make the purchase even if it was out of their budget if they liked the social media post they saw. Combining this 25% with 37% who said they would save up to make the purchase, it can be seen that social media marketing is quite successful at influencing people to make food purchase decisions which are out of their budget as well.

Thus, social media platforms have a visible effect on all participants irrespective of their mode of purchase, generation, and income brackets.

REFERENCES

Abdul, S. B., Soundararajan, V., & Parayitam, S. (2022). The Relationship between Social Media Influence, EWOM, and E-satisfaction of Consumers in India: A Moderated Moderated-mediation Conditional Model. *Global Business Review, 097215092211301*. Advance online publication. doi:10.1177/09721509221130153

Akbarov, S. (2020). The Impact of Social Media Marketing on Consumer - Moderating Role of Gender and Income. Scholedge International Journal of Multidisciplinary & Allied Studies, 7(7), pp. 147-163. https://doi.org/doi:10.19085/sijmas070701

Ananda, J., Karunasena, G. G., & Pearson, D. (2023). A comparison of online and in-store grocery shopping behaviour and its effects on household food waste. *Technological Forecasting and Social Change*, *194*, 122698. https://doi.org/doi:10.1016/j.techfore.2023.122698

Andreani, F., Gunawan, L., & Haryono, S. (2021). *SOCIAL MEDIA INFLUENCER, BRAND AWARENESS, AND PURCHASE DECISION AMONG GENERATION Z IN SURABAYA*. *Jurnal Manajemen Dan Kewirausahaan*. E-journal., doi:10.9744/jmk.23.1.18-26

Asgari, H., Azimi, G., Titiloye, I., & Jin, X. (2023). Exploring the influences of personal attitudes on the intention of continuing online grocery shopping after the COVID-19 pandemic. *Travel Behaviour & Society*, *33*, 100622. doi:10.1016/j.tbs.2023.100622 PMID:37396502

Balakrishnan, B. K., Dahnil, M. I., & Yi, W. T. (2014). The Impact of Social Media Marketing Medium toward Purchase Intention and Brand Loyalty among Generation Y. *Procedia: Social and Behavioral Sciences*, *148*, 177–185. doi:10.1016/j.sbspro.2014.07.032

Bandura, A. (1977). *Social learning theory*. Prentice Hall.

Bandura, A. (1986). *Social foundations of thought and action: A social cognitive theory*. Prentice-Hall, Inc.

Bandura, A., Ross, D., & Ross, S. A. (1961). Transmission of aggression through the imitation of aggressive models. *Journal of Abnormal and Social Psychology*, *63*(3), 575–582. doi:10.1037/h0045925 PMID:13864605

Barysevich, A. (2020b). How social media influence 71% consumer buying decisions. Search Engine Watch. https://www.searchenginewatch.com/2020/11/20/how-social-media-influence-71-consumer-buying-decisions/

Bolton, R. N., Parasuraman, A., Hoefnagels, A., Migchels, N., Kabadayi, S., Gruber, T., Loureiro, Y. K., & Solnet, D. (2013). Understanding Generation Y and their use of social media: A review and research agenda. *Journal of Service Management*, *24*(3), 245–267. doi:10.1108/09564231311326987

Campo, K., & Breugelmans, E. (2015). Buying Groceries in Brick and Click Stores: Category Allocation Decisions and the Moderating Effect of Online Buying Experience. *Journal of Interactive Marketing*, *31*, 63–78. https://doi.org/doi:10.1016/j.intmar.2015.04.001

Dabija, D.-C., Bejan, B. M., & Tipi, N. (2018). Generation X versus Millennials communication behavior on social media when purchasing food versus tourist services. *E+M. Ekonomie a Management*, *21*(1), 191–205. doi:10.15240/tul/001/2018-1-013

Ewing, M. (2019, June 28). 71% More Likely to Purchase Based on Social Media Referrals [Infographic]. *Blog.Hubspot*. https://blog.hubspot.com/blog/tabid/6307/bid/30239/71-More-Likely-to-Purchase-Based-on-Social-Media-Referrals-Infographic.aspx

· *Food And Grocery Retail Market Size, Share, Opportunities & Forecast*. (2022, November 9). Verified Market Research. https://www.verifiedmarketresearch.com/product/food-grocery-retailmarket/#:~:text=Food%20And%20Grocery%20Retail%20Market%20is%20a%20store%20that%20sells,%2C%20frozen%20foods%2C%20and%20more

Garner, B., & Mady, A. (2023, March 27). · Garner, B., & Mady, A. (2023). Social media branding in the food industry: Comparing B2B and B2C companies' use of sustainability messaging on Twitter. *Journal of Business and Industrial Marketing*. Advance online publication. doi:10.1108/JBIM-09-2022-0418

Khaleeli, M. (2020). The Effect Of Social Media Advertising And Promotion On Online Purchase Intention. *ResearchGate* https://www.researchgate.net/publication/344337458_THE_EFFECT_OF_SOCIAL_MEDIA_ADVERTISING_AND_PROMOTION_ON_ONLINE_PURCHASE_INTENTION

Knezevic, K., Davidaviciene, D., & Skrobot, S. (2017). Social networks as a communication tool in social supermarkets. *SOTICS 2017 : The Seventh International Conference on Social Media Technologies, Communication, and Informatics*. (pp.5-10).

Momin, A. (2023, June 8). Grocery Industry Analysis: What is the Future of Grocery Stores? *PESTLE Analysis*. https://pestleanalysis.com/grocery-industry-analysis/

Naeem, M. (2021). Do social media platforms develop consumer panic buying during the fear of Covid-19 pandemic. *Journal of Retailing and Consumer Services, 58*, 102226. https://doi.org/ doi:10.1016/j.jretconser.2020.102226

Pauliene, R., & Sedneva, K. (2019). The Influence of Recommendations in Social Media on Purchase Intentions of Generations Y and Z. *Organizations and Markets in Emerging Economies*, *10*(2), 227–256. doi:10.15388/omee.2019.10.12

Peeroo, S., Samy, M., & Jones, B. (2017). Facebook: A blessing or a curse for grocery stores? *International Journal of Retail & Distribution Management*, *45*(12), 1242–1259. doi:10.1108/IJRDM-12-2016-0234

Prasad, S., Garg, A., & Prasad, S. K. (2019). Purchase decision of generation Y in an online environment. *Marketing Intelligence & Planning*, *37*(4), 372–385. doi:10.1108/MIP-02-2018-0070

Pütter, M. (2017). The Impact of Social Media on Consumer Buying Intention. *Journal of International Business Research and Marketing*, *3*(1), 7–13. doi:10.18775/jibrm.1849-8558.2015.31.3001

Ramanathan, U., Subramanian, N., & Parrott, G. (2017). Role of social media in retail network operations and marketing to enhance customer satisfaction. *International Journal of Operations & Production Management*, *37*(1), 105–123. https://doi.org/doi:10.1108/IJOPM-03-2015-0153

Sashi, C. (2012). Customer engagement, buyer-seller relationships, and social media. *Management Decision*, *50*(2), 253–272. doi:10.1108/00251741211203551

Sokolova, K., & Kefi, H. (2020). Instagram and YouTube bloggers promote it, why should I buy? How credibility and parasocial interaction influence purchase intentions. *Journal of Retailing and Consumer Services*, *53*, 101742. doi:10.1016/j.jretconser.2019.01.011

· Sulthana, A. N., & Shanmugam, V. (2021). USAGE OF SOCIAL MEDIA ON PURCHASE DURING COVID-19. *ResearchGate*. https://www.researchgate.net/publication/348349944_USAGE_OF_SOCIAL_MEDIA_ON_PURCHASE_DURING_COVID-19

The Effect of Promotional Push Notifications from Supermarket Branded Apps on Purchase Behavior - ProQuest. (n.d.). https://search.proquest.com/openview/cf96a2c8a801b6187359f136ca12ed13/1?pq-origsite=gscholar&cbl=2026366&diss=y&casa_token=XXF8MrJyw34AAAAA:WbWQlr48FvV7c-X4S0kJk_Eg0RhcCbrTUGpqr0d9UmoIxAXY7spFrp1HLdVHwnSqPNYex7qHEY8

The next horizon for grocery e-commerce: Beyond the pandemic bump. (2022, April 29). McKinsey & Company. https://www.mckinsey.com/industries/retail/our-insights/the-next-horizon-for-grocery-ecommerce-beyond-the-pandemic-bump#/

Thoumrungroje, A. (2014). The Influence of Social Media Intensity and EWOM on Conspicuous Consumption. *Procedia: Social and Behavioral Sciences, 148*, 7–15. doi:10.1016/j.sbspro.2014.07.009

Thoumrungroje, A. (2014). The Influence of Social Media Intensity and EWOM on Conspicuous Consumption. *Procedia: Social and Behavioral Sciences, 148*, 7–15. doi:10.1016/j.sbspro.2014.07.009

Timothy, D. (2019). The influence of social media on consumer buying behavior: a case study of Ho Technical University, Ho. *ResearchGate*. https://www.researchgate.net/publication/333852892_The_influence_of_social_media_on_consumer_buying_behavior_a_case_study_of_Ho_Technical_University_Ho

Zhang, J., & Du, M. (2020). Utilization and effectiveness of social media message strategy: How B2B brands differ from B2C brands. *Journal of Business and Industrial Marketing, 35*(4), 721–740. doi:10.1108/JBIM-06-2018-0190

Zhang, T., Omran, B. A., & Cobanoglu, C. (2017). Generation Y's positive and negative eWOM: Use of social media and mobile technology. *International Journal of Contemporary Hospitality Management, 29*(2), 732–761. doi:10.1108/IJCHM-10-2015-0611

Zolfaghari, A., Thomas-Francois, K., & Somogyi, S. (2022a). Consumer adoption of digital grocery shopping: What is the impact of consumer's prior-to-use knowledge? *British Food Journal, 125*(4), 1355–1373. doi:10.1108/BFJ-02-2022-0187

KEY TERMS AND DEFINITIONS

Digital Acceptance: The acknowledgment and adoption of automated services in the digital era. Being a digital literate describes a person who is eligible to reap benefit by using cybernated services.

Digital Supermarket: Digital Supermarket is a new concept of purchasing groceries and other necessaries online

Consumers' Purchase Decisions: The consumers' become conscious of what they purchase and identify their necessaries & requirements. With the available alternate products, the consumers make their own purchase decisions.

APPENDIX: SURVEY QUESTIONS

Email

1. Name of Respondent
2. Occupation of the respondent
   a. Employed
   b. Student
   c. Homemaker
   d. Self Employed
   e. Retired
3. Please select the age group you belong to ?
   a. Generation Z (1997-2012)
   b. Generation Y (1981-1996)
   c. Generation X (1965-1980)
   d. Generation Alpha (2013-2025)
4. Please Specify your gender
   a. Male
   b. Female
5. Income per annum
   a. ₹0 - ₹2,50,000
   b. ₹2,50,000 - ₹7,50,000
   c. More than Rs. 7,50,000
6. Do you think social media influences your decisions while purchasing food and grocery ?
   a. Yes
   b. Maybe
   c. No
7. Which of the below mentioned platforms do you use often to know more about food and grocery ?
   a. Facebook
   b. Instagram
   c. Twitter
   d. Youtube
   e. Swiggy
   f. Zomato
8. Do you think there is a shift in food habits post COVID-19 era ?
   a. Yes
   b. No
   c. Maybe

9. Have you ever got influenced by any blogs/ memes/ videos and ordered food/ went to a restaurant
   a. 1 Strongly Agree
   b. 2
   c. 3
   d. 4
   e. 5 Strongly Disagree
10. Which Generation do you think is highly influenced by social media while making their decision to purchase food and grocery?
   Choose multiple
   a. Generation X (1965-1980)
   b. Generation Y (1981-1996)
   c. Generation Z (1997-2012)
   d. Generation Alpha (2013-2025)
11. People choose online purchase of food and grocery because:
   a. Comfortable and Convenient
   b. Feeling Lazy and Tired
   c. Lack of Time
12. Do these kinds of notifications persuade you to buy food online or at restaurants?

Figure 10.

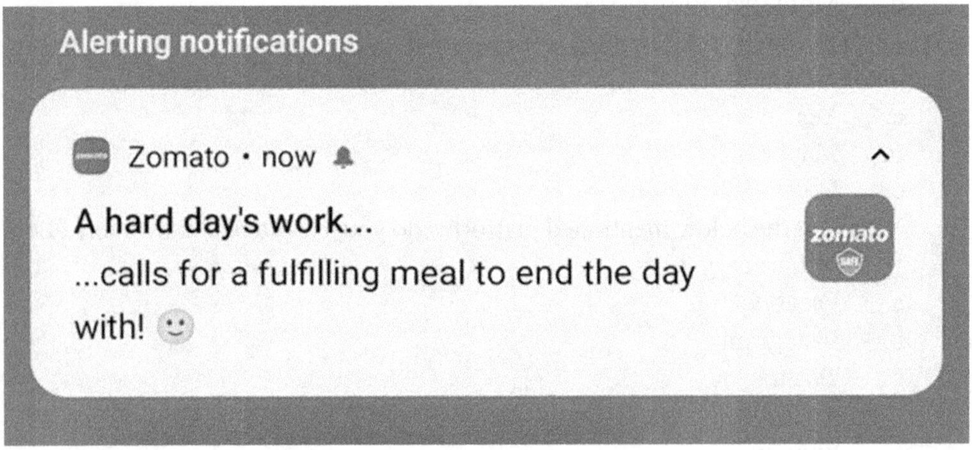

A. 1 Strongly Agree
B. 2
C. 3
D. 4
E. 5 Strongly Disagree

13. Do the offers and discounts advertised over the social media platforms tempt you to purchase food/grocery at that particular shop?

Figure 11.

a. Yes
b. No
c. Maybe

14. How many times do you order food/grocery online in a month?
    a. 0 - 10 times
    b. 11 - 25 times
    c. More than 26 times
15. You saw an Instagram video which showed a restaurant and the food varieties they offer. You instantly liked it and wanted to visit there immediately. But the rates are a bit costlier in comparison to your budget, will you still make it to that restaurant?
    a. Yes I will definitely visit that restaurant
    b. I will save money and make it to that restaurant in a month or two
    c. No I will never make it
    16. How often do you go to restaurants in a month ?
        a. < 4 times
        b. 5 - 15 times
        c. More than 15 times

Chapter 3
Greek Consumers' Perceptions on Sponsored Food Advertisement Through Social Media and Its Effects on Their Purchasing Behavior

Nikolaos Sklavounos
International Hellenic University, Greece & Perrotis College, American Farm School of Thessaloniki, Greece

George Kartsiotis
Perrotis College, American Farm School of Thessaloniki, Greece

Konstantinos Rebholz
Perrotis College, American Farm School of Thessaloniki, Greece

ABSTRACT

As the usage of social media becomes more and more infused in the daily life of billions of individuals, paid advertisement via them offers companies an enormous degree of visibility and exposure. This research investigates the perceptions, attitudes and behavioral responses of young Greek consumers regarding sponsored food products in order to determine the impact of this advertising method on their purchasing behavior. This study applies quantitative research methods to collect primary data besides the review of secondary sources from the existing literature. The collected data are analysed with the appropriate statistical tools and the research findings are discussed thoroughly. The results of the study reveal indicators and information about how food brands and sponsored food advertisement on social media are perceived by young social media users and how users respond and behave when in contact with sponsored advertisements while browsing on social media platforms. Finally, recommendations for future research are also presented.

DOI: 10.4018/978-1-6684-8868-3.ch003

INTRODUCTION

As the usage of social media becomes more and more infused in the daily life of billions of individuals, paid advertisement via them offers companies an enormous degree of visibility and exposure, with food companies included. Social media are defined as "*a group of Internet-based applications that build on the ideological and technological foundations of Web 2.0 and allow the creation and exchange of User Generated Content*" (Kaplan & Haenlein, 2010, p. 61). Social media has become an essential component of our daily lives in today's digitally connected world. It has changed the way we communicate, share information, and even make purchases. As social media platforms gain popularity, businesses, including the food industry, are increasingly using them to promote their products and services. Sponsored food commercials, particularly those found on social media, have emerged as a common marketing approach used by food firms to communicate with consumers and influence their purchase behavior (Kucharczuk et al., 2022).

However, despite the prevalence of sponsored food advertisements on social media, there is a lack of research focusing on Greek consumers' perceptions of such advertisements and their consequent implications on purchasing behavior. To the best of the authors' knowledge, there is limited prior literature in this general context such as the qualitative study of Tsimonis and Dimitriadis (2014) regarding the brand marketing strategies in social media of 14 companies operating in the Greek market and the recent review of Tsochantaridou et al. (2023) regarding the possible influence of nutrition-related advertisements through television, social media, or video games on the choice and consumption of unhealthy foods and drinks in adolescents. This study intends to fill this research gap by shedding light on Greek consumers' opinions regarding sponsored food marketing on social media, as well as the impact of these advertisements on their purchase behavior. Understanding how Greek consumers perceive these adverts and how they influence their shopping decisions is critical for firms looking to optimize their digital marketing strategy.

Furthermore, cultural and social aspects have a considerable impact on customer perceptions and behaviors (Madhavan & Kaliyaperumal, 2015). Greece, with its rich history and distinct cultural heritage, provides an exceptional setting for researching consumer responses to sponsored food marketing on social media. The Greek people have a strong affinity to traditional culinary practices and food values. Investigating young Greek consumers' perceptions of sponsored food advertisements in the context of their cultural and historical background may provide useful insights into the effectiveness of these advertisements and their alignment with local values.

The main incentive for this research project is to investigate the perception, attitudes and behavioral responses of young Greek consumers regarding sponsored social media content about food products. The purpose of this research is to determine the impact of this advertising method and the exploration of the responses of the targeted group. Furthermore, the research aim is to establish whether social media campaigns are beneficiary for food products, to what extend and to investigate the perceived risk, trust and probability of purchase by the young Greek consumers.

This study applies quantitative research methods to collect primary data besides the review of secondary sources from the existing literature. The research questionnaire was completed by accessing respondents through online channels. The findings were analysed through SPSS, where calculations and tests (correlations and descriptive statistics) were used to obtain a better understanding of the data. The findings of this study contribute to the growing body of knowledge in the field of consumer behavior and social media advertising while providing practical implications for marketers and policymakers alike. By understanding how Greek consumers respond to sponsored food advertisements, businesses can refine their marketing strategies and foster meaningful connections with their target audience in the Greek market.

LITERATURE REVIEW

Advertising intends to stimulate a market towards achieving more sales of a service or product. The word advertising roots back the Latin "Ad vertere", which is translated into "to turn one's attention to". A more recent definition of advertising is "*paid, owned, and earned mediated communication, activated by an identifiable brand and intent on persuading the consumer to make some cognitive, affective or behavioural change, now or in the future*" (Kerr & Richards, 2021, p. 25). According to Richards et al. (2009), advertising is designed to persuade the reader to take some meditated action, now or in the future, due to the fact that the message is conveyed from sender to receiver through a medium (social media in this case), dissimilar to in person communication. Advertisement can be broken down in two categories, direct and indirect. In the former, the potential consumer/receiver understands that the sender is trying to persuade towards the purchase of a product, while in indirect advertisement it is more difficult for the consumer to acknowledge being a marketing target. Indirect advertisement aims more towards the awareness building of a brand (McQuarrie & Phillips, 2005).

The methods used for marketing, advertisement and for the persuasion of the consumer practices are regulated in the EU by the Consumer Protection Law, the EU Consumer and Marketing Law and the European Advertising Standards Alliance (EASA). These legal segments are established to voice on advertising issues and ensure that ads are legal, decent, honest and truthful (European Economic and Social Committee, 2023; European Commission, 2023).

In the past, marketers used the traditional means of advertisement such as radio, television, press, cinema, etc., which have been proven empirically successful for the advertising firms. The consumers of today became more sceptical, due to the abundance of advertisements surrounding them. Social media platforms offer businesses the opportunity to advertise to a specific target group in a more inconspicuous manner (Boerman et al., 2017a). This can be implemented either through sponsored advertisement directly through the platform, or via affiliation with popular social media users.

Social Media

A social media platform can be characterized as software that uses the existing functions of the internet for the creation and demonstration of user generated content (Kietzmann et al., 2011). These researchers believe in the essentiality of social media as a critical and substantial method of communication between individuals, communities and organizations after the introduction of the internet. The characteristics of social media are being dissected by Kietzmann et al. (2011) into 7 brackets. The presence of all seven is not mandatory, but this honeycomb represents the aspects of social media user experiences and its implication for firms (Kietzmann et al., 2011).

The most popular social media websites are currently Facebook, YouTube, WhatsApp, Instagram, WeChat and Tik Tok (Statista, 2023a). As of 2022, the average internet user spent 147 minutes every day on social media, the daily usage of 2021 was 145 minutes (Statista, 2023b). The number of social media users in 2022 was over 4.59 billion people and is expected to grow to almost 6 billion in 2027. Globally 6 out of every 10 people use social media, in southern Europe the social network penetration as of January 2023 is up to 76.7% (Statista, 2023c).

With the invention of social media, the manner of communication amongst people was redefined, which inevitably led to a change in advertisement techniques and impacted consumer behavior. The internet, especially with the introduction of Web2.0, which can be characterised as the total of internet based applications allowing the creation and exchange of user generated content, established a two-way and many-to-many communication system allowing consumers to connect, create, produce, and share media content (Kaplan & Haenlein, 2010). This digital interaction of user generated content created an electronic word of mouth, appearing more influential than the traditional word of mouth, which is considered to be the one of the most significant factors impacting consumer decision making processes (Selvi & Thomson, 2016).Nowadays, the consumer is able to look up the social media account of a brand, read comments other people made about the brand, see other people's ratings and form an opinion based on all of these. Due to the constant communication, interaction

Figure 1. Social media functionalities
(Kietzmann et al. 2011)

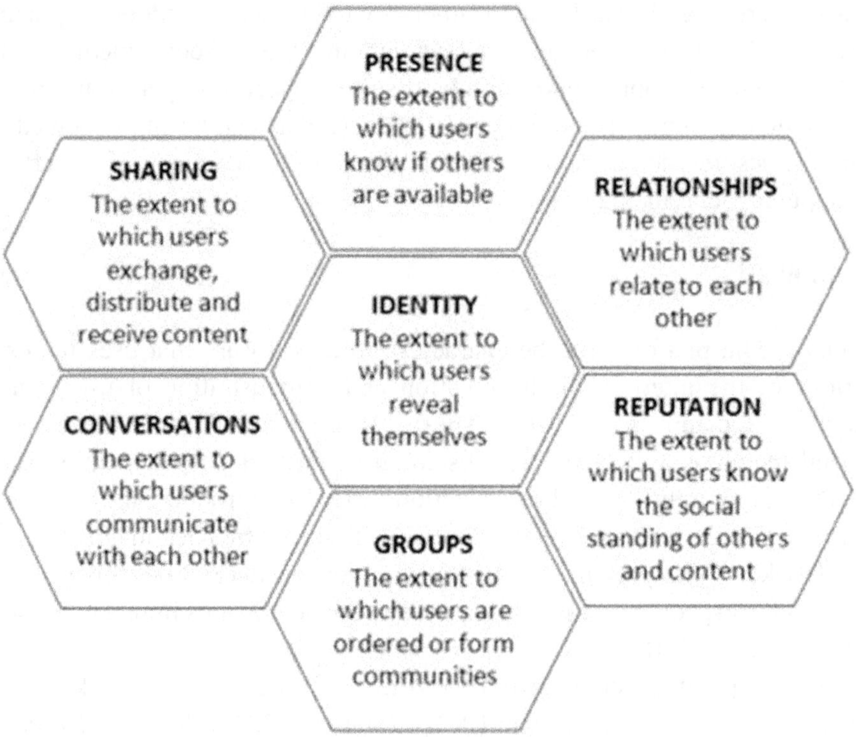

and openness of the brand via social media, the consumer-brand relationship gains elements and qualities of interpersonal relationships, closer, more intimate and emotion-driven (Labrecque, 2014). Labrecque finds that consumers involved in such relationships tend to be more loyal towards those brands.

Social media, especially after the turn of the century, has infiltrated our daily lives, becoming the most used activity on the internet. Inevitably, consumer-oriented companies started to engage and influence consumers throughout social media usage. Social media provide a cheaper and easier path for businesses to engage with their customer base, compared to traditional advertising (Anderson et al., 2011). Social media provide new ways for brands to create customer value, primarily throughout the possibility of interactions between the brand and the consumer and between the consumer and other consumers (Hamilton et al., 2016), thus gaining customer value in terms of exposure, increasing the brand loyalty and overall bringing consumers closer to the brand. This can be achieved with the increase of the frequency of information shared on social media, the enhancement of the relevance of the published information and the extended interaction between the company and the individual (Adjei et al., 2012). Studies have shown that interactions of millennials with brands via social media are not only triggered for the purpose of gathering information about the product, but also for *"fun"* (interaction for entertainment) and also consumers initiate interaction with a brand "*to identify with or psychologically connect to a brand*" (Rohm et al., 2013, p. 301).

Nowadays, social media are considered as very effective interaction mechanisms between brands and consumers. Social media offer the brands a space to advertise direct and indirect, to build up a brand name, to maintain constant customer relations and to influence consumer behavior and perception (Alalwan et al. 2017). A brand outside of social media lacks communication with the consumer and potential customer. Fundamentally, social media enable communication. By building a virtual community, the brand benefits in terms of knowledge sharing, participation of the consumer in the brand and by gaining information about the consumer (Weinberg et al., 2013).

Social Media and Consumer Perception

Social media engages with a person's behavior (Bleier & Eisenbeiss 2015; Steinfield et al., 2008; Mattke et al. 2020; Arora et al., 2020; Ma et al., 2022; Lütjens et al., 2022), interfering with the consumers not only on a cognitive level (Lütjens et al., 2022), but also on an emotional level (Ma et al., 2022), manipulating self-esteem (Steinfield et al., 2008) and providing the individual with a sense of belonging into a group (Mattke et al., 2020). Purchasing behaviors can be boosted through social media content that leads to the engagement with the customer (Malthouse et al. 2016). Different types of brand posts lead to influencing different aspects of consumer behavioral, cognitive or emotional engagement (Ma et al., 2022).

Mattke et al. (2020) debated that in social media there are evident examples of herd behavior, interpreting that a user is more likely to subscribe, investigate and purchase a page, product or service, if it is liked by either a close friend or a great number of individuals. According to Mattke et al. (2020, p. 11), *"when a user sees a sponsored content, "liked" by others, the behavior of others influences a user's behavior"*. This is the great illusion a firm can achieve via social media marketing, especially via sponsored marketing.

Social Media Sponsored ads

Sponsored advertisement via Instagram and Facebook from the perspective of the brand can be either achieved directly through Instagram ads and Facebook ads, which are offered directly from the platform and give the brand a plethora of customization possibilities, such as the selection of the target audience, the location and the range of the advertisement, the frequency, the time period and the format of the advertisement. Alternatively, brands can advertise products or services through a popular user of the platform via user generated content. In both advertisement methods, it is mandatory to be visible that the ad is sponsored (most commonly with the word sponsored appearing on the top of the post or story) by the Federal Trade Commission in the US and by consumer protection laws in Europe (Boerman et al., 2018).

The effects on sponsored advertisement has been proven double-sided. The positive outcome is the engagement of the receiver with the brand, raising the knowledge he/she possesses about the brand and ultimately being persuaded to consume the brand's products. The engagement with the brand happens when the consumer navigates into the brand's account by clicking on the advertisement. Concerning the restaurants and the food sector, the average click-through rate across Google Ads, Facebook, Instagram, Twitter and LinkedIn in 2023 is 8.37% (Chaffey, 2023).

However, the sponsored disclaimer raises the suspicion of the consumer regarding the brand. This can hurt the perception of the consumer regarding the brand's trustworthiness (Kim et al., 2019). Distrusting beliefs about the post can appear because the consumer connects with a sponsored advertisement without consent. The fact that the consumer gets in contact with an advertisement while browsing social media can also raise a feeling of irritation. This irritation can be transmitted towards the brand, affecting negatively the brand's image (Boerman et al., 2017b).

METHODOLOGY

Research, Questionnaire and Sample Description

The aim of this research is to gain insights into consumers' perceptions regarding the presence of food brands and sponsored food advertisement on social media. To investigate this issue a quantitative research approach was selected. Quantitative methods fundamentally involve the collection, processing, description and analysis of data, with the objective of the explanation of a case (Kolb, 2008), and by definition involve the use of numerical data and statistical tools in order to research different phenomena (Nunan et al., 2020).

Prior research indicates that web surveys compared to mail surveys are faster, less expensive, offer easy access to wide dispersed respondents and provide data in numerical form in real time (Dillman et al., 2014). Thus, all data for this research was collected via an online survey with the questionnaire forwarded through email and social media accounts (private messaging and posts). Google Forms were used to generate the online version of the questionnaire and the resulting spread sheet was migrated to and processed with SPSS Version 28.

The questionnaire included 17 questions. The first four were demographical oriented (gender, age, occupation, residency), followed by six questions about social media preferences and usage, two binary type questions about perceptions of food brands sponsored content, and finally five questions (answered in a 5-Likert scale) again about perceptions of food brand sponsored content. The questionnaire is included in the Appendix. The research sample consists of 200 young adults, aged from 18 to 39, which are separated into three age groups so as to categorize them into two generations. In the first age group, 18 to 24, fall respondents of Generation Z, while the other two are composed of Millennials, which for the purposes of this research were split into two sub-groups, ages 25 to 30, and ages 31 to 39.

ANALYSIS AND RESULTS

Frequency Tables

Most of the correspondents (52%) identified as female, 46% identified as male, 1% as non-binary and 1% did not want to disclose their gender identity; the difference between female and male participants is small. Regarding age, the majority (70.5%) of the respondents were in the 18-24 group, and thus belong to generation Z, which are the digital natives growing up in a world where social media were pre-existing. The second and third age groups, from 25 to 30 and from 31 to 39 respectively, accounted for 22% and 7.5%. Participants belonging in those age groups are Millennials. These individuals witnessed the development of the internet and social media, making themselves digital immigrants. Each generation approaches and perceives social

Table 1. Gender and age group frequency

	Gender		Age group					
			18-24		25-30		31-39	
	Frequency	Percent	Frequency	Percent	Frequency	Percent	Frequency	Percent
Female	104	52	76	53.9	19	43.18	9	60
Male	92	46	63	44.68	24	54.55	5	33.3
Other	2	1	1	0.71	0	0	1	6.67
Prefer not to say	2	1	1	0.71	1	2.27	0	0
Total	200	100	141	100	44	100	15	100

Table 2. Occupation frequency

Occupation	Frequency	Percent
Enlisted	2	1
Full-time working	52	26
Part-time working	11	5.5
Self-employed	12	6
Student	81	40.5
Unemployed	4	2
Working Student	38	19
Total	200	100

Table 3. Residency frequency

Residency	Frequency	Percent
City (over 100.000 in population)	138	69
Urban area / town / village (under 100.000 in population)	62	31
Total	200	100

media dissimilar and differentiates regarding food buying behavior (Kamenidou et al., 2020; Fietkiewicz et al., 2016; Childers & Boatwright, 2020; Leung, 2013).

From Table 2 and Table 3, we deduct that the majority of the correspondents are students (40.5% students and 19% being working students), 26% of them work full-time, 5.5% work part-time, 6% are self-employed, 2% are unemployed and 1% are enlisted. Also, it is observed that more than two out of three (69%) respondents live in high populated environments, with a population of over 100,000 and that the remaining 31% live in low populated areas, towns and villages. This provides indicators for both groups; hence, both data sets are relatively well sized.

From Table 4 it is deduced that there is a clear preference for Instagram amongst the respondents (68.5%), followed by Tik Tok with 12.5% and YouTube with 10.5%, while that Facebook received only 4.5% of the answers. These results are in accordance with the findings of the leading audience targeting company for the global marketing industry GWI which show that younger people are more likely to say that Instagram is their "favourite" social media platform (GWI, 2022).

From Table 5 it is deduced that the majority of the respondents (42%) use social media for 3-4 hours, 24% for 4-6 hours and 7.5% use social media for more than 6 hours per day. Also, 46% of the participants notice sponsored food advertisement

Table 4. Social media platforms usage (multiple answers allowed) and preferences (single answer)

	Usage		Preference	
Social Media platform	**Frequency**	**Percent**	**Frequency**	**Percent**
Facebook	117	19.9	9	4.5
Instagram	188	32	137	68.5
Tik Tok	110	18.7	25	12.5
YouTube	132	22.4	21	10.5
Twitter	29	4.9	6	3
Other	12	2	2	1
Total	588	100	200	100

Table 5. How much time do you spent on social media per day and how often do you notice a sponsored food advertisement?

Time spent	Frequency	Percent	Notice a sponsored food ad	Frequency	Percent
1-2 hours	53	26.5	**More than 6 times per day**	4	2
3-4 hours	84	42	**Once per 4-5 days**	49	24.5
4-6 hours	48	24	**Once per week**	92	46
Over 6 hours	15	7.5	**Once to 5 times per day**	55	27.5
Total	200	100	**Total**	200	100

once a week, 24.5% once per 4 to 5 days, 27.5% once to five times per day and only 2% see this type of advertisements more than 6 times per day, i.e., most of the respondents do not often encounter sponsored food advertisement.

In Table 6 it is observed that the majority of the respondents (58%) agree or strongly agree that they feel annoyed/ irritated when a sponsored ad appears while I they are using social media. Also, Table 7 outlines that 65.5% of the participants were negative regarding purchasing a food product or service after watching an advertisement. This could be an indicator towards consumer distrust in regard to food advertisement on social media.

Table 9 shows the answers about the perception of the participants regarding the trustworthiness of a food brand appearing in sponsored advertisement in social media. More specifically, 59% are neutral, 27.5% consider a brand or a food product that appears in a sponsored ad as unreliable (8,5% very unreliable, 19%

Table 6. Consumers irritation regarding sponsored food advertisement while browsing frequency

	Frequency	Percent	Cumulative percent
Strongly disagree	9	4.5	4.5
Disagree	18	9	13.5
Neutral	57	28.5	42
Agree	49	24.5	66.5
Strongly Agree	67	33.5	100
Total	200	100	

Table 7. Purchase of food product or service after contact with an advertisement in social media

	Frequency	Percent
No	131	65.5
Yes	69	34.5
Total	200	100

Table 8. How trustworthy do you consider a brand or a food product that appears in a sponsored ad?

	Frequency	Percent
Very unreliable	17	8.5
Unreliable	38	19
Neutral	118	59
Reliable	21	10.5
Very reliable	6	3
Total	200	100

Table 9. Would you purchase a food product that you do not know but appears as a sponsored advertisement in your social media?

	Frequency	Percent
Definitely not	34	17
Probably not	70	35
Neither yes or no	67	33.5
Probably yes	25	12.5
Definitely yes	4	2
Total	200	100

*Table 10. Gender identity * Time spent on social media per day cross tabulation table chart*

			Time spent on social media per day				Total
			1-2 hours	3-4 hours	4-6 hours	> 6 hours	
Gender identity	Female	Count	18	44	33	9	104
		% within Gender identity	17.3%	42.3%	31.7%	8.7%	100%
		% within Time spent on social media per day	34%	52.4%	68.8%	60%	52%
		% of Total	9%	22%	16.5%	4.5%	52%
	Male	Count	34	38	14	6	92
		% within Gender identity	37%	41.3%	15.2%	6.5%	100%
		% within Time spent on social media per day	64.2%	45.2%	29.2%	40%	46%
		% of Total	17%	19%	7%	3%	46%
	Other	Count	1	1	0	0	2
		% of Total	0.5%	0.5%	0%	0%	1%
	Prefer not to say	Count	0	1	1	0	2
		% of Total	0%	0.5%	0.5%	0%	1%
Total		Count	53	84	48	15	200
		% within Gender identity	26.5%	42%	24%	7.5%	100%
		% within Time spent on social media per day	100%	100%	100%	100%	100%
		% of Total	26.5%	42%	24%	7.5%	100%

unreliable) and the remaining 13.5% consider them as reliable (10.5% reliable, 3% very reliable). Thus, the percentage of respondents that trust a brand displayed via an advertisement is small.

Cross tabulation

Regarding gender identity in correlation with the time spent on social media, from the given options of the questionnaire, only the female and male gender identities will be studied, because the data set contains very few answers for the other categories. Table 10 displays that the great majority of female participants either spend 3-4 hours (42.3%), or 4-6 hours (31.7%) online. Concerning male participants, 41.3% spend 3-4 hours on social media and 37% spend 1-2 hours. It is noted that 64.2% of the users that spend 1-2 hours on social media are men and that from the participants

*Table 11. Age group * Time spent on social media per day cross tabulation table chart*

			Time spent on social media per day				Total
			1-2 hours	3-4 hours	4-6 hours	Over 6 hours	
Age group	18-24	Count	28	64	38	11	141
		% within Age group	19.9%	45.4%	27%	7.8%	100%
		% within Time spent on social media per day	52.8%	76.2%	79.2%	73.3%	70.5%
		% of Total	14%	32%	19%	5.5%	70.5%
	25-30	Count	18	16	8	2	44
		% within Age group	40.9%	36.4%	18.2%	4.5%	100%
		% within Time spent on social media per day	34%	19%	16.7%	13.3%	22%
		% of Total	9%	8%	4%	1%	22%
	31-39	Count	7	4	2	2	15
		% within Age group	46.7%	26.7%	13.3%	13.3%	100%
		% within Time spent on social media per day	13.2%	4.8%	4.2%	13.3%	7.5%
		% of Total	3.5%	2%	1%	1%	7.5%
Total		Count	53	84	48	15	200
		% within Age group	26.5%	42%	24%	7.5%	100%
		% within Time spent on social media per day	100%	100%	100%	100%	100%
		% of Total	26.5%	42%	24%	7.5%	100%

that spent 4-6 hours on social media (68.8%) identify as female, and the ones who spend over 6 hours (60%) also identify as female.

From the cross tabulation of the age groups and the time spent daily on social media displayed in Table 11, it is observed that the youngest age group, Gen Z's, 45.4% spend 3 to 4 hours daily on social media and 27% within that age group use social media for 4-6 hours. Regarding the second age group, from 25-30, 40.9% of the participants use social media for 1-2 hours daily, this percentage being 46.7% for the third age group (31-39). For the 25-30-year-old participants, 36.3% spend 3-4 hours daily on social media. Assumptions about correlations between the age groups would be inconclusive, due to the great difference in the numbers of participants in each age group.

Table 12 illustrates the percentages of the respondents that feel annoyed or irritated when sponsored content appears in relation with the daily time spent on social media. For the 1-2 hours group the disagree rates are 7.6% (1.9% strongly

*Table 12. Time spent on social media * Consumers irritation regarding sponsored food advertisement while browsing cross tabulation table chart*

			I feel annoyed/ irritated when a sponsored ad appears while I am using social media.					Total
			Strongly disagree	Disagree	Neutral	Agree	Strongly Agree	
Time spent on social media	1-2 hours	Count	1	3	15	17	17	53
		% within Time spent on social media	1.9%	5.7%	28.3%	32.1%	32.1%	100%
		% of Total	0.5%	1.5%	7.5%	8.5%	8.5%	26.5%
	3-4 hours	Count	4	9	21	21	29	84
		% within Time spent on social media	4.8%	10.7%	25%	25%	34.5%	100%
		% of Total	2%	4.5%	10.5%	10.5%	14.5%	42%
	4-6 hours	Count	4	3	17	11	13	48
		% within Time spent on social media	8.3%	6.3%	35.4%	22.9%	27.1%	100%
		% of Total	2%	1.5%	8.5%	5.5%	6.5%	24%
	Over 6 hours	Count	0	3	4	0	8	15
		% within Time spent on social media	0%	20%	26.7%	0%	53.3%	100%
		% of Total	0%	1.5%	2%	0%	4%	7.5%
Total		Count	9	18	57	49	67	200
		% within Time spent on social media	4.5%	9%	28.5%	24.5%	33.5%	100%
		% of Total	4.5%	9%	28.5%	24.5%	33.5%	100%

disagree, 5.7% disagree), the 3-4 hours group 15.5% (4.8% strongly disagree, 10.7% disagree), the 4-6 hours group 14.6% (8.3% strongly disagree, 6.3% disagree) and the over 6 hours group 20% (0% strongly disagree, 20% disagree). Vice versa, the agree rate, within the time spent on social media, drops when the hours of social media browsing increase.

Table 13 provides information about the time spent on social media in relation to whether the participants would purchase goods after them getting advertised on social media, or not. It is observed that 22.6% of the participants that use social media for 1-2 hours answered positively. Respondents that spend 3-4 hours on social media (31%) answered yes, while those that answered 4-6 hours of usage (45.8%) answered yes and 60% with over 6 hours usage group answered positively. Thus, as the time of social media usage grows the percentage of people that would purchase

*Table 13. Time spent on social media * Purchase of food product or service after contact with an advertisement in social media cross tabulation table chart*

			Do you purchase a food product or service after seeing the advertisement on a social media platform?		Total
			No	**Yes**	
Time spent on social media	**1-2 hours**	**Count**	41	12	53
		% within Time spent on social media	77.4%	22.6%	100%
		% of Total	20.5%	6%	26.5%
	3-4 hours	**Count**	58	26	84
		% within Time spent on social media	69%	31%	100%
		% of Total	29%	13%	42%
	4-6 hours	**Count**	26	22	48
		% within Time spent on social media	54.2%	45.8%	100%
		% of Total	13%	11%	24%
	Over 6 hours	**Count**	6	9	15
		% within Time spent on social media	40%	60%	100%
		% of Total	3%	4.5%	7.5%
Total		**Count**	131	69	200
		% within Time spent on social media	65.5%	34.5%	100%
		% of Total	65.5%	34.5%	100%

increases. It is noted that regarding the last group (over 6 hours), the information given can be inconclusive and serves only as an indication, due to the small number bodying that group (15).

Table 14 includes information gathered from the participants aged between 18-24 when asked if they would purchase goods after seeing a sponsored advertisement. It is observed that 1.4% answered definitely yes, 11.3% probably yes, 32.6% neither yes or no, 39.7% probably not and 14.9% definitely not. From the 25-30-year old respondents, 4.5% answered definitely yes, 20.5% probably yes, 27.3% neither yes

*Table 14. Age group * Would you purchase an unknown food product that appears as sponsored advertisement cross tabulation table chart*

			Would you purchase a food product that you do not know but appears as a sponsored advertisement in your social media?					Total
			Definitely not	Probably not	Neither yes or no	Probably yes	Definitely yes	
Age group	18-24	Count	21	56	46	16	2	141
		% within Age group	14.9%	39.7%	32.6%	11.3%	1.4%	100%
		% of Total	10.5%	28%	23%	8%	1%	70.5%
	25-30	Count	8	13	12	9	2	44
		% within Age group	18.2%	29.5%	27.3%	20.5%	4.5%	100%
		% of Total	4%	6.5%	6%	4.5%	1%	22%
	31-39	Count	5	1	9	0	0	15
		% within Age group	33.3%	6.7%	60%	0%	0%	100%
		% of Total	2.5%	0.5%	4.5%	0%	0%	7.5%
Total		Count	34	70	67	25	4	200
		% within Age group	17%	35%	33.5%	12.5%	2%	100%
		% of Total	17%	35%	33.5%	12.5%	2%	100%

or no, 29.5% probably not and 18.2% definitely not. The last group of participants, due to its small size (15 people), cannot be taken into consideration.

Spearman Correlation

Spearman's correlation was used to investigate the association between time spent on social media and the possibility of the participant's engagement with a sponsored food advertisement on social media. As displayed in Table 15, there is a weak positive monotonic relationship between the two variables (0.177), which is statistically significant ($p=0.012<0.05$). The associated stacked bar charted is shown in the following Figure 2.

Spearman's correlation was also used to investigate and measure the association of purchase probability of an unknown food product that appears as sponsored and food brands using sponsored advertisement. As displayed in Table 16, there is a moderate positive monotonic relationship between the variables (0.457), which

Table 15. Time spent and possibility of engagement Spearman correlation

			Time spent on social media daily	When you stumble upon a sponsored food advertisement how possible is it for you to navigate into the brand's social media account
Spearman's rho	Time spent on social media daily	Correlation Coefficient	1.000	.177*
		Sig. (2-tailed)	.	.012
		N	200	200
	When you stumble upon a sponsored food advertisement how possible is it for you to navigate into the brand's social media account	Correlation Coefficient	.177*	1.000
		Sig. (2-tailed)	.012	.
		N	200	200

Figure 2. Time spent and possibility of engagement Spearman correlation stacked bar chart

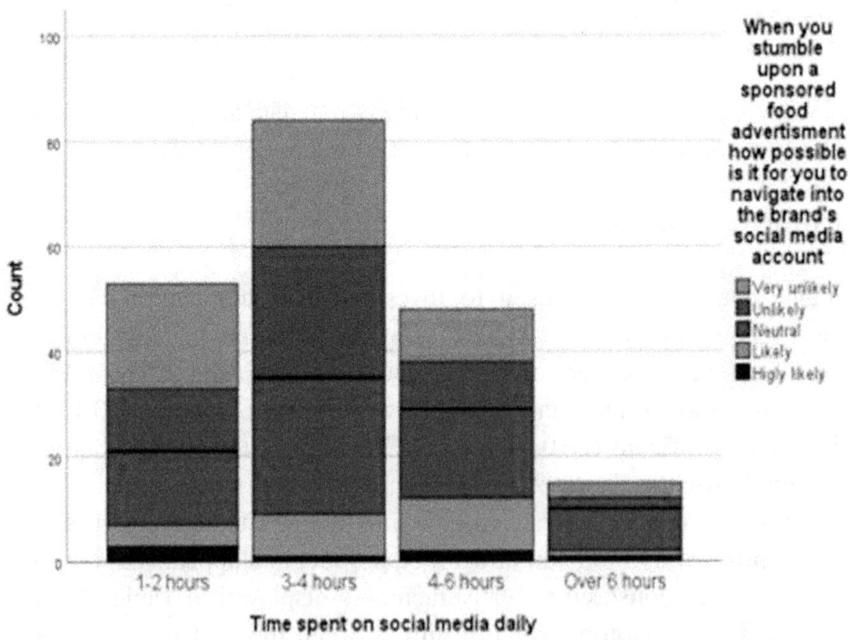

Table 16. Possibility of purchase of an unknown food product and trustworthiness Spearman correlation

			Would you purchase a food product that you do not know but appears as a sponsored advertisement in your social media?	How trustworthy do you consider a brand or a food product that appears in a sponsored ad?
Spearman's rho	Would you purchase a food product that you do not know but appears as a sponsored advertisement in your social media?	Correlation Coefficient	1.000	.457**
		Sig. (2-tailed)	.	<.001
		N	200	200
	How trustworthy do you consider a brand or a food product that appears in a sponsored ad?	Correlation Coefficient	.457**	1.000
		Sig. (2-tailed)	<.001	.
		N	200	200

Figure 3. Possibility of purchase of an unknown food product and trustworthiness stack bar chart

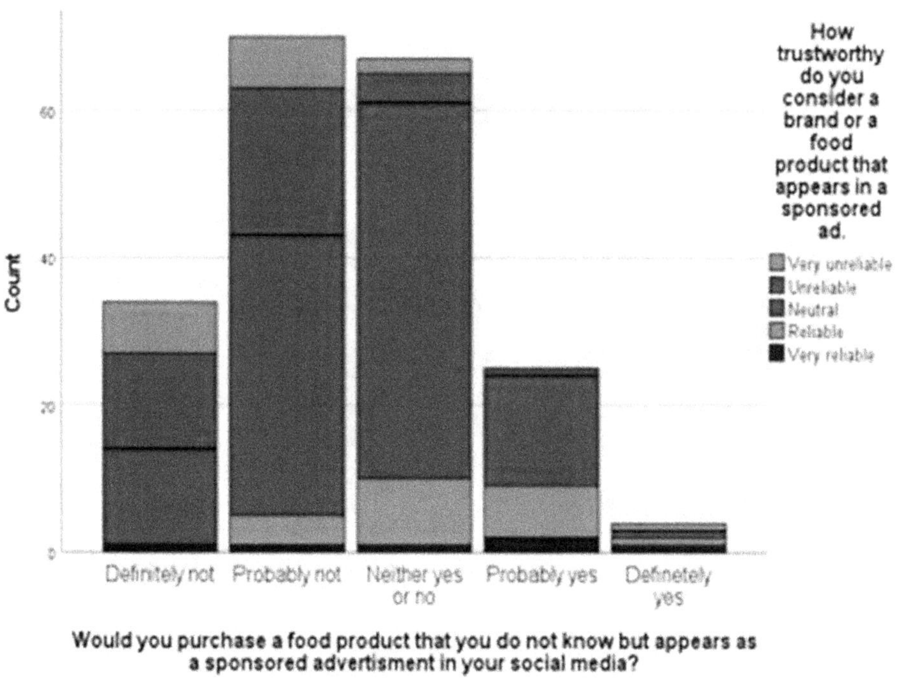

Table 17. Possibility of purchase of an unknown food product and social media engagement and consumer perception spearman correlation

			Would you purchase a food product that you do not know but appears as a sponsored advertisement in your social media?	Do you consider a food brand with more followers/ likes/ comments more trustworthy?
Spearman's rho	Would you purchase a food product that you do not know but appears as a sponsored advertisement in your social media?	Correlation Coefficient	1.000	.203**
		Sig. (2-tailed)	.	.004
		N	200	200
	Do you consider a food brand with more followers/ likes/ comments more trustworthy?	Correlation Coefficient	.203**	1.000
		Sig. (2-tailed)	.004	.
		N	200	200

Figure 4. Probability of purchase of an unknown food product and social media engagement and consumer perception stacked bar chart

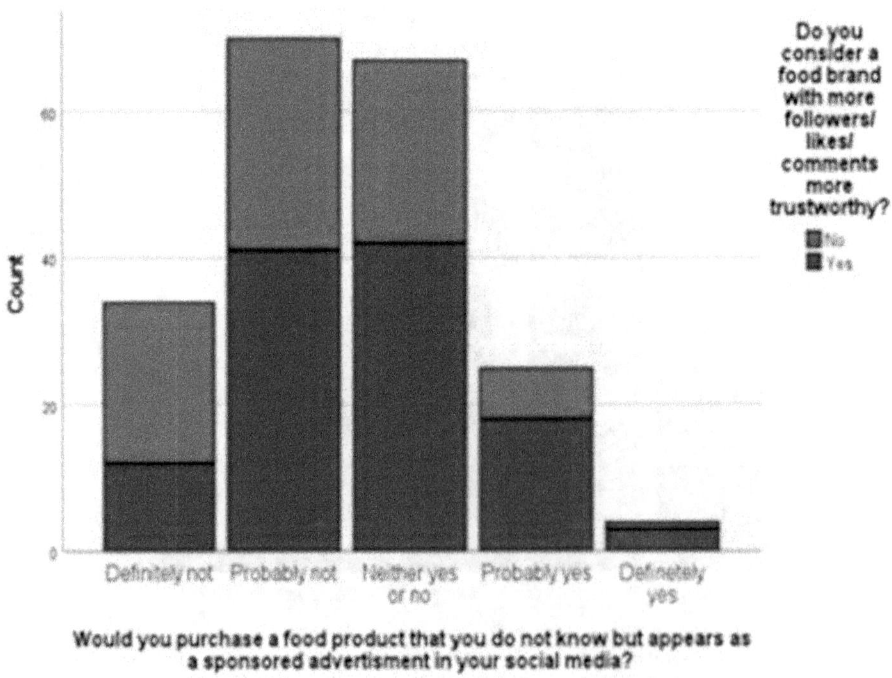

Table 18. Possibility of engagement and probability of purchase of an unknown food product spearman correlation

			When you stumble upon a sponsored food advertisement how possible is it for you to navigate into the brand's social media account	Would you purchase a food product that you do not know but appears as a sponsored advertisement in your social media?
Spearman's rho	When you stumble upon a sponsored food advertisement how possible is it for you to navigate into the brand's social media account	Correlation Coefficient	1.000	.407**
		Sig. (2-tailed)	.	<.001
		N	200	200
	Would you purchase a food product that you do not know but appears as a sponsored advertisement in your social media?	Correlation Coefficient	.407**	1.000
		Sig. (2-tailed)	<.001	.
		N	200	200

Figure 5. Possibility of engagement and probability of purchase of an unknown food product stacked bar chart

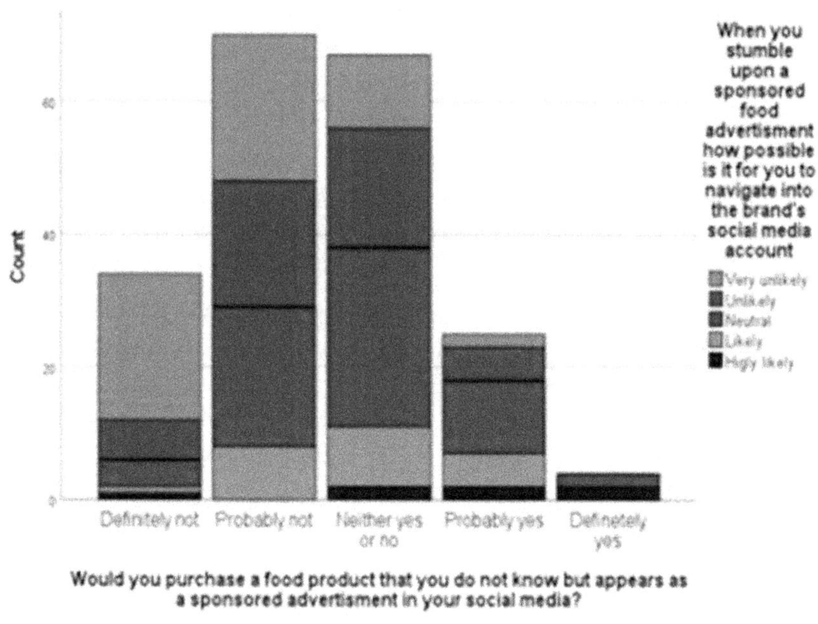

is viewed as highly statistically significant ($p<0.001$). The associated stacked bar charted is shown in the following Figure 3.

Spearman's correlation was additionally used to investigate and measure the association of purchase probability of an unknown food product that appears as sponsored and consumers' perception about social media engagement for food brands. As displayed in Table 17, there is a weak positive correlation between the variables (0.203), which is highly statistically significant ($p=0.004<0.01$). The associated stacked bar charted is shown in the following Figure 4.

Spearman's correlation was also used to investigate and measure the association of the possibility of participants' engagement with a sponsored food advertisement in social media and purchase probability of an unknown food product that appears as sponsored. As displayed in Table 18, there is a moderate positive monotonic relationship (spearman's correlation coefficient at 0.407), being of high statistical significance ($p<0.001$). The associated stacked bar charted is shown in the following Figure 5.

DISCUSSION

This study provides a good starting point for more discussions and further research. The results of the study reveal indicators and information about how food brands and sponsored food advertisement on social media are perceived by young social media users and how users respond and behave when in contact with sponsored advertisements while browsing on social media platforms. From the 200 young individuals taking part in the research, it was possible to establish connections between the most used social media platforms and the overlap percentage of the platforms amongst the participants. Indicators of links between user engagement in/under food brand accounts and the perception of trustworthiness respectively have been discovered. These indicators could potentially validate a perceived herd behavior construct amongst the social media user as found in previous work (Lee & Hong, 2016). Correlations between gender identity and usage of social media have been established, showing that the majority of the participants browsing over four hours identify as women. In addition, the percentage of participants actually following food brands and the percentage of participants observing sponsored food advertisement in social media were measured.

Furthermore, the click-through percentage was investigated, when sponsored food ads appear during the usage of social media, with the outcome suggesting that a very small percentage navigates towards the sponsoring brands social media accounts. This leads to the conclusion that sponsored advertisement is inadequate to generate online traffic on their websites or accounts, as previously partially discussed by Mattke et al. (2020). Out of the participants, a very small number (30%) would be willing to navigate into a food brand's social media account, creating traffic in this way. Additionally, it was found that the possibility of participants' engagement with a sponsored food advertisement on social media and the purchase probability of an unknown food product that appears as sponsored are correlated.

This study contributes to the establishment of links between social media sponsored advertisement efficiency, in terms of engagement and potential purchase after contact with the consumer and the time spent on social media by the users. Proportionally, individuals that browse social media longer are more likely to engage (click-through) on a sponsored food advertisement and to purchase an unknown product that appears as a sponsored advertisement. In addition, time spent on social media was correlated with the perception of participants regarding trustworthiness of brands, advertising through sponsored advertisement and irritation of the advertisement target, showing that individuals that browse longer feel less irritated when a sponsored advertisement appears. This could be due to the fact that persons browsing for longer times are used to coming across sponsored advertisement more often.

Regarding the probability of purchase of an unknown food product appearing as sponsored advertisement, it was found that it grows with the growth of social media usage. The same applies also to the probability of purchase of a food product or service after contact with an advertisement on social media. From a marketer's perspective, this information could be useful when promoting a food product, to create the advertisement to target specific groups (age, gender, use of social media, etc.), for the planning of the advertising strategy of the food brand and to aim for consumer engagement for the food brand's account.

MANAGERIAL IMPLICATIONS, LIMITATIONS AND RECOMMENDATIONS

This research work contributes additional indications to the pre-existing literature. Concerning consumers' perceptions and behavior about sponsored food advertisement through social media, the findings of this research make valuable practical contributions. Nevertheless, this study consists only of indicators regarding perceptions and behaviors. The factors that affect consumer behavior stretch out, surpassing the knowledge that can be gathered via a questionnaire. The data set of 200 young individuals can lead to inconclusive information; users may not be representative of the young consumer population. Future studies should include a larger sample size to enable for the generalization of results (Comrey & Lee, 2013). Furthermore, out of the age groups of the participants a difference in capacities can be recognized, which did not offer the complete picture to the researchers. In addition, every social media platform uses different tactics regarding sponsored advertisement, it has different overlay and is used for its specific functions by the users. A consumer feeling of trust is not only affected by the online presence of the individual, but also has to be looked upon in a more holistic way. Hence, all surroundings and experiences of an individual may shift one's consumption behavior.

Furthermore, results were gathered through online fixed questions. This method was selected since it was inexpensive and easy to share and distribute to the target audience. Online surveys may contain inaccurate responses due to a misunderstanding of the questions (Bryman, 2016). As a result, it is possible that useful information has remained unavailable and future studies should include both online and in-person surveys.

Finally, future research may look into different features offered for advertisement from social media platforms and consumer perceptions. All platforms have different strategies regarding sponsored advertisement and their influence on consumer behavior and the rates of favourable outcomes should be researched. The importance of user engagement regarding different types of food products and services, the functionalities of different social media platforms and ways to achieve a growth in user engagement rate are all fields that should be examined in detail in future research.

REFERENCES

Adjei, M. T., Noble, C. H., & Noble, S. M. (2012). Enhancing Relationships With Customers Through Online Brand Communities. *MIT Sloan Management Review*, *53*(4), 22.

Alalwan, A. A., Rana, N. P., Dwivedi, Y. K., & Algharabat, R. (2017). Social Media In Marketing: A Review And Analysis Of The Existing Literature. *Telematics and Informatics*, *34*(7), 1177–1190. doi:10.1016/j.tele.2017.05.008

Anderson, M., Sims, J., Price, J., & Brusa, J. (2011). Turning "like" to "buy" social media emerges as a commerce channel. *Booz & Company Inc*, *2*(1), 102–128.

Arora, T., Kumar, A., & Agarwal, B. (2020). Impact of social media advertising on millennials buying behaviour. *International Journal Of Intelligent Enterprise*, *7*(4), 481–500. doi:10.1504/IJIE.2020.110795

Bleier, A., & Eisenbeiss, M. (2015). Personalized online advertising effectiveness: the interplay of what, when, and where. *Marketing Science*, *34*(5), 669–688. doi:10.1287/mksc.2015.0930

Boerman, S. C., Helberger, N., Van Noort, G., & Hoofnagle, C. J. (2018). Sponsored blog content: what do the regulations say: and what do bloggers say. *Journal Of Intellectual Property, Information Technology And Electronic Commerce Law*, *9*, 146.

Boerman, S. C., Willemsen, L. M., & Van Der Aa, E. P. (2017). "This post is sponsored" effects of sponsorship disclosure on persuasion knowledge and electronic word of mouth in the context of facebook. *Journal of Interactive Marketing*, *38*(1), 82–92. doi:10.1016/j.intmar.2016.12.002

Bryman, A. (2016). Social research methods, 5th ed.; oxford university press: Oxford, UK

Chaffey, D. (2023). *2023 Average ad click through rates (CTRS) for paid search, display and social media*. Smart Insights. Retrieved May 17, 2023, From https://www.smartinsights.com/internet-advertising/internet-advertising-analytics/display-advertising-clickthrough-rates/

Childers, C., & Boatwright, B. (2021). Do digital natives recognize digital influence? Generational differences and understanding of social media influencers. *Journal of Current Issues and Research in Advertising*, *42*(4), 425–442. doi:10.1080/10641734.2020.1830893

Comrey, A. L., & Lee, H. B. (2013). A first course in factor analysis. 2nd Edition, Hillsdale: Psychology Press

Dillman, D. A., Smyth, J. D., & Christian, L. M. (2014). Internet, phone, mail, and mixed-mode surveys: the tailored design method. John wiley & sons.

European Commission. (2023). *Consumer Protection Law*. Retrieved May 17, 2023, from https://commission.europa.eu/law/law-topic/consumer-protection-law_en

European Economic And Social Committee. (2023). *EU consumer and marketing law*. Retrieved May 17, 2023, from https://www.eesc.europa.eu/en/our-work/opinions-information-reports/information-reports/eu-consumer-and-marketing-law

fietkiewicz, k. J., lins, e., baran, k. S., & stock, w. G. (2016, january). Inter-generational comparison of social media use: investigating the online behavior of different generational cohorts. In *2016 49th hawaii international conference on system sciences (hicss)* (pp. 3829-3838). IEEE.

Franses, P. H., & Paap, R. (2001). Quantitative models in marketing research. Cambridge university press.

GWI. (2023). *Global social media statistics*. Retrieved may 4, 2023, from https://datareportal.com/social-media-users

Hamilton, M., Kaltcheva, V. D., & Rohm, A. J. (2016). Social media and value creation: the role of interaction satisfaction and interaction immersion. *Journal of Interactive Marketing*, *36*(1), 121–133. doi:10.1016/j.intmar.2016.07.001

Kamenidou, I., Stavrianea, A., & Bara, E. Z. (2020). Generational differences toward organic food behavior: insights from five generational cohorts. *Sustainability (Basel)*, *12*(6), 2299. doi:10.3390u12062299

Kaplan, A. M., & Haenlein, M. (2010). Users of the world, unite! The challenges and opportunities of social media. *Business Horizons*, *53*(1), 59–68. doi:10.1016/j.bushor.2009.09.003

Kerr, G., & Richards, J. (2021). Redefining advertising in research and practice. *International Journal of Advertising*, *40*(2), 175–198. doi:10.1080/02650487.2020.1769407

Kietzmann, J. H., Hermkens, K., Mccarthy, I. P., & Silvestre, B. S. (2011). Social media? Get serious! Understanding the functional building blocks of social media. *Business Horizons*, *54*(3), 241–251. doi:10.1016/j.bushor.2011.01.005

Kim, S. J., Maslowska, E., & Tamaddoni, A. (2019). The paradox of (dis) trust in sponsorship disclosure: the characteristics and effects of sponsored online consumer reviews. *Decision Support Systems*, *116*, 114–124. doi:10.1016/j.dss.2018.10.014

Kolb, B. (2008). Marketing research: a practical approach. *Sage (Atlanta, Ga.)*.

Kucharczuk, A. J., Oliver, T. L., & Dowdell, E. B. (2022). Social media's influence on adolescents′ food choices: a mixed studies systematic literature review. *Appetite*, *168*, 105765. doi:10.1016/j.appet.2021.105765 PMID:34687823

Labrecque, L. I. (2014). Fostering consumer–brand relationships in social media environments: the role of parasocial interaction. *Journal of Interactive Marketing*, *28*(2), 134–148. doi:10.1016/j.intmar.2013.12.003

Lee, J., & Hong, I. B. (2016). Predicting positive user responses to social media advertising: the roles of emotional appeal, informativeness, and creativity. *International Journal of Information Management*, *36*(3), 360–373. doi:10.1016/j.ijinfomgt.2016.01.001

Leung, L. (2013). Generational differences in content generation in social media: the roles of the gratifications sought and of narcissism. *Computers in Human Behavior*, *29*(3), 997–1006. doi:10.1016/j.chb.2012.12.028

Lütjens, H., Eisenbeiss, M., Fiedler, M., & Bijmolt, T. (2022). Determinants of consumers' attitudes towards digital advertising–a meta-analytic comparison across time and touchpoints. *Journal of Business Research, 153*, 445–466. doi:10.1016/j.jbusres.2022.07.039

Ma, L., Ou, W., & Lee, C. S. (2022). Investigating consumers' cognitive, emotional, and behavioral engagement in social media brand pages: a natural language processing approach. *Electronic Commerce Research and Applications, 54*, 101179. doi:10.1016/j.elerap.2022.101179

Madhavan, M., & Kaliyaperumal, C. (2015). Consumer buying behavior-an overview of theory and models. *St. Theresa journal of humanities and social sciences, 1*(1), 74–112.

Malthouse, E. C., Calder, B. J., Kim, S. J., & Vandenbosch, M. (2016). Evidence that user-generated content that produces engagement increases purchase behaviours. *Journal of Marketing Management, 32*(5-6), 427–444. doi:10.1080/0267257X.2016.1148066

Mattke, J., Maier, C., Reis, L., & Weitzel, T. (2020). Herd behavior in social media: the role of facebook likes, strength of ties, and expertise. *Information & Management, 57*(8), 103370. doi:10.1016/j.im.2020.103370

Mcquarrie, E. F., & Phillips, B. J. (2005). Indirect persuasion in advertising: how consumers process metaphors presented in pictures and words. *Journal of Advertising, 34*(2), 7–20. doi:10.1080/00913367.2005.10639188

Nunan, D., Malhotra, N. K., & Birks, D. F. (2020). *Marketing research.* Pearson UK.

Richards, J., Daugherty, T., & Logan, K. (2009). Advertising History. *Encyclopedia Of Journalism*, 1-15.

Rohm, A., & Kaltcheva, D., VMilne, G.R. (2013). A mixed-method approach to examining brand-consumer interactions driven by social media. *Journal of Research in Interactive Marketing*, 7(4), 295–311. doi:10.1108/JRIM-01-2013-0009

Selvi, B. M., & Thomson, J. E. (2016). An exploratory study on the electronic word of mouth communication in promoting brands in the online platforms. *Intelligent Information Management, 8*(5), 115–141. doi:10.4236/iim.2016.85010

Statista. (2023A). *Biggest Social Media Platforms 2023.* Retrieved May 3, 2023, from https://www.statista.com/statistics/272014/global-social-networks-ranked-by-number-of-users/

Statista. (2023B). *Global Daily Social Media Usage 2022*. Retrieved May 3, 2023, from https://www.statista.com/statistics/433871/daily-social-media-usage-worldwide/

Statista. (2023C). *Number Of Worldwide Social Network Users 2027*. Retrieved May 3, 2023, from https://www.statista.com/statistics/278414/number-of-worldwide-social-network-users/

Steinfield, C., Ellison, N. B., & Lampe, C. (2008). Social capital, self-esteem, and use of online social network sites: a longitudinal analysis. *Journal of Applied Developmental Psychology*, *29*(6), 434–445. doi:10.1016/j.appdev.2008.07.002

Tsimonis, G., & Dimitriadis, S. (2014). Brand strategies in social media. *Marketing Intelligence & Planning*, *32*(3), 328–344. doi:10.1108/MIP-04-2013-0056

Tsochantaridou, A., Sergentanis, T. N., Grammatikopoulou, M. G., Merakou, K., Vassilakou, T., & Kornarou, E. (2023). Food advertisement and dietary choices in adolescents: an overview of recent studies. *Children (Basel, Switzerland)*, *10*(3), 442. doi:10.3390/children10030442 PMID:36980000

Weinberg, B. D., De Ruyter, K., Dellarocas, C., Buck, M., & Keeling, D. I. (2013). Destination social business: exploring an organization's journey with social media, collaborative community and expressive individuality. *Journal of Interactive Marketing*, *27*(4), 299–310. doi:10.1016/j.intmar.2013.09.006

APPENDIX: QUESTIONNAIRE

1. To which gender identity do you most identify?
    - Female
    - Male
    - Other
    - Prefer not to say
2. What is your age group?
    - 18-24
    - 25-30
    - 31-39
3. What is your occupation?
    - Student
    - Self-employed
    - Part-time working
    - Full-time working
    - Working Student
    - Enlisted
    - Unemployed
4. Where do you live?
    - In a city (over 100.000 in population)
    - In an urban area / town / village (under 100.000 in population)
5. Which social media do you use?
    - Facebook
    - Instagram
    - Tik Tok
    - YouTube
    - Twitter
    - Other
6. How much time do you spend daily on social media?
    - I do not use social media
    - 1-2 hours
    - 3-4 hours
    - 4-6 hours
    - Over 6 hours

7. Which social media do you prefer?
    - Facebook
    - Instagram
    - Tik Tok
    - YouTube
    - Twitter
    - Other
8. Why are you using social media platforms?
    - For finding connections
    - To get information about brands
    - To get information about products/services
    - To catch up on the latest news/gossip
    - Entertainment
    - Other
9. Do you follow food brands on social media?
    - Yes
    - No
10. How frequently do you read or pay attention to a sponsored food advertisement?
    - Once to 5 times per day
    - More than 6 times per day
    - Once per 4-5 days
    - Once per week
11. Do you purchase a food product or service after seeing the advertisement on a social media platform?
    - Yes
    - No
12. Do you consider a food brand with more followers/ likes/ comments more trustworthy?
    - Yes
    - No
13. On a scale from 1 to 5 how much does the below phrase represent your opinion. **I feel annoyed/ irritated when a sponsored ad appears while I am using social media.**
    - 1 Strongly disagree
    - 2
    - 3
    - 4
    - 5 Strongly agree

14. When you stumble upon a sponsored food advertisement how possible is it for you to navigate into the brand's social media account
    - 1 Very unlikely
    - 2
    - 3
    - 4
    - 5 Highly likely
15. How trustworthy do you consider a brand or a food product that appears in a sponsored ad?
    - 1 Very unreliable
    - 2
    - 3
    - 4
    - 5 Very reliable
16. Would you purchase a food product that you do not know but appears as a sponsored advertisement in your social media?
    - 1 Definitely No
    - 2
    - 3
    - 4
    - 5 Definitely Yes
17. Do you believe that sponsored advertisements with food products that you see in social media are relevant to you?
    - 1 Definitely No
    - 2
    - 3
    - 4
    - 5 Definitely Yes

Chapter 4
Moderating Effects of Likelihood to Use In-Store Technology in Grocery Stores:
Perceived Value of Retailtainment

Adesegun Oyedele
University of the Incarnate Word, USA

Fuat Firat
The University of Texas-Rio Grande Valley, USA

Monica Hernandez
https://orcid.org/0000-0001-8906-928X
Texas Lutheran University, USA

Emily Goenner Munson
https://orcid.org/0000-0002-0598-4075
St. Cloud State University, USA

ABSTRACT

The purpose of this study is the assessment of the moderating effects of consumers' likelihood to use instore technologies on the relationship between retailtainment value and satisfaction with retailtainment in physical grocery stores. A questionnaire designed to test our model was administered to 332 undergraduate students. The data were analyzed using AMOS-SEM. The results show that perceived benefit, enjoyment, and unique values of retailtainment were significant in explicating satisfaction with retailtainment. Regarding the interaction effects of likelihood to use instore technology, the results reveal the positive relationship between human interactivity-instore, benefits, and unique values, and the dependent variable satisfaction with retailtaiment are stronger for individuals with low likelihood to use instore technologies. Results confirmed that retailtainment, which provides enjoyment and perceived informative benefits in terms of experience with the consumption of products, is likely to increase satisfaction and improve loyalty as well as propensity to return to the store.

DOI: 10.4018/978-1-6684-8868-3.ch004

INTRODUCTION

Fulberg (2003) describes retailtainment as an attempt by retailers to provide entertainment experiences to customers through staging instore performances to enhance the value of their product/service offerings. In this study, we research the case of physical retail grocery stores, and we describe retailtainment as the instore entertainment activities used by physical grocery stores to connect, entertain, and increase customers' interest in their merchandise. So far, retailtainment events have generally included free product tasting/sampling, product demonstrations, instore cooking shows, instore artist appearances, live shows, and pop-up events. For instance, HEB stores, one of the largest grocery stores in the U.S., stages pop-up cooking events offering customers the opportunity to meet and interact with local celebrity chefs to share cooking ideas.

Previously, Hede and Kellett (2011) posited that retailers, particularly grocery retailers, have focused on retailtainment strategies or strategies to enhance consumers' instore experiences and engagement. They advocated for more studies to explicate consumers' perceptions of and attitude toward retailtainment. Sands et al. (2015) argued there is a gap in the literature on consumers' perceived value of instore retailtainment and the effects of perceived value on satisfaction with retailtainment. They urged scholars to develop studies to assess and test consumer factors that moderate the relationship between perceived retailtainment value and satisfaction.

Developing such studies is relevant, particularly in the grocery store context, because instore retailtainment drives engagement and promotes employee-customer interaction during the shopping process. Employee interaction with customers provides more opportunities for relationships and experiential value creation in grocery stores. Experiential and relational value are the main factors that allow for creation of unique value that will maximize perceived instore value and satisfaction (Jara et al., 2018).

The current forms of retailtainment promote engagement with store employees or product demonstrators making consumers' preference for human interactivity in the physical grocery store environment relevant in explaining satisfaction with the retailtainment experience and customers' satisfaction with physical grocery stores (Florenthal & Shoham, 2010). Despite the logical link between preference for human interactivity and satisfaction with retailtainment, no study in the literature has assessed the effects of human interactivity-instore on satisfaction with retailtainment.

Pantano and Vannucci (2019) argued more studies are needed to understand retailers' and consumers' responses to increased adoption and usage of instore technologies in physical retail stores. Similarly, a recent study by Grewal et al. (2020) alluded to the need for researchers to assess the potential interaction effects of consumers' likelihood to use instore technologies on the relationship between perceived retailtainment value and satisfaction with retailtainment. The human interactivity demands of retailtainment events would conflict with the anticipated desires of consumers with high likelihood to use instore technologies that are currently largely designed for shopping efficiency and convenience.

In contrast, the human interactivity demands of retailtainment should align well with the expected relational value desired by consumers with low likelihood to use such instore technologies. Therefore, we anticipate consumers' perceived value and satisfaction with retailtainment will be different for consumers with high versus low likelihood to use instore technologies. So far, the moderating effects of likelihood to use instore technologies on the relationship between perceived retailtainment value and satisfaction with retailtainment has not been reported in the literature.

We begin by investigating the influence of preference for human interactivity-instore and perceived retailtainment value on satisfaction with retailtainment. In addition, we evaluate the effects of satisfaction with retailtainment on word-of-mouth and revisit intention to shop in a physical grocery store. We test the moderating effects of high versus low likelihood to use instore technologies on the relationship between perceived retailtainment value and satisfaction with retailtainment to help assess potential for and hurdles to new retailtainment technologies. The moderating variable is defined as likelihood to use instore technologies deployed by retailers to aid the convenience of locating information and product search instore and transaction convenience in the payment stage.

This study does not seek to explain attitudes and perceptions towards instore use of technology. Rather, we are interested in understanding how consumers' likelihood to use instore technologies interacts with the relationship between perceived retailtainment value and satisfaction with retailtainment in a physical grocery store situation. Thus, theories we find most relevant for this study are the Stimulus-Organism-Response (S-O-R) framework (Mehrabian & Russell, 1974), perceived value (Holbrook, 1999), and human interactivity mode in physical grocery stores (Florenthal & Shoham, 2010).

Our findings will help to understand the influence of instore technologies on consumers' perceived value and satisfaction with retailtainment in a physical grocery store environment. This offers insight on the role of instore customer engagement programs such as retailtainment and preferences for human interactivity-instore on consumer loyalty behavior in a physical grocery store environment.

This chapter is organized as follows: first, we briefly discuss the literature on interactivity modes in retail stores, and retail atmospherics and perceived value in thephysical retail environment. Second, we present the study hypotheses and the conceptual model in the study. Third, we discuss the study methodology, results from the study, and implications for retailtainment technology use in physical stores.

Finally, we present a discussion on the study limitations and recommendations for future research.

BACKGROUND

Interactivity

Interactivity is one dimension of retailtainment. Consumers' preferences for different interactivity modes should affect customer satisfaction (Burke, 2002). Florenthal and Shoham (2010) proposed several modes of interacting, including two modes of interactivity that are relevant for consideration in physical grocery store situations: product interactivity and human interactivity. Product interactivity describes the consumers' experience with a product that engages their senses. Physical stores provide greater product interactivity than online stores because consumers have the option to engage their senses and touch products. Human interactivity describes personal interactions among humans throughout their shopping experience, including interactions with store employees, customer service representatives, friends, instore performers, and other shoppers.

Atmosphere

Many studies of retail atmosphere have employed the Stimulus-Organism-Response (S-O-R) framework from psychology to evaluate consumers' perceptions and behavioral responses (e.g., Mehrabian & Russell, 1974). According to Turley and Milliman (2000), the S-O-R framework proposes that the environment produces Stimuli (S) that trigger organismic/internal (O) changes in individuals and result in approach or avoidance responses (R) (Mehrabian & Russell, 1974; Sands et al., 2015). The proposed S-O-R framework (Turley and Milliman, 2000) substantiates the effects of tactile, aural, olfactory, and visual cues on consumer behavior and accounts for responses of approach and avoidance. The three fundamental components of this framework are arousal, pleasure, and dominance. Evidence from previous studies (e.g., Donovan et al., 1994) show limited support for the effects of dominance. Consequently, studies on the S-O-R framework in consumption situations are more focused on assessing the arousal and pleasure dimensions than evaluating dominance effects.

Mehrabian and Russell (1974) defined arousal as a measure of an individual's feelings of excitement, stimulation, and alertness to a stimulus in the environment. Pleasure is a measure of an individual's feelings of happiness, joyfulness, and satisfaction with a stimulus in the environment. Pleasure assesses the extent of enjoyment perceived by the individual in an environment (Yalch & Spangenberg, 2000). For example, staging food-tasting shows in a grocery store may enrich the consumers' pleasure; on the other hand, staging a hard sell instore event to pressure customers to buy a new product may lead to consumers' displeasure.

Kaltcheva and Weitz's (2006) study showed that consumers with recreational shopping motives are more likely than consumers with task-oriented motives to enjoy the experience of shopping in stores that exhibit high arousal stimuli. Traditionally, retailtainment events in physical grocery stores display high arousal stimuli. Consumers' low likelihood to use instore technologies may imply preference for recreational experiences and the need for interaction with others in the grocery store, including employees. Following this logic, given the current efficiency-and-convenience-oriented nature of instore technologies, we anticipate that consumers with low likelihood, rather than high likelihood, to use instore technologies would be more receptive to high arousal stimuli from retailtainment. That is, we argue that engagement with technology and desire for retailtainment will be contingent on the nature of the technology in use.

Consumers who are driven by task-oriented motivations would attain satisfaction mainly from the shopping outcome as opposed to deriving satisfaction from the shopping activities. The goal of shoppers with task-oriented motivations is to execute the shopping activity in an efficient manner without expending too much energy or time (van Rompay et al., 2012; Kaltcheva & Weitz, 2006). Vieira and Torres (2014) found that shoppers characterized by task-oriented motives tend to perceive high arousal retail environments to be challenging in shopping situations, which may lead to negative emotions or unpleasant feelings. Task-oriented consumers attain satisfaction from accomplishing a task. Therefore, the utility value rather than the hedonic value of a shopping situation is more important to task-oriented consumers.

Drawing insight from Kaltcheva and Weitz (2006), we posit that consumers with high likelihood to use instore technologies and task-oriented consumers share common characteristics including the need for efficiency and timeliness in a grocery store shopping situation. This argument is logical because, as we already mentioned, most contemporary instore technologies that have smart capabilities in grocery stores allow customers to efficiently and conveniently search for products and checkout products in a timely manner.

Gelbrich et al.'s (2014) study on the factors that influence the use of self-service technology (SST) in public, such as in grocery stores, suggests that the likelihood to use SSTs is strongly linked to task-oriented behavior. Other related studies, such as the works of Collier et al. (2015), also show that task-oriented behavior rather than recreational influences (e.g., retailtainment) positively affects high likelihood to use instore technologies. Thus, we expect consumers with high rather than low likelihood to use instore technologies would be less responsive to arousal/enjoyment from retailtainment.

Perceived Value

A review of the literature reveals that the theories of consumption value and multidimensional perspectives of perceived value (e.g., Babin et al., 1994; Holbrook, 1999; Sheth et al., 1991) are relevant in understanding consumers' perceived value of retailtainment in physical retail stores. Functional value denotes consumers' perceived utility from assessing the physical and functional attributes of a product/service. Sweeney and Soutar (2001) conceptualized two types of functional value: monetary functional value (economic value) and performance functional value (convenience value).

In this study, functional value relates to deriving economic and convenience values and ease of completing task-related activities that consumers need to accomplish when they shop in a physical grocery store. Economic value may be derived from receiving coupons and free product samples from participation in retailtainment events. Perceived convenience value accounts for the consumer's need to derive some form of utility or functional outcome from shopping at a physical store. An example of convenience value in this context is customers obtaining timely information about new product deals from product demonstrators staging retailtainment events.

Perceived emotional value is defined as the outcome of consumers' responses to the visual aesthetic and affective attributes of a product (Veryzer, 1993). Sheth, Newman & Gross (1991) contend consumers may perceive emotional value if the product/service stimulates affective experiences or feelings. Hirschman (1980) contended feelings or affective experiences might be positive or negative. Positive emotional value is derived from the capacity of the product to stimulate playful and fun experiences (Holbrook, 1994; Sheth, Newman & Gross, 1991). General dimensions of positive affective experiences are happiness, fun, playfulness, joy, etc. Negative affective experiences are indicated through anger, fear, and distress.

Regardless of the situation, the perceived emotional value of a retail environment, a retail grocery store, is largely related to the visual appeal of the retail setting, as determined by the physical attractiveness and the design of the retail environment (Holbrook, 1994; Mathwick, Malhotra & Rigdon, 2001). Customers derive experiential and emotional values from retailtainment through their interactions with the physical environment, relational interactions with store employees and through the shopping tips they get from talking to product demonstrators and other customers.

Figure 1. Moderating effects of likelihood to use instore technologies on the relationship between perceived retailtainment value and satisfaction with retailtainment

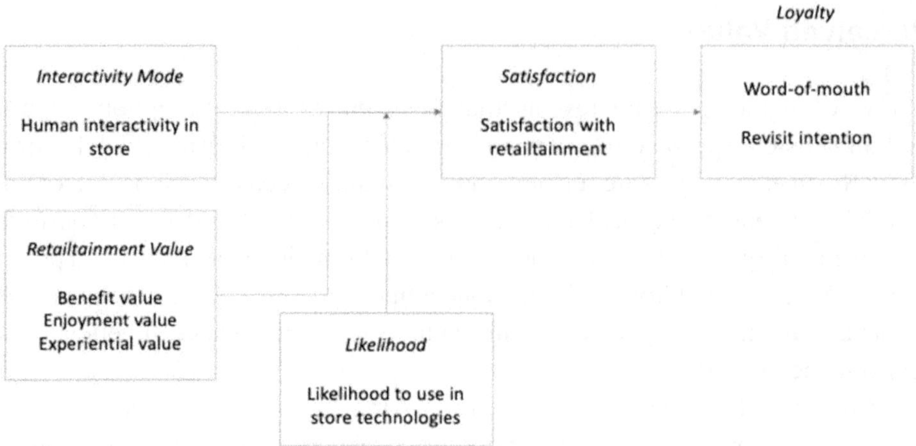

CONCEPTUAL FRAMEWORK AND HYPOTHESES

Relevant Theories

Our review of the literature and relevant theories shows the pleasure-arousal models (e.g., Donovan et al., 1994), perceived value theory (e.g., Holbrook, 1994), and perspectives on interactivity mode in physical retail stores (e.g., Florenthal & Shoham, 2010) are relevant for explicating consumers' perceptions and responses to environmental cues in a physical retail store. We integrate knowledge from perceived value, pleasure-arousal models, and human interactivity needs in physical retail stores to explain the effects of perceived value of retailtainment and human interactivity-instore on satisfaction with retailtainment, and additionally, we assess the effects of satisfaction on word-of-mouth and revisit intention. We test the moderating effects of likelihood to use instore technologies on the relationship between perceived retailtainment value and satisfaction with retailtainment. The study model is presented in Figure 1.

Human Interactivity-instore

Consumers may have high levels of interpersonal communication during their visits to physical grocery stores where they can interact with customer service representatives, as opposed to shopping online which only offers them mediated communication. Beatty et al. (1996) investigated the relationship between customer loyalty, repeat customer-engagement, and relationship selling activities of customer service representatives in retail stores. The outcome of their study suggests that instore activities that promote human interactivity and personal interaction between customers and store employees (e.g., retaitainment) positively affect loyalty behavior and customer satisfaction.

Similarly, Merrilees and Miller (2001) examined the relationship between physical interactivity variables, such as customers' instore interactivity, design, and instore atmosphere, on store loyalty. The results of their study suggest that consumer preferences for human interactivity-instore has a positive impact on customer satisfaction, and that superstores, compared to traditional specialist stores, tend to prioritize self-service and store atmosphere over personal interactions with customers.

As noted earlier, human interactivity tendencies, such as socializing with store employees, should be weaker in consumers with high, rather than those with low, likelihood to use instore technologies. For consumers with high likelihood to use instore technologies, leveraging the efficiency of instore technologies rather than seeking human interactivity would be crucial for completing their shopping tasks. In contrast, consumers with low likelihood to use instore technologies are expected to leverage opportunities for human interactivity rather than use instore technologies for shopping related tasks in physical grocery stores. Based on this background, we propose:

H_{1a}: Human interactivity-instore is positively related to consumers' satisfaction with retailtainment.

H_{1b}: The effects of the positive relationship between human interactivity-instore and satisfaction with retailtainment will be stronger for consumers with low, rather than those with high, likelihood to use instore technologies.

Perceived Benefit Value

Perceived benefit relates to consumers' need to derive functional value (convenience and economic values) from their visit to the grocery store (Sweeney & Soutar, 2001). Perceived convenience value is defined as consumers' perception of the location benefits and the time savings obtained from purchasing or using a product/service (Berry et al., 2002). For service delivered through a physical grocery store, convenience value may be attained through ease of obtaining information and acquiring a product in the grocery store. Zeithmal and Bitner (2000) point out that higher perception of time scarcity results from performing tasks associated with purchasing a product and consuming a service. Therefore, convenience value is linked to perceived reduction in the time and effort required to acquire and consume a service.

Consumers may attain ease of use and convenience values from instore events or retailtainment that can aid them in completion of their shopping task in a timely manner (Jain & Bagdare, 2009). Examples of retailtainment that facilitate ease of use and convenience values include instore information events at store entrances and product demonstrations. Retailtainment events focused on product demonstration could help ease the effort and time required to search for new product options or compare products. Economic value may be derived from retailtainment through instore pop-up events that offer coupons and exclusive discounts on high demand products during specific store operating hours. In addition, economic benefit could be attained through coupon offers that are broadly linked to customer participation in product sampling events (Davis & Hodges, 2002).

Broadly, most instore retailtainment promotes human interactivity, which demands engagement with store employees or customer service representatives (Jain & Bagdare, 2009). Consequently, we anticipate the human interaction demand of retailtainment may reduce perception of benefit value for consumers with high likelihood to use instore technologies. This is because the human-interactivity demand of retailtainment would be perceived as a hindrance to attaining the convenience value of using instore technologies for completing the pending buying tasks. In contrast, the effect of this relationship should increase for consumers with low likelihood to use instore technologies because the human interactivity aspects of retailtainment are likely to be prioritized over the efficiency of using instore technology to accomplish the pending shopping tasks. Therefore, we hypothesize the following:

H_{2a}: The perceived benefit value of retailtainment is positively related to consumers' satisfaction with retailtainment.

H_{2b}: The effects of the positive relationship between perceived benefit value of retailtainment and satisfaction with retailtainment will be reduced for consumers with high, rather than those with low, likelihood to use instore technologies.

Perceived Enjoyment and Unique Values

Numerous perceived value researchers have noted that consumers' perceived enjoyment of shopping experiences is connected to the different dimensions of hedonic value (Holbrook & Hirschman, 1982) and satisfaction (Falk & Campbell, 1997). Along this line, Ridgway et al (1990) found that perceived enjoyment is positively related to Mehrabian and Russell's (1974) emotional state model or PAD model. Hedonic value of retailtainment may be derived from the friendly, personal interactions with product demonstrators staging a retailtainment event. Numerous scholars argue consumers and store employees are active collaborative participants of enjoyment value in consumption situations (e.g., Deighton & Grayson, 1995;

Gummesson, 1998). Huizinga (1955) points out that enjoyment value is related to escapism, and escapism enables consumers to temporarily withdraw from the stressful demands of day-to-day activities.

Experiential and relational situations create value that is unique and memorable and will maximize customer value. Perceived unique value in the grocery store context refers to consumers' perception of unique experiential and relational benefits offered by a store, compared to competing or other stores. Bagdare and Jain (2013) posit retailers can distinguish themselves from their competition by enhancing their customer experience through influencing perceptions of the store by making the store unique in its environment and making the store experience memorable. Retailtainment events such as product demonstrations can help the retailer facilitate service differentiation and unique shopping experiences instore that are enjoyable and entertaining (Franke & Schreier, 2008).

In grocery stores, experiential benefits are generally linked with the consumer-retailer relationship, which is influenced by the layout of the store, interactions with store employees, and staging of retailtainment events. Employee interaction during the retailtainment event should influence consumers' perception of and satisfaction with the grocery store. Drawing insight from the above discussion suggests a retailtainment event can enhance consumers' perception of the store and increase enjoyment value and perceived uniqueness of the grocery store. Therefore, we expect perceived enjoyment and unique values of retailtainment to have a positive effect on satisfaction with retailtainment. We anticipate the effects of the positive relationship between perceived retailtainment enjoyment and unique values on satisfaction with retailtainment will be stronger for consumers with low, rather than high, likelihood to use instore technologies. Thus:

H_{3a}: The perceived enjoyment value of retailtainment is positively related to consumers' satisfaction with retailtainment.

H_{3b}: The effects of the positive relationship between perceived enjoyment value of retailtainment and satisfaction with retailtainment will be reduced for consumers with high, rather than those with low, likelihood to use instore technologies.

H_{4a}: The perceived unique value of retailtainment is positively related to consumers' satisfaction with retailtainment.

H_{4b}: The effects of the positive relationship between perceived unique value of retailtainment and satisfaction with retailtainment will be reduced for consumers with high, rather than those with low, likelihood to use instore technologies.

Satisfaction

A review of past studies showed that satisfaction is an important dependent variable for explicating consumers' perceptions of retail engagement and experience (Bitner, 1992; Booms & Bitner, 1982). The definition of satisfaction hinges on a relative judgement of a selected standard and on disconfirming or confirming meeting the expectation of that performance standard. Consumers may experience dissatisfaction if they perceive the service experience in a retail store is substandard or if the performance of a retail service experience is perceived to be below the expected standard.

Numerous studies have assessed factors that predict satisfaction with a retail store service and satisfaction with a product/service and customer engagement experience (Abbott et al., 2000). Consumers' satisfaction with the environment in a physical retail store affects their perceptions, attitude, and behavioral responses toward the retail store (Iacobucci et al., 1995). Woodruff et al. (1983) find that consumers' satisfaction with a retail store's environment and retailtainment related engagement positively affects their loyalty behavior (e.g., revisit intention and word-of-mouth) toward the retail store. Based on this background information, we posit:

H_5: Customer satisfaction with retailtainment is positively related to word-of-mouth intentions towards a grocery store that offers retailtainment experiences.

H_6: Customer satisfaction with retailtainment is positively related to revisit intention to shop in a grocery store that offers retailtainment experiences.

METHODOLOGY

Survey Questionnaire

The questionnaire used in this study consists of three sections. The first section is the consent to participate in the study statement, definition of retailtainment, and examples of retailtainment activities. Next, we provided a brief guideline on how to complete the survey questionnaire. For example, one of the narratives in the guidelines reads as follows: "This study and survey questions are designed to determine your perception about retailtainment customer experiences in physical grocery stores. Retailtainment describes the instore entertainment activities used by physical grocery stores to connect, entertain and increase customers' interest in their merchandise. Retailtainment events include free product tasting/sampling, product demonstration, instore cooking shows, instore artist appearances, live shows, and pop-up events."

Table 1. Scale items and measurement values

Construct and items	Mean	SD	Load	CR	AVE	α
Human interactivity-instore (adapted from Florenthal and Shoham, 2010)	3.37	0.67		0.86	0.60	0.82
I can conduct an intelligent discussion with customer-service reps. in a grocery store that provides RE experiences (e.g., sampling).			0.62			
I can have an interpersonal dialogue with customer-service reps. in a grocery store that provides RE experiences (e.g., sampling).			0.73			
I can have an engaging discussion with customer-service reps. in a grocery store that provides RE experiences (e.g., sampling).			0.74			
I can socialize with customer-service reps. in a grocery store that provides RE experiences (e.g., sampling).			0.75			
Benefit value (adapted from Kim and Kankanhalli, 2009)	3.19	0.75		.88	0.66	0.83
I can get better experiences shopping for groceries in a grocery store that provides RE experiences (e.g., sampling).			0.81			
I think shopping for groceries in a grocery store that provides RE experiences (e.g., sampling) is easy compared to shopping at other grocery stores.			0.71			
I can save money by shopping for groceries in a grocery store that provides RE experiences (e.g., sampling).			0.70			
I feel shopping for groceries in a physical grocery store that provides RE experiences (e.g., sampling) is convenient.			0.85			
Enjoyment value (adapted from Ligas and Chaudhuri, 2012)	3.38	0.77		0.87	0.67	0.86
I would enjoy shopping for groceries in a grocery store that provides RE experiences (e.g., sampling).			0.81			
The actual process of shopping for groceries would be pleasant in a grocery store that provides RE experiences (e.g., sampling).			0.77			
I would enjoy watching live cooking demonstrations if they occurred at a grocery store.			0.70			
I would have fun shopping for groceries in a grocery store that provides RE experiences (e.g., sampling).			0.80			
Unique value (adapted from Ligas and Chaudhuri, 2012)	3.54	0.66		0.82	0.60	0.77
I believe a grocery store that offers RE experiences is different from other stores in a positive way.			0.84			
I believe a grocery store that offers RE experiences is unique in a good way.			0.84			
I believe a grocery store that offers RE experiences provides benefits that no other store offers.			0.63			
Satisfaction (adapted from Hsu et al. 2006)	3.39	0.68		0.82	0.60	0.82

Table 1. Continued

Construct and items	Mean	SD	Load	CR	AVE	α
I would be satisfied with retailtainment customer experiences offered by a grocery store.			0.76			
I would be very pleased with retailtainment customer experiences offered by a grocery store.			0.81			
On an overall basis, retailtainment customer experiences offered by a grocery store would fulfill my expectations.			0.74			
Word-of-mouth (adapted from Lee et al. 2019)	3.44	0.73		0.79	0.60	0.79
I would speak favourably about retailtainment customer experiences to others.			0.72			
I would say positive things about retailtainment customer experiences to others.			0.76			
I would assist other customers with retailtainment customer experiences if they need my help.			0.60			
Revisit Intention (adapted from Lee et al. 2019)	3.40	0.74		0.82	0.60	0.81
Given the chance, I intend to shop in a grocery store that offers retailtainment customer experiences.			0.83			
I am willing to shop in a grocery store that offer retailtainment customer experiences in the near future.			0.75			
I will frequently shop in a grocery store that offers retailtainment customer experiences.			0.74			
Likelihood to use technology (adapted from Oyedele and Simpson, 2017)	3.33	0.83		0.86	0.60	0.76
I would use computer tablets in the aisles in a grocery store to learn more about the store's products.			0.52			
I would purchase a good if I find a coupon or discover a discount on a grocery store's interactive kiosk.			0.71			
I would use interactive kiosks in a grocery store to seek information on specials and deals for customers.			0.74			
I would use a grocery store's app that lets me check r myself out using my mobile phone.			0.60			
I would use a mobile check out option that allows the grocery store staff to scan items in your cart and speed transactions from anywhere in the store.			0.61			

*SD = Standard deviation, Load = Factor loadings, CR = Composite reliability, α = Cronbach's alpha
Model fit indices: Chi-square = 1155.403/338, χ^2/df = 3.41, p = 0.00
GFI = .94, NFI = .92, CFI = .91, RMSEA = 0.08

The second section of the questionnaire contains the survey Likert type scales/ constructs. The constructs used in the study are adapted from prior research (See Table 1). The human interactivity-instore measures are from the work of Florenthal and Shoham (2010), and the perceived benefit value scale is adapted from Kim and Kankanhalli (2009). The enjoyment value and unique value scales are adapted from Ligas and Chaudhuri (2012). Satisfaction is adapted from the work of Hsu et al. (2006), and revisit intention and word-of-mouth scales are adapted from Lee et al.'s (2019) study on food shopping experience. The scale measuring likelihood to use instore technologies is adapted from Oyedele and Simpson's (2007) measure of usage frequency of self-service technologies. With the exception of demographic variables, all of the scale items are rated on a 1-5-point Likert type scale where '1' = Strongly Disagree and '5' = Strongly Agree. The third section of the questionnaire contained standard socio-demographic questions (e.g., age, gender, education, etc.).

Procedure and Sample

College students were considered suitable for this study because recent studies on market trends in the retail industry suggest that instore self-service technologies are popular among college-age students, between 18–25 years old. Young consumers may derive value from using instore technologies because it gives them some control over their shopping experience (Hooker, 2020). Also, the college student sample was deemed suitable for this study because college students tend to be representative of others within the same age group (Fry et al., 1973; Xu et al., 2004). Therefore, the survey questionnaire was administered to 332 undergraduate business students in classes at a Midwestern U.S. university. Participation in the study was voluntary and no incentives for participation were provided. The questionnaire contained Likert scale items and standard demographic questions. A total of 312 questionnaires were completed and used in the analysis. All survey respondents were recruited using convenience sampling. A majority of the study's respondents were single (92%), white (63%), and female (51%); the average age was 23 years old.

ANALYSIS AND RESULTS

Measurement Model

The measurement and structural models were evaluated using AMOS structural equation modeling software (AMOS-SEM). The study constructs were evaluated for reliability, convergent and discriminant validity. All Cronbach's alphas were above the .70 recommended value. The composite reliability results ranged from .70 to .80, which exceeds Bagozzi and Yi's (1989) recommended value of .60. Discriminant validity was evaluated using Fornell-Larcker's (1981) benchmark whereby if all the squared correlations between the latent constructs are less than their AVEs, then discriminant validity is confirmed (See Table 2). The Goodness-of-Fit Index (GFI)

Table 2. Discriminant validity: Average variance extracted and construct correlations

Construct	Mean	Std Dev	1	2	3	4	5	6	7	8
Human interactivity-instore	3.37	0.66	**0.77**							
Benefit value	3.22	0.74	0.37	**0.81**						
Enjoyment value	3.41	0.77	0.38	0.70	**0.82**					
Unique value	3.55	0.65	0.29	0.56	0.70	**0.77**				
Satisfaction	3.40	0.68	0.37	0.66	0.69	0.70	**0.77**			
Word-of-Mouth	3.46	0.72	0.33	0.58	0.64	0.62	0.70	**0.77**		
Revisit Intention	3.42	0.74	0.35	0.70	0.68	0.61	0.71	0.79	**0.77**	
Likelihood to use technology	3.27	0.81	0.26	0.29	0.35	0.37	0.32	0.33	0.40	1

Note: The square root of the AVEs are on the diagonal, and construct correlations are below the diagonal.

Table 3. Structural model results

	Hypothesized paths	Path coefficient	t-values	p-values	Hypothesis Supported?
H1a	Human interactivity-instore àSatisfaction	0.08	1.64	0.10	No
H2a	Benefit-value àSatisfaction	0.32	3.12	0.00	Yes
H3a	Enjoyment value àSatisfaction	0.31	2.45	0.00	Yes
H4a	Uniqueness value àSatisfaction	0.30	3.60	0.00	Yes
H5	Satisfaction à Word-of-mouth	0.87	12.12	0.00	Yes
H6	Satisfaction à Revisit intention	0.95	11.19	0.00	Yes
	Variable	R^2			
	Satisfaction	0.79			
	Word-of-mouth	0.77			
	Revisit Intention	0.95			
	Model fit indices: Chi-square = 677.181/226, χ^2/df = 2.99, p = 0.00 GFI = .93, NFI = .93, CFI = .91, RMSEA = 0.07				

is .94, the Normed Fit Index (NFI) is .92, and the Comparative Fit Index (CFI) is .91. The GFI, NFI and the CFI values exceed the recommended threshold of .90 (Bentler, 1990). The chi-square value computation for the measurement model is 1155.403 and the degrees of freedom are 338, resulting in a chi-square/df ratio of 3.41 (See Table 3)

Structural Model

The results from testing the structural model show the RMSEA value is within the limit for reasonable fit of 0.07. The Goodness-of-Fit Index (GFI) is .93, the Normed Fit Index (NFI) is .93, and the Comparative Fit Index (CFI) is .91. The GFI, NFI and the CFI values exceed the recommended threshold of .90 (Bentler, 1990). Overall, the fit indices (e.g., CFI, GFI, and NFI) indicate the data fit the hypothesized model well. The chi-square value computation for the structural model is 677.181 and the degrees of freedom are 226, resulting in a chi-square/df ratio of 2.99, which is within the desirable value of between 1 and 3 (Bentler, 1990).

The significance levels for each path coefficient and the R^2 values from testing the structural model offer useful understanding about the hypothesized relationships in the study's model. The results presented in Table 3 show the R^2 of satisfaction is 0.79; revisit intention is 0.95; and word of mouth is 0.77. The recommended R^2 value for consumer behavior studies is 0.20 (Hair et al., 2011). Following this criterion of 0.20, the R^2 for satisfaction, revisit intention, and word of mouth are significant.

With the exception of the relationship between human interactivity-instore and satisfaction, the results of the path coefficients show all coefficients are significant at the 0.05 significance level. For instance, the results show that benefit value (β=0.32, t=3.12, p=0.00), enjoyment value (β=0.31, t=2.45, p=0.00), and unique value (β=0.30, t=3.60, p=0.00) significantly affect satisfaction with retailtainment. The hypothesized relationships between satisfaction and word-of-mouth (β=0.87, t=12.12, p=0.00), and satisfaction on revisit intention (β=0.95, t=11.19, p=0.00) are significant at the 0.05 significance level.

A closer look at the results shows the coefficient of the relationship between benefit value and satisfaction (0.32) is greater than the coefficient of the relationship between human interactivity-instore and satisfaction with retailtainment (0.08). This indicates the value of the instore experience, or the value derived from instore retailtainment experiences, to be relatively more influential than consumers' internal characteristics (e.g., preference for human interactivity-instore) in the prediction of satisfaction with retailtainment. One implication of this result is that retail managers can broadly enhance their customer satisfaction initiative by increasing the benefit and pragmatic value of instore retailtainment events. This may include a safe shopping environment or other factors to ensure the instore experience is as fast and as safe as possible. The benefit value of retailtainment could be enhanced by offering free product samples, promotional discounts and coupons, and highlighting safety actions taken by store personnel. As seen in the items listed in Table 1, these benefits are perceived as experientially attained.

Based on Hair et al.'s (2011) R^2 criterion of 0.20, the results about the effects of satisfaction with retailtainment as an independent variable in the proposed model are powerful for explaining both revisit intentions and word-of-mouth behavior. In particular, a closer look at the R^2 values of revisit intention (.91) and word-of-mouth (.77) show a significant proportion of the variance in the dependent variables is explained by the independent variable satisfaction with retailtainment.

In relation to the hypothesized moderating effects of high vs. low likelihood to use instore technologies, we created an aggregate measure of likelihood to use instore technologies scale items (see Table 1). We used the aggregate measure to create two groups in SPSS: high versus low likelihood to use instore technologies. We used each group to compute multi-group analysis in AMOS to determine the possible differences between high vs. low likelihood to use instore technologies (See Table 4). The chi-square difference test result from the multi-group analysis was significant with a p value of 0.00. The result is significant at $p < 0.05$.

As hypothesized, the result of the moderation analysis of likelihood to use instore technologies on the relationship between human interactivity-instore and satisfaction with retailtainment is stronger and significant for low (β=0.18, t=2.24, p=0.00) rather than for high (β= -0.06, t= -0.83, p=0.40) likelihood to use instore technologies. This finding implies that individuals with low likelihood to use instore

Table 4. Multigroup analysis: Low vs. High likelihood to use instore technologies.

		Low likelihood			High likelihood		
Paths		Path Coefficients	t-values	p-values	Path Coefficients	t-values	p-values
H1b	Human interactivity à Satisfaction	0.18	2.24	0.00	-0.06	-0.83	0.40
H2b	Benefit-value à Satisfaction	0.44	2.63	0.00	0.18	1.51	0.13
H3b	Enjoyment-value à Satisfaction	0.07	0.33	0.75	0.51	2.97	0.00
H4b	Uniqueness value à satisfaction	0.37	2.98	0.00	0.33	2.37	0.02
Variable		R^2			R^2		
Satisfaction		0.76			0.79		

technologies are more likely than individuals with high likelihood to use instore technologies to perceive strong levels of satisfaction with retailtainment. The strong levels of retailtainment satisfaction perceived by individuals with low likelihood to use instore technologies may be connected to their greater preference to gain tangible benefits from retailtainment events.

The results of the path coefficient in Table 4 show the interaction analysis of likelihood to use instore technologies on the relationships between benefit value and satisfaction with retailtainment: Low (β=0.44, t=2.63, p=0.00) vs. High (β= 0.18, t= 1.51, p=0.31); enjoyment value and satisfaction with retailtainment: Low (β=0.07, t=0.33, p=0.75) vs. High (β= 0.51, t= 2.97, p=0.00) and unique value and satisfaction with retailtainment: Low (β=0.37, t=2.98, p=0.00) vs. High (β= 0.33, t= 2.37, p=0.02). As anticipated, with the exception of enjoyment value, these results are stronger for consumers who are low on likelihood to use instore technologies compared to individuals who are high on likelihood to use instore technologies. Overall, with exception of H_{1a} and $H_{3b,}$ all hypothesized relationships in the proposed model were significant (H_{1b}, H_{2a}, H_{2b}, H_{3a}, H_{4a}, H_{4b}, H_5 and H_6 were supported).

DISCUSSION

This study contributes to the literature of perceived value and the emerging stream of research on consumer engagement by evaluating the interaction effects of consumers' likelihood to use instore technologies on the relationship between perceived retailtainment value and satisfaction with retailtainment. We find that perceived benefit, enjoyment, and unique values of retailtainment were significant in explicating satisfaction with retailtainment in a physical grocery store context. This finding is consistent with previous studies on the role of perceived value in predicting satisfaction. For instance, Sands et al. (2015) found that functional and hedonic values are important predictors of satisfaction with both education and entertainment focused retailtainment events. Previous studies show that benefits and unique value derived from instore product sampling campaigns and instore information events (Franke & Schreier, 2008; Hu & Jasper, 2006) positively affect satisfaction with retailtainment.

Surprisingly, our analysis concerning the relationship between human interactivity-instore and satisfaction with retailtainment was not significant, suggesting that consumers' ability to interact with store employees or others in the store does not necessarily lead to satisfaction with retailtainment. This contradicts the findings from previous studies (e.g., Merrilees & Miller, 2001) which suggest preferences for human interaction instore positively affect loyalty behavior.

We also find positive relationships between the independent variables (human interactivity-instore, benefits, and unique values) and the dependent variable satisfaction with retailtaiment are stronger for individuals with low, rather than high, likelihood to use instore technologies. We attribute this to the fact that current technologies in use in grocery stores are geared toward time and effort efficiencies rather than entertainment and experiential benefit value-oriented information. This also explains why, contrary to the hypothesized relationships, analyses revealed that the relationship between enjoyment value and satisfaction with retailtainment is stronger for individuals with high, rather than low, likelihood to use technologies.

Individuals with high likelihood to use instore technologies may attain a strong level of satisfaction from the enjoyment value of retailtainment due to their lack of knowledge about the tangible benefits of retailtainment events. This lack of knowledge probably stems from their currently limited interactions with store employees and product demonstrators – since these consumers are more interested in shopping efficiently and quickly. They have limited interaction with people who have the necessary expertise and knowledge to offer shoppers advice about the benefits of an ongoing retailtainment event (e.g., product sampling). Therefore, individuals with high likelihood to use instore technologies may construe or imagine occasional encounters with store employees and product demonstrators as fun rather than beneficial.

Managerial Implications

Based on our findings above, we know that physical retail store customers, whether they have a low or a high likelihood to use technology, derive greater satisfaction from retailtainment that they perceive to provide enjoyment and benefits in an experiential setting. We also know that human interactivity is not a significant contributor to satisfaction with retailtainment, especially for customers with high likelihood to use technology for whom satisfaction with retailtainment becomes significantly higher when they perceive enjoyment value in using technology.

These results indicate to us that retailtainment technologies, which provide enjoyment and perceived informative benefits in terms of experience with the consumption of products, are likely to increase satisfaction and improve loyalty as well as propensity to return to the store. Interestingly, human interaction is not a necessarily sought element, but interactive technologies seem likely to increase immersion in enjoyable shopping experiences.

Grocery retailers need to create new retailtainment experiences that are well adapted to the reality of contactless and no-touch customer experiences by leveraging the features of immersive technologies to facilitate enjoyable and benefit-providing shopping experiences. We refer to these technologies as retailtainment technologies.

Retailtainment technologies should facilitate instore immersive shopping experiences to give customers opportunities to experience the physical grocery store and provide prior experiences with the products they are likely to purchase in unique ways. We suggest instore use of interactive kiosks, computer tablets in aisles, in-app check out, instore use of the retailer website to shop & purchase, and click-and-collect technologies that are enhanced with touch-safe accessories, such as gloves and self-cleansing or self-replacing surfaces, will be helpful to improve satisfaction.

Retailers can deploy machine-like robots to connect with customers through their cellphones to offer information about new products and price information. A machine-like robot in the aisle of the store could have features that allow customers to use their cellphones to interact with store brands in a unique way. For example, Kroger Co., a big box store in the U.S., recently completed a test of A.I. powered retailtainment technologies that allow the products and the shelves in the grocery store to engage individual customers through their cellphones. The technology can offer customers recommendations customized to their dietary needs or dietary limitations. In addition, the technology is able to connect with the shopping lists on the customers' cellphones to electronically display dietary and pricing information, availability, and product coupons.

FUTURE RESEARCH DIRECTIONS

The study's convenience sample of undergraduate university students may create bias as the sample is composed of young respondents who are usually more willing to use technology.

The generalizability of this study is limited by a number of factors including its use of a student sample, its survey questionnaire methodology and other weaknesses usually linked with survey research including study measures, and so on. While these study limitations affect the generalizability of the findings the limitations also offer opportunities for future research by employing different methodologies such as experiments in the field or laboratory and different measures. Future research should replicate this study with respondents of different ages and different technology self-efficacy.

REFERENCES

Abbott, M., Chiang, K. P., Hwang, Y. S., Paquin, J., & Zwick, D. (2000). The process of on-line store loyalty formation. *Advances in Consumer Research. Association for Consumer Research (U. S.)*, *27*, 145–150.

Babin, B. J., Darden, W. R., & Griffin, M. (1994). Work and/or fun: Measuring hedonic and utilitarian shopping value. *The Journal of Consumer Research*, *20*(4), 644–656. doi:10.1086/209376

Bagozzi, R. P., & Yi, Y. (1989). On the use of structural equation models in experimental designs. *JMR, Journal of Marketing Research*, *26*(3), 271–284. doi:10.1177/002224378902600302

Barsade, S. G. (2002). The ripple effect: Emotional contagion and its influence on group behavior. *Administrative Science Quarterly*, *47*(4), 644–675. doi:10.2307/3094912

Beatty, S. E., Mayer, M., Coleman, J. E., Reynolds, K. E., & Lee, J. (1996). Customer-sales associate retail relationships. *Journal of Retailing*, *72*(3), 223–247. doi:10.1016/S0022-4359(96)90028-7

Bentler, P. M. (1990). Comparative fit indexes in structural models. *Psychological Bulletin*, *107*(2), 238–246. doi:10.1037/0033-2909.107.2.238 PMID:2320703

Berry, L. L., Seiders, K., & Grewal, D. (2002). Understanding service convenience. *Journal of Marketing*, *66*(3), 1–17. doi:10.1509/jmkg.66.3.1.18505

Bitner, M. J. (1992). Servicescapes: The impact of physical surroundings on customers and employees. *Journal of Marketing*, *56*(2), 57–71. doi:10.1177/002224299205600205

Booms, B. H., & Bitner, M. J. (1982). Marketing services by managing the environment. *The Cornell Hotel and Restaurant Administration Quarterly*, *23*(1), 35–40. doi:10.1177/001088048202300107

Collier, J. E., & Barnes, D. C. (2015). Self-service delight: Exploring the hedonic aspects of self-service. *Journal of Business Research*, *68*(5), 986–993. doi:10.1016/j.jbusres.2014.09.036

Davis, L., & Hodges, N. (2012). Consumer shopping value: An investigation of shopping trip value, in-store shopping value and retail format. *Journal of Retailing and Consumer Services*, *19*(2), 229–239. doi:10.1016/j.jretconser.2012.01.004

Deighton, J., & Grayson, K. (1995). Marketing and seduction: Building exchange relationships by managing social consensus. *The Journal of Consumer Research*, *21*(4), 660–676. doi:10.1086/209426

Donovan, R. J., Rossiter, J. R., Marcoolyn, G., & Nesdale, A. (1994). Store atmosphere and purchasing behavior. *Journal of Retailing*, *70*(3), 283–294. doi:10.1016/0022-4359(94)90037-X

Falk, P., & Campbell, C. (Eds.). (1997). *The Shopping Experience*. Routledge. doi:10.4135/9781446216972

Florenthal, B., & Shoham, A. (2010). Four-mode channel interactivity concept and channel preferences. *Journal of Services Marketing*, *24*(1), 29–41. doi:10.1108/08876041011017871

Fornell, C., & Larcker, D. F. (1981). Structural equation models with unobservable variables and measurement error: Algebra and statistics. *JMR, Journal of Marketing Research*, *18*(3), 382–388. doi:10.1177/002224378101800313

Franke, N., & Schreier, M. (2008). Product uniqueness as a driver of customer utility in mass customization. *Marketing Letters*, *19*(2), 93–107. doi:10.100711002-007-9029-7

Fry, J. N., Shaw, D. C., von Lanzenauer, C. H., & Dipchand, C. R. (1973). Customer loyalty to banks: A longitudinal study. *The Journal of Business*, *46*(4), 517–525. doi:10.1086/295575

Fulberg, P. (2003). Using sonic branding in the retail environment—An easy and effective way to create consumer brand loyalty while enhancing the in-store experience. *Journal of Consumer Behaviour*, *3*(2), 193–198. doi:10.1002/cb.132

Gelbrich, K., & Sattler, B. (2014). Anxiety, crowding, and time pressure in public self-service technology acceptance. *Journal of Services Marketing*, *28*(1), 82–94. doi:10.1108/JSM-02-2012-0051

Grewal, D., & Roggeveen, A. L. (2020). Understanding retail experiences and customer journey management. *Journal of Retailing*, *96*(1), 3–8. doi:10.1016/j.jretai.2020.02.002

Gummesson, E. (1998). Implementation requires a relationship marketing paradigm. *Journal of the Academy of Marketing Science*, *26*(3), 242–249. doi:10.1177/0092070398263006

Hair, J. F. Jr, Ringle, C. M., & Sarstedt, M. (2011). PLS-SEM: Indeed a silver bullet. *Journal of Marketing Theory and Practice*, *19*(2), 139–151. doi:10.2753/MTP1069-6679190202

Hede, A. M., & Kellett, P. (2011). Marketing communications for special events: Analysing managerial practice, consumer perceptions and preferences. *European Journal of Marketing*, *45*(6), 987–1004. doi:10.1108/03090561111119930

Heeter, C. (2000). Interactivity in the context of designed experiences. *Journal of Interactive Advertising*, *1*(1), 3–14. doi:10.1080/15252019.2000.10722040

Hirschman, E. C. (1980). Innovativeness, novelty seeking, and consumer creativity. *The Journal of Consumer Research*, *7*(3), 283–295. doi:10.1086/208816

Holbrook, M. B. (1994). The nature of customer value: An axiology of services in the consumption experience. *Service Quality: New Directions in Theory and Practice*, *21*, 21–71. doi:10.4135/9781452229102.n2

Holbrook, M. B. (1999). *Consumer value: A framework for analysis and research.* Routledge.

Holbrook, M. B., & Hirschman, E. C. (1982). The experiential aspects of consumption: Consumer fantasies, feelings, and fun. *The Journal of Consumer Research*, *1*(2), 132–140. doi:10.1086/208906

Hooker, L. (2020). How can retailers thrive in a changing landscape? A review of 2019 and our expectations for 2020. *The Retailer* (winter edition), 28-29.

Hsu, M. H., Yen, C. H., Chiu, C. M., & Chang, C. M. (2006). A longitudinal investigation of continued online shopping behavior: An extension of the theory of planned behavior. *International Journal of Human-Computer Studies*, *64*(9), 889–904. doi:10.1016/j.ijhcs.2006.04.004

Hu, H., & Jasper, C. R. (2006). Social cues in the store environment and their impact on store image. *International Journal of Retail & Distribution Management*, *34*(1), 25–48. doi:10.1108/09590550610642800

Huizinga, J. (1955). *Homo ludens: A study of the play element inculture*. The Beacon Press. International Data Corporation.

Iacobucci, D., Ostrom, A., & Grayson, K. (1995). Distinguishing service quality and customer satisfaction: The voice of the consumer. *Journal of Consumer Psychology*, *4*(3), 277–303. doi:10.120715327663jcp0403_04

Iacopini, I., Petri, G., Barrat, A., & Latora, V. (2019). Simplicial models of social contagion. *Nature Communications*, *10*(1), 1–9. doi:10.103841467-019-10431-6 PMID:31171784

Jain, R., & Bagdare, S. (2009). Determinants of customer experience in new format retail stores. *Journal of Marketing Communications*, *5*(2), 34–44.

Jara, M., Vyt, D., Mevel, O., Morvan, T., & Morvan, N. (2018). Measuring customers benefits of click and collect. *Journal of Services Marketing*, *32*(4), 430–442. doi:10.1108/JSM-05-2017-0158

Kaltcheva, V. D., & Weitz, B. A. (2006). When should a retailer create an exciting store environment? *Journal of Marketing*, *70*(1), 107–118. doi:10.1509/jmkg.70.1.107.qxd

Kim, H. W., & Kankanhalli, A. (2009). Investigating user resistance to information systems implementation: A status quo bias perspective. *Management Information Systems Quarterly*, *33*(3), 567–582. doi:10.2307/20650309

Lee, H., Jang, Y., Kim, Y., Choi, H. M., & Ham, S. (2019). Consumers' prestige-seeking behavior in premium food markets: Application of the theory of the leisure class. *International Journal of Hospitality Management*, *77*, 260–269. doi:10.1016/j.ijhm.2018.07.005

Ligas, M., & Chaudhuri, A. (2012). The moderating roles of shopper experience and store type on the relationship between perceived merchandise value and willingness to pay a higher price. *Journal of Retailing and Consumer Services*, *19*(2), 249–258. doi:10.1016/j.jretconser.2012.01.006

Mathwick, C., Malhotra, N., & Rigdon, E. (2001). Experiential value: Conceptualization, measurement and application in the catalog and internet shopping environment. *Journal of Retailing*, *77*(1), 39–56. doi:10.1016/S0022-4359(00)00045-2

Mehrabian, A., & Russell, J. A. (1974). *An approach to environmental psychology*. The Massachusetts Institute of Technology.

Merrilees, B., & Miller, D. (2001). Superstore interactivity: A new self-service paradigm of retail service? *International Journal of Retail & Distribution Management*, *29*(8/9), 379–389. doi:10.1108/09590550110396953

Oyedele, A., & Simpson, P. M. (2007). An empirical investigation of consumer control factors on intention to use selected self-service technologies. *International Journal of Service Industry Management*, *18*(3), 287–306. doi:10.1108/09564230710751497

Pantano, E., & Vannucci, V. (2019). Who is innovating? An exploratory research of digital technologies diffusion in retail industry. *Journal of Retailing and Consumer Services*, *49*, 297–304. doi:10.1016/j.jretconser.2019.01.019

Ridgway, N. M., Dawson, S. A., & Bloch, P. H. (1990). Pleasure and arousal in the marketplace: Interpersonal differences in approach-avoidance responses. *Marketing Letters*, *1*(2), 139–147. doi:10.1007/BF00435297

Sands, S., Oppewal, H., & Beverland, M. (2015). How in-store educational and entertaining events influence shopper satisfaction. *Journal of Retailing and Consumer Services*, *23*, 9–20. doi:10.1016/j.jretconser.2014.11.004

Sheth, J. N., Newman, B. I., & Gross, B. L. (1991). Why we buy what we buy: A theory of consumption values. *Journal of Business Research, 22*(2), 159–170. doi:10.1016/0148-2963(91)90050-8

Sweeney, J. C., & Soutar, G. N. (2001). Consumer perceived value: The development of a multiple item scale. *Journal of Retailing, 77*(2), 203–220. doi:10.1016/S0022-4359(01)00041-0

Turley, L. W., & Milliman, R. E. (2000). Atmospheric effects on shopping behavior: A review of the experimental evidence. *Journal of Business Research, 49*(2), 193–211. doi:10.1016/S0148-2963(99)00010-7

Van Rompay, T. J. L., Tanja-Dijkstra, K., Verhoeven, J. W. M., & van Es, A. F. (2012). On store design and consumer motivation: Spatial control and arousal in the retail context. *Environment and Behavior, 44*(6), 800–820. doi:10.1177/0013916511407309

Veryzer, R. W. (1993). Aesthetic response and the influence of design principles on product preferences. In L. McAllister & R. Rothschild (Eds.), *Advances in consumer research* (Vol. 20, pp. 224–231). Association for Consumer Research.

Vieira, V. A., & Vaz Torres, C. (2014). The effect of motivational orientation over arousal-shopping response relationship. *Journal of Retailing and Consumer Services, 21*(2), 158–167. doi:10.1016/j.jretconser.2013.11.008

Woodruff, R. B., Cadotte, E. R., & Jenkins, R. L. (1983). Modeling consumer satisfaction processes using experience-based norms. *JMR, Journal of Marketing Research, 20*(3), 296–304. doi:10.1177/002224378302000308

Xu, J., Shim, S., Lotz, S., & Almeida, D. (2004). Ethnic identity, socialization factors, and culture-specific consumption behavior. *Psychology and Marketing, 21*(2), 93–112. doi:10.1002/mar.10117

Yalch, R. F., & Spangenberg, E. R. (2000). The effects of music in a` retail setting on real and perceived shopping times. *Journal of Business Research, 49*(2), 139–147. doi:10.1016/S0148-2963(99)00003-X

Zahorik, A. J., & Rust, R. T. (1993). Customer satisfaction, customer retention, and market share. *Journal of Retailing, 69*(2), 193–215. doi:10.1016/0022-4359(93)90003-2

Zeithaml, V. A., & Bitner, M. J. (2000). *Services marketing: Integrating customer focus across the firm* (2nd ed.). Irwin/McGraw-Hill.

Chapter 5
Exploring Mexican Attitudes Toward the Front Labeling System for Food and Beverages:
A Twitter Analysis

Monica D. Hernandez
https://orcid.org/0000-0001-8906-928X
Texas Lutheran University, USA

Edith Galy
The University of Texas-Rio Grande Valley, USA

ABSTRACT

Recently, the Mexican government implemented a simple labeling system that would apply to 85% of the food products. The aim of the system is to report high amounts of calories, sugars, sodium, fats and trans fats. Labels are displayed on the front of the package individually or in groups. No studies have been conducted to analyze public attitudes toward the labeling system. In order to fill this gap, the purpose of the study is to conduct an exploratory analysis of the Mexican attitudes toward the new labeling system on Twitter. The Twitter API was used to collect tweets published between January 01, 2020 to June 30, 2021. QSR NVivo 12 software was used to conduct thematic content analysis. The emerged themes were related to consumer education, impact on the industry and businesses, and support or rejection to the labeling system. A category emerged as reflection of the unique cultural traditions.

DOI: 10.4018/978-1-6684-8868-3.ch005

INTRODUCTION

Obesity and chronic diseases are the leading causes of mortality in Mexico (WHO, 2018). These linked factors are prevalent among the population and continue on the rise. The latest national survey indicated 36.1% of Mexican adults are considered obese, whereas only 23.5% has a healthy weight (Barquera & Rivera, 2020). The situation is attributable to a shift of the Mexican diet over the past 40 years, shifting from mainly fresh and organic foods to ultra-processed products high in sugar, salt and fat. Arguably, the best example is the soda consumption. Mexico has one of the highest global rates of soda consumption (Colchero et al., 2016), averaging 137 liters consumed individually per year (Galvez, 2020).

The recent pandemic has exacerbated the public health problem. The large number of individuals with COVID-19, and more important, the large number of mortality rates (now exceeding the US, UK and Italy rates according to Statista, 2020) can be explained by the unhealthy habits of the population. In particular, the consumption of sugary beverages has been identified as a possible culprit (Bello, 2020). In response, the government implemented a "National Strategy for the Prevention and Control of Overweight, Obesity, and Diabetes" sponsored by corporate funding. The strategy would cover innovation and research in order to promote a healthier lifestyle (Secretaria de Salud, 2013).

Recently, the Mexican government implemented a simple labeling system that would apply to 85% of the food products consumed in the country. The Front Labeling System for Food and Beverages (SEFAB in Spanish) was implemented on October 1, 2020. This system was developed by the National Institute of Public Health and led to the update of the official Mexican standard NOM-051-SCFI/SSA1-2010. The implemented system consist of black octagons with white letters (see Figure 1). The aim of the system is to report high amounts of calories, sugars, sodium, fats and trans fats. Labels are displayed on the front of the package individually or in groups.

Figure 1. Legends/warning labels
(Caloric excess; sodium excess; trans-fat excess; sugars excess; saturated fats excess).

Due to its recency, no studies have been conducted to analyze public attitudes toward the most recent labeling system or any other recent effort. Researchers called for investigations of consumer perceptions of the information provided on food labels and the resulting consumer decisions (Andrews et al., 2021; Przyrembel, 2004). In order to fill this gap, the purpose of the study is to conduct an exploratory analysis of the Mexican attitudes toward the new labeling system on Twitter. Moreover, in response to the United Nations' goals for Sustainable Development #2 Zero Hunger (Improved nutrition), #3 Good Health and Well-Being and #12 Responsible Consumption and Production, the present study reports on investigations of Mexican consumer perceptions of the new format on food and beverage labels (as posted to Twitter) and the resulting consumer decisions.

BACKGROUND

Chile was the first country to jointly require front-of-package warning labels, restrict food promotion directed to children, and ban sales in schools of products having excess of calories, sugars, sodium and fats. Implemented in 2016, the labeling system had a significant impact on the consumer. According to Taillie et al. (2020), at the time the measure was implemented, a decline of 24% on purchases of labeled beverages was observed. These authors noted that this effect on purchases could be attributed to the industry, consumer behavior or both.

Although the original purpose of food labeling was to avoid the misleading of consumers, there was a shift towards the consumer education via labeling as the US American Nutrition Labeling and Education Act (1993) illustrated (Przyrembel 2004). The introduction of the Chilean-style labeling system using the "Stop Sign" symbols was considered a threshold for consumer education and communication effort (Andrews et al. 2021).

METHODOLOGY

This study performed a content analysis including both hashtag analysis (hashtag frequency) as well as word analysis (word frequency, word combination frequency as well as cluster document-level analysis) of tweets. Three stages of the study included: (1) Data collection using Twitter API v2/Postman; (2) Data analysis using QSR Nvivo 12 and (3) Reporting of thematic analysis findings.

The Twitter API was used to collect historical tweets regarding the recently implemented labeling system. The following terms in Spanish were given as input to collect Tweets published between January 01, 2020 to June 30, 2021.

Figure 2. Methodology

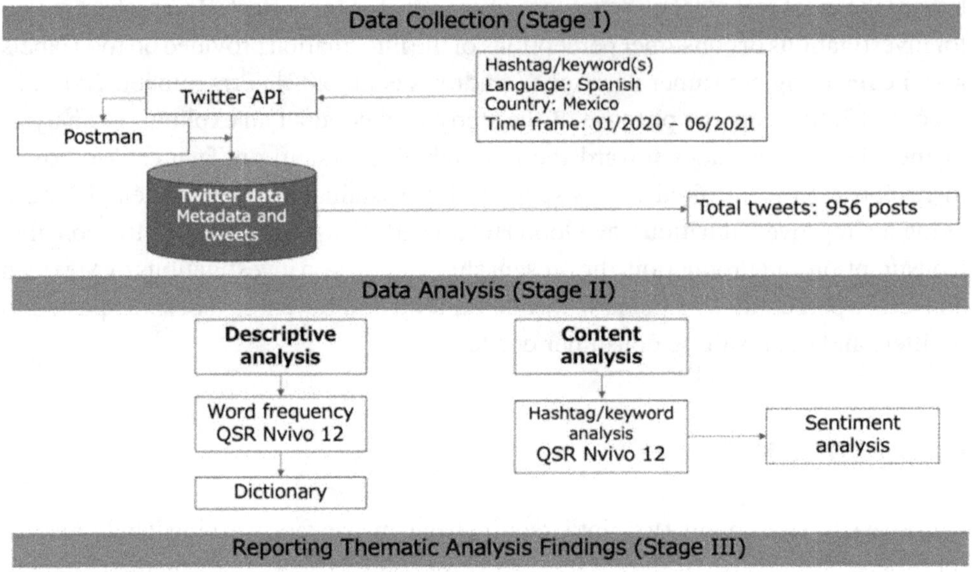

1. Hashtags: #etiquetadoparalasalud #etiquetadoclaroya #etiquetadonutrimental #NOM051
2. Keywords: nuevo etiquetado; etiquetado de alimentos; etiquetado nutricional; etiquetado frontal; etiquetado frontal de advertencia; etiquetado frontal octagonal; etiquetado nutrimental.

Language was restricted to Spanish and country of origin was Mexico. The country of origin was necessary as similar regulations are being implemented in other Spanish speaking countries (e.g. Colombia, Spain). In total, 956 posts were pulled from Twitter.

To analyze the sample, the QSR NVivo 12 software was used to conduct thematic content analysis. The software allows to obtain a preliminary visualization of themes, a precise thematic organization using predefined themes, and the integration of themes emerged from the data. First, a dictionary of themes was developed based on Word frequency. Next, a series of patterns emerged from the data after initial coding.

RESULTS

Three major categories were identified and named according to the central themes across the data set. The themes ranged from messages related to consumer education, impact on the industry and businesses, and support or rejection to the labeling system.

The themes included in the first category represented different circumstances and attempts to foster consumer education. To illustrate, tweets mentioned a series of workshops to educate consumers about the meaning and benefits of the system, as well as efforts in the classroom to educate the young consumers. The category also included messages highlighting the insufficient information about the purpose and scope of the labeling system. Since the implementation occurred during the COVID pandemic, some messages reinforced the need to make better food choices after the negative impact of the pandemic in Mexico.

Another emerged theme focused on the effects on the junk food industry and businesses, such as product reformulation, changes on packages, modified advertising, just to name a few. Messages related to the theme expressed the public benefits of the implementation of the system by uncovering the realities of a number of products that on surface appear as healthy options. A related group of messages celebrated the reformulation of many food offerings for a better consumer health.

Other salient category focused on the negative aspects of the implementation of the systems. One of the categories simply rejected the idea and covered a series of cynical messages. These messages revolved around the realization that the introduction of the system may not change the habits acquired early in life or the preferences of the consumer. A series of jokes and memes by the absence of the typical illustrations or mascots originally featured in the package were also frequent. Some jokes made reference to the null effect on consumer decisions because of the changes on packaging.

DISCUSSION

The present study reaffirms the potential of social media as a tool for uncovering attitudes toward the implementation of efforts to combat the obesity and chronic diseases. In particular, Twitter data demonstrated the advantages of sourcing an ample range of information to uncover and classify a series of themes. The focus on attitudes toward the recently implemented Front Labeling System for Food and Beverage emphasize the mixed reactions to the government initiative. The findings show that tweets were used to educate the consumer, highlight the benefits of the labeling system, highlight the impact on the food industry and businesses, as well as express a series of rejection and cynical messages.

Przyrembel (2004) identified three interrelated aims of food labeling, citing (1) information to the consumer; (2) protection to the consumer and (3) fairness in trade. Previous studies concluded that the use of nutritional labels is associated with an improved nutrition knowledge (An et al. 2021). Accordingly, food labeling would provide "correct information on the identity, nature and composition of the food should prevent the consumer to make choices which are inappropriate for a healthy diet and should guarantee equal opportunities for the marketing of comparable foods." (p. 360). Therefore, the uncovered themes frequently cited at least one of these interrelated aims. Therefore, it is safe to conclude that the majority of tweets revolved around the topics previously identified by Przyrembel (2004).

Notably, the third salient category was not previously identified in the literature as it appears to be a unique form of expression of the Mexicans or perhaps Latinx. Stanton (2019) found that Mexicans exhibit strong ties to traditions in food preparations while also display interest in modern conveniences. This was also evident in a series of tweets expressing some form of rejection to the new system because the preservation of Mexican traditions in meal preparations or consumption.

In sum, the uncovered themes were mixed, including positive, neutral (e.g. facts, announcements) and negative messages. This is indicative that not all the consumers are embracing the new system. The labeling system is currently being implemented, so it remains to see if the effects on consumer purchases are similar to that achieved in Chile.

Future work may include a sentiment analysis dealing with people's opinions, attitudes and emotions. A sentiment analysis may report an alternative measure of the perception of the public. Also, future research may include an analysis of illustrations or videos posted to other social media platforms. As different segments of the population navigate specific platforms because of their interests or opinions, it would be interesting to compare the attitudes expressed on different social media. As other countries (Colombia and Spain) undergo the implementation of similar systems, it would be useful to conduct similar analyses in these countries. A comparison of the emerged themes across World regions can also be a fruitful avenue for research.

In sum, our findings draw some implications for government, organizations, researchers and consumers:

- The study confirms that the government use of social media has evolved to educate and engage the population.
- The effects of the system on product reformulations and other adaptation to marketing efforts (packaging, advertising, etc.) are still developing. So, affected companies should maintain meaningful exchanges with consumers in social media to increase the customer knowledge about the reformulation and their impact on their health.

- Social media may provide consumers with the opportunity to learn more about the benefits of the system implemented by the government and the food industry response.
- Twitter API v2 has a great potential as a data source as well as a predictive system. In particular, this tool allows researchers to obtain real-time data, which provides means to identify changes in public perceptions over time.

The study has a series of limitations due to the inherent shortcomings arising from the common uses of the Twitter platform. As Twitter appears to serve as a platform for some people to criticize, complain and generate conflict among groups, the rationale for the emerged negative themes may need to be further scrutinized. Another consideration is that social media appears to serve for the spread of fake news. Therefore, the social media expressions need to be analyzed within the appropriate context. Last but not least, the use of NVivo software poses the limitation that classification of messages into categories cannot identify sarcasm or irony. Despite its limitations, the present study presents preliminary findings on the Mexican consumer perceptions of the new food labels and the resulting consumer decisions.

REFERENCES

An, R., Shi, Y., Shen, J., Bullard, T., Liu, G., Yang, Q., Chen, N., & Cao, L. (2021). Effect of front-of-package nutrition labeling on food purchases: A systematic review. *Public Health*, *191*(February), 59–67. doi:10.1016/j.puhe.2020.06.035 PMID:33517247

Andrews, J. C., Netemeyer, R., Burton, S., & Kees, J. (2021). What consumers actually know: The role of objective nutrition knowledge in processing stop sign and traffic light front-of-pack nutrition labels. *Journal of Business Research*, *128*, 140–155. doi:10.1016/j.jbusres.2021.01.036

Barquera, S., & Rivera, J. A. (2020). Obesity in Mexico: Rapid epidemiological transition and food industry interference in health policies. *Lancet*, *8*(9), 746–747. PMID:32822599

Bello. (2020). Politicians step up the fight against Mexico's Coca-Cola habit. *The Economist*, October, 29.

Colchero, M. A., Rivera-Dommarco, J., Popkin, B. M., & Ng, S. W. (2017). In Mexico, evidence of sustained consumer response two years after implementing a sugar-sweetened beverage tax. *Health Affairs*, *36*(3), 564–571. doi:10.1377/hlthaff.2016.1231 PMID:28228484

Galvez, A. (2020). Taking Susto seriously: A critique of behavioral approaches to diabetes. *American Anthropologist*, *122*(3), 647–648. doi:10.1111/aman.13443

Przyrembel, H. (2004). Food labelling legislation in the EU and consumers information. *Trends in Food Science & Technology*, *15*(7-8), 360–365. doi:10.1016/j.tifs.2003.12.006

Secretaria de Salud. (2013). Estrategia Nacional para Prevencion y Control de Sobrepeso, Obesidad y Diabetes [National Strategy for the Prevention and Control of Overweight, Obesity and Diabetes]. Gobierno de la Republica, Available: https://www.gob.mx/cms/uploads/attachment/file/200355/Estrategia_nacional_para_prevencion_y_control_de_sobrepeso_obesidad_y_diabetes.pdf

Stanton, J. V. (2019). Changing consumer preferences in emerging markets: Food market challenges in Central Mexico. *Journal of Food Products Marketing*, *25*(4), 378–403. doi:10.1080/10454446.2019.1566807

Statista. (2022). Coronavirus (COVID-19) deaths worldwide per one million population as of April 26, 2022, by country. Available: https://www.statista.com/statistics/1104709/coronavirus-deaths-worldwide-per-million-inhabitants/

Taillie, L. S., Reyes, M., Colchero, M. A., Popkin, B., & Corvalán, C. (2020). An evaluation of Chile's Law of Food Labeling and Advertising on sugar-sweetened beverage purchases from 2015 to 2017: A before-and-after study. *PLoS Medicine*, *17*(2), 1–22. doi:10.1371/journal.pmed.1003015 PMID:32045424

Chapter 6
Impact of Social Media Platforms on the Consumer Decision-Making Process in the Food and Grocery Industry

Tanu Gupta
KR Mangalam University, India

Pallavi Pandey
KR Mangalam University, India

Yogita Yashveer Raghav
https://orcid.org/0000-0003-0478-8619
KR Mangalam University, India

ABSTRACT

The rise of online social networking platforms has created a network around the globe among people for communicating and interacting with each other. Customer's view of an organization's contributions and brand are probably going to impact a buy choice. This idea is the focus of an investigation into trends, entertainment, customization, electronic word-of-mouth, and interactivity, additionally, fadedness, risk, interactivity, and personalization were perceived; keywords were also examined in order to test social media marketing in the insurance industry. Moreover, few additional metrics are used to evaluate the success of social media marketing, such as immediacy, accessibility, responses, information, interactivity, entertainment, perceived risk, trendiness, and customizability are all important factors. Also due to sudden hit of covid-19, the change in trend of customer purchase behaviour and interest is also discussed.

DOI: 10.4018/978-1-6684-8868-3.ch006

INTRODUCTION

Customers now have new opportunities to participate in online interactions through social media, creating content and communicating with other users. Businesses have recognized the benefits of social media and established dedicated teams or departments to manage their online projects. The shift towards online marketing is evident, with a projected 33% of global advertising spending in digital channels by 2017. Consequently, consumer research must focus on understanding consumer behavior in digital environments, particularly on mobile and social media platforms. This discussion will explore the influence of social media on customer marketing, the importance of brand promotion for customer satisfaction, and the changes in marketing trends on social media following the Covid-19 pandemic, specifically within the Food and Grocery (F&G) industry.

Social media has the potential to establish an authentic connection between brands and users, positively impacting brand results. Customers' previous experiences and the ability of a product to meet their specific needs often influence their purchasing decisions. Social media marketing can take various forms, such as pictures, videos, micro-blogging, weblogs, and wikis. The way a brand markets itself directly affects the buying process, and a distinctive brand with positive recommendations develops a strong image. This connection between a brand's strength and its image leads to brand loyalty, where customers repeatedly choose and purchase the brand.

The sudden onset of the Covid-19 pandemic had a profound impact on businesses, forcing many to close their doors. The web and social media platforms have become crucial for customer engagement and communication, offering convenience to businesses of all sizes, especially during a pandemic. Researchers are interested in understanding how businesses adapt to the new normal and continue to be successful. They aim to explore what drives consumers to make food purchases solely through social media advertisements, as online advertisements have a significant influence. Social media marketing has gained popularity in the fast food industry, with various businesses utilizing platforms like Twitter, Facebook, Instagram, and YouTube to reach a wider audience and sell their products. This chapter will discuss how the Food and Grocery (F&G) industry utilizes social media as a marketing tool.

This study will outline the evolution of social media and social media marketing, compare it with conventional marketing approaches, examine the impact of brand promotion on customer satisfaction, and analyze the changes in consumer purchasing patterns within the F&G industry following the Covid-19 pandemic. The chapter is divided into the following sections: literature review, expansion and evolution of social media marketing, the influence of brand promotion on customer satisfaction, and the impact of the Covid-19 pandemic on consumer purchasing behaviour in the food and grocery industry.

2. IMPACT OF DIGITAL SOCIAL PLATFORM FOR CUSTOMER SATISFACTION IN FOOD INDUSTRY

Due to how far innovation has advanced, social media is becoming increasingly vital to modern businesses. Since almost everyone now has a personal online space on a variety of platforms, direct customer interaction with businesses has significantly improved their performance by providing them with useful insights into the needs, expectations, and recommendations to increase customer satisfaction levels of their current and potential customers.

Many research have been conducted before you to investigate how customers make decisions utilising social media marketing. Consumer restaurant selection, on the other hand, has received little attention. The majority of research focuses on the factors that influence consumer decisions; studies [1] have identified service quality, meal quality, cost, and food provenance as significant contributions. Greater insights into customers' consumption experiences and restaurant decision-making and are still required with widespread of usage of social media as mobile technologies [2]. Previous studies, on the other hand, used a quantitative research approach. This study on impact of social media usage on consumer experiences at restaurants is conducted as, these days consumer's decision on picking locations leverages the benefit of reviews and rating on social media. The specific research questions of this study are: (a) investigate the vital elements associated with using social media on mobiles for picking up restaurant and the utility of social media for picking up restaurant; and (b) examine how consumers use online entertainment for their experience at various stages i.e. at home, on the go and in the restaurant. By providing answers to these research questions, the current study is anticipated to provide stakeholders in the food and grocery sector with useful recommendations for the development of efficient social media marketing campaigns.

2.1 Related Work

2.1.1 Consumers' Decision Making Process

Recognizing a problem or need for a service, product, or experience is the opening in the typical consumer decision making process. Next, they look for information to help them make a purchase [3]. According to Crotts, throughout their lives, customers must make multiple decisions when purchasing goods [4]. As a result, academics have spent more than 50 years researching consumer decision-making [5]. Most prior research on customer dynamic cycles in the assistance area has zeroed in on characterizing recognizing characteristics of administrations in contrast with highlights of products look for data to direct their purchase [6]. It has been recommended that purchasers' data search ways of behaving be concentrated on to completely grasp and expect shoppers' dynamic cycles in the assistance area in light of the fact that the climate wherein buyers settle on choices contrasts from that in the item areas [7]. Because of the inborn flightiness and elusiveness of administrations, clients' data looking for ways of behaving are more significant in the assistance area than in the product sector (including restaurant industry) [8]. In light of this idea, consumers' decision-making processes in the restaurant industry ought to be studied in a manner distinct from that of the product industry in order to comprehend how customers act when selecting the appropriate restaurant.

2.1.2 Restaurant Customers' Choices and Experiences

Previous study has showed that restaurant selections are considered as the most flexible activity among several trip features [9]. This proposes that data got through the pursuit cycle, as well as different factors, may strongly affect eatery choices. When compared to other choices for services or products in this industry, restaurant decisions are perceived to be less risky in terms of time and distance; Typically, restaurant decisions are limited to a single occasion, indicating that customers' perspectives may differ from those of other food industry decisions [10]. In other words, restaurant decision makers may have a smaller opportunity cost than a customer who must choose a more costly travel restaurant. On the other hand, despite the fact that group decision-making in restaurants is now commonplace, little research has been done on group decision-making processes in restaurants. The characteristics that the majority of previous research on group decision-making in the restaurant industry has focused on family restaurant decision-making; only a couple of studies have investigated café decision making among non-family bunch individuals, which is viewed as an exploration hole. For instance, Labrecque and Ricard (2001) researched youngsters' and guardians' view of kids' effect on family eating out choices and found that youngsters will generally underrate their impact [11]. The findings of the study indicate that the type of family is a significant factor in restaurant selection; however, a child's age is more influential than the type of family. In addition, the gender of the child is a factor at fast-food restaurants but not at casual dining establishments. Children play a major role in the decision-making phases when choosing the type of restaurant, the particular restaurant, and food ordering, according to Chen et al.'s investigation of the involvement of children in family group dining-out selections [12]. However, in a digitalized environment where technologically developed platforms enable restaurant decision-makers to access a variety of information, there are multiple opportunities to investigate the group restaurant decision-making processes in action. Although a child's age is more influential than family type, the study found that the type of family is a significant factor in restaurant selection. In addition, the gender of the child is a factor at fast-food restaurants but not at casual dining establishments. Chen et al researched the association of kids in family bunch feasting out determinations and found that youngsters have a significant impact in the dynamic stages while choosing on the sort of eatery, the particular café, and food requesting [12]. In any case, there are a few opportunities to examine bunch café dynamic cycles in real life, especially in a digitalized climate where eatery leaders might get to an assortment of data by means of mechanically produced stages. Thus, there is a need to research top to bottom how and why customers' café related choices are made as per their different utilization stages; moreover, what the advanced time might mean for purchasers' dynamic cycles and café feasting encounters with the wide extension of innovation based instruments ought to be explored. Buyers have generally high levels of vulnerability in their café determinations when contrasted with buying items, notwithstanding eatery picking qualities. As a consequence of this, customers are more likely to conduct information searches in order to lessen the perceived risk associated with their choices; Instead of sticking to the initial planned decision, they keep the option open to convert their decisions based on the context they are in, such as data from outside sources [13,14].

2.2 Modern Marketing Tool: Social Media

Social media marketing is a strategy that seeks to promote and adapt social media marketing strategy in conjunction with several other types of theories that impact social behaviours of a society and a person in order to perform a more useful social deed. The completeness of social media for marketing purposes is a major concern in this digital 21st century. Customers had limited options for engaging specific organisations about their products or services prior to the emergence of Web 2.0, therefore enterprises had to invest money to promote the brand profile. In [15], the marketing theory says, that the organisation should stand apart among a large number of worldwide locales to accomplish memorability and last deals. The introduction of social media has furnished those traditional methods obsolete. There are a number of commercial strategies for getting your brand out there on social media. Consistent use of social media is critical to its success. Using effective methods such as word-of-mouth (WoM), connecting and influencing with customers and good communication all have a significant impact on the success of any organisation. [15]

The major effects of social media in business include increased traffic, dedicated fans, increased visibility and the creation of business intelligence. Each of the benefits listed above is applicable to both business-to-consumer (B2C) and business-to-business (B2B) marketing. Similarly, intelligent leadership is usually employed in B2B, but every marketer needs to know about the capacity and quality of their product.

Improved search ranking and increased business collaboration are important in every company operation. Finally, improving sales and lowering marketing expenses are at the bottom of the list of social media marketing benefits [16].

2.3 Social Media Platforms

The word social media refers to online portal such as websites and applications that allow users, whether organisations or people, to communicate, create and share material in various ways [17]. Some kinds of social media include microblogging, discussion forums, social networking, wiki, video sharing, photo sharing, and social reviewing. Some social platforms are easier to access and as a result, more comfortable using mobile applications. Facebook, LinkedIn, Instagram, Twitter, Pinterest, and YouTube are among the most popular social media sites. Anyone with an electronic device and an internet connection can now create their own social media pages.

No matter what the various long range informal communication destinations accessible, most of them start with a client making a profile, frequently by giving a username and email address. Following that, the client can either share existing substance or make new satisfied. Users can have friends, followers, and subscribers, depending on the type of the social media platform; They can respond to the published content in a number of ways, including sharing, commenting, liking, and even reporting if they consider the content irrelevant [18]. Social media sites can be used for a variety of things, including keeping in touch with friends, family, acquaintances, and associates and sharing information or ideas. The majority of people now have more than one digital profiles, whereas in the past, social media was only popular with younger people. In addition, the term “social media influencer” was created as a result of the wide use of social media. Influencers are people who have a large number of followers because of the entertaining and useful content they post online. In parallel, influencers are extremely active on their channels, posting journals, videos, images, and a wide range of other types of content that piques users’ interest and encourages further interaction, resulting in a solid reputation [19].

The use of social media has increased the necessity for organisations to create their own pages on social media platforms and sites in order to establish communities around them [20]. Similarly, companies are aware of the rising relevance of social media since they want to use these sites for promotion and marketing. Despite being a low cost strategy, it is obvious that the vast majority of social media users have boosted the performance of many firms’ brand recognition and consumer engagement. The majority of businesses have their own websites with share options and social features like a comment box for likes. By doing so, their pages build strong relationships with existing clients while also reaching out to future ones[18]. Users often scroll through a social media site and determine whether or not to pay attention to a piece of material based on how pleasant it seems in their "feed." The algorithm used by social media to determine the order of profile pages that appear in other users' feeds based on information from the profile page is influenced by a variety of factors, including the location of the restaurant and the type of services offered. [21].

3. INFLUENCE OF PROMOTION OF BRAND ON SOCIAL MEDIA ON CUSTOMER BEHAVIOUR IN FOOD AND GROCERY INDUSTRY

Social media platforms like facebook, instagram and others are used to frame online circle where users can interact and meet is particularly referred to as one of these .Tablets, smart phones and other smart devices with Internet access are just a few of the simple-to-use platforms that social media offers, and they provide many sides open for creating a genuine conversation between the customers and market sides. It also makes it easier to interact and communicate with customers in a direct and more personalized way and enables them to participate in the marketing, design, and production of products and services together [22]. Virtual entertainment is overwhelmed by client created content, which is believed to be more dependable and solid than the substance on sites oversaw by genuine organizations [23]. The positive connection has an impact on the outcomes of the brand. This study aims to investigate the link between brand commitment, brand loyalty, and brand trust, as well as three additional prospects that are very significant in the customer pleasure with a brand and relationship marketing literature, and. We pay special attention to the emotive component of commitment since research consistently shows that this kind of commitment has the greatest influence on the hospitality industry [24].

This study focus at brand loyalty in terms of customers' propensity to make repeat purchases as well as their propensity to suggest services . The linkages indicated above are looked at in the hospitality sector, more especially in the brands of fast food chains. Since most services are highly experienced, it can be difficult for buyers to judge the quality of a service before making a purchase. Visitors use social media to engage and read each other's reviews and comments in that situation prior to making a purchase decision [25].

However, as recently stated by [26], there is still a significant lot of uncertainty regarding the impact of internet evaluations on the hotel sector, which is why more attention to the topic from marketing academics and practitioners may be beneficial. This study attempts to solve this issue by investigating the effects of user generated online reviews on social media on brand satisfaction, emotional commitment, trust, and loyalty. This specific setting was chosen because, together with lodging (fast food), restaurants accurately reflect the features of the hospitality business.

More precisely, a 2007 research by comScore and The Kelsey Group [27] found that 41% of readers of restaurant reviews went to the restaurant in question after reading the review, while 40% of perusers of lodging survey remained at the inn being referred to. However, the same survey found that although 79% of readers of restaurant reviews said that the review had an impact on their restaurant visit, 87% of hotel review users said that the review had a major impact on their decision to make a purchase. According to this finding, customers of fast food restaurants have a relevant impact from online reviews, but not as much as hotel guests do. This is likely because the services provided by fast-food chain brands are more commoditized and less experiential, which may lessen the impact of user-generated online reviews and consumer uncertainty

3.1 Related Work

In previous studies, a person's decision to choose a company's product or service over its rivals was referred to as a "buy decision" [28]. Consumer purchasing decisions may be influenced by internal or external marketing factors. Internal elements include perceptions, attitudes, personalities, knowledge, roles, and status as well as attitude and beliefs. External, on the other hand, culture, affinity groups, and socioeconomic status are all contributing variables. Service providers realised that it is very difficult to acquire and maintain good connections with important clients to ensure their continuing development and presence in the marketplace since consumers today have become exposed to a variety of product or service offers and different alternatives [29]. The majority of service providers have their own social media pages so that they can interact with customers online and foster positive brand perceptions. Marketers have also noticed that consumers are more comfortable connecting with one another through online platforms like social media. Before weighing the benefits of choosing a brand over alternatives and making a purchase, customers typically look for additional information about a brand online when they become more aware of what it offers [30].

Due to this, social media platforms have lately become a potent method for connecting and interacting with clients electronically and at a lesser cost. Companies may increase consumer involvement by using social media networks, swiftly contact the target market, easily distribute key marketing messages [31]. Customers will have the chance to express their views and influence others through online reviews and comments, and WoM marketing as a result of their experiences [32]. Consumers' preparedness to depend on a brand to fulfil a stated promise was expressed as brand assurance in previous research [33]. It therefore occurs as a outcome of a company's goodness in working in the interests of its customers in order to frame fruitful relations with them. There is brand trust when customers have faith in a service provider's dependability and moral character. Customer response to various brand interactions in the virtual world are effected by customer trust and brand awareness. In [34] researchers said that social media interactions are crucial for promoting brand trust. The writers went on to say that these interactions may be created through content produced by a company as well as through online reviews and social media data. Businesses will find it simpler to deliver their targeted marketing messages and create positive perceptions of their brands in the minds of customers at the point when brand trust among buyers in the objective market increments. Jadil et al. [35] reported that consumers' behaviour is largely influenced by online trust. Pop et al., [36] also demonstrated that brand trust influences buying decisions favourably.

4. HOW CONSUMER BEHAVIOUR IN THE FOOD AND GROCERY INDUSTRIES IS AFFECTED BY ADVERTISEMENTS ON SOCIAL MEDIA DURING COVID-19?

The sudden erupt of novel virus Covid-19 mark big hit on various industries all over the world. As Coronavirus pandemic is a new peculiarity, data about its effect via web-based entertainment promoting rehearses is limited [37]. Because of this Covid-19 limitation on direct contact, the job of web-based entertainment in purchaser spending may increment since it can interface clients all over the planet. Due to the findings of a previous survey, which indicate that the pandemic has a significant impact on consumer purchasing, decision-making processes and behaviour, it is essential to investigate the pandemic's impact on consumer behaviour. This could result in significant shifts in marketing strategies. As the 21st century starts, specialists expect the Web will act as an extension between business associations and customer inside the world. At the point when the world is compeling to hold a more segregated distance, web-based entertainment make up for this shortfall, permitting individuals to stay in contact with each person and association [38]. Besides, social media marketing has recently regained prominence in 2020. Because of this change in shopper conduct, F&B organizations have made online entertainment a basic component of arising advertising patterns [39]. In order to conduct social activities with the target customers and improve the business, it is also necessary to estimate long-established social media channels [40]. Therefore, this study will assist in determining the impact of COVID-19 on consumer behaviour and the continuing trend of using social media as a new marketing channel in the food and beverage industry.

4.2 Conceptual framework:

This chapter discusses certain hypothesis given in existing related work to investigate the opportunities that social media marketing can bring to the food and grocery industry, as well as its impact on consumer behaviour during COVID-19. The conceptual framework (figure1) supporting the hypothesis is given below:

Hypothesis 1: In food and grocery (F&G), a significant relationship between social media advertising and consumer behaviour is observed.

Due to the suppression of the desire to go to public places by social distance and hygiene measures, it is anticipated that restaurant consumption behaviour will significantly change following this COVID-19 outbreak [41]. Consumer attitudes toward online shopping have improved as a result of the growing market share held by e-commerce businesses through the use of social media advertising. [42] states that over 200 million posts have been tagged with the hash tag #foodandgrocery, making F&G posts one of the most popular content types on social media. This study demonstrated that social media has also emerged as an important source of marketing data regarding consumer preferences for online-based goods and services. Consumer perceptions of legitimacy, content utility, non-irritating social media advertising and entertainment influence consumer behaviour, according to a survey [43].

Hypothesis 2: A critical connection is observed between E-WoM and consumer conduct in F&G industry during Covid 19.

According to marketers, electronic word-of-mouth (E-WOM) has taken the place of WoM in social media, enabling the most successful advertising strategy to reach a larger population of target consumers through low-cost marketing channels [40]. All businesses, including those in the food and beverage sector, are able to increase

Figure 1. Conceptual framework of hypothesis

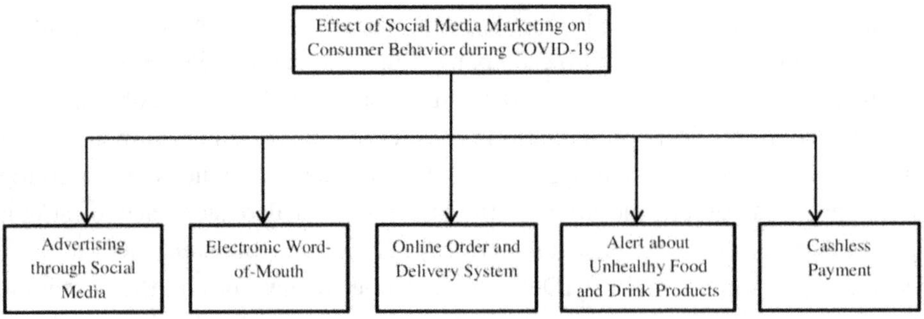

brand awareness through social media marketing because E-WOM is the primary platform for obtaining media coverage today. Through online platforms that are open to discussion, researchers have discovered that social media marketing can help establish connections with customers, build relationships, and influence consumer decisions [44]. E-WOM information, in contrast to WOM, can be easily accessed and enhanced with the addition of features like emoji and images [40]. However, it has also been demonstrated that interaction, socialization, innovation, and experiences all contribute to the spread of E-WOM through social media marketing. Since web-based entertainment showcasing is an instrument for E-WOM advertising, the organization ought to utilize it for its potential benefit by effectively advancing its item and administration via virtual entertainment to try not to be overwhelmed by rivals.

Hypothesis 3: During Covid-19, correlation between online order and delivery system and consumer behaviour in F&G industry.

During the pandemic, scientists researched how virtual entertainment stages changed customer conduct by showing a 300% increment popular for DeliverEat. my, and Get Food riders likewise expressed that their conveyances expanded by upto 30% [45]. In light of the serious pandemic, the drawing in relationship with the web-based entertainment stage fills in as an informal notice to urge more individuals to arrange and get food from different cafés on the web. According to a study, online ordering is preferred by customers due to its convenience and increased level of control [46]. A complete food ordering system demonstrates never ending control by notifying customers when their order is complete and allowing them to monitor their meal status. Researchers in [46], elements of online request and conveyance frameworks impact the purchaser conduct like apparent costs, limits, and advancements, accommodation, and food and administration. Nevertheless, the study also revealed that convenience is a significant factor in consumer satisfaction and online purchasing behaviour. Since purchaser fulfilment is the essential errand for organizations to acquire a cutthroat advantage in the F&B business, they should embrace online request and conveyance frameworks to answer changing purchaser conduct

Hypothesis 4: The affinity between consumer behaviour and cashless payment in F&G industry during Covid-19.

Consumer attitudes about the value of money are changing as a result of progressive innovation, distinguished digital safety, social impact, facilities, and performance accomplishment [47]. Previously Coronavirus pandemic, credit only instalment had been energized in Malaysia in any case, it was not commonly known among individuals, which just saw that as 36% of Malaysians involved e-wallets before the flare-up in a review [47]. Notwithstanding, Bank Negara Malaysia (BNM) detailed that credit only instalment exchanges expanded by 131% in 2020, arriving at 600 million exchanges [48]. Given the ongoing pandemic circumstance, worldwide clients, including Malaysians, are stressed over the security of different buying choices. As a result, due to the big rise in e-users and the necessity of social distance, cashless payment has been strongly recommended through the new social media marketing [49]. Perceived convenience, facilitating factors, and perceived security were identified as the three factors that increase consumer willingness to use cashless payment in the study cited in [50]. As a result, it is concluded that the sudden and important shifts in the new normal and lifestyle have prompted customers to use a simpler payment gateways to lower their risk of infection.

Hypothesis 5: Differentiate between healthy and unhealthy food and drink products using sentiment analysis of social media content.

During COVID-19, various unhealthy food and drink product brands started using social media platforms for promotions to vulnerable population during time of increased hardship and stress. Due to lack of monitoring and rules and regulations social media is a popular channel for selling harmful foods and beverages. The emotion detection of content and comments about products on brand page help social media users examine the utility of product. The judgement and attitude promoted by feeling towards certain entity is generated by content posted on micro-blogs, forum and other social networking sites [51]. The detection of positive, negative and neutral emotions helps in promoting and restricting the products among consumers and also alerting them with detriment of product if it is identified with negative emotion.

5. METHODOLOGY

The basic steps followed in existing work to perform conceptual research on impact of social media on customer satisfaction and behaviour in food and grocery industry is discussed below along with figure 2:

Figure 2. General research design of the methodology

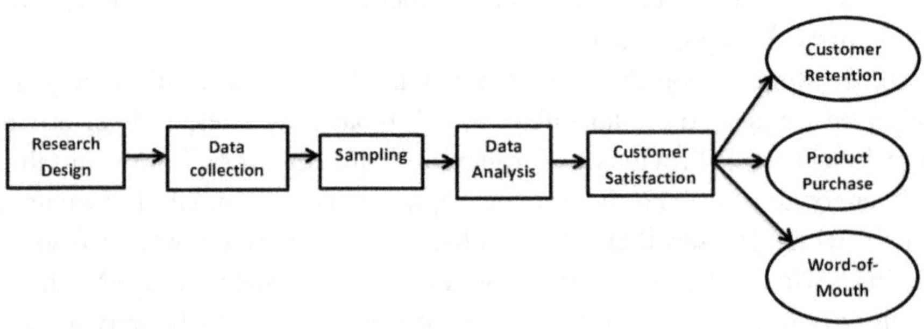

5.1 Research Design

The theoretical foundation of the study will be followed in the research project on F&G consumer behaviour and expectations on social media applied to a case firm. The primary purpose of the research is to get a full understanding of the segmentation of the local market for restaurant clients in Finland's major cities. The Juicy Rolly food truck will be utilised as a case study, and its social media operation will be studied for future possibilities. An exploratory and descriptive research strategy will be used for this empirical portion of the chapter. While descriptive research identifies features of certain things, such as a phenomena or a group of individuals, exploratory research allows for the study and discovery of previously unknown theories. Observations, case studies and database information analysis are examples of exploratory research methodologies. There will be an overall analysis of the example company's social media IMC performance under each post, including details on the firm's internal implementation and the extent of public reaction. The study will use exploratory research methodologies such as observation and historical result analysis to identify the advantages and downsides of Juicy Rolly's IMC efforts. In addition to the preceding research, a study of F&G customers' social media behaviour will be done. The important question for this chapter is how social media improves F&B business success in relation to consumer pleasure. Because the study focuses on the behaviours and characteristics of a specific group of individuals, a descriptive research approach will be employed for the project's analysis, which will include a customer survey.

5.2 Research Method

The subjects addressed by research methodology are data collecting and analysis. The most common forms of research are quantitative and qualitative methodologies. Quantitative research is a numerical and measurable way to highlighting an issue that employs computing and statistical data. In comparison, qualitative research entails gathering conclusive and descriptive data from personal observation and experience. In other words, qualitative research is about an idea, expression, attitude, or point of view, whereas quantitative research is about data. The focus of research methodology is data collection and analysis. The most common study kinds are quantitative and qualitative research approaches. In quantitative research, which is a quantitative and measurable technique, an issue may be found using computations and statistical data. In comparison, qualitative research comprises gathering data from personal experience and observation. In other words, qualitative research is concerned with a expression, notion, attitude, or point of view, whereas quantitative research is concerned with data and numbers.

5.3 Population and Sample

The subjects addressed by research methodology are data collecting and analysis. The most common forms of research are quantitative and qualitative methodologies. Quantitative research is a numerical and measurable way to highlighting an issue that employs computing and statistical data. In comparison, qualitative research entails gathering conclusive and descriptive data from personal observation and experience. In other words, a qualitative study relates to a notion, expression, attitude, or point of view, whereas a quantitative study operates. A population is a group from whom a researcher expects to draw broad conclusions. In a study, the term "population" does not always relate to individuals; it may also refer to objects like metrics, events, organisations, and so on. When a population is big enough that access to all data is problematic, it is common practise to choose a sample that correctly represents the population and evaluate the data from that sample. Using the concept of data sampling, analysts may take a small subset of data from a vast population and use it to make conclusions and discover new information. The obstacles of sampling for big data analysis might include bias, mistake, and complexity in sample, which analysts must take into account [53].

5.4 Designing the Questionnaire

The poll will be developed with Google Forms, an online questionnaire tool, and will be disseminated over Facebook, Messenger, Instagram, and WhatsApp in the future. The survey is accessible in English. The questionnaire is divided into four areas by the author: respondent basic information, social media usage, dining habits, and social media consumer behaviour. This will be stated in the form as instructions for participants. The survey uses closed-ended questions such as multiple choices and rating scale, as well as phrasing them with clear and straightforward wording, to ensure that respondents fully understand the goal of the survey. The questionnaire is divided into four areas by the author: respondent basic information, social media usage, dining habits, and social media consumer behaviour. This will be stated in the form as instructions for participants. The survey uses closed-ended questions such as multiple choice and rating scale, as well as phrasing them with clear and unambiguous wording, to ensure that respondents fully understand the goal of the survey.

5.5 Data collection and Analysis

The customer survey responses of participants will be meticulously assessed and converted into graphs and charts to provide a clear picture of the situation utilising visual effects. The primary data will be utilised to support the study results and conclusions on the behaviour and expectations of the target group. The collection of primary data from the case company's social media using exploratory research methods. By examining the company's social media implementation, the researcher wants to get relevant knowledge for future conclusions on the issue. Secondary data, on the other hand, comprises sources referenced in the literature review section, data accessible by the case firm, and background information about the case company and its rivals obtained through social media. Depending on the various degrees of company requirements, the data is collected from various sources and then data analysis techniques and tools are offered to them to find the deep insight in voluminous data. The tools operate using a logic intended for analysis, which involves data sampling, pre-processing, transformation, mining and evaluation of hidden patterns. The open source, proprietary, offline and real time tools are the major categories of social media analytics tools [52]. Using data analysis tools, social media data can be analysis in many forms such as; predictive, statistical, text, diagnostic and others [54].

5.6 Validity and Reliability

The validity of research measures, what need to be examined, is the degree of accuracy of the research study. Meanwhile, research dependability refers to the consistency and stability of a study regardless of the amount of attempts made. The questionnaire, which is based on the theoretical background of the topic gathered from academic and professional books and articles, ensures the validity and reliability of the research project in this chapter. The sources of which are available on the website of Satakunta University of Applied Sciences Library. To eliminate implicit assumptions and prejudice, the questionnaire's wording and phrasing are carefully chosen, as is the number of feasible options for each close-ended question. The language of choice will be English. Furthermore, many consultation meetings with the thesis supervisor are undertaken to evaluate the validity of the questionnaire content. At the same time, the author met with the example company's management a few times to ensure that the survey analysis stayed on track with the company's goals.

6. CONCLUSION

The aim of this chapter is to provide a comprehensive conceptual picture of the impact of social media marketing and advertising on restaurant consumers' satisfaction and behaviour in food and grocery industry. In the fast-food and restaurant (F&B) industry, where individual customers are at the center of attention, the use of social media to boost customer fulfillment is unquestionably significant. By conveying reliable and straightforward messages all through each channel, giving significant and dynamic proposals as well as really taking care of correspondence as in criticisms and grievances, organizations will probably be capable to maintain client relationships and in this manner, further develop showcasing efficiency and productivity. YouTube, Facebook and Instagram are the most promising social media channels for food and beverage businesses, according to the literature review and data. The importance of e-WOM in today's business world makes it one of the most important factor for any company, especially in the food and beverage sector. E-WoM methods like food blogs, ratings, and reviews show how consumer behaviour is influenced by feedback, complaints, and online information. Furthermore, Sharing food sources and premises, offers and limits in web-based entertainment destinations are the keys to draw in clients and, the time utilization in virtual entertainment is very low. The purpose for is the eateries have no devoted representative who is simply answerable for dealing with virtual entertainment locales. As a result, handling these issues effectively will undoubtedly result in improved profitability and a positive brand image. This chapter also verify the characteristics of fast-food brands' social media marketing on consumer decision-making. The outcomes showed that virtual entertainment destinations address significant stages for cheap food brands to accomplish their ideal promoting goals, for example assembling brand trust and affecting shoppers' buy choice. When it comes to mediating the link between two of the selected social media marketing traits—informativeness and interactivity—and a purchase decision, brand trust plays a crucial role. Hence, it is critical to consistently share intelligent reviews and brand data via virtual entertainment destinations that are most often utilized by the clients of food and staple to expand their certainty to them. As the vital target of showcasing publicizing and advancement is to fabricate brand trust and animate shopper buy conduct, web-based entertainment showcasing exercises are additionally considered to significant for create effective associations with clients and achieving these goals. These discoveries propose that arrangement creators ought to support their presence via web-based entertainment and consistently search about evolving buyers' requirements, then creating offer for meeting them. Besides this, we have also examined four factors such as; e-advertising on social media, E-WoM, cashless payment and online ordering and delivery system, have influenced the customer behaviour and satisfaction in food and grocery industry during Covid-19 using hypothesis. The theoretical implication of this study yield the association between e-marketing on social media and change in customer behaviour towards adjusting with new normal.

REFERENCES

Ahmad, M., & Lasi, M. (2020). The Attitudes on Consumer Perceptions towards Viral Marketing: A Study on Foodpanda Food Delivery in Malaysia. *International Journal of Research and Scientific Innovation*, *7*(9), 251–255.

Ban, O. I., Ancusa, V., Bogdan, V., & Tara, I. G. (2015). Empirical social research to identify clusters of characteristics that underlie the online evaluation of accommodation services. *Revista de Cercetare si Interventie Sociala*, 50.

Barker, M., Barker, D. I., Bormann, N. F., & Neher, K. E. (2012). *Social media marketing: A strategic approach*. CENGAGE learning.

Baron, S., Conway, T., & Warnaby, G. (2010). *Relationship marketing: A consumer experience approach*. Sage Publications. doi:10.4135/9781446251096

Barry, M., & Jan, M. T. (2018). Factors influencing the use of m-commerce: An extended technology acceptance model perspective. *International Journal of Economics. Management and Accounting*, *26*(1), 157–183.

Berné Manero, C., Ciobanu, A. V., & Pedraja Iglesias, M. (2020). The electronic word of mouth as a context variable in the hotel management decision-making process.

Berthon, P. R., Pitt, L. F., Plangger, K., & Shapiro, D. (2012). Marketing meets Web 2.0, social media, and creative consumers: Implications for international marketing strategy. *Business Horizons*, *55*(3), 261–271. doi:10.1016/j.bushor.2012.01.007

Calefato, F., Lanubile, F., & Novielli, N. (2015). The role of social media in affective trust building in customer–supplier relationships. *Electronic Commerce Research*, *15*(4), 453–482. doi:10.100710660-015-9194-3

Cao, B., & Reilly, J. (2019). Major Challenges and Limitations of Big Data Analytics. *Personalized Psychiatry: Big Data Analytics in Mental Health*, 15-36.

Chen, Y. S., Lehto, X., Behnke, C., & Tang, C. H. (2016). Investigating children's role in family dining-out choices: Evidence from a casual dining restaurant. *Journal of Hospitality Marketing & Management*, *25*(6), 706–725. doi:10.1080/19368623.2016.1077368

Choi, J., & Yoo, D. (2021). The impacts of self-construal and perceived risk on technology readiness. *Journal of Theoretical and Applied Electronic Commerce Research*, *16*(5), 1584–1597. doi:10.3390/jtaer16050089

Choudhury, D. (2021). Artificial Intelligence in the Hospitality Sector. In Insights, Innovation, and Analytics for Optimal Customer Engagement (pp. 257-278). IGI Global. doi:10.4018/978-1-7998-3919-4.ch013

Crotts, J. (1999). Consumer decision making and prepurchase information search. *Consumer behavior in travel and tourism, 11*(3), p149-168.

Davis, C. H. III, Deil-Amen, R., Rios-Aguilar, C., & González Canché, M. S. (2015). Social media, higher education, and community colleges: A research synthesis and implications for the study of two-year institutions. *Community College Journal of Research and Practice, 39*(5), 409–422. doi:10.1080/10668926.2013.828665 PMID:31511765

Davis, C. H. III, Deil-Amen, R., Rios-Aguilar, C., & González Canché, M. S. (2015). Social media, higher education, and community colleges: A research synthesis and implications for the study of two-year institutions. *Community College Journal of Research and Practice, 39*(5), 409–422. doi:10.1080/10668926.2013.828665 PMID:31511765

Dwivedi, Y. K., Ismagilova, E., Hughes, D. L., Carlson, J., Filieri, R., Jacobson, J., Jain, V., Karjaluoto, H., Kefi, H., Krishen, A. S., Kumar, V., Rahman, M. M., Raman, R., Rauschnabel, P. A., Rowley, J., Salo, J., Tran, G. A., & Wang, Y. (2021). Setting the future of digital and social media marketing research: Perspectives and research propositions. *International Journal of Information Management, 59*, 102168. doi:10.1016/j.ijinfomgt.2020.102168

Fang, X., & Zhan, J. (2015). Sentiment analysis using product review data. *Journal of Big Data, 2*(1), 1–14. doi:10.118640537-015-0015-2

Ghani, N. A., Hamid, S., Hashem, I. A. T., & Ahmed, E. (2019). Social media big data analytics: A survey. *Computers in Human Behavior, 101*, 417–428. doi:10.1016/j.chb.2018.08.039

Gregory, S., & Kim, J. (2005). Restaurant choice: The role of information. *Journal of Foodservice Business Research, 7*(1), 81–95. doi:10.1300/J369v07n01_06

Hanaysha, J. R. (2022). Impact of social media marketing features on consumer's purchase decision in the fast-food industry: Brand trust as a mediator. *International Journal of Information Management Data Insights, 2*(2), 100102. doi:10.1016/j.jjimei.2022.100102

Howard, J. A., & Sheth, J. N. (1969). The theory of buyer behavior. New York, 63, 145.

Huang, L., Clarke, A., Heldsinger, N., & Tian, W. (2019). The communication role of social media in social marketing: A study of the community sustainability knowledge dissemination on LinkedIn and Twitter. *Journal of Marketing Analytics*, *7*(2), 64–75. doi:10.105741270-019-00053-8

Hudson, M. (2019). What Is Social Media: The Balance Small Business.

Hwang, J., Park, S., & Woo, M. (2018). Understanding user experiences of online travel review websites for hotel booking behaviours: An investigation of a dual motivation theory. *Asia Pacific Journal of Tourism Research*, *23*(4), 359–372. doi:10.1080/10941665.2018.1444648

Jadil, Y., Rana, N. P., & Dwivedi, Y. K. (2022). Understanding the drivers of online trust and intention to buy on a website: An emerging market perspective. *International Journal of Information Management Data Insights*, *2*(1), 100065. doi:10.1016/j.jjimei.2022.100065

Kee, D. M. H., binti Mohd Nazri, N. F., binti Misbah, N., binti Nazril, N. A., binti Musa, N. H., & binti Abdul Hamid, N. F. (2021). The impact of COVID-19 on the fast-food industry in Malaysia. [JCDA]. *Journal of the Community Development in Asia*, *4*(2), 44–57. doi:10.32535/jcda.v4i2.1072

Kim, W. G., Lim, H., & Brymer, R. A. (2015). The effectiveness of managing social media on hotel performance. *International Journal of Hospitality Management*, *44*, 165–171. doi:10.1016/j.ijhm.2014.10.014

Kumar, J., Konar, R., & Balasubramanian, K. (2020). The impact of Social Media on Consumers' purchasing behaviour in Malaysian Restaurants. *Journal of Spatial and Organizational Dynamics*, *8*(3), 197–216.

Labrecque, J., & Ricard, L. (2001). Children's influence on family decision-making: A restaurant study. *Journal of Business Research*, *54*(2), 173–176. doi:10.1016/S0148-2963(99)00088-0

Lai, H. B. J., Abidin, M. R. Z., Hasni, M. Z., Ab Karim, M. S., & Ishak, F. A. C. (2020). Key adaptations of SME restaurants in Malaysia amidst the COVID-19 Pandemic. *International Journal of Research in Business and Social Science (2147-4478)*, *9*(6), 12-23.

Liu, H., Jayawardhena, C., Osburg, V. S., Yoganathan, V., & Cartwright, S. (2021). Social sharing of consumption emotion in electronic word of mouth (eWOM): A cross-media perspective. *Journal of Business Research*, *132*, 208–220. doi:10.1016/j.jbusres.2021.04.030

Mail, M. (2020). *Data expert shares tips to empower SMEs in surviving MCO.* Malay Mail.

Mason, A. N., Narcum, J., & Mason, K. (2021). Social media marketing gains importance after Covid-19. *Cogent Business & Management*, *8*(1), 1870797. doi:10.1080/23311975.2020.1870797

McKechnie, S. (1992). Consumer buying behaviour in financial services: An overview. *International Journal of Bank Marketing*, *10*(5), 5–39. doi:10.1108/02652329210016803

Mozeik, C. K., Beldona, S., Cobanoglu, C., & Poorani, A. (2009). The adoption of restaurant-based e-service. *Journal of Foodservice Business Research*, *12*(3), 247–265. doi:10.1080/15378020903158525

Nanda, P., & Kumar, V. (2021). Social media analytics: Tools, techniques and present day practices. *International Journal of Services Operations and Informatics*, *11*(4), 422–436. doi:10.1504/IJSOI.2021.120691

Nguyen, G. (2021). Social Media Impacts on Customer Satisfaction in Food and Beverage Business: Case of Juicy Rolly.

Ozdemir-Guzel, S., & Bas, Y. N. (2021). Gen Z tourists and smart devices. In *Generation Z Marketing and Management in Tourism and Hospitality: The Future of the Industry* (pp. 141–165). Springer International Publishing. doi:10.1007/978-3-030-70695-1_6

Park, S., & Fesenmaier, D. R. (2014). Travel decision flexibility. *Tourism Analysis*, *19*(1), 35–49. doi:10.3727/108354214X13927625340154

Pop, R. A., Săplăcan, Z., Dabija, D. C., & Alt, M. A. (2022). The impact of social media influencers on travel decisions: The role of trust in consumer decision journey. *Current Issues in Tourism*, *25*(5), 823–843. doi:10.1080/13683500.2021.1895729

Pop, R. A., Săplăcan, Z., Dabija, D. C., & Alt, M. A. (2022). The impact of social media influencers on travel decisions: The role of trust in consumer decision journey. *Current Issues in Tourism*, *25*(5), 823–843. doi:10.1080/13683500.2021.1895729

Rahman, M., Ismail, I., & Bahri, S. (2020). Analysing consumer adoption of cashless payment in Malaysia. *Digital Business*, *1*(1), 100004. doi:10.1016/j.digbus.2021.100004

Richardson, N., & Gosnay, R. M. (2010). *A quick start guide to social media marketing: High impact low-cost marketing that works*. Kogan Page Publishers.

Salem, M. Z. (2018). Effects of perfume packaging on Basque female consumers purchase decision in Spain. *Management Decision*, *56*(8), 1748–1768. doi:10.1108/MD-04-2017-0363

Salleh, N. H., Abd Patah, M. O. R., Samsudin, A., & Piah, Z. H. M. (2017). Restaurant advertisement through social media: Examining followers' responses. *Journal of Tourism. Hospitality & Culinary Arts*, *9*(2), 411–424.

Sharma, A., Dwivedi, Y. K., Arya, V., & Siddiqui, M. Q. (2021). Does SMS advertising still have relevance to increase consumer purchase intention? A hybrid PLS-SEM-neural network modelling approach. *Computers in Human Behavior*, *124*, 106919. doi:10.1016/j.chb.2021.106919

Sharmin, F., Sultan, M. T., Badulescu, D., Badulescu, A., Borma, A., & Li, B. (2021). Sustainable destination marketing ecosystem through smartphone-based social media: The consumers' acceptance perspective. *Sustainability (Basel)*, *13*(4), 2308. doi:10.3390u13042308

Sigala, M., Christou, E., & Gretzel, U. (Eds.). (2012). *Social media in travel, tourism and hospitality: Theory, practice and cases*. Ashgate Publishing, Ltd.

Sotelo, E. N. (2017). Social and cultural implications of the new communications technologies: its human rights education challenges in the current century. *Rights and Science: R&S*, 81-100.

Tan, H., & Kim, V. W. E. (2021). Examining the factors that Influence consumer satisfaction with online food delivery in Klang Valley, Malaysia. *The Journal of Management Theory and Practice (JMTP)*, 88-95.

Tatar, Ş. B., & Eren-Erdoğmuş, İ. (2016). The effect of social media marketing on brand trust and brand loyalty for hotels. *Information Technology & Tourism*, *16*(3), 249–263. doi:10.100740558-015-0048-6

Timilsina, M. (2017). Impacts of social media in restaurant businesses: A case study of restaurants based on Oulu region.

Wigmore, I. 2020. Definition social media. TechTarget Network. Referred 11.2.2021. https://whatis.techtarget.com/definition

Zhang, Z., Ye, Q., Law, R., & Li, Y. (2010). The impact of e-word-of-mouth on the online popularity of restaurants: A comparison of consumer reviews and editor reviews. *International Journal of Hospitality Management*, *29*(4), 694–700. doi:10.1016/j.ijhm.2010.02.002

Chapter 7
How Customer Rating on Digital Restaurant Guides Influence Consumer Satisfaction:
The Zomato Platform Experience

Alexandre Duarte
https://orcid.org/0000-0002-2665-864X
ICNOVA, FCSH, Universidade Nova de Lisboa, Portugal

Joana Fernandes
Catholic University of Portugal, Portugal

Claudia Pernencar
ICNOVA, FCSH, Universidade Nova de Lisboa, Portugal

ABSTRACT

Nowadays, anybody is a potential food critic, only requiring a smartphone to write an opinion and evaluate a restaurant through a digital app. As people trust other people's opinions - even strangers - more than the service provider's own marketing strategies, restaurant recommendation apps are great tools to analyze and improve performance. This keeps up with a recent consumer behaviour: gathering opinions that have impact on both ends of the consumer-organization relationship. This research aims to identify the relevant factors when classifying a restaurant and understand if Zomato app influences a restaurant choice, by identifying the features that lead a consumer to choose restaurant X over Y, whether it's a workday lunch, family lunches, dinners with friends or a romantic dinner. The chapter analyzes Zomato's case study: competition along catering industry dimension and the competitive position. Results point to how consumers perceive restaurant experience and how they influence others' decisions with online evaluating.

DOI: 10.4018/978-1-6684-8868-3.ch007

1. INTRODUCTION

The advance of the digital world has changed how the individual participates in the production, communication and choice of a product or service, going from a mere spectator to an active participant (Duarte & Dias, 2021). On the internet, companies have relinquished control over information that is shared and have become dependent on others' opinions. With this transformation, the individual has become a producer of content of topics that are of interest to them, namely brands, services, or institutions (Phillips & Young, 2009). This means that existing content is no longer entirely of the brand's responsibility (Li, Larimo & Leonidou, 2021) and individual behaviour has also changed. Individuals presently wish to feel satisfaction when sharing experiences of all kinds on social networks (Fabretti, 2012). Any experience, positive or negative, becomes content.

As technology evolves to keep up with recent consumer behaviour, digital spaces that gather opinions and are specialised in different business areas have been created. These spaces have an impact on both ends of the consumer-organization relationship. For the consumers, these digital platforms are a source of shared disseminated information that help them during a decision-making process prior to a purchase, whilst for companies they are a way to analyse how a product or service is received by the public (Parikh et al., 2014). Consequently, the consumer research influences and is influenced during the purchasing process, with there being an increase of *reviews* websites and mobile applications, where they may share and evaluate their experience related to the quality of a product/service, namely in the catering sector, which is heavily influenced by *Word-Of-Mouth*. Nowadays, to be a food critic, only requires a smartphone to write an opinion and evaluate a restaurant through a digital application (Hopper, 2013). It is also known that people trust other people's opinions, even those of strangers (Siegrist, 2021), more than the service provider's own marketing strategies (Chen & Xie, 2008), making restaurant recommendation applications great tools for analysing and improving performance.

This study aims to understand whether the Zomato application has an influence on an individual's decision when choosing a restaurant, as well as to identify the attributes offered in the application that matter the most to users, in various situations: individual lunch on weekdays, family lunch, dinner with friends and romantic dinner. It also aims to understand what are the most important dimensions that make up a user's satisfaction when evaluating a restaurant after a consumption experience. Additionally, a characterization of the Zomato user profile was carried out.

The present chapter is organized in four sections. Firstly, to deepen understand how social media has led to users becoming active participants in the decisions of another when choosing a restaurant, a narrative literature review was carried out, with special focus on the *Word-Of-Mouth* Influence; the factors that influence a restaurant selection; those who influence the consumer satisfaction in restaurants; and finally, the online platforms and their importance and reviews in the culinary sector.

Secondly, the Zomato case study was analyzed, following four steps: First, a competitive dimension with applications description that are focused on the category industry; Second, an investigation of the competitive position using a benchmark study of the competition (Stapenhurst, 2009). Third, a SWOT analysis to outwit the competitors' pros, cons, opportunities, and treats, and, at least, a quantitative method allowing the researchers to obtain information to correlate the variables present and determine behavioural patterns, using dependent or independent variables (Moreira et al., 2009) among hypotheses (H1-H4f). The quantitative method chosen was a questionnaire, the data was collected between 28/October and 28/November of 2020 using Google Forms, and the 320 valid answers were analyzed afterwards in SPSS.

Thirdly, the results were presented, and a discussion was carried out. A multiple logistic regresa specific variablec variable to study the sociodemographic variables that influence of being a Zomato user were used. The research questions were:

- Q1. How can the Zomato users be characterized?
- Q2. Using Zomato influences restaurant selections?
- Q3. What is the impact of the different criteria that Zomato has when selecting a restaurant, in different situations? (Pre-consumption)?
- Q4. What is the importance of each evaluation criteria for consumer (after use)?

Fourthly, the limitations of the study, conclusions and future guidelines are presented.

2. THEORETICAL BRACKGROUND

The rise of social media has led to users becoming active participants, with the possibility to immediately co-create, share and react to thoughts and opinions via *microblogs, vlogs, podcasts, networking sites*, content sharing sites, content creation or evaluation sites (Tarabasz, 2013).Whilst consumers were previously more easily persuaded by marketing campaigns, social relationships (family, friends, and social networks) presently have a much greater influence than company marketing communication. This is one of the reasons for the growth of public evaluation systems like TripAdvisor or Yelp, as the concept of trust has shifted from vertical to horizontal. This means that the consumer should be viewed as a colleague or friend by a brand, which should be genuine and true to its values.

2.1 The *Word-of-Mouth* Influence

Word-Of-Mouth (WOM) communication has been identified as being one of the most influential forms of transmitting information since society first started to form (Godes & Mayzlin, 2004; Keller, 2007; Duan et al., 2008; Kozinets et al., 2010). WOM can influence consumer behaviour, especially their expectations, perceptions, and attitudes (Buttle, 1998). It is considered one of the ways that most influences consumer behaviour, being more trustworthy and credible when compared with the organization's communication as it is seen as impartial (Chen, 2011; Cheung & Thadani, 2012). This level of influence grows when it is actively sought for by the consumer (Bansal & Voyer, 2000). Villanueva et al. (2008) state that clients that learned of the brand through WOM generated greater long-term value for the companies than clients gained through traditional channels.

With the increase of internet use, WOM has reached a new level, designated *Electronic Word-Of-Mouth* (eWOM). Hennig-Thurau et al. (2004, p. 39) define eWOM as "a positive or negative statement made by potential, current or former clients about a product or company that is available to many people and institutions via the internet". Rodgers & Wang (2011) extended the definition to any combination of positive, negative, or neutral comments, recommendations or statements about companies, brands, products, or services, discussed or shared between users on digital or electronic formats. It is through research and evaluation platforms that consumers share their experiences of restaurants, developing a connection that eventually form communities (Fogel, 2010). Kotler et al. (2017) characterizes present day consumers as being more connected and being surrounded by a lot of information, thereby being more "distracted". They are individuals that place greater value on the opinion of the *F-Factors*: *Friends, Family, Fans e Followers.* The best way to be close to this consumer is via WOM and the opinion of these *F-Factors*.

The concept of consumption is no longer considered an individual but social act, where experience and feedback are constantly being shared. In the bibliography review, a scarcity of information related to the characterization of restaurant application users was found, with this being, as well as their sociodemographic characteristics, one of the objectives of this research.

2.2 Factors that Influence Restaurant Selection

There have been various studies that have sought to understand which factors influence consumer restaurant selection, but so far there has not been any evidence found on how a restaurant is chosen based on the use of restaurant recommending digital applications.

According to Lewis (1981) there are four main factors: food quality, menu variety, ambiance, and convenience. In this study the importance of these factors varied according to the type of restaurant. Nonetheless, food quality was considered the most important. Later June & Smith (1987) identified nine main criteria: price, ambiance, liquor licensing, service, client rotation, location, food quality, service quality and food type. For Auty (1992) factors that influence selecting a restaurant are: food type, food quality, cost-benefit, image and ambiance, location, service speed, recommendation, whether it is a new experience, working hours and installations for children. To check if the type of restaurant varied according to the occasion, Auty also analyzed four occasions: a celebration (e.g., anniversary); a social gathering; the convenience/need for a fast meal, and a business meal. The study concluded that food type was the most important factor when choosing a restaurant, followed by its quality, price-quality relationship, image and ambiance, service speed, and recommendation.

Jillian, Lester, and Robert (1992) defend that the factors that influence consumer restaurant selection are meal prices, past experiences with similar restaurants, relative restaurant's reputation, the convenience of the location, if there was any striking announcement and employee presentation. In this study price plays a lower role, with service and WOM dominating consumer perception.

According to Dulen (1999), there are six factors that lead to a consumer choosing a restaurant: food quality, cleanliness, service, variety, convenience, and ambiance. For Sulek and Hensley (2004), the main influencing factors are food quality, ambiance, service quality and employee interpersonal skills, whilst for Martin and Frumkin (2005) the key factors are: the comfort of the space, location convenience, food variety and finally the price. Duecy (2006) considers that demographics may also influence consumer selection. Consumers over 65 tend to say that their choice is motivated by price, whilst those between 18 and 34 consider themselves "food explorers", wishing to try out new food and restaurants.

2.3 Factors that Influence Consumer Satisfaction in Restaurants

According to Jeong& Jang (2011), one of the most important characteristics of a restaurant experience is its perceived quality. However, consumer experience is holistic and multidimensional, i.e., it integrates cognitive, affective, emotional, and physical responses (Verhoef et al., 2009). Given that the concept of "experience" incorporates the knowledge or observation of events through involvement or exposure, client experience in a restaurant is acquired during the culinary experience and are considered positive or negative depending on how the client judges current or prior experiences. The ability to judge if an experience was good or bad related to trying

Figure 1. Factors that influence the perceived quality of a restaurant and the motivation for WOM and e-WOM

Authors	**Attributes**				
	Food Quality	Service Quality	Ambiance	Motivation for WOM	Motivation for e-WOM
Jeong & Jang, 2011	x	x	x	x	x
Ha & Jang, 2010	x	x	x	x	x
Jang & Namkung, 2009	x	x	x	x	x
Liu & Jang, 2009	x			x	x
Namkung & Jang, 2007	x			x	x
Pettijohn et al., 1997	x			x	
Qin & Prybutok, 2008	x			x	x
Sulek & Hensley, 2004	x			x	x
Liu & Jang, 2009	x			x	x
Qu, 1997				x	
Kim et alr., 2009		x		x	x
Yuksel & Yuksel, 2003		x		x	x

or using a service is called the perceived quality of a service, a general or judgement towards that service (Parasuraman et al., 1988; Zeithaml, Bitner & Gremler, 2000) and can influence WOM and e-WOM. Figure 1 helps with the comprehension of which factors are influencing the perceived quality of a restaurant and the motivation for WOM and e-WOM according to some authors.

In Kalgi and Mamta (2017) literature review, they outlined the factors that affect the perceived quality of a restaurant using the following figure. The data range between 1992 and 2014 presents a broader view of these factors. Analysing the results' review with a summary of 30 articles referred, food quality is the factor that most lead to a consumer choosing a restaurant with 22 references. The factor identified as less relevant is work hours.

Figure 2. Factors that influence the perceived quality of a restaurant
(Shah & Brahmbhatt, 2017).

AUTHORS	FACTORS								
	Food Quality (including flavour and temperature)	Price	Physical Ambiance	Cleanliness	Speed and precision	Location	Staff behaviour / friendliness	Work hours	Restaurant image
Tan et al. (2014)	X	X	X		X		X		X
Hwang et al. (2013)					X				
Yunus et al. (2013)	X	X			X	X	X		
Harrington et al. (2013)	X			X	X		X		
Zhang et al. (2013)	X								
Ryu et al. (2012)	X		X						X
Haghighi et al. (2012)	X	X	X	X	X	X	X	X	
Wen et al. (2011)		X	X		X		X		X
Harrington et al. (2011)					X				
Jo and Oh (2011)	X								
Barber and Scarcelli (2010)				X					
Qin et al. (2010)	X	X	X		X		X		X
Pantelidis (2010)	X	X	X		X				
Ha and Jang (2010)	X		X		X				
Qin and Prybutok (2009)	X								
Namkung and Jang (2008)	X		X		X				
Meng et al. (2008)	X	X	X				X		
Roseman e Niblock (2007)	X								
Grupta et al. (2007)	X								
Andaleeb et al (2007)	X		X	X	X		X		
Kim, Lee and Yoo (2006)	X	X	X				X		
Reich et al al. (2005)	X								
Park (2004)	X								
Soriano (2002)	X	X			X	X			
Bernhardt et al. (2000)				X	X				
Walz and Niehoff (2000)	X				X				
Clark and Wood (1999)					X		X		
Stevens et al.1995)			X						
Aaty (1992)					X				
Campos e Nobrda (n.d)	X	X			X		X	X	

2.4 Online Platforms and the Importance of Classifications and Reviews in the Culinary Sector

The progress of social networks has led consumers to feel included and have a greater sense of belonging to a community (Kotler et al., 2017). An important benefit of this is that it provides consumers with support throughout the purchasing decision making process, given that classifications influence, either positively or negatively, consumer choice (Tucker, 2017). There are two types of users: those that only read the comments, and those that contribute actively to the content (Fernandes, 2015). Most of the time individuals research other consumer's opinions before deciding. Nowadays, it is almost impossible to not use the internet, specially through mobile environment, to find opinions on matters of personal interest. Many ecommerce companies like Amazon and eBay implement *online* classification systems to motivate users to publish opinions related to purchased products, as they believe in the public value this information (Wu, 2013). As such, this sharing of information means that the consumer both influences and is influenced.

Consumers are primarily concerned with the result, but the way they are treated during a service also has a significant impact on their satisfaction (Patterson et al., 2011). For Hussain et al. (2015), satisfaction is an immediate response to consumption, with the evaluation platforms helping to create expectation. When a service corresponds to consumer expectations then the quality is satisfactory. On the other hand, if a service exceeds consumer expectations, then that client will recognize the quality of the service/product and will wish to repeat the experience.

Living in the digital information era means that a person does not have to wait to talk with friends or family to discover if a restaurant is good ("How Many Customers Use Mobile Devices to Find Restaurants?", 2019). Nowadays, consumers can be informed on whatever they want, and can share their experience and opinions with other consumers, which is a consequence of the huge variety of available internet services and social networks. McFadden and Train (1996) state that third person evaluations and decisions influence other people's decision making. In the culinary sector, *online* consumer analysis and classification has an important role in helping others make decisions before consuming, due to the intangibility of the service, leading to potential clients often using online evaluations or classifications to reduce uncertainty (Pan, Maclaurin, & Crotts, 2007). Furthermore, consumers can easily access the internet using mobile devices, researching information about restaurants from any location and can decide based on other people's classifications and evaluations (Chevalier & Mayzlin, 2006; Liu, 2006; Zhu & Zhang, 2010).

Mobile experience sharing is fundamental in the culinary industry. Younger generations consider a restaurant experience to go beyond that of mere food quality, as it encompasses all its moments that may be shared via photographs or messages on social networks (Flatters, 2015). Ha, Park & Park (2016) concluded that a restaurant classification significantly influences choice intent, regardless of the type of restaurant, given that participants demonstrated a greater desire to choose restaurants when they scored highly. As indicated in previous studies on the effect of evaluations or classifications of products or services on consumer decision making (Sparks & Browning, 2011; Stringam & Gerdes, 2010), the classification of a restaurant was considered to be a critical factor in its selection.

According to the National Association of American Restaurants[1], 92% of active users of social networks eat at a restaurant at least once a month, and 32% of consumers use their mobile device while visiting, meaning that a third of all visitors are sharing the meal with their followers via social networks (Storms, 2014), with this sharing potentially influencing other consumers which in turn will influence others, and so on. Curiously, the use of mobile devices during a meal to share on social media is considered by others to be less appropriate than sending text messages or answering calls (Moser, Schoenebeck & Reinecke, 2016)

In accordance with Everett (2019), 33% read *online* comments before choosing a restaurant to visit. When consumers only have a limited amount of information pertaining to a restaurant, there is a greater tendency to be previously informed (Parikh et al., 2014). The three main reasons that consumers share their experiences (*reviews*) on social networks are because: they want to truly share a positive experience, they want to be seen as leaders in a specific area, or because they wish to brag about where they go or what they do. No matter the reason, they are creating and sharing content related to the restaurant and giving their testimony (Tucker, 2017), which as has already been seen has a greater weight on others than communication made by the brand (Fogel, 2010). The consumer usually writes a *review* when they either have a very positive or very negative experience. Nonetheless, it is easier for a consumer to write a negative *review*, as their expectations have been crushed. A strategy to increase the number of positive evaluations is to directly ask consumers to comment on their visit if they liked it, or to use cards or signal where they can do it. A limited or non-existent number of *reviews* are also negative for a restaurant as it may discourage potential visitors (Tucker, 2017).

In terms of the culinary sector, *reviews* are extremely important as more than 80% of consumers are believed to trust recommendations that they obtain from others (Libai et al., 2010). As stated by Fehrer et al. (2018), the interactions between customers are essential to raise the level of engagement behaviours.

In the tourism and hospitality sector, consumer decision making is highly influenced by eWOM (Gretzel, 2017; Yeh & Choi, 2011). WOM and positive *reviews* are the most effective way to attract consumers to visit the restaurant: *Word-Of-Mouth* is the oldest, cheapest, and most powerful form of publicity (Fields, 2014) and consumers believe the *reviews* of other consumers as much as they do their friend's or family's opinions (Tucker, 2017). Lu, Ba, Huang & Feng (2013) refer to the published reviews on research and evaluation platforms as having a strong impact on restaurant sales. They proved that, on one hand, positive *reviews*, as well as a large number of reviews lead to higher sales, whiles negative *reviews* led to a fall in the number of clients.

To consolidate what literature referred, Zomato case was selected to build a perspective of a Portuguese case regarding what consumers most value when selecting a restaurant. Based on the literature review, three research objectives were defined: understand if Zomato has, or not, influence on restaurant selection; understand which information provided by the application is most important during restaurant selection, and lastly, understand which factors related to consumer satisfaction are most important, when a consumer evaluates a restaurant after their experience. Additionally, Zomato's profile will be characterised under the following hypotheses:

- H1. Zomato influences restaurant selection.
- H2. Different Zomato criteria influence restaurant selection according to the situation.
- H3. The criteria are of different importance to the consumer when evaluating a restaurant experience.
- H4a. There is no difference between genders of a Zomato user.
- H4b. There is no difference between school education levels of a Zomato user.
- H4c. There is no difference between marital status of a Zomato user.
- H4d. There is no difference between levels of financial comfort of a Zomato user.
- H4e. There is no difference between dietary restrictions of a Zomato user.
- H4f. There is no difference between age of a Zomato user.

3. CASE STUDY – ZOMATO

Applications that are focused on the catering industry, such as Zomato, TripAdvisor and The Fork, allow important information from restaurants to be gathered, as well as consumer critique that influence their selection (Sage Portugal, 2016). Applications of this kind can be advantageous for both restaurants and consumers. The consumers can make reservations, compare establishments, and place orders (Fields, 2014), as well as search for promotions or special offers. Conversely, restaurants can optimise their digital resources (Sage Portugal, 2016) and increase profits. Notwithstanding, Hopper (2013) states that there are many managers that don't like this type of tool because they can't control the *reviews* that are published.

This article focuses on Zomato[2], an application that is exclusively dedicated to the culinary sector. Founded in India, it has since 2013 been greatly adhered to in Portugal. It is available in 24 countries and is the leader in 19 of these, being one of the biggest sources of culinary information. The application enables its users to not only consult and search for service providers but also has social functions, with users being able to follow and have access to other opinions, the locations they have visited, and in some countries the delivery service (Zomato, 2019).

It has been increasingly used in Portugal, having around 840.000 users and has the second largest market share (Publituris, 2016). Its mission is to "take better food to more people", creating strategies that help promote and group all useful information, enabling consumers to easily access information on a restaurant before visiting it: score, photographs, menus, and comments made by other clients, making it also a social network (Ribeiro, 2019). This is an application that has an influence on restaurant businesses. As Miguel Ribeiro (2019), Country Manager of Zomato Portugal claims: "What makes us most proud is when restaurant owners say that by "deactivating" Zomato services they felt a decrease of their daily client affluence".

Zomato was chosen as the object of this study as it not only was considered one of the ten best applications in the "Food and Drinks" category, but it is also, according to Ribeiro (2019), the application in the category that is most used in Portugal, and which has a social networking component.

3.1 Competition Along the Catering Industry Dimension

3.1.1 TheFork

The Fork[3] gathers opinions and comments of thousaplatforms, soorms so that everything related to any of the restaurants on their platform can be known. It allows users to instantly book a table and offers excluding promotions and discounts of up to 50% at adhering restaurants. It has a reservation points system, called Yums, which can be traded in for discounts of future meals.

3.1.2 TripAdvisor

TripAdvisor[4] is the largest in the world, and it enables travellers to make the most of each trip. It has more than 661 million evaluations and opinions on the most varied of global trips (approximately 7,7 million lodgings, airlines, experiences, and restaurants). TripAdvisor provides travellerswith other user's experiences, helping them to decide how to fly, where to stay, and what to do and eat. TripAdvisor also compares more than 200 hotel reservation sites so that travellers can find the lowest price in their ideal hotel. Its sites are available in 49 markets and consists of the largest travel community in the world, with an average of over 456 million monthly visitors, where all are seeking to get the most out of each trip (…)".

3.1.3 Yelp

This social network[5] was founded in 2014 with the sole purpose of informing users about companies that provide the best treatment and services. This platform includes a wide range of sectors such as real estate, education, and services, among others, and has an average of 120 million users per month (Esfahani, 2015). Users can consult work hours of each service provider and user multiple filters, write comments and evaluate companies.

3.2 Analysis of the Competitive Position

3.2.1 *Benchmark* Analysis

The Yang et al. (2021) technique to develop the *Benchmark* was used, which compares various applications. In the present research, the following protocol was defined:

- Research source: Apple Store
- Categories analyzed: Restaurant sector *apps*
- Keywords: culinary; restaurants; reservations, food, lunch, dinner
- Characteristics of the analyzed applications: name, description, downloads, number of evaluations, the evaluation score, version, shop, provider, shop *link*, category, free *vs.* paid, and the ranking of the apps in the category
- Inclusion criteria: be a restaurant recommendation or evaluation application
- Exclusion criteria: not meet the above criteria.

The results of this *Benchmark* conducted in May 2021 were consolidated in the above Figure 3. As seen The Fork is the mobile app that presents the higher score, with a 42 k rating and a 4.8 score and is a TripAdvisor Company. This is a global evaluation not focused only on Portugal marketplace.

3.2.2 SWOT Analysis

Despite the three applications being recommendation guides and evaluating restaurants, they are all positioned differently in the market. TripAdvisor is a travel guide; The Fork is more geared towards promotions, and Yelp is a platform that includes multiple services and is not only focused on the culinary sector. To succinctly highlight their pros and cons, a SWOT Analysis was made (Sarsby, 2016). Figure

Figure 3. Benchmark results

Characteristics				
Name	zomato	Tripadvisor	thefork	yelp
Description	Whether you're looking for biryani to feed your desi cravings, soul comforting pizzas and burgers, or even a salad with a cup of chai or coffee, Zomato is the only app you need for the quickest doorstep delivery of your favourites. With over 1.5 million restaurants and 265 million ratings and reviews, discover the best around you in no time – only on the Zomato app.	As a company of recommendations related to travel, TripAdvisor joins people interests and locations. We want you to be a better traveller, from the planning stage to the booking, not forgetting the trip itself. Our application allows you to make the most of your trip, whether you are planning it or are on location. Find out where to stay and where to eat based on millions of recommendations made by travellers that have already visited the locations. Find hotel promotions, book experiences, reserve tables in fantastic restaurants and discover incredible places nearby. Independent of the type of trip you are looking for, TripAdvisor helps your planning as well as it enables you to help other.	TheFork gives you access to more than 80 000 restaurants available at any moment and with the best prices, in Portugal and more than 21 countries! Consult more than 20 million client opinions which will help you find the ideal restaurant!	Aren't we yet on your phone? What are you waiting for? Download the Yelp app to always be up to date with the best local deals in your city. Furthermore, you will be part of a community that likes, defends and promotes local commerce and has fun sharing experiences via evaluations, photographs, videos, tips, and much more.
N° of evaluations	10,1 mil	6,8 mil	40,8	29
Score	4,7	4,6	4,8	4,2
Version	15.7.6	42.1	18.7.0	12.86.0
Last *update*	Our latest update comes with bug fixes and performance enhancements to ensure a seamless experience across our app. Update your app now and give it a spin!	We have revamped our app to improve your traveling experience, from planning to booking. This is what you can do: • Obtain advice on where to stay, what to eat and where to eat from travellers that have been to those places • Access COVID-19 health and safety information of hotels, restaurants and experiences • Reserve hotels and experiences with free cancelations • Store, organize and share ideas with Trips • Discover nearby places on the map	It's with enormous pleasure that we inform you that there is a new update available for TheFork. We are always thinking of how to improve your experience! Culinary greetings!	Bug fixes and other improvements
Provider	Zomato Media Pvt. Ltd.	TripAdvisor	**La Fourchette**	Yelp, Inc.
Store link	Zomato: Food Delivery & Dining in the App Store (apple.com)	TripAdvisor: plan and book on the App Store (apple.com)	TheFork restaurants in the App Store (apple.com)	Yelp in the App Store (apple.com)
Category	Food and drinks	Travel	Food and drinks	Food and drinks
Free vs. Paid	Free	Free	Free	Free
Category ranking	#8	#15	#6	#42

Figure 4. SWOT analysis involving TheFork, TripAdvisor and Yelp apps

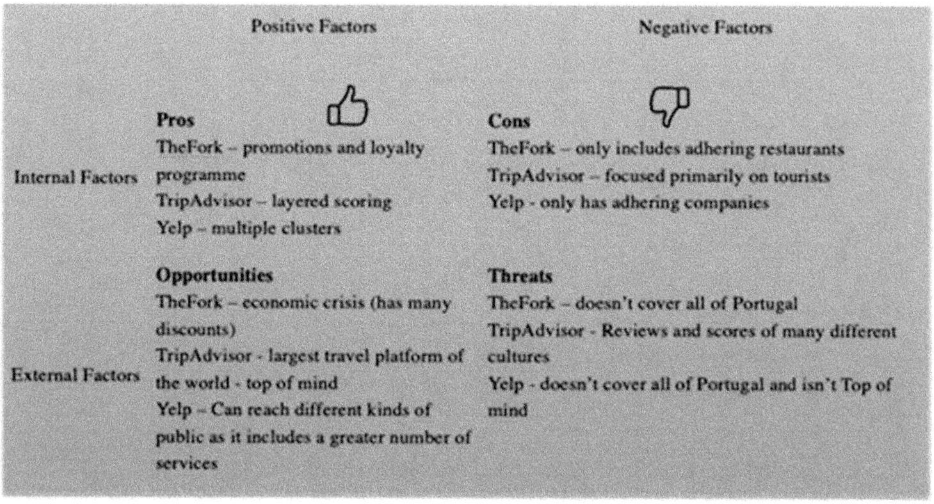

	Positive Factors	Negative Factors
Internal Factors	**Pros** TheFork – promotions and loyalty programme TripAdvisor – layered scoring Yelp – multiple clusters	**Cons** TheFork – only includes adhering restaurants TripAdvisor – focused primarily on tourists Yelp - only has adhering companies
External Factors	**Opportunities** TheFork – economic crisis (has many discounts) TripAdvisor - largest travel platform of the world - top of mind Yelp – Can reach different kinds of public as it includes a greater number of services	**Threats** TheFork – doesn't cover all of Portugal TripAdvisor - Reviews and scores of many different cultures Yelp - doesn't cover all of Portugal and isn't Top of mind

4 presents the article' authors' analysis of what are the positive and negative issues in the internal and external factors:

3.3 A quantitative analysis of Zomato Experience

Before start answering the hypotheses (H1-H4f), a quantitative analysis was conducted. It involved a sample of 320 answered questionnaires. On the next section, the results of the quantitative analysis are discussed to support answering the research questions.

It showed that only 219 consumers claimed to be Zomato users (Table 1).

- **H1 and H3 - The influence of Zomato on restaurant selection and its position in terms of other factors**

In terms of the first question, "Are you a Zomato user?" 68% (219) answered yes, and 31% (101) answered "No" as Figure 5 shows.

After, they were characterized by sociodemographic criteria and for those that answered no in the first question the questionnaire was concluded. The rest of the questionnaire was exclusively for the Zomato users (68%). The following question was to understand if Zomato can, or not, influence decision making when selecting a restaurant (Figure 6).

In terms of Zomato's position relative to other influential factors, the variable with most importance is friends and family (4,7 ± 0,43) as Table 2 reveals.

Table 1. Sociodemographic characteristics (N=219)

	N	%
Gender		
Male	79	36.1
Female	140	63.9
Age (M; DP)	29.7	10.6
School Education		
Professional course	6	2.7
Secondary school	10	4.6
Bachelor's degree	90	41.1
Postgraduate	21	9.6
Master's degree	84	38.4
PhD	8	3.7
Marital Status		
Single	163	74.4
Married	47	21.5
Divorced	9	4.1
Financial situation		
Sufficient	41	18.7
Comfortable	156	71.2
Very comfortable	22	10.0

Figure 5. "Are you a Zomato user?"

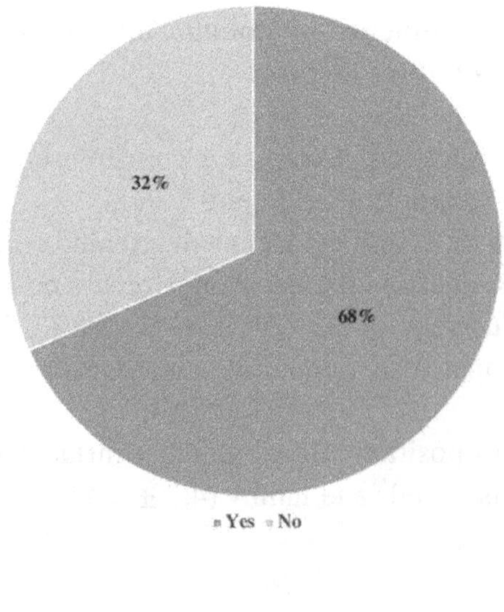

Figure 6. "Does Zomato influence your choice when selecting a restaurant?"

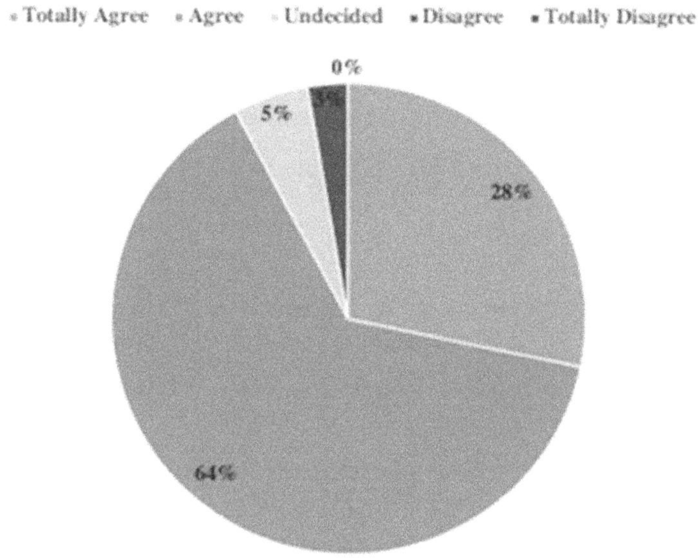

Table 2. "Classify how important the following recommendations are when choosing a restaurant"

	M	DP
Friends and family	4.7	.43
Online influencers	2.9	1.09
Zomato	4.0	.75
Other applications (TripAdvisor, Google My Business, ...	3.4	.89
Magazines/newspapers	3.0	.95
Tv shows/reports	3.0	1.03

Table 3. "When looking for a restaurant, how often do you use the following sources"

	M	DP
Friends and family	4,55	,68
Online influencers	2,71	1,27
Zomato	4,25	,74
Other applications (TripAdvisor, Google My Business,...	3,29	1,03
Magazines/newspapers	2,05	,99
Tv shows/reports	2,26	1,04

The aim of the next question was to understand how often they used the same variables when choosing a restaurant, and the conclusion was that "Friends and Family" (4,55±0,68) came first (Table 3)

- **H3 - Evaluation of the criteria made available by Zomato, in different situations**

The questionnaire respondent is now faced with various situations – an individual lunch on a weekday, a family lunch, dinner with friends and a romantic dinner – and they must evaluate the importance of different application criteria, shown previously in an image with an uncharacterized restaurant, when choosing a restaurant (Table 4).

- **H4 - Evaluation of a restaurant experience**

The next question seeks to understand how often they evaluate the restaurants after their experience (Figure 7).

The last question before the sociodemographic characterization aims to understand what factors most influence restaurant classification (Table 5).

Table 4. The most important attributes for each situation

Attribute	Situation			
	Individual lunch on a week day	Family lunch	Dinner with friends	Romantic dinner
Average Price	4.51	4.19	4.65	3.94
Type of food	4.37	4.53	4.32	4.53
Classification	4.14	4.48	4.11	4.59
If there is a menu	4.03	4.17	4.18	4.20
Photographs of the food	3.58	3.96	3.83	4.05
Photographs of the venue	3.56	4.08	3.97	4.53
Location	4.29	4.24	4.36	4.30
Possibility of making a reservation	3.17	4.10	4.18	4.20
Number of opinions	3.32	3.60	3.41	3.75
Opinions	3.61	3.84	3.64	3.99

Figure 7. "Do you usually evaluate/classify restaurants on digital recommendation/ evaluation platforms?"

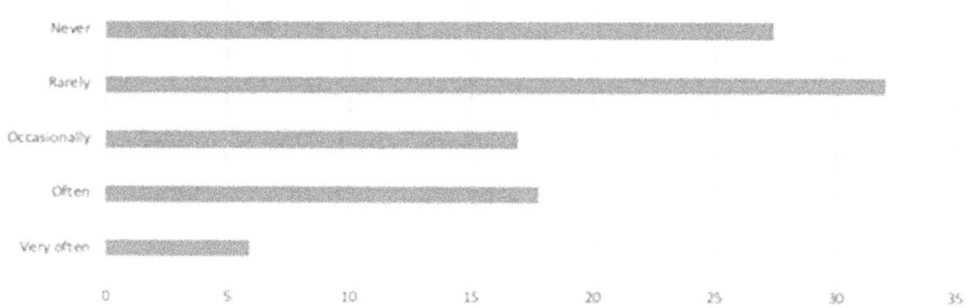

Table 5. "To classify the experience, please rank the following categories"

	M	DP
Food quality (including flavour and temperature)	4.87	.35
Physical environment	4.35	.64
Cleanliness	4.78	.46
Average price	4.19	.73
Speed and precision	4.33	.69
Behaviour/friendliness of the staff	4.68	.58
Restaurant working hours	3.76	.86
Restaurant aspect	4.04	.87
Location	3.98	.91

4. RESULTS AND DISCUSSION

- **Q1 -How can the Zomato users be characterized?**

To better understand Zomato user's profile, a multiple logistical regression was done, with the variable "being a Zomato user" as the dependent variable, and gender, age, education, marital status, and dietary restrictions as the independent variable. This enabled the study of the sociodemographic variables that influence the probability of being a Zomato user. The final model presents a correct classification percentage of 77,8%, which is higher than the constant (68.4%). As such, as age increases the probabilities that the subjects are Zomato users decreases, and those with higher educations have a greater chance of being Zomato users than those without (Table 6).

The Zomato user tends to be younger, with more than 12 years of formal education. There is no statistical difference between gender, financial situation, marital status, and dietary restrictions (Table 7).

- **Q2 -Using Zomato influences restaurant selection?**

Just as the literature revision indicates, this type of platform influences client selection. The greatest benefit is to provide support to the consumer through all stages of the decision-making process (Tucker, 2017). This was confirmed in the results: question 2 of the questionnaire "Does Zomato influence your decision when

Table 6. Logistical regression

	B	S.E.	Wald	df	Sig.	Exp(B)	95% C.I.for EXP(B)	
							Lower	Upper
Age	-.052	.016	10.388	1	.001***	.949	.919	.980
Marital status(single)	-.171	.471	.132	1	.716	.843	.335	2.120
Education(upper)	1.905	.379	25.206	1	.001***	6.719	3.194	14.133
Financial situation	-.220	.234	.882	1	.348	.803	.508	1.270
Gender (female)	-.172	.284	.365	1	.546	.842	.483	1.470
Dietary_restr. (yes)	.058	.517	.012	1	.911	1.059	.384	2.919
Constant	1.787	1.090	2.689	1	.101	5.974		

Table 7. Summary of the hypothesis testing 1

Hypothesis	Hypothesis test
H4a. There is no difference between genders of a Zomato user.	Not rejected
H4b. There is no difference between school education levels of a Zomato user.	Rejected
H4c. There is no difference between marital status of a Zomato user.	Not rejected
H4d. There is no difference between levels of financial comfort of a Zomato user.	Not rejected
H4e. There is no difference between dietary restrictions of a Zomato user.	Not rejected
H4f. There is no difference between age of a Zomato user.	Rejected

selecting a restaurant" (Figure 6) – as 92% of the respondents agreed or totally agreed that it did, with only 3% disagreeing. Figure 10 shows how the respondents answered in terms of ordering the recommendations for choosing a restaurant, with the most frequent answers being highlighted in a light ash tone. The recommendation that is of most importance to them is that Friends and Family (4.75) which reinforces McKinsey's study (2015), which concludes that *Word-Of-Mouth* evaluations and recommendations from friends and family are fundamental in the decision-making process (Court *et al.*, 2009). The recommendation that is of less importance was of

Figure 8. The importance of the other recommendations when choosing a restaurant

	1	2	3	4	5	M	DP
Friends and family	0.0	0.0	0.0	25.1	74.9	4.75	.43
Online influencers	12.3	20.5	37.4	23.3	6.4	2.91	1.09
Zomato	0.0	2.7	20.1	51.6	25.6	4.00	.75
Other applications (TripAdvisor, Google My Business, ...	1.8	13.2	33.3	42.9	8.7	3.43	.89
Magazines/newspapers	5.5	21.9	37.9	30.6	4.1	3.06	.95
Television programs/reports	9.6	18.3	37.4	29.7	5.0	3.02	1.03

Figure 9. Frequency of restoring to sources

	1	2	3	4	5	M	DP
Friends and family	0.0	0.5	9.1	25.1	65.3	4.55	.68
Online influencers	21.5	23.7	27.4	16.9	10.5	2.71	1.27
Zomato	0.0	2.7	10.0	47.0	40.2	4.25	.74
Other applications (TripAdvisor, Google My Business, ...	4.6	20.1	26.0	40.6	8.7	3.29	1.03
Magazines/newspapers	36.1	32.4	22.8	7.8	0.9	2.05	.99
Television programs	25.1	39.3	22.8	9.6	3.2	2.26	1.04

online influencers (2.91), despite these having a positive influence on the consumer and giving the opportunity to learn of new and different experiences (Philip, 2016). The Zomato application has a significantly higher evaluation, then the other competing applications, Z = -7.604, p = .001. To obtain these results, a *Wicoxon* test for paired samples was done, comparing the average between two ordinal variables: Zomato and the other applications (Figures 8 and 9).

When looking for a restaurant, the respondents resorted more regularly to friends and family (4.55), Zomato (4.26) or other applications like TripAdvisor, Google My Business, Facebook, The Fork (3.29). Zomato has a significantly better evaluation than its competition Z = -9.473, p = .001, possibly because of its greater use in

Portugal (Ribeiro, 2019), and because it is the first in the sector with a strong social component (Itchannel, 2014).

Therefore, it is possible to accept **H1 - Zomato has an influence on restaurant selection**.

- **Q3 -What is the impact of the different criteria that Zomato has when selecting a restaurant, in different situations? (pre-consumption)**

When the respondents have a romantic dinner, they considered the information provided of more importance, whilst considering it of less importance when having lunch on their own (Table 8). The difference in averages between the level of importance attributed to the two situations is statistically significant, $t\ (219) = -8.017, p = .001$. The level of importance attributed to sources of information when they are having lunch with family or have a romantic dinner is significantly higher than the evaluation level *Important* (4.00), ($p < .001$).

The different attributes of the app have varying levels of importance according to the situation, perhaps due to eating no longer being a strictly physiological need, but also being a meaningful experience. Eating out is an indispensable part of a person's routine (Walker, 2014). The type of food is the most referred variable, irrespective of the occasion. The same can also be seen in Auty's study (1992). The context of having a romantic dinner is the only situation where photographs of the venue are one of the most important attributes when selecting a restaurant. This can be explained by the fact that the influence that the ambiance has when going to a restaurant for hedonic reasons is greater than when utilitarian (Ryu & Jang, 2008).

In the culinary field, online consumer analysis and classifications have an important role to play when others are deciding prior to consumption, due to the intangibility of the service, with restaurant clients using *online* evaluations or classifications to reduce uncertainty (Pan, Maclaurin, & Crotts, 2007). Although it may be impossible for this

Table 8. Descriptive statistics

[No Title]	Minimum	Maximum	Average	Standard deviation
Importance of the information provided by the app (Individual lunch)	2.20	5.00	3.85	0.53
Importance of the information provided by the app (Family lunch)	2.10	5.00	4.11	0.50
Importance of the information provided by the app (dinner w/friends)	2.00	5.00	4.06	0.54
Importance of the information provided by the app (romantic dinner)	2.09	5.00	4.14	0.46

Figure 10. The most important attributes for each situation

Attribute	Situation			
	Individual lunch on a week day	Family lunch	Dinner with friends	Romantic dinner
Average Price	4.51	4.19	4.65	3.94
Type of food	4.37	4.53	4.32	4.53
Classification	4.14	4.48	4.11	4.59
If there is a menu	4.03	4.17	4.18	4.20
Photographs of the food	3.58	3.96	3.83	4.05
Photographs of the venue	3.56	4.08	3.97	4.53
Location	4.29	4.24	4.36	4.30
Possibility of making a reservation	3.17	4.10	4.18	4.20
Number of opinions	3.32	3.60	3.41	3.75
Opinions	3.61	3.84	3.64	3.99

study to determine whether the classification of a restaurant is more important in a family lunch or romantic dinner, possibly because they are both special occasions. Ha, Park & Park (2016) concluded that the classification of a restaurant significantly influences selection, regardless of restaurant type.

When considering individual lunches on weekdays, the three most important factors for the user are average price, type of food and location. However, the same was not observed either in Kivela's et al. study (1999) or in Auty's study (1992). Nowadays, these attributes may be more important for Zomato users due to being a meal of convenience or with a utilitarian purpose. The possibility of being able to make a reservation is the least important reason, perhaps for the same reason.

The number of opinions is the less importance attribute when selecting a restaurant in three of the four situations. Nonetheless, opinions provide useful information for potential future clients when selecting a restaurant (Titz et al., 2004). These evaluations provide a variety of information, simplifying the user's decision-making process. By analysing this information, consumers can obtain detailed information on attributes such as restaurant ambiance, quality of food and service. According to Everett (2019), 33% read *online* comments before choosing a restaurant. In this study, although opinions are important, the number of opinions is not as influential an attribute in selecting a restaurant when compared to the others.

Upon concluding this statistical analysis, it is possible to accept **H2 - Different Zomato criteria influence restaurant selection according to the situation**.

- **Q4. What is the importance of each evaluation criteria for a consumer (after use)?**

The proportion of respondents that indicate that they rarely or never evaluate/classify a restaurant on digital recommendation/evaluation platforms is 59.4%, whilst the percentage of those that do so frequently or very frequently is 23.7%. Figure 11 shows that the factors that are considered most important when classifying an experience were food quality (4.87), cleanliness (4.78), and behaviour/friendliness of the staff (4.53), with the least important being restaurant working hours (3.76).

Figure 11. Classification of the experience

	1	2	3	4	5	M	DP
Food quality (including flavour and temperature)	0.0	0.0	0.5	11.9	87.7	4.87	.35
Physical environment	0.0	0.5	7.8	47.9	43.8	4.35	.64
Cleanliness	0.0	0.0	1.8	18.7	79.5	4.78	.46
Average price	0.0	2.7	10.5	52.1	34.7	4.19	.73
Speed and precision	0.0	0.5	11.0	43.8	44.7	4.33	.69
Behaviour/friendliness of the staff	0.0	0.9	3.2	23.3	72.6	4.68	.58
Restaurant working hours	1.4	6.4	24.7	50.2	17.4	3.76	.86
Restaurant aspect	0.5	4.1	21.0	40.2	34.2	4.04	.87
Location	1.8	4.6	17.4	46.1	30.1	3.98	.91

Concluding the statistical analysis, it is possible to confirm that **H3 - Criteria have varying importance to the consumer when evaluating a restaurant experience** is true.

The result concurs with that in the literature review: for some authors, food quality is the main factor for the consumer to feel satisfied and desire to return to the restaurant, as well as being the greatest motivator for WOM and E-WOM (Liu & Jang, 2009; Jang & Namkung,2009; Qin & Prybutok, 2008). Barber and Scarcelli

(2010), indicate that clients recommend or return to an establishment based on its cleanliness. The present research shows that cleanliness is the second most important factor for overall satisfaction with a restaurant experience. The importance of the physical environment, the creation of an image and influence of consumer behaviour is very pertinent in the catering industry.

Nonetheless, consumers don't evaluate a restaurant experience based only on food quality, but also on the quality of the service (Jeong & Jang, 2011), also confirmed in the current study. Various studies have shown that the quality of a service has an impact on client satisfaction, as well as their behavioural intentions such as WOM (Kim et al., 2009; Ladhari et al., 2008; Liu & Jang, 2009). Considering DINESERV, Ladhari et al. (2008) model, the perceived quality of a service affects client satisfaction, resulting in positive or negative emotions and influencing behaviour after the meal. Jeong and Jang (2011) concluded that if the clients were satisfied with the food quality and employee service, then they were more willing to help the restaurant by sharing their experience on evaluation sites. Liu and Jang (2009) used the DINESERV criteria to measure the service quality of a discovered that attributes such as friendliness and reliability as part of staff behaviour, are the attributes that most influence client satisfaction and their intentions after the experience.

5 LIMITATIONS OF THE STUDY

Being based on a convenience sample is the first limitation of this study. By not being random, the sample can't be considered to completely represent Zomato users in Portugal. Another limitation has to do with data structuring, as the attributes that were considered are not the only attributes to influence restaurant selection and its classification. The third limitation is related to there being limited literature on behaviour using digital recommendation platforms for restaurants, and how they influence the consumer.

6 CONCLUSION AND FUTURE GUIDELINES

One conclusion is that the Zomato user tends to be younger and has more than 12 years of formal education. There was no statistical difference between gender, financial situation, marital status, or dietary restrictions. Furthermore, Zomato does have an influence on restaurant selection, although recommendations from family and friends continue to have the greatest effect on a consumer's decision.

By analysing the importance of the application's attributes, it is possible to understand what consumers most value when selecting a restaurant, which can be significant to design future marketing and communications strategies. This study enables restaurants to focus on the most relevant attributes according to their objectives: e.g., if a restaurant manager perceives their establishment to be most used for convenience lunches, it may create lunch menus with affordable average prices or include promotions. Additionally, when on a romantic dinner, individuals consider the information provided by the application to be of greater importance than when having lunch alone.

The application provides a general score of the restaurant without specifying what this value refers to. As such, different factors presented in the literature were used for those considered to influence a client's experience in a restaurant, and which were of most importance when classifying a restaurant. The literature puts them into three main groups: food quality, service quality, and ambiance. According to this study, the three most important factors are: food quality, cleanliness, and staff behaviour/friendliness, with the least important being restaurant work hours. This means that restaurant managers should pay special attention to the former three factors as they have an important role to play in their business' classification. However, evaluating/classifying restaurants on digital recommendation/evaluation platforms is not frequently done by Zomato users, making it important that the restaurant promotes WOM.

As consumers rely on shared experiences to reduce the perceived risk associated with services (Verma & Yadav, 2021), WOM, and especially eWOM, plays a very important role in influencing consumer's behaviour. Because of that, a better understanding of the reasons and the items that customers use to make their choices in these digital evaluating platforms will help the restaurant managers to better define and implement their marketing actions.

REFERENCES

Auty, S. (1992). Consumer choice and segmentation in the restaurant industry. *Service Industries Journal*, *12*(3), 324–339. doi:10.1080/02642069200000042

Bansal, H. S., & Voyer, P. A. (2000). Word-of-mouth processes within a services purchase decision context. *Journal of Service Research*, *3*(2), 166–177. doi:10.1177/109467050032005

Barber, N., & Scarcelli, J. M. (2010). Enhancing the assessment of tangible service quality through the creation of a cleanliness measurement scale. *Managing Service Quality*, *20*(1), 70–88. doi:10.1108/09604521011011630

Bughin& Jacques. (2015). McKinsey & Company: Brand success in an era of Digital Darwinism. Retrieved March 22, 2021, from https://www.mckinsey.com/ industries/ high-tech/our-insights/brand-success-inanera-of-digital-darwinism

Buttle, A. (1998). Word of mouth: Understanding and managing referral marketing. *Journal of Strategic Marketing*, *6*(3), 241–254. doi:10.1080/096525498346658

Chen, H. (2011). The relationship between comments and recommendation system and online shopper buying behaviour. [). Trans Tech Publications Ltd.]. *Advanced Materials Research*, *204*(210), 197–200. doi:10.4028/www.scientific.net/AMR.204-210.197

Chen, Y., & Xie, J. (2008). Online consumer review: Word-of-mouth as a new element of marketing communication mix. *Management Science*, *54*(3), 477–491. doi:10.1287/mnsc.1070.0810

Cheung, M., & Thadani, R. (2012). The impact of electronic word-of-mouth communication: A literature analysis and integrative model. *Decision Support Systems*, *54*(1), 461–470. doi:10.1016/j.dss.2012.06.008

Chevalier, J. A., & Mayzlin, D. (2006). The effect of word of mouth on sales: Online book reviews. *JMR, Journal of Marketing Research*, *43*(3), 345–354. doi:10.1509/jmkr.43.3.345

Court, D., Elzinga, D., Mulder, S., & Vetvik, O. J. (2009). McKinsey & Company. Retrieved January 24, 2021, fromhttps://www.mckinsey.com/business- functions/ marketing-andsales/ourinsights/the-consumer-decision-journey

Duan, W., Gu, B., & Whinston, A. B. (2008). The dynamics of online word-of-mouth and product sales—An empirical investigation of the movie industry. *Journal of Retailing*, *84*(2), 233–242. doi:10.1016/j.jretai.2008.04.005

Duarte, A., & Dias, P. (2021). TikTok: Usos e motivações entre adolescentes em Portugal. Chasqui. *Chasqui*, *1*(147), 81–103. doi:10.16921/chasqui.v1i147.4419

Duecy, E. (2006). NPD: Dinners look for menu variety, 'buzz' in full-service eateries. *Nation's Restaurant News*, *40*(4), 14.

Dulen, J. (1999). Quality control. *Restaurants & Institutions*, *109*(5), 38–44. PMID:10558057

Esfahani, S. (2015). Investigating Information Adoption Tendencies of Restaurants' User-Generated Content Utilizing a Hypothesized Information Adoption Model (Doctoral dissertation, Kent State University).

Everett, H. (2019). Digital Marketing for Restaurants: How to Get Found Online. Retrieved March 26, 2020, from: https://upserve.com/restaurantinsider/ digital-marketing- restaurants

Fabretti, P. (2012). Community Management. Share This Too: More Social Media Solutions for PR Professionals, 79-87.

Fehrer, J. A., Woratschek, H., Germelmann, C. C., & Brodie, R. J. (2018). Dynamics and drivers of customer engagement: Within thedyad and beyond. *Journal of Service Management*, *29*(3), 443–467. doi:10.1108/JOSM-08-2016-0236

Fernandes, R. (2015). A indústria hoteleira e as reclamações online: o caso do TripAdvisor.

Fields, R. (2014). *Restaurant Success by the Numbers: A Money-guy's Guide to Opening the Next New Hot Spot*. Ten Speed Press.

Flatters, P. (2015). Eating Out - Today and Tomorrow Consumer Survey. Retrieved January 25, 2021, from https://trajectorypartnership.com/wpcontent/uploads/2015/07/ SaclaReport_v19FINAL.pdf

Fogel, S. (2010). Issues in Measurement of Word of Mouth in Social Media Marketing. *International Journal of Integrated Marketing Communications*, *2*(2), 54–60.

Godes, D., & Mayzlin, D. (2004). Using online conversations to study word-of-mouth communication. *Marketing Science*, *23*(4), 545–560. doi:10.1287/mksc.1040.0071

Gretzel, U. (2017). Influencer marketing in travel and tourism. In *Advances in social media for travel, tourism, and hospitality* (pp. 147–156). Routledge. doi:10.4324/9781315565736-13

Ha, J., & Jang, S. S. (2010). Effects of service quality and food quality: The moderating role of atmospherics in an ethnic restaurant segment. *International Journal of Hospitality Management*, *29*(3), 520–529. doi:10.1016/j.ijhm.2009.12.005

Ha, J., Park, K., & Park, J. (2016). Which restaurant should I choose? Herd behavior in the restaurant industry. *Journal of Foodservice Business Research*, *19*(4), 396–412. doi:10.1080/15378020.2016.1185873

Hennig-Thurau, T., Gwinner, K. P., Walsh, G., & Gremler, D. D. (2004). Electronic Word-of-Mouth via Consumer-Opinion Platforms: What Motivates Consumers to Articulate Themselves on the Internet? *Journal of Interactive Marketing*, *18*(1), 38–52. doi:10.1002/dir.10073

Hopper, C. (2013). *Selling Eating*. Young &Laramore, Inc.

Jang, S., & Namkung, Y. (2009). Perceived quality, emotions, and behavioral intentions: Application of an extended Mehrabian–Russell model to restaurants. *Journal of Business Research*, *62*(4), 451–460. doi:10.1016/j.jbusres.2008.01.038

Jeong, E., & Jang, S. (2011). Restaurant experiences triggering positive electronic word-of-mouth (eWOM) motivations. *International Journal of Hospitality Management*, *30*(2), 356–366. doi:10.1016/j.ijhm.2010.08.005

Jillian, S., Lester, J., & Robert, A. (1992). The Effect of Cues on Service Quality Expectations andService Selection in a Restaurant Setting. *Journal of Services Marketing*, *6*(4).

June, P., & Smith, L. (1987). Service attributes and situational effects on customer preferences for restaurant dining. *Journal of Travel Research*, *26*(2), 20–27. doi:10.1177/004728758702600205

Keller, E. (2007). Unleashing the power of word of mouth: Creating brand advocacy to drive growth. *Journal of Advertising Research*, *47*(4), 448–452. doi:10.2501/S0021849907070468

Kim, W. G., Ng, C. Y. N., & Kim, Y. S. (2009). Influence of institutional DINESERV on customer satisfaction, return intention, and word-of-mouth. *International Journal of Hospitality Management*, *28*(1), 10–17. doi:10.1016/j.ijhm.2008.03.005

Kivela, J., Inbakaran, R., & Reece, J. (1999). Consumer research in the restaurant environment, Part 1: A conceptual model of dining satisfaction and return patronage. *International Journal of Contemporary Hospitality Management*, *11*(5), 205–222. doi:10.1108/09596119910272739

Kotler, P., Bowen, J. T., Makens, J. &Baloglu, S. (2017). Marketing for hospitality and tourism.

Kozinets, V., De Valck, K., Wojnicki, C., & Wilner, J. (2010). Networked narratives: Understanding word-of-mouth marketing in online communities. *Journal of Marketing*, *74*(2), 71–89. doi:10.1509/jm.74.2.71

Ladhari, R. (2008). Alternative measures of service quality: A review. *Managing Service Quality*, *18*(1), 65–86. doi:10.1108/09604520810842849

Ladhari, R., Brun, I., & Morales, M. (2008). Determinants of dining satisfaction and post-dining behavioral intentions. *International Journal of Hospitality Management*, *27*(4), 563–573. doi:10.1016/j.ijhm.2007.07.025

Lewis, R. (1981). Restaurant advertising: Appeals and consumers' intentions. *Journal of Advertising Research*, *21*(5), 69–74.

Li, F., Larimo, J., & Leonidou, L. C. (2021). Social media marketing strategy: Definition, conceptualization, taxonomy, validation, and future agenda. *Journal of the Academy of Marketing Science*, *49*(1), 51–70. doi:10.100711747-020-00733-3

Libai, B., Bolton, R., Bügel, M. S., De Ruyter, K., Götz, O., Risselada, H., & Stephen, A. T. (2010). Customer-to-customer interactions: Broadening the scope of word-of-mouth research. *Journal of Service Research*, *13*(3), 267–282. doi:10.1177/1094670510375600

Liu, Y. (2006). Word of mouth for movies: Its dynamics and impact on box office revenue. *Journal of Marketing*, *70*(3), 74–89. doi:10.1509/jmkg.70.3.074

Liu, Y., & Jang, S. (2009). Perceptions of Chinese restaurants in the US: What affects customer satisfaction and behavioural intentions? *International Journal of Hospitality Management*, *28*(3), 338–34. doi:10.1016/j.ijhm.2008.10.008

Lu, X., Ba, S., Huang, L., & Feng, Y. (2013). Promotional marketing or word-of-mouth. Evidence from online restaurant reviews. *Information Systems Research*, *24*(3), 596–612. doi:10.1287/isre.1120.0454

Martin, R., & Frumkin, P. (2005). Consumer trends: What do they want (and why). *International Journal of Contemporary Hospitality Management*, *39*(21), 58–63.

McFadden, L., & Train, E. (1996). Consumers' evaluation of new products: Learning from self and others. *Journal of Political Economy*, *104*(4), 683–703. doi:10.1086/262038

Moreira, A., Sá, P., & Costa, A. P. (2009). Metodologias de Investigação.

Moser, C., Schoenebeck, Y., & Reinecke, K. (2016). Technology at the table: Attitudes about mobile phone use at mealtimes. In *Proceedings of the 2016 CHI Conference on Human Factors in Computing Systems*,1881-1892. 10.1145/2858036.2858357

Pan, B., Maclaurin, T., & Crotts, J. (2007). Travel blogs and the implications for destination marketing. *Journal of Travel Research*, *46*(1), 35–45. doi:10.1177/0047287507302378

Parasuraman, A., Zeithaml, A., & Berry, L. (1988). Servqual: A multiple- item scale for measuring consumer perc. *Journal of Retailing*, *64*(1), 12.

Parikh, A., Behnke, C., Vorvoreanu, M., Almanza, B., & Nelson, D. (2014). Motives for reading and articulating user-generated restaurant reviews on Yelp. com. *Journal of Hospitality and Tourism Technology*, *5*(2), 160–176. doi:10.1108/JHTT-04-2013-0011

Patterson, P., Wirtz, J., Walker, R., Pearce, G., & Lovelock, C. (2011). Services marketing.

Philip, L. (2016). Impact of food blogs on the readers. *Journal of Mass Communication and Journalism*, *6*(2), 1–3. doi:10.4172/2165-7912.1000300

Phillips, D., & Young, P. (2009). *Online public relations: A practical guide to developing an online strategy in the world of social media*. Kogan Page Publishers.

Portugal, S. (2016). Os desafios da Restauração Moderna. [Ebook] Lisboa: Sage. Retrieved June 1, 2021, from: https://www.sage.pt/~/media/markets/pt/LP-Software-Restaurantes/EBook-Os-desafios-da restauracaomoderna.pdf

Qin, G., & Prybutok, R. (2008). Determinants of customer-perceived service quality in fast-food restaurants and their relationship to customer satisfaction and behavioural intentions. *The Quality Management Journal*, *15*(2), 35–50. doi:10.1080/10686967.2008.11918065

Ribeiro, M. (2019). Zomato em Portugal: A história contada por Miguel Ribeiro. (2019). Retrieved July 20, 2020, from https://medium.com/zomatoblogportugal/zomatoem-portugal-a-hist%C3%B3ria-contada-por-miguel-ribeiro-86925735f3e3

Rodgers, S., & Wang, Y. (2011). Electronic word of mouth and consumer generated content: From concept to application. In *Handbook of research on digital media and advertising: User generated content consumption* (pp. 212–231). IGI Global. doi:10.4018/978-1-60566-792-8.ch011

Ryu, K., & Jang, S. (2008). DINESCAPE: A scale for customers' perception of dining environments. *Journal of Foodservice Business Research*, *11*(1), 2–22. doi:10.1080/15378020801926551

Sarsby, A. (2016). *SWOT analysis – A guide to SWOT for business studies students* (1st ed.). Spectaris Ltd.

Shah, K. & Brahmbhatt, M. (2017). A Literature Review On Factors Affecting Service Quality In Restaurants

Siegrist, M. (2021). Trust and risk perception: A critical review of the literature. *Risk Analysis*, *41*(3), 480–490. doi:10.1111/risa.13325 PMID:31046144

Sparks, B. A., & Browning, V. (2011). The impact of online reviews on hotel booking intentions and perception of trust. *Tourism Management*, *32*(6), 1310–1323. doi:10.1016/j.tourman.2010.12.011

Stapenhurst, T. (2009). *The benchmarking book*. Routledge. doi:10.4324/9780080943329

Storms, D. (2014). Social Media Influence on the Restaurant Industry - Social Media. Retrieved December 22, 2020 from, disponível em: https://www.socialmedialink.com/ uncategorized/social-media-influence-on-therestaurant-industry/

Stringam, B. B., & Gerdes, J. Jr. (2010). An analysis of word-of-mouse ratings and guest comments of online hotel distribution sites. *Journal of Hospitality Marketing & Management*, *19*(7), 773–796. doi:10.1080/19368623.2010.508009

Tarabasz, A. (2013). The revaluation of communication in customer approach–towards marketing 4.0.

Titz, K., Lanza-Abbott, A., & Cruz, Y. (2004). The anatomy of restaurant reviews: An exploratory study. *International Journal of Hospitality & Tourism Administration*, *5*(1), 49–65. doi:10.1300/J149v05n01_03

Tucker, K. (2017). *Social media marketing for restaurants* (1st ed.).

Verhoef, C., Lemon, N., Parasuraman, A., Roggeveen, A., Tsiros, M., & Schlesinger, L. A. (2009). Customer experience creation: Determinants, dynamics, and management strategies. *Journal of Retailing*, *85*(1), 31–41. doi:10.1016/j.jretai.2008.11.001

Verma, S., & Yadav, N. (2021). Past, present, and future of electronic word of mouth (EWOM). *Journal of Interactive Marketing*, *53*(1), 111–128. doi:10.1016/j.intmar.2020.07.001

Villanueva, J., Yoo, S., & Hanssens, M. (2008). The impact of marketing-induced versus word-of-mouth customer acquisition on customer equity growth. *JMR, Journal of Marketing Research*, *45*(1), 48–59. doi:10.1509/jmkr.45.1.48

Walker, R. (2014). *Exploring the Hospitality Industry, 2/e*. Pearson Education India.

Wu, F. (2013). In search of negativity bias: An empirical study of perceived helpfulness of online reviews. *Psychology and Marketing*, *30*(11), 971–984. doi:10.1002/mar.20660

Yang, F., Heemsbergen, L., & Fordyce, R. (2021). Comparative analysis of China's Health Code, Australia's COVIDSafe and New Zealand's COVID Tracer Surveillance Apps: A new corona of public health governmentality? *Media International Australia, Incorporating Culture & Policy*, *178*(1), 182–197. doi:10.1177/1329878X20968277

Yeh, H., & Choi, M. (2011). MINI-lovers, maxi-mouths: An investigation of antecedents to eWOM intention among brand community members. *Journal of Marketing Communications*, *17*(3), 145–162. doi:10.1080/13527260903351119

Zeithaml, A., Bitner, J., & Gremler, D. (2000). *Services Marketing: integrating customer focus across the Firm.* Tata-McGraw-Hall.

Zhu, F., & Zhang, X. (2010). Impact of online consumer reviews on sales: The moderating role of product and consumer characteristics. Journalof marketing, 74(2), 133-148.

ENDNOTES

1 https://restaurant.org/home

2 https://www.zomato.com/pt/grande-lisboa

3 https://www.thefork.pt/

4 https://www.tripadvisor.pt/

5 https://www.yelp.pt/lisboa

Chapter 8
Grocery E-Commerce Transformation

Maria Kalyvaki
Minnesota State University, Mankato, USA

ABSTRACT

This chapter traces the evolution of grocery shopping, spotlighting the rise of e-commerce in the sector, particularly since 2020 due to COVID-19. The pandemic accelerated digital sales growth, condensing a decade's progress into mere months. This shift towards convenient, time-saving shopping methods was instrumental in integrating e-commerce into the food industry, including the fresh fruit and vegetable market. Amid COVID-19 restrictions, e-commerce became a vital food distribution tool, bolstering supply chain resilience. The chapter reviews the status of online grocery shopping, discussing customer hesitations and strategies to boost market share. Urging retailers to modernize business models, restructure supply chains, and develop efficient, eco-friendly local food delivery systems. Policy suggestions and vital investment areas for sustainable e-commerce development are presented. It advocates for urban governments to foster a supportive environment that capitalizes on e-commerce while minimizing its adverse impacts on traditional retail, traffic, and greenhouse gas emissions.

INTRODUCTION

The popularity of online grocery sales took a considerable amount of time to gain traction. In 2019, it was reported that 81% of US consumers had never purchased groceries online (Morgan, 2020). However, the outbreak of the COVID-19 pandemic caused a significant shift in this trend. In 2020, 79% of US consumers started ordering

DOI: 10.4018/978-1-6684-8868-3.ch008

their groceries online, resulting in a surge in online grocery sales from 1.2 billion USD in August 2019 to 7.2 billion USD in June 2020 (Morgan, 2020). Günday et al. (2020) consistently reports that 15% of European consumers have adopted new online grocery services, and 12% of consumers have switched to different grocery stores after experiencing home deliveries or click-and-collect services (Günday et al., 2020). These new customer segments have demonstrated continued use of online grocery services even beyond the initial spike caused by the pandemic (Hurtig, 2021).

Online grocery shopping refers to the act of purchasing groceries online through click-and-collect or home delivery services (Brand et al., 2020; Tyrväinen & Karjaluoto, 2022). Various empirical studies have examined consumer intentions toward online grocery shopping from different perspectives within marketing and information systems research since the early 21st century (Tyrväinen & Karjaluoto, 2022). A review of the existing literature on online grocery retailing reveals that the focus has primarily been on technological perspectives, relying heavily on models such as the technology acceptance model (TAM) and the unified theory of acceptance and use of technology (UTAUT), as well as psychological models such as the theory of planned behavior (TPB). Researchers have also incorporated emotional aspects, such as entertainment, enjoyment, or hedonic shopping motivation, into these technological frameworks. However, despite the research interest in online grocery shopping, there is still a lack of a unified meta-analytical framework that combines the key determinants influencing this phenomenon, highlighting the need for meta-analytical research. Therefore, this meta-analysis aims to synthesize previous studies incorporating both technological and emotional perspectives to resolve inconsistencies and provide a comprehensive understanding of the factors that significantly impact online grocery services. The results of this analysis will provide valuable insights for managers regarding the attributes they should emphasize when it comes to online grocery services.

According to Günday et al. (2020), only approximately 15% of consumers in Italy, Germany, and France express satisfaction with their online grocery services. This suggests that despite the forced adoption of online grocery services due to the COVID-19 pandemic, there is still a considerable need for improvement in these services. Therefore, this meta-analysis not only seeks to identify the critical factors that influence consumers' attitudes and contribute to their continued online grocery purchases post-pandemic, but it also aims to examine the mediating effects of attitudes and perceived usefulness on the relationship between determinants and behavioral intentions. Including these mediation mechanisms in a meta-analytical study helps researchers evaluate the potential risk of overestimating or underestimating the impact of determinants (Iyer et al., 2020). Investigating these mediators can assist retailers in emphasizing the valuable attributes of their online grocery services. The sudden impact of COVID-19 has compelled consumers to alter their habits and prioritize online channels for shopping (Pan et al., 2020; Pantano et al., 2020; Sheth, 2020). The grocery sector, in particular, has experienced a significant shift towards online channels as a result of the pandemic (Pantano et al., 2020). With the growing popularity of online grocery shopping, research interest in evaluating the pandemic's impact on consumer behavior has increased in the field of marketing science (He & Harris, 2020; Roggeveen & Sethuraman, 2020).

LITERATURE REVIEW

Impact of E-commerce on the Grocery Industry

The proliferation of e-commerce in the grocery industry has brought about a significant shift in traditional grocery retail, instigating both positive and negative outcomes. From the consumer's perspective, e-commerce has simplified and expanded the possibilities of grocery shopping. It permits customers to make purchases from the comfort of their homes or workplaces, at any time of the day, and have their groceries delivered straight to their doorstep. This flexibility and convenience have proven to be a major advantage, particularly considering the COVID-19 pandemic, where safety concerns led many to avoid public spaces like grocery stores. The ability to order groceries online has provided a safer alternative, allowing consumers to continue purchasing their daily essentials without risking exposure to the virus. Moreover, e-commerce has opened new avenues for grocery retailers to attract and engage with a broader range of customers. With the option of online shopping, retailers can now cater to those who may have been unable to visit their physical stores due to geographical or time constraints. This expanded reach not only increases the potential customer base for retailers but also presents opportunities for increased sales and revenue growth. However, the advent of e-commerce has also posed substantial challenges for the traditional brick-and-mortar grocery stores. The comfort and affordability offered by online shopping have disrupted the traditional retail model, making it difficult for physical stores to compete. Many such retailers have found it tough to transition to this new era of digital commerce, experiencing a decline in sales and a dwindling market share as a result. Beyond the retailers, the impact of e-commerce extends to grocery suppliers too. They are now required to navigate an increasingly intricate and competitive online marketplace. This entails ensuring the delivery of high-quality products at competitive prices, alongside maintaining a robust online presence for effective customer outreach. In summary, while the advent of e-commerce in the grocery industry has disrupted traditional retail practices, it has also brought about new opportunities and challenges. Its impacts are multi-faceted, influencing consumers, retailers, and suppliers alike. E-commerce is a transformative force in the grocery industry and is poised to continue shaping its future trajectory.

Walmart's E-Commerce Evolution Example and its Effects on the Grocery Industry

Walmart, an American multinational retail corporation, is renowned as the world's largest company by revenue, with over USD 500 billion as of 2020. Founded by Sam Walton in 1962 in Rogers, Arkansas, Walmart has transformed from a single discount store into a global retail giant, with over 11,000 stores in 27 countries operating under 55 different names (Volpe & Boland, 2022). Walmart's business model was initially built around physical 'brick-and-mortar' stores, where it became known for its 'Every Day Low Prices'. Over the years, Walmart has remained committed to saving people money to help them live better, a philosophy that has guided its evolution and growth. However, the rise of the internet and e-commerce in the late 1990s and early 2000s presented a new challenge and opportunity for Walmart. The company recognized that to maintain its leading position in the retail industry, it needed to adapt to changing consumer behaviors and expectations influenced by digital technology.

In the early 2000s, Walmart launched its e-commerce platform, Walmart.com, offering a wide range of products for online purchase. But it was not until the late 2010s that Walmart began a more aggressive push into the online retail space, recognizing the growing importance of e-commerce in the retail landscape. This was marked by key strategic moves, such as the acquisition of Jet.com in 2016, which significantly boosted its online presence and expertise. One of the most transformative aspects of Walmart's digital evolution has been in the grocery sector. Realizing the convenience that online shopping could provide for busy consumers, Walmart began offering online grocery shopping, home deliveries, and pickup services. The company leveraged its expansive physical store network to provide 'click and collect' services, allowing customers to order groceries online and pick them up at a nearby store, a strategy that few competitors could match.

The digitalization of Walmart's grocery business has fundamentally changed consumer behavior. Customers could now effortlessly compare prices, read product reviews, and make informed purchasing decisions from their homes' comfort. This prompted Walmart to prioritize customer satisfaction even more, leading to personalized services and improved customer engagement. In addition to transforming its customer-facing operations, Walmart's foray into e-commerce required a radical rethink of its supply chain management. The company introduced innovative delivery methods to ensure efficient order fulfillment, even experimenting with drone deliveries. Furthermore, to guarantee the freshness of groceries, Walmart invested heavily in advanced packaging techniques and cold chain logistics. The e-commerce shift has proven to be a profitable venture for Walmart. As of 2021, Walmart's e-commerce sales in the U.S. grew by 80%. This growth can be attributed to its grocery pickup and delivery services, which have been particularly important during the COVID-19 pandemic when many consumers have opted for contactless shopping options. Walmart's e-commerce evolution has had a profound impact not only on its operations but also on the broader grocery industry. The shift has led to increased digitalization, changes in consumer behavior, and enhancements in supply chain management. As the e-commerce landscape continues to evolve, other grocery retailers can learn valuable lessons from Walmart's successful digital transformation.

RESEARCH METHODS

This book chapter aims to review the existing literature on retail formats, present a framework for customer-centric retail formats in the future, explore ongoing and potential trends in retail formats, and suggest areas of future research in this field. Our proposed framework outlines two potential strategies for retail formats to remain competitive and relevant. The first strategy is to enhance the customer experience, and the second is to reduce customer friction. It is worth noting that retailers may choose to adopt both strategies if their resources allow. This research comprehensively reviews the existing literature from the past three decades focusing on the challenges and opportunities associated with the e-grocery industry. The data is collected from a variety of sources including industry reports, books, case studies, academic journals, and market analysis to delve deeper into the current landscape of the e-grocery sector.

The keywords used for sourcing relevant material for this research include "e-grocery," "online grocery shopping," "consumer behavior," "supply chain," "e-commerce," "digital transformation," "customer experience," "online retail," and "COVID-19 impact." These keywords are utilized to search for pertinent sources in databases like JSTOR, Google Scholar, and business research databases. Alongside the databases, a thorough search of the World Wide Web was also conducted to ensure that all relevant industry reports, case studies, and articles pertaining to the challenges and opportunities in the e-grocery industry were identified. The articles and reports obtained from these searches were meticulously reviewed to confirm their relevance to the research topic. The gathered data were analyzed to identify recurring themes and patterns related to the e-grocery industry's challenges and opportunities, and potential strategies to address them are identified. The research is conducted using a qualitative approach, employing thematic analysis to identify patterns and themes in the data.

The conclusion summarizes the findings, underlining the necessity for interdisciplinary approaches to understand and address the complexities of the e-grocery industry, and the significance of creating strategic plans and policies that balance the diverse interests of various stakeholders within the industry. To understand the future evolution of grocery formats, we will delve into the challenges faced by groceries by exploring a) How has the COVID-19 pandemic impacted consumer attitudes towards online grocery shopping, particularly in the fresh fruits and vegetables (FFV) market, and what factors contribute to or hinder its wider adoption? b) What strategies and investments are necessary for retailers and policymakers to promote sustainable development of groceries e-commerce, while addressing its potential adverse effects on the traditional retail sector, traffic congestion, and greenhouse gas emissions?

FINDINGS

Grocery shopping has undergone a significant transformation over the past few decades. Historically, grocery shopping involves physically visiting a local grocery store to purchase household essentials and food items. However, with the advent of technology and the internet, people's grocery shopping has changed dramatically. The emergence of e-commerce in the grocery industry has enabled consumers to shop for groceries online, often from the comfort of their own homes. The first online grocery stores began to appear in the 1990s (Tyrväinen & Karjaluoto, 2022). Still, it wasn't until the widespread adoption of smartphones and the growth of fast and reliable delivery services that e-commerce grocery shopping became more widespread. As more and more consumers have embraced the convenience and accessibility of online grocery shopping, the grocery industry has been forced to adapt to the changing landscape. Today, e-commerce grocery is a rapidly growing market, with many traditional grocery retailers launching their online grocery platforms or partnering with existing e-commerce providers. The trend toward e-commerce groceries is expected to continue as consumers become increasingly comfortable purchasing groceries online, and retailers seek to meet this demand. Overall, the evolution of grocery shopping and e-commerce in the grocery industry has profoundly impacted how people shop for groceries. This transformation is set to continue in the years to come.

The growth of food e-commerce has accelerated significantly since 2020, largely due to the COVID-19 pandemic, which has been described as having compressed ten years of digital sales penetration into three months (Luo et al., 2023). Prior to the pandemic, the expansion of e-commerce was already anticipated, with Euromonitor International projecting that e-commerce would account for over half of the global retail sector between 2020 and 2025 (Bourlier & Gomez, 2016; Gružauskas & Burinskienė, 2022). The transformation of consumer food demand patterns towards more convenient and time-saving shopping methods had been contributing to the penetration of e-commerce in the food industry, including the fresh fruits and vegetables (FFV) market. Interestingly, a similar surge in e-commerce was observed during China's 2003 Severe Acute Respiratory Syndrome (SARS) outbreak, yet the boom accompanying the COVID-19 pandemic has presented unprecedented challenges and opportunities.

The e-commerce sector has seen a significant increase in the prominence of groceries as a category. In 2021, groceries, electronics, and apparel drove 41.8% of the overall e-commerce market. The pandemic has had a notable impact on each of these categories, and in particular, groceries experienced a breakout year in 2020, with online spending reaching $73.7 billion, an increase of 103%. While the category continues to grow, it now represents 8.9% of the overall e-commerce market, up from 6.3% in 2019, but slightly down from the surge in demand seen in 2020. On average, consumers now spend $6.7 billion per month on groceries, up from $3.1 billion pre-pandemic. There are projects that the category will surpass $85 billion in 2022 (Verdon, 2022).

In the face of lockdowns and other measures aimed at reducing the spread of COVID-19, e-commerce emerged as a crucial means of food distribution, thereby strengthening food supply chains and enhancing their resilience against the disruptive effects of the pandemic, particularly in mature food economies (Gomes & Lopes, 2022; Reardon et al., 2023). Although the pace of e-commerce expansion varies, the growth trend persists even as restrictions ease, driving a significant transformation of the retail sector. This transformation is evident in the emergence of new actors, services, and business models, which are currently undergoing a process of adaptation and consolidation due to the lack of comprehensive regulation.

Focusing on the sale of FFV, this chapter discusses the rapid surge and evolution of e-commerce based on an analysis by the Food and Agriculture Organization of the United Nations and the European Bank for Reconstruction and Development (Reardon et al., 2023). The report offers policy recommendations and highlights strategies and key investment areas essential for the sustainable development of FFV e-commerce. Governments, particularly urban authorities, are encouraged to create a supportive institutional, regulatory, and business environment that maximizes e-commerce opportunities while mitigating its negative impacts on the traditional retail sector, traffic congestion, and greenhouse gas (GHG) emissions. To successfully adapt to the e-commerce landscape, retailers must invest in upgrading their business models, reorganizing supply chains, and establishing efficient, environmentally-sustainable systems for delivering local and healthy food products (Food and Agriculture Organization of the United Nations, 2023). The history and current state of online grocery shopping is a fascinating topic that has been researched and discussed by many experts in the field. Online grocery shopping lags behind other areas of eCommerce in the US, with only 3% of groceries being purchased online, compared to 40% of consumer electronics (Kamel et al., 2022).

In the early days of eCommerce, pioneers like NetMarket, Amazon, and eBay paved the way for a revolution in shopping. Amazon, which began as an online bookstore, sold books to people in all 50 states and 45 foreign countries in its first month of operation (Hartmans, 2021). eBay was started as AuctionWeb, an open marketplace for sellers and buyers of used items (eBay Inc., n.d.). Both companies have come a long way in the past two decades and are now among the largest global online retailers. The potential of eCommerce to revolutionize shopping was clear from the beginning, offering convenience, customization, and potential savings, despite concerns about online payment and privacy (Rigby, 2011). The entry of Alibaba in 1999 was a game changer, as they believed that online shopping could enable small businesses to reach a larger market, and Chinese manufacturers to sell globally (Carsten, 2013; Reardon et al., 2021).

The failure of Webvan, the first online grocery store, was a high-profile setback, but it did not stop others from trying (Barr, 2013). Webvan raised $375 million in a public offering in November 1999 and decided to build high-tech storage warehouses and develop delivery systems in 26 locations (Aspray et al., 2013; Delaney-Klinger et al., 2003; Lunce et al., 2006) . However, they filed for bankruptcy less than two years later. England's Ocado, founded in 2000, partnered with Waitrose and has been successful, constantly innovating with new services like price matching and introducing an own-brand range. The UK is the leading market for online grocery sales, with 48% of people aged 35-44 buying groceries online in 2018 (Galante et al., 2013). In conclusion, online grocery shopping has seen great innovation in recent years, with the introduction of devices like Amazon Dash and voice-activated services like Alexa, making eCommerce more accessible and flexible. Retailers are investing in site layout, graphics, AI, and widgets to make shopping more attractive and easier. The ability to make and store lists, vouchers, price matching services, and other money-saving ideas make online grocery shopping more appealing to customers (Zehavi, 2019).

The intersection of technology and retail has been progressively evolving, with each epoch-making a significant impact on how we shop. The first major shift was the introduction of universal product codes in 1974, which streamlined retail operations, and set the stage for more advanced retail technologies. This was followed by the emergence of the Home Shopping Network in 1985, a revolutionary step that brought together television and shopping, offering a unique, non-store shopping format that did not rely on traditional brick-and-mortar stores. However, the real game-changer was the launch of Amazon in 1995, which ushered in a new era by selling its first book online (Gauri et al., 2021; Ratchford et al., 2022). This pivotal event changed the face of retailing forever, introducing consumers to the convenience and variety of online shopping. As each new retail format emerges, it creates a ripple effect, necessitating the evolution and adaptation of older formats. In their heyday, groceries stores revolutionized retailing by enhancing the shopping experience. They provided a wide variety of products divided into distinct departments, thereby catering to diverse customer needs under one roof. However, during the latter half of the 20th century, grocery stores found it challenging to compete with discount stores and category-killers, who were able to offer lower prices due to superior economies of scale.

DISCUSSION

The advent of internet retailing further complicated the landscape, posing a significant threat to all brick-and-mortar retailers, henceforth referred to as offline retailers. Internet retailing brought vast product options and the convenience of shopping from anywhere. To stay relevant, older retail formats have been striving to adopt the features and technologies of the newer formats while also returning to their roots and leveraging their unique strengths. Groceries, once seen as the ultimate shopping destination where shopping was a leisure activity, are now forced to redefine themselves. In an age where consumers can easily browse a retailer's product range and compare prices from the comfort of their homes, these stores are endeavoring to stand out. They are doing so by redesigning their store layouts, meticulously curating their product offerings, investing in value-added services to lure customers, and introducing innovative concepts like the store-within-a-store.

Meanwhile, discount stores and category-killers, who once capitalized on their ability to offer lower prices, are now being outpriced by online retailers. To counter this, they are investing in matching the convenience and product range offered by online retailers. Conversely, several online retailers are venturing into the physical store arena to enhance customer experience and expedite product acquisition. This shift towards omnichannel retailing is leading to increased costs for larger players, paving the way for smaller, independent stores - reminiscent of the mom-and-pop stores of the past, albeit with a significant emphasis on technology. Additionally, these new retail formats offer a blend of services and features from both offline and online channels.

PRACTICAL AND MANAGERIAL IMPLICATIONS

Types of E-commerce Grocery Models

As the digital age continues to evolve, the grocery industry has witnessed the emergence of various e-commerce models, each with its unique characteristics, advantages, and disadvantages. The three primary models dominating the landscape are Pure Play E-commerce, Click and Collect, and Delivery Services.

a. Pure Play E-commerce

Pure Play E-commerce model represents businesses that operate exclusively online, without a physical presence or brick-and-mortar stores. Companies operating under this model conduct all their transactions, sales, and customer interactions through digital platforms such as websites or mobile applications. Renowned pure-play e-commerce grocery retailers include Amazon Fresh and Walmart+. Pure Play E-commerce has become increasingly prevalent in the digital age, driven by advancements in technology, internet accessibility, and changing consumer preferences (Grover & Vriens, 2006; Rasheed, 2009). Pure Play E-commerce companies offer a wide range of products and services, including retail goods, digital content, software, subscriptions, and more. By leveraging the power of the internet, they provide customers with the convenience of shopping from anywhere at any time, along with various benefits such as competitive pricing, extensive product selections, personalized recommendations, and seamless shopping experiences. One of the key advantages of Pure Play E-commerce is its ability to reach a global customer base. Without the constraints of physical stores, these businesses can expand their reach and target customers across different geographic locations. They can employ various marketing strategies, including search engine optimization, social media marketing, and targeted online advertising, to attract and engage customers on a global scale. Pure Play E-commerce companies also rely heavily on technology to manage their operations. They invest in robust e-commerce platforms, secure payment gateways, inventory management systems, logistics and fulfillment services, and customer relationship management tools. By utilizing these digital tools and systems, they streamline processes, enhance efficiency, and provide customers with seamless online experiences (Grover & Vriens, 2006; Rasheed, 2009).

However, Pure Play E-commerce companies face unique challenges. They must establish a strong online presence, build trust and credibility with customers, and ensure secure transactions and data protection. They also need to address logistical issues, such as efficient order fulfillment, shipping, and returns. Moreover, competition in the online marketplace can be intense, requiring Pure Play E-commerce businesses to continuously innovate, differentiate themselves, and deliver exceptional customer experiences to stay ahead. However, this model isn't without drawbacks. Delivery costs often appended to the grocery prices can make this option more expensive. Furthermore, the lack of physical interaction may not appeal to customers who prefer to inspect their groceries before purchase.

b. Click and Collect

The Click and Collect model bridges the gap between online shopping and brick-and-mortar stores. Customers order their groceries online and pick them up at a designated location, such as a store or a pickup point. Tesco and Sainsbury's are prime examples of grocery retailers offering this service.

In the grocery industry, Click&collect is an emerging channel that has gained popularity. Research on this topic has been conducted by private sector companies, focusing on the comparison between online and physical shopping experiences. Consumer profiling is also a prevalent theme, providing opportunities for research on the factors that drive e-commerce. The market share of grocery Click&collect has been steadily increasing, with 48 percent of shoppers having used the service in 2015, doubling from 2010 (Davies et al., 2019; Wollenburg et al., 2018). This growth is expected to continue as online grocery services offer tangible benefits such as avoiding checkout queues and crowded stores. France has seen high usage of drive-through collection facilities, thanks to significant investments made to avoid home delivery and last-mile costs (Davies et al., 2019; Jara et al., 2018). The UK has also invested heavily in Click&collect, but the perishable nature of groceries presents infrastructure challenges. Click&collect is considered a supplementary channel, with physical stores playing a central role. The shopping process involves online research and additional product information availability.

Multichannel offerings can enhance traditional store performance and efficiency in the grocery retail environment. The UK grocery industry, known for its efficiency, has adapted retail stores to serve as multifaceted hubs, acting as distribution centers for online operations. Successful e-commerce operations require efficient distribution networks and last-mile delivery. Customers interact with the retailer through online platforms and at the collection point, requiring real-time product and stock information. Design and accurate information are crucial to avoid out-of-stock situations and unnecessary costs. Click&collect must combine these factors to create a buying environment that enhances customer purchase probability, while considering cost, service quality, and efficiency. Retail stores are traditionally classified based on location and size. Large flagship stores in prime locations have the resources to implement expensive facilities. For example, Sainsbury's grocery Click&collect service reserves the most expensive format, Canopy, for high-revenue stores. Research suggests that online shopping is used for comparison purposes, while physical stores are still preferred for making purchases. Retailers are adopting multichannel strategies to target customers and provide multiple routes to purchase. However, this increases the complexity of measuring store performance. Traditional measures include profit, store traffic, and return on sales, but recent measures have expanded to include factors like checkout waiting times and online order item substitutions. This model balances convenience and cost-effectiveness. Customers enjoy the comfort of ordering from home and the freedom to pick up their groceries at a suitable time, eliminating waiting for deliveries. However, it necessitates customers to travel to the pickup location, which might not suit everyone, particularly those with mobility issues or without access to convenient transportation.

c. Delivery Services

In the Delivery Services model, customers order their groceries online, and the items are delivered directly to their doorstep. These services can be offered by traditional grocery retailers branching into e-commerce or specialized delivery companies like Instacart and Shipt.

Delivery services have become increasingly popular in the grocery industry, providing customers with the convenience of ordering groceries online and having them delivered directly to their doorstep. This model involves customers selecting their desired items through an online platform or app and choosing a delivery time slot that suits their schedule. Traditional grocery retailers have embraced this trend by incorporating their own delivery services, while specialized delivery companies like Instacart and Shipt have also emerged as major players in the market. These delivery service providers operate by employing a network of personal shoppers who fulfill the orders and deliver them to the customers' specified locations.

Instacart, a prominent delivery service, holds the largest share of online grocery and pickup transactions in the United States, accounting for 63% of the market as reported in June 2021(Griesbach et al., 2019; Millan et al., 2022). With its wide reach and convenience, Instacart has established itself as a preferred choice for customers seeking efficient and reliable grocery delivery services. By leveraging its extensive network of shoppers and partnering with various retailers, Instacart has successfully captured a significant portion of the online grocery market, catering to the growing demand for convenient shopping experiences. This model offers high convenience as customers receive their groceries at their doorstep, saving them the trouble of commuting to a store. However, this model might entail longer delivery times, especially during peak hours or bad weather conditions. Additionally, the delivery costs can potentially be higher compared to the other models. In essence, each e-commerce grocery model has its pros and cons. Pure Play E-commerce offers unparalleled convenience and wide reach, but might be costlier. Click and Collect provides a balance of convenience and cost but requires customers to pick up their orders. Delivery Services bring groceries to the doorstep but may include higher costs and longer waiting times. The choice between these models depends on individual customer needs, preferences, and circumstances. As the e-commerce landscape continues to evolve, we may witness the emergence of new models or hybrid approaches that combine the best features of existing ones.

Online purchasing complements traditional physical shopping, but its penetration is continually increasing. Understanding e-commerce is crucial, as consumer patronage decisions are influenced by various factors such as time, effort, risk, financial cost, and efficiency. Online channels provide convenience by eliminating the need to go in-store, but they introduce the inconvenience of accepting deliveries. Socio-economic factors also influence brand loyalty. While recent research has shed light on consumer purchase channel selection, the need for further innovation and investigation remains. Store performance is also influenced by competition, as multichannel offerings can cannibalize demand from traditional channels. Market saturation is limited by the finite nature of demand and the characteristics of the retail environment. Planning must consider store characteristics, socio-economic profiles, and competition to optimize resources and develop effective multichannel strategies.

NEW CHALLENGES

Future of Grocery E-commerce

Artificial Intelligence (AI) and automation have the potential to significantly impact the future of grocery e-commerce. Advancements in machine learning and data analytics allow retailers to personalize online shopping experiences, provide tailored product recommendations, and streamline the order fulfillment process. AI-powered chatbots and virtual assistants can also enhance customer service by addressing inquiries and resolving issues in real-time. Furthermore, automation technologies such as robotics and autonomous vehicles enable efficient warehouse operations and last-mile deliveries, reducing costs and improving speed and accuracy. Sustainability has become a key consideration for consumers, and it will continue to shape the future of grocery e-commerce. With growing awareness of environmental issues, shoppers are seeking more sustainable options in their purchasing decisions. This includes preferences for eco-friendly packaging, locally sourced products, and reduced carbon emissions in the supply chain. Retailers will need to prioritize sustainable practices, such as optimizing delivery routes, implementing green packaging solutions, and offering eco-friendly product alternatives, to attract and retain environmentally conscious customers. The integration of online and offline experiences, often referred to as omnichannel retailing, is a significant trend in the grocery industry. Retailers are recognizing the importance of providing a seamless shopping journey across different channels. This involves enabling customers to switch effortlessly between online and in-store shopping, offering options like click-and-collect services and in-store returns for online purchases. By integrating online and offline experiences, retailers can enhance convenience and provide a more holistic shopping experience that caters to customers' preferences and needs.

The growth of e-commerce has been substantial, but the COVID-19 pandemic has acted as a catalyst, further accelerating this trend. The market for online food, beverages, and groceries has experienced explosive growth, with notable examples such as Instacart reporting a staggering 500% year-over-year increase in April 2020 (Unnikrishnan & Figliozzi, 2020). This shift towards e-commerce and home delivery has significant implications not only for the job market but also for the transportation sector and the environment. The increase in online shopping and home deliveries translates into a substantial volume of packages being transported. In the United States alone, over 13 billion packages were delivered, and household-based grocery shopping trips exceeded 15 billion in 2018. With such large numbers, even small percentage changes in e-commerce and home delivery can result in significant shifts in travel patterns and transportation-related emissions. It is essential to consider the environmental impact of this growing trend and explore ways to mitigate and minimize the associated emissions.

The impact of these trends on the grocery industry will require retailers to adapt their strategies to remain competitive. Embracing AI and automation can improve operational efficiency, optimize inventory management, and enhance customer engagement. Implementing sustainable practices will be crucial to meet the demands of eco-conscious consumers and align with regulatory requirements. Furthermore, retailers must invest in technology and infrastructure to enable seamless integration of online and offline channels, ensuring a consistent and personalized experience for shoppers. Those who successfully navigate these trends will have a competitive advantage in the evolving landscape of grocery e-commerce. In conclusion, the transformation of the grocery industry driven by e-commerce has revolutionized the way consumers shop for groceries and presented both opportunities and challenges for retailers. Embracing technology, focusing on sustainability, and providing seamless omnichannel experiences will be key to remaining competitive in the evolving landscape of grocery e-commerce.

Policy Recommendations and Strategies for Sustainable FFV E-commerce Development

There are several policy recommendations and underscores strategies for fostering the sustainable growth of fruits, vegetables, and flowers (FFV) e-commerce. This aims to give an overview to governments, especially urban authorities, in creating a conducive institutional, regulatory, and business landscape that enhances e-commerce potential while limiting its adverse impacts on the traditional retail sector, traffic congestion, and greenhouse gas (GHG) emissions.

The first recommendation is for urban authorities to establish a balanced institutional and regulatory environment that supports the growth of FFV e-commerce without damaging the traditional retail sector. The introduction of e-commerce in the FFV sector should not lead to a zero-sum game where the gains of one sector translate into the losses of another. Instead, the objective should be a healthy coexistence where e-commerce complements traditional retail, encouraging competitive pricing, product diversity, and improved customer service. Regulation could include policies that ensure fair competition between e-commerce and traditional retail, like preventing predatory pricing and ensuring market access for all businesses. Furthermore, authorities can implement regulations to encourage e-commerce platforms to source a certain percentage of their products from local suppliers, thereby supporting local economies.

The second recommendation pertains to nurturing a supportive business environment. This involves the provision of public goods and services that reduce transaction costs for e-commerce businesses, such as digital infrastructure, logistics services, and consumer protection laws. It also involves investing in capacity-building initiatives, like digital literacy training for small-scale farmers and vendors, to help them tap into e-commerce opportunities. The advent of e-commerce, while advantageous in many respects, has inadvertently led to a surge in delivery vehicles, contributing to traffic congestion and GHG emissions. Authorities should therefore create regulations that encourage the adoption of green logistics practices. This could include the use of electric vehicles for deliveries, route optimization software to minimize travel distances, and packaging reduction measures. Congestion pricing schemes could be considered to manage peak delivery times in busy urban areas. Investment in digital infrastructure is key to the growth of e-commerce. This includes broadband internet access, digital payment systems, and cybersecurity measures. Expanding the digital infrastructure will ensure that all citizens, including those in remote and rural areas, can participate in and benefit from e-commerce. Investments in training and education are also crucial. Capacity-building programs for digital literacy, e-commerce business models, and sustainable practices should be implemented. These programs could help small-scale farmers and local vendors leverage e-commerce platforms, contributing to the growth of the sector while promoting sustainability.

Lastly, the government should foster public-private partnerships. Private sector expertise and resources can be leveraged to expand digital infrastructure, develop green logistics solutions, and provide training programs. Public-private partnerships (PPP)s can be instrumental in bridging the digital divide, driving innovation, and promoting sustainable growth in the FFV e-commerce sector. In summary, authorities have a significant role to play in shaping the future of FFV e-commerce. By providing a supportive institutional, regulatory, and business environment, they can help maximize the potential benefits of e-commerce while mitigating its negative impacts. Furthermore, strategic investments and collaborations with the private sector can lead to a vibrant, inclusive, and sustainable FFV e-commerce ecosystem.

FUTURE RESEARCH

Factors Driving the Growth of Online Grocery Shopping

Several factors are contributing to the growth of online grocery shopping, including increased access to technology, changing consumer preferences, and the convenience offered by online shopping. The growth of online grocery shopping can be attributed to several factors. Firstly, increased access to technology, with the widespread adoption of smartphones and improved internet connectivity, has made online shopping more accessible to a broader range of consumers. This has allowed consumers to easily browse and purchase groceries using their mobile devices or computers. Changing consumer preferences also play a significant role, as more consumers, particularly younger generations, are embracing e-commerce due to its convenience and efficiency. The COVID-19 pandemic has further accelerated this shift in preferences, with many consumers planning to continue shopping for groceries online even after the pandemic subsides. Convenience is another key driver, as online grocery shopping eliminates the need for travel and waiting in lines, allowing customers to shop at any time from the comfort of their homes. The broader product selection available online, along with personalized recommendations based on browsing and purchasing history, also attracts consumers. Price comparison and the ability to find better deals online further contribute to the growth of online grocery shopping. Technological advancements, such as artificial intelligence and machine learning, enhance the online shopping experience by offering more personalized and efficient options. Lastly, the expansion of delivery and pickup options, including same-day delivery and curbside pickup, makes online grocery shopping even more convenient and accessible for consumers. Overall, these factors have propelled the growth of online grocery shopping and are likely to continue shaping the future of the industry.

The market is expected to continue growing in the coming years, driven by ongoing technological advancements and the increasing adoption of e-commerce by both consumers and retailers. As a result, the online grocery market represents a significant opportunity for both established players and new entrants seeking to capitalize on this expanding sector. The growth of online grocery shopping represents a significant shift in the way consumers purchase groceries and how the industry operates. This transformation has impacted multiple aspects of the grocery shopping experience, from the convenience of online shopping to the challenges faced by traditional brick-and-mortar retailers in the era of e-commerce. The transformation of the grocery industry through e-commerce has significant implications for both consumers and the industry. For consumers, the growth of online grocery shopping offers increased convenience, access to a broader range of products, and the ability to compare prices and make more informed purchasing decisions. This has led to a more efficient and personalized shopping experience, with many consumers embracing the convenience and flexibility that online grocery shopping provides. For the grocery industry, the rise of e-commerce presents both opportunities and challenges. While traditional brick-and-mortar retailers face increased competition and the need to adapt to the changing landscape, the growth of online grocery shopping also offers new opportunities for market expansion and innovation. As the online grocery market continues to grow, both established players and new entrants can capitalize on this expanding sector by offering innovative solutions and services that cater to the evolving needs and preferences of consumers. The future of the grocery industry will be shaped by the continued growth of e-commerce and the evolving preferences and needs of consumers. As technology continues to advance, innovations such as artificial intelligence, machine learning, and data analytics will enable retailers to offer even more personalized and efficient shopping experiences. These advancements can range from personalized product recommendations to optimized delivery routes and inventory management, enhancing the overall customer experience. In addition, the expansion of delivery and pickup options will continue to make online grocery shopping more convenient and accessible for consumers. Retailers are likely to invest in logistics and fulfillment infrastructure to improve delivery speed and efficiency, offering same-day or next-day services to meet consumer expectations. Curbside pickup and in-store pickup options will also be expanded to provide greater convenience and flexibility for shoppers. However, the industry will also face challenges, such as increased competition, the need to invest in online platforms and delivery infrastructure, and the changing preferences of consumers. Brick-and-mortar retailers will need to continue adapting their strategies to compete in the e-commerce era. This may involve enhancing the in-store experience by incorporating technologies like self-checkout systems, interactive displays, or creating unique atmospheres that cannot be replicated online. Furthermore, sustainability and environmental concerns will play an increasingly important role in the future of the grocery industry. As consumers become more aware of the environmental impact of their purchasing decisions, retailers will need to address issues such as packaging waste, food waste, and the carbon footprint of delivery services. Implementing sustainable practices and offering eco-friendly alternatives will be crucial to meet consumer expectations and regulatory requirements.

Overall, the future of the grocery industry will be shaped by the continued growth of e-commerce, technological advancements, and the evolving needs and preferences of consumers. Retailers who can successfully navigate these opportunities and challenges will be well-positioned to thrive in the changing landscape of the grocery industry. Adaptation, innovation, and a focus on providing exceptional customer experiences will be key to remaining competitive and capturing the growing market share of online grocery shopping.

CONCLUSIONS

The metamorphosis of the grocery industry brought about by the advent of e-commerce has had profound implications that extend to both the consumers and the industry. The ease of access and convenience offered by online grocery shopping have turned out to be a boon for consumers, offering them a viable and time-saving alternative to conventional brick-and-mortar stores. Today's consumers enjoy the luxury of shopping from the warmth and comfort of their homes, have access to a broader array of products than ever before, and are on the receiving end of personalized recommendations which cater to their unique tastes and preferences. This fundamental shift in consumer behavior has brought about a major transformation in the industry, creating new challenges for traditional retailers who must now adapt to the ever-evolving digital landscape to remain relevant and competitive. As we gaze into the future, it is clear that the contours of the grocery industry will continue to be defined by further advancements in technology, an increased confluence of online and offline experiences, and the rising need for sustainability. The ascent of artificial intelligence and automation will persist in making operations more efficient, augmenting customer experiences, and optimizing supply chains. For retailers, significant investment in digital infrastructure will be necessary to keep pace with the burgeoning demand for e-commerce. In addition, the blending of online and offline shopping experiences will become increasingly crucial. Retailers will need to offer seamless omnichannel shopping journeys that afford consumers both convenience and flexibility. The importance of sustainability as a key driver in the future of the grocery industry cannot be overstated. As consumers grow more and more conscious of the environmental repercussions of their shopping habits, retailers will need to put sustainable practices at the forefront to align with these expectations. This means implementing strategies such as eco-friendly packaging, reducing food waste, and optimizing delivery routes to minimize carbon footprints. Even though the e-commerce arena in the grocery sector presents ample opportunities for growth and innovation, it isn't without its challenges. Traditional retailers will have to traverse the intricate path of digital transformation, guarantee data security and privacy, and carve out unique value propositions in a fiercely competitive market. Moreover, bridging the digital divide and ensuring equitable access to e-commerce for all consumers will be crucial considerations moving forward.

REFERENCES

Aspray, W., Royer, G., & Ocepek, M. G. (2013). *Food in the internet age*. Springer. doi:10.1007/978-3-319-01598-9

Barr, A. (2013, June 18). From the ashes of Webvan, Amazon builds a grocery business. *Reuters*. https://www.reuters.com/article/ctech-us-amazon-webvan-idCABRE95H1CC20130618

Bourlier, A., & Gomez, G. (2016). *Strategies for expanding into emerging markets with e-commerce*. Unctad.Org. https://unctad.org/system/files/non-official-document/dtl-eWeek2017c08-euromonitor_en.pdf

Brand, C., Schwanen, T., & Anable, J. (2020). 'Online omnivores' or 'willing but struggling'? Identifying online grocery shopping behavior segments using attitude theory. *Journal of Retailing and Consumer Services*, *57*, 102195. Advance online publication. doi:10.1016/j.jretconser.2020.102195

Carsten, P. (2013, October 13). Alibaba to transform China's "e-conomy" with $500 bln marketplace. *Rueters*. https://www.reuters.com/article/alibaba-retail/alibaba-to-transform-chinas-e-conomy-with-500-bln-marketplace-idUSL4N0HY29Y20131013

Davies, A., Dolega, L., & Arribas-Bel, D. (2019). Buy online collect in-store: Exploring grocery click & collect using a national case study. *International Journal of Retail & Distribution Management*, *47*(3), 278–291. doi:10.1108/IJRDM-01-2018-0025

Delaney-Klinger, K., Boyer, K. K., & Frohlich, M. (2003). The return of online grocery shopping: A comparative analysis of Webvan and Tesco's operational methods. *The TQM Magazine*, *15*(3), 187–196. doi:10.1108/09544780310469334 eBay Inc. (n.d.). *Our history*. Retrieved June 10, 2023, from https://www.ebayinc.com/company/our-history/

Food and Agriculture Organization of the United Nations. (2023). Impact assessment of the COVID-19 pandemic in relation to food value chains in the Lori and Tavush regions. *Policy Brief*. Advance online publication. doi:10.4060/cc0477en

Galante, N., García López, E., & Munby, S. (2013, March 1). The future of online grocery in Europe. *McKinsey & Company*. https://www.mckinsey.com/industries/retail/our-insights/the-future-of-online-grocery-in-europe

Gauri, D. K., Jindal, R. P., Ratchford, B., Fox, E., Bhatnagar, A., Pandey, A., Navallo, J. R., Fogarty, J., Carr, S., & Howerton, E. (2021). Evolution of retail formats: Past, present, and future. *Journal of Retailing*, *97*(1), 42–61. doi:10.1016/j.jretai.2020.11.002

Gomes, S., & Lopes, J. M. (2022). Evolution of the online grocery shopping experience during the COVID-19 pandemic: Empiric study from Portugal. *Journal of Theoretical and Applied Electronic Commerce Research*, *17*(3), 909–923. doi:10.3390/jtaer17030047

Griesbach, K., Reich, A., Elliott-Negri, L., & Milkman, R. (2019). Algorithmic control in platform food delivery work. *Socius: Sociological Research for a Dynamic World*, *5*, 1–15. doi:10.1177/2378023119870041

Grover, R., & Vriens, M. (Eds.). (2006). *The handbook of marketing research: Uses, misuses, and future advances*. SAGE Publications, Inc., doi:10.4135/9781412973380

Gružauskas, V., & Burinskienė, A. (2022). The development of sustainable transportation for e-grocery. *Journal of Management*, *38*(1), 69–74. doi:10.38104/vadyba.2022.1.08

Günday, G., Kooij, S., Moulton, J., Karabon, M., & Omeñaca, J. (2020, December 2). How European shoppers will buy groceries in the next normal. *McKinsey & Company*. https://www.mckinsey.com/industries/retail/our-insights/how-european-shoppers-will-buy-groceries-in-the-next-normal

Hartmans, A. (2021, July 2). Jeff Bezos originally wanted to name Amazon 'Cadabra,' and 14 other little-known facts about the early days of the e-commerce giant. *Insider*. https://www.businessinsider.com/jeff-bezos-amazon-history-facts-2017-4

He, H., & Harris, L. (2020). The impact of Covid-19 pandemic on corporate social responsibility and marketing philosophy. *Journal of Business Research*, *116*, 176–182. doi:10.1016/j.jbusres.2020.05.030 PMID:32457556

Hurtig, K. (2021, August 6). Time edges out COVID concerns for buying groceries online. *Winsight Grocery Business.* https://www.winsightgrocerybusiness.com/industry-partners/time-edges-out-covid-concerns-buying-groceries-online

Iyer, G. R., Blut, M., Xiao, S. H., & Grewal, D. (2020). Impulse buying: A meta-analytic review. *Journal of the Academy of Marketing Science*, *48*(3), 384–404. doi:10.100711747-019-00670-w

Jara, M., Vyt, D., Mevel, O., Morvan, T., & Morvan, N. (2018). Measuring customers benefits of click and collect. *Journal of Services Marketing*, *32*(4), 430–442. doi:10.1108/JSM-05-2017-0158

Kamel, M.-A., de Montgolfier, J., Athanassiou, M., & De Mol, A. (2022, March 16). Online grocery strategy: A reality check for disruptors and incumbents. *Bain & Company.* https://www.bain.com/insights/online-grocery-strategy/

Lunce, S. E., Lunce, L. M., Kawai, Y., & Maniam, B. (2006). Success and failure of pure-play organizations: Webvan versus Peapod, a comparative analysis. *Industrial Management & Data Systems*, *106*(9), 1344–1358. doi:10.1108/02635570610712618

Luo, Q., Forscher, T., Shaheen, S., Deakin, E., & Walker, J. L. (2023). Impact of the COVID-19 pandemic and generational heterogeneity on ecommerce shopping styles – A case study of Sacramento, California. *Communications in Transportation Research*, *3*, 100091. Advance online publication. doi:10.1016/j.commtr.2023.100091

Millan, J., Phakamad, B., Rhodes, S., & Tipon, C. (2022). *Instacart - Accessibility usability evaluation of grocery delivery website for the visually impaired.* https://static1.squarespace.com/static/61b27d1fa32231228c041e6e/t/61b7a9245380f5602fc75808/1639426341268/instacartreport.pdf

Morgan, B. (2020). Lasting changes to grocery shopping after Covid-19. *Forbes.* https://www.forbes.com/sites/blakemorgan/2020/12/14/3-lasting-changes-to-grocery-shopping-after-covid-19/?sh=3158c55754e7

Pan, S. L., Cui, M., & Qian, J. (2020). Information resource orchestration during the COVID-19 pandemic: A study of community lockdowns in China. *International Journal of Information Management*, *54*, 102143. Advance online publication. doi:10.1016/j.ijinfomgt.2020.102143 PMID:32394997

Pantano, E., Pizzi, G., Scarpi, D., & Dennis, C. (2020). Competing during a pandemic? Retailers' ups and downs during the COVID-19 outbreak. *Journal of Business Research*, *116*, 209–213. doi:10.1016/j.jbusres.2020.05.036 PMID:32501307

Rasheed, H. S. (2009). Contrasting e-commerce business models: Performance implications for small enterprises. *Journal of Developmental Entrepreneurship*, *14*(1), 89–101. doi:10.1142/S1084946709001168

Ratchford, B., Soysal, G., Zentner, A., & Gauri, D. K. (2022). Online and offline retailing: What we know and directions for future research. *Journal of Retailing*, *98*(1), 152–177. doi:10.1016/j.jretai.2022.02.007

Reardon, T., Belton, B., Liverpool-Tasie, L. S. O., Lu, L., Nuthalapati, C. S. R., Tasie, O., & Zilberman, D. (2021). E-commerce's fast-tracking diffusion and adaptation in developing countries. *Applied Economic Perspectives and Policy*, *43*(4), 1243–1259. doi:10.1002/aepp.13160

Reardon, T., Tomatis, F., & Pedersen, E. (2023). *Evolution of food e-commerce during the COVID-19 pandemic* [Investment brief]. Food and Agricultural Organization of the United States., doi:10.4060/cc3650en

Rigby, D. (2011). The future of shopping. *Harvard Business Review*. https://hbr.org/2011/12/the-future-of-shopping

Roggeveen, A. L., & Sethuraman, R. (2020). How the COVID-19 pandemic may change the world of retailing. *Journal of Retailing*, *96*(2), 169–171. doi:10.1016/j.jretai.2020.04.002

Sheth, J. (2020). Impact of Covid-19 on consumer behavior: Will the old habits return or die? *Journal of Business Research*, *117*, 280–283. doi:10.1016/j.jbusres.2020.05.059 PMID:32536735

Tyrväinen, O., & Karjaluoto, H. (2022). Online grocery shopping before and during the COVID-19 pandemic: A meta-analytical review. *Telematics and Informatics*, *71*, 101839. Advance online publication. doi:10.1016/j.tele.2022.101839 PMID:35607591

Unnikrishnan, A., & Figliozzi, M. (2020). *A study of the impact of COVID-19 on home delivery purchases and expenditures* [Working paper]. Portland State University. https://pdxscholar.library.pdx.edu/cengin_fac/557

Verdon, J. (2022, March 15). The pandemic changed how we shop for groceries, Adobe report shows. *Forbes*. https://www.forbes.com/sites/joanverdon/2022/03/15/the-pandemic-changed-how-we-shop-for-groceries-adobe-report-shows/?sh=1006da814bb1

Volpe, R., & Boland, M. A. (2022). The economic impacts of Walmart supercenters. *Annual Review of Resource Economics*, *14*(1), 43–62. doi:10.1146/annurev-resource-111820-032827

Wollenburg, J., Hübner, A., Kuhn, H., & Trautrims, A. (2018). From bricks-and-mortar to bricks-and-clicks: Logistics networks in omni-channel grocery retailing. *International Journal of Physical Distribution & Logistics Management*, *48*(4), 415–438. doi:10.1108/IJPDLM-10-2016-0290

Zehavi, G. (2019, April 16). Online grocery shopping: Past & present. *Medium*. https://gadzehavi.medium.com/online-grocery-shopping-past-present-ace5f21b9598

KEY TERMS AND DEFINITIONS

Online Grocery Shopping: The act of purchasing groceries through online platforms, often facilitated by click-and-collect or home delivery services. This method of shopping has gained popularity due to its convenience and accessibility, allowing consumers to shop from the comfort of their own homes.

Technology Acceptance Model (TAM): A theoretical model in information systems research that explains how users come to accept and use a technology.

Unified Theory of Acceptance and Use of Technology (UTAUT): A theoretical framework that aims to explain user intentions towards using an information system and subsequent usage behavior. This model is often used in research to understand consumer adoption of new technologies, such as e-commerce platforms.

Theory of Planned Behavior (TPB): A psychological theory that links beliefs and behavior. It suggests that human action is guided by three kinds of considerations: behavioral beliefs, normative beliefs, and control beliefs.

Meta-analysis: A statistical technique for combining the findings from independent studies to assess the overall trend of the research. It is often used in research to resolve inconsistencies among individual studies and to identify common factors or determinants.

E-commerce: A business model that involves transactions taking place on the internet. The term covers a wide range of businesses, from consumer-based retail sites to business exchanges trading goods and services between corporations.

Food Supply Chains: The network of all the individuals, organizations, resources, activities, and technology involved in the creation and sale of food products, from the delivery of seed and inputs to the production sectors to final delivery to the consumers.

Chapter 9
Review and the Use of PROMETHEE Methods in Marketing (Problems)

Theodore K. Tarnanidis
https://orcid.org/0000-0002-4836-3906
University of Macedonia, Greece

Jason Papathanasiou
University of Macedonia, Greece

Maro Vlachopoulou
University of Macedonia, Greece

Bertrand Mareschal
Université Libre de Bruxelles, Belgium

ABSTRACT

The method of PROMETHEE belongs to Multiple Criteria Decision Making (MCDM) techniques, which helps decision-makers to examine problems where there are multiple and conflicting criteria calculated in different parameters and units. Furthermore, they help people in assessing all the information included in a problem from a realistic and pragmatic viewpoint (Vincke, 1992).The next table shows a classification of the most widely used MCDM methods. According to relevant scholars (Triantaphyllou et al., 1998; Georgiadis et al., 2013) the general format of a PROMETHEE task involves the construction of the measurement analysis of the problem with the identification of relevant criteria and alternatives, the estimation of the relative importance and impact of the weights (i.e. statistical measures), and the final stage involves the decision of the best evaluations that comes from the ranking/assessment of each alternative.

DOI: 10.4018/978-1-6684-8868-3.ch009

1. INTRODUCTION

The method of PROMETHEE belongs to Multiple Criteria Decision Making (MCDM) techniques, which helps decision-makers to examine problems where there are multiple and conflicting criteria calculated in different parameters and units. Furthermore, they help people in assessing all the information included in a problem from a realistic and pragmatic viewpoint (Vincke, 1992).The next table shows a classification of the most widely used MCDM methods.

According to relevant scholars (Triantaphyllou et al., 1998; Georgiadis et al., 2013) the general format of a PROMETHEE task involves the construction of the measurement analysis of the problem with the identification of relevant criteria and alternatives, the estimation of the relative importance and impact of the weights (i.e. statistical measures), and the final stage involves the decision of the best evaluations that comes from the ranking/assessment of each alternative.

2. PROMETHEE II OVERVIEW AND DESCRIPTION

This section briefly describes PROMETHEE II, which is intended to provide a complete ranking of a finite set of feasible alternatives from the best to the worst. This method is fundamental to implement the other PROMETHEE methods and the majority of researchers have referred to this version of the PROMETHEE methods. The basic principle of PROMETHEE II is based on a pairwise comparison of alternatives along each recognized criterion. Alternatives are evaluated according to different criteria, which have to be maximized or minimized. The implementation of the PROMETHEE II requires the determination of the weight PROMETHEE II assumes that the decision-maker is able to weigh the criteria appropriately, at least when the number of criteria is not too large (Macharis et al., 2004). Additionally, it requires the selection of the preference function for each criterion, so to translate the difference between the evaluations obtained by two alternatives into a preference degree ranging from zero to one. In order to facilitate the selection of a specific preference function, Vincke and Brans (1985) proposed six basic types: (1) usual criterion, (2) U-shape criterion, (3) V-shape criterion, (4) level criterion, (5) V-shape with indifference criterion and (6) Gaussian criterion. These six types are particularly easy to define. For each criterion, the value of an indifference threshold, q; the value of a strict preference threshold, p; and the value of an intermediate value between p and q, s, has to be fixed (Brans and Mareschal, 1992). In each case, these parameters have a clear significance for the decision-maker. The procedure is started to determine deviations based on pair-wise comparisons. It is followed by using a relevant preference function for each criterion in Step 2, calculating global preference index in Step 3, and calculating positive and negative outranking flows for each alternative and partial ranking in Step 4. The procedure is come to an end with the calculation of net outranking flow for each alternative and complete ranking.

The PROMETHEE method includes the outranking evaluations, applying different mechanisms. It includes the PROMETHEE I for partial ranking of the alternatives and the PROMETHEE II for complete ranking of the alternatives. The specific mechanisms were initial built by Brans in 1982 at a conference organized at the University Laval, Quebec, Canada (Brans, 1982, Mareschal, 1986). Later on, it was included the mechanism of:

- PROMETHEE III for ranking based on interval,
- PROMETHEE IV for complete or partial ranking of the alternatives when the set of solutions is continuous,
- PROMETHEE V for problems with segmentation constraints (Brans and Mareschal,1992),
- PROMETHEE VI for the human brain representation (Brans and Mareschal, 1995),
- PROMETHEE GDSS for group decision- making (Macharis et al., 1998), and the
- Visual interactive module GAIA (Geometrical Analysis for Interactive Aid) for graphical representation were developed to help in more complicated decision-making situations (Mareschal & Brans, 1988; Brans and Mareschal,1994; Brans and Mareschal, 2005).

Figueira et al. (2004) has recently proposed two extended approaches on PROMETHEE, called as the PROMETHEE TRI for dealing with sorting problems and the PROMETHEE CLUSTER for nominal classification. All these various mechanisms have been applied various examinations. The success of the PROMETHEE methods is due to their mathematical properties (Brans and Mareschal, 2005).

Two PROMETHEE software packages, including PROMCALC and DECISION LAB, have been developed to facilitate the PROMETHEE process. PROMCALC was published by the authors of the method (Mareschal and Brans, 1986). It was provided for all types of multi- criteria problems, the PROMETHEE I, II, V, VI as well as the GAIA visual module. DECISION LAB, developed in collaboration with the Canadian company Visual Decision (Decision Lab, 2000, 1999), is the current software implementation of the PROMETHEE and GAIA methods. It replaces the PROMCALC software that the authors had previously developed. By using DECISION LAB, decision-makers can improve the quality and reliability of the decision-making processes, because of the structured procedure, accompanied by computational help, and the analytical aids (Geldermann and Zhang (2001).

Figure 1. Number of papers published per year from 1982 to 2020

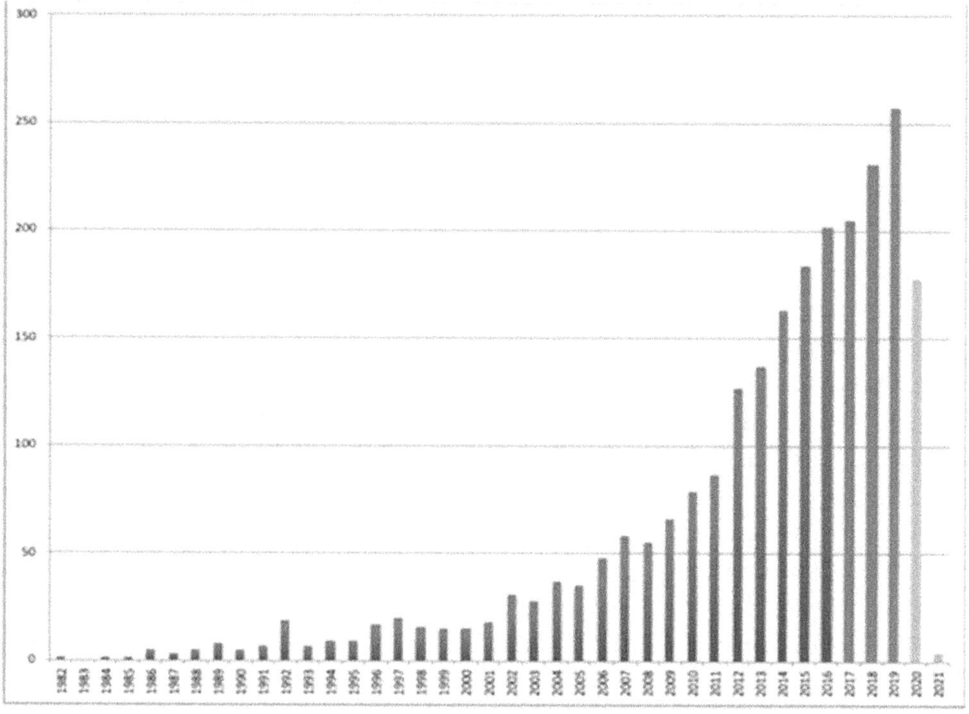

According to the website of Professor Mareschal (http://en.promethee-gaia.net/), the number of publications with the use of PROMETHEE is 2393 since September 2020 (next figure).

It can be seen that from the year of 2012 till 2020, there is an increase of the number of papers published. The majority of the published papers according to Mareschal website are related to applications of PROMETHEE in different fields, like

- 469 papers (19.6%) are related to services and/or public applications.
- 457 papers (19.1%) are related to environmental problems.
- 347 papers (14.5%) are related to industrial applications.
- 227 papers (9.5%) are related to energy.
- 153 papers (6.4%) are related to water.
- 124 papers (5.2%) are related to finance.
- 116 papers (4.8%) are related to transportation.
- 77 papers (3.2%) are related to procurement.
- 75 papers (3.1%) are related to health care.
- 30 papers (1.3%) are related to mining.

- 101 papers (4.2%) are related to other fields of application.

Finally, a large number of publications are made in the scientific fields of the environment, energy, water, public goods/services and health.

3. REVIEW OF MCDM AND PROMETHEE METHODS

MCDM methods have been used in different areas, like: water and waste management (Garcia -Garcia, 2022; Coban et al., 2018; Hadipour et al., 2015; Qin, et al., 2008); Chandrakar and Limje, 2018), engineering and computer industries for the selection of materials and other manufacturing processes (Sandström, 1985; Brown and Wright,1998; Ghaleb et al., 2020; Zhu et al., 2021), Economics/econometrics and finance (Zavadskas and Turski, 2011; Yıldız and Aybar, 2019; Zopounidis et al., 2015; Yuksel et al., 2018; Kowalski, et al., 2009), medicine and health sector (Frazão et al., 2018; Adunlin et al., 2015; Kahraman et al., 2020; Afshari and Khorsand, 2020;) education (Malik et al., 2021; Ayyildiz et al., 2022; Bhattacharyya and Chakraborty, 2014; Alias, et al., 2008), environmental science (Zavadskas et.al., 2014; Geldermann, et al., 2000; Vaillancourt and Waaub, 2004; Huang et al., 2011; Afrasiabi et al., 2022), and other researches in business, management and accounting. What is more, MCDM and PROMETHEE has been implemented in the analysis of agricultural- and environmental-related decision making, ranging from farm selection problems to management decision making.

Based on the above researches and according to recent systematic reviews implemented by other practitioners for the use of MCDA methods (i.e., Asadabadi et al., 2019; Namin et al., 2022), it is noticed that throughout the last decade the majority of the researchers were made in the scientific fields of engineering, computing, mathematics and decision-sciences. Furthermore, it should be mentioned that the evolution of the techniques are focusing on capturing the uncertainty factors of the decision-making tasks with the use of hybrid methods, like the modelling of human preferences and judgement (Rekik et al., 2016). However, MCDM is used more in Europe and USA, whereas it has not been widely examined in other continents, like the Australia and New Zealand (Hajkowicz, and Higgins, 2008; Kabir et al., 2014; Sotoudeh-Anvar, 2022).

In addition, decision-makers (DM) use MCDM methods in order to manage and solve complex decisions with multiple tasks and criteria defined (i.e. alternative choices, ranking and sorting evaluations). More explicitly, the MCDM methodologies (shown in table 1) provides to DMs accurate key steps/or paths for the examination of their objectives/goals. More and more, several authors examined various studies for the applicability of which tools are useful for the coherence in a pragmatic business context (Ishizaka and Siraj, 2018; Majumder et al., 2019; Cavallo et al., 2019). For example, complex techniques and methods are more appropriate for competitive industries/sectors, e.g. problems with production, location, supply chains, high tech and electric problems (Stoycheva et al., 2018; Fattoruso, 2022; Jacobides et al., 2015). Supplementary experiments with the use of MCDM methodologies were targeted to operational and management levels, such as lean processes and total quality directions (Mumani et al., 2022; Yahya et al., 2016; Zeynali et al., 2012).

Specifically, the method of the Analytic Hierarchy Process (AHP) is applicable to problems assessing the performance of resources and strategy planning. The method of ELECTRE helps in the evaluation of environmental management problems (i.e. energy, water, mobility and transportation). The MOORA has been successfully used to multi-attribute problems in the field of engineering, agriculture, and finance. The TOPSIS technique is best suited to problems related to supply chain management, manufacturing, human resources, and other soft managerial examinations. Fuzzy set theory is appropriate to complex evaluations with different weights and criteria (like in the field of construction-engineering, medical and economics).

Finally yet importantly, the PROMETHEE method examines the evaluation of the different parameters and criteria set by the decision maker, and thus is it is applicable to various fields like environmental, transportation, manufacturing, management, and marketing.

4. MARKETING PROBLEMS AND PROMETHEE

What is more, related to marketing problems, MCDM methods are applied for the selection of different products, where multiple criteria exist, and decision-makers have to manage conflicting goals, by analyzing the relevant criteria to the case examined (Baczkiewicz, 2022). The next table includes the methods applied for the selection of products.

We can see that MCDM methods have been successfully used in solving purchasing problems, i.e. of choosing different products with multiple criteria. However, according to our knowledge there is little on the application of MCDM to marketing problems, i.e., how to choose between approaches or techniques in analyzing the usefulness of the various processes in developing and assessing the impact of marketing strategies (like promotional techniques for campaigns). The MCDM process is generally similar for all approaches, but there are differences in the way the information on alternatives, criteria and relative significance of the criteria is elicited, specified and analyzed (Belton & Stewart 2002; Papathanasiou and Ploskas, 2018: Mareschal and Tsaples, 2021).

Table 1. MCDM methods in consumer products

Purchased problems	MCDM methods/concept
General Product/service development	Fuzzy numbers, Entropy theory (Chen and Hung, 2021; Wang et al., 2020), BIM, Multi-attribute Utility Theory (El-Sawalhi, and Agha, 2017; Kumar and Tiwari, 2021)
General consumer choices	COMET, TOPSIS, VIKOR and PROMETHEE II (Paradowski et., 2021; Brans and Vincke, 1985), Hierachical Scaling (Saaty, 1977), Sentiment analysis (Kumar and Parimala, 2020)
Car selection	AHP and TOPSIS (Ulkhaq et al., 2018)
Electric vehicles,car selection	COMET (Sałabun and Karczmarczyk, 2018; Shekhovtsov and Sałabun, 2020), PROMETHEE II (Watróbski et al., 2017; Ziemba, 2020)
Electric scooter	Fuzzy AHP, TOPSIS, and COMET (Kizielewicz and Dobryakova, 2020),Fuzzy AHP-MABAC (Biswas and Das, 2019; Biswas and Saha, 2019)ELECTRE III (Kubik, (2022)
Hydrid car	Fuzzy TOPSIS (Khan et al., 2020)
Electric bike	COMET (Kaczyńska et al., 2022; Sałabun, et al., 2019), TOPSIS and VIKOR (Shekhovtsov et al., 2020)
Laptop	MULTIMOORA and MOOSRA (Adalı and Isık, 2017), Fuzzy AHP (Mitra, et sl., 2019), DEMATEL and Fuzzy AHP (Çakır and Pekkaya, 2020), TOPSIS and MOORA (Kecek, and Demirag, 2016), AHP and TOPSIS (Goswami and Behera, 2021a), TOPSIS (Kalyani et al., 2016; Kusnadi and Kurniawan, 2017), AHP, PROMETHEE I, PROMETHEE II (Goswami, 2020)
Mobile phone	AHP-COPRAS and AHP-ARAS (Goswami and Mitra, 2020), Fuzzy TOPSIS (Büyüközkan and Güleryüz, 2016; Saqlain et al., 2020), AHP and TOPSIS (Singh et al., 2020), Fuzzy ARAS and TOPSIS [Rani et al., 2019], TOPSIS and MOORA (Kumar et al., 2020), Fuzzy AHP and PROMETHEE II (Goswami and Behera, 2021a; Mohd et al., 2019), PROMETHEE (Samantraj et al., 2020)
Promotion/advertising content	COMET (Lewandowska et al., 2019;Multiple Regression Analysis (Tjahjadi and Hendijani, 2020; Lammers, 2020)
Football, players evaluation	COMET, TOPSIS (Sałabun et al., 2020; Palczewski, and Sałabun, 2019)
Power production	Fuzzy AHP (Nieto -Morote, 2011; Bottani, 2008)

From a more recent scanning of the literature on the use of PROMETHE, we identified 2634 papers until the end of 2022 from different reliable sources, like the ScienceDirect, Scopus, Google Scholar, Research Gate, EBSCO, SpringerLink, DOA (Directory of Open Access Journals), and other published works from members of the PROMETHEE community. Surprisingly we found that more than half publications were during the last 7 years, around 1300 papers. By examining further the country distribution of publications, we found seven (7) countries out of thirty one (31) with minimum number of citation 5 have produced more than 100 papers.

Publication per country (31 countries, 4 clusters). 2181 documents, minimum number of citation 5

Figure 2. Geographical distributions

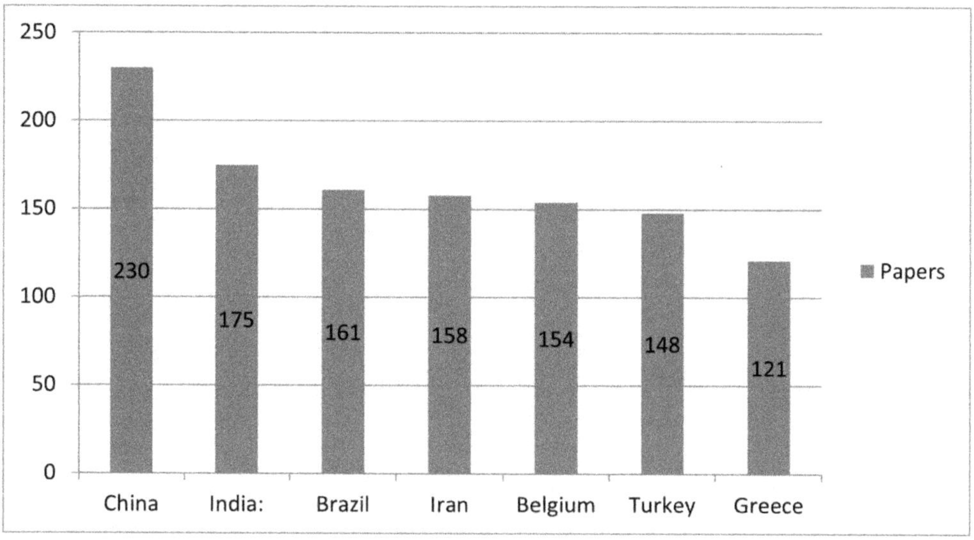

Figure 3. Citations per countries

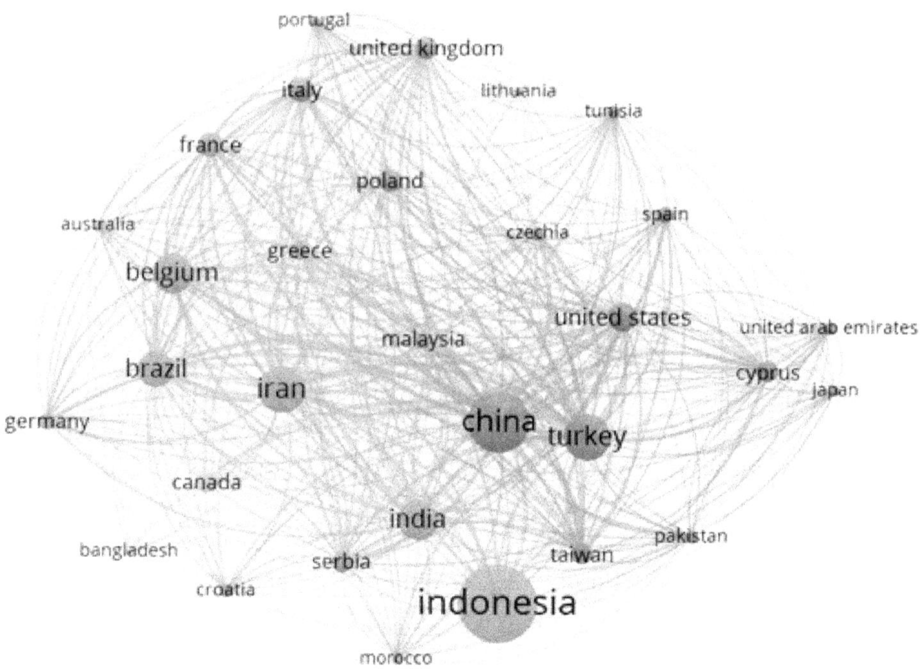

Figure 4. Key steps of the systematic review process

Publication years:	2021-2022
Citation years:	1 (2021-2022)
Papers:	241
Citations:	324
Cites/year:	324.00
Cites/paper:	1.34
Authors/paper:	3.08
h-index:	9
g-index:	12
hI,norm:	5
hI,annual:	5.00
hA-index:	9

Publication per country (31 countries, 4 clusters). 2181 documents, minimum number of citation 5

There is still a lot of activity related to PROMETHEE into management and marketing decision problems. Next, we concentrate the systematic review process for synthesizing and analyzing the data on published works for the last two years, 2021-2022. The process was accomplished by collecting relevant data, analyzing the data and reporting the results (Tranfield et al., 2003; Becheikh et al., 2006). The review process is shown in the next figure (Figure 4) and was based on specific keywords and themes related to PROMETHEE, i.e. social media, marketing, consumer behavior, purchase, digital marketing

The bounding of search criteria included an initial ad hoc reading of abstracts that focus on the use of PROMETHEE II method with a combination of other marketing concepts, such as social media strategies and campaigns, advertising strategies. As exclusion criteria included the absence of marketing strategies with the use of social media and other digital marketing tools. We found around 201 Journal publications (some are in European Journal of Operational Research-23, Expert Systmes wih Applications-13, Journal of Intelligent and Expert Systems-12, Sustainability-14, International Journal of Engineering and Engineering Management-14, International Journal of Multicriteria Decision-Making-29, Research Papers in Economics-17, Journal of Physics-12, Advances in Intelligent Systems and Computings), 14 conference proceedings (Arnallynda et al., 2022: Sypplier selection, fuzzy-AHP, PROMETHEE; Khan and Purohit, 2022: Webservice domain, PROMETHEE and TOPSIS critique; Guler et al., 2021: Wind power plant, TOPSIS and PROMETHEE; Tarnanidis, 2021: Social media campaign, PROMETHEE II) and 26 book chapters (Bertrand and Tsaples, 2021: The present and future of PROMETHEE; Angitha and Supriya, 2022: Ranking of educational institution, AHP-PROMETHEE; Mirzael et al., 2021: Management and Prevention of Covid 19, Fuzzy PROMETHEE; Jitesh and Thakkar, 2021: Analyzing PROMETHEE; Bareto et al., 2021: Decision making in stroke diagnosis with PROMETHE)

5. REFERENCES

Lewandowska, A., Jankowski, J., Sałabun, W., & Wątróbski, J. (2019). Multicriteria selection of online advertising content for the habituation effect reduction. In Intelligent Information and Database Systems: 11th Asian Conference, ACIIDS 2019, Yogyakarta, Indonesia, April 8–11, 2019 [Springer International Publishing.]. *Proceedings*, *11*(Part II), 499–509.

Adunlin, G., Diaby, V., & Xiao, H. (2015). Application of multicriteria decision analysis in health care: A systematic review and bibliometric analysis. *Health Expectations*, *18*(6), 1894–1905. doi:10.1111/hex.12287 PMID:25327341

Afrasiabi, A., Tavana, M., & Di Caprio, D. (2022). An extended hybrid fuzzy multi-criteria decision model for sustainable and resilient supplier selection. *Environmental Science and Pollution Research International*, *29*(25), 37291–37314. doi:10.100711356-021-17851-2 PMID:35050472

Afshari, A., & Khorsand, M. (2020). APPLICATION OF MULTI CRITERIA DECISION MAKING IN. *Health Care*.

Alias, M. A., Hashim, S. Z. M., & Samsudin, S. (2008). Multi criteria decision making and its applications: A literature review. *Jurnal Teknologi Maklumat*, *20*(2), 129–152.

Asadabadi, M. R., Chang, E., & Saberi, M. (2019). Are MCDM methods useful? A critical review of Analytic Hierarchy Process (AHP) and Analytic Network Process (ANP). *Cogent Engineering*, *6*(1), 1623153. doi:10.1080/23311916.2019.1623153

Ayyildiz, E., Murat, M., Imamoglu, G., & Kose, Y. (2022). A novel hybrid MCDM approach to evaluate universities based on student perspective. *Scientometrics*. Advance online publication. doi:10.100711192-022-04534-z PMID:36339521

Bączkiewicz, A., & Wątróbski, J. (2022). A Multi-Criteria Approach to Sustainable Energy Management Evaluation Focusing on Renewable Energy Sources. *Procedia Computer Science*, *207*, 4640–4650. doi:10.1016/j.procs.2022.09.528

Becheikh, N., Landry, R., & Amara, N. (2006). Lessons from innovation empirical studies in the manufacturing sector: A systematic review of the literature from 1993–2003. *Technovation*, *26*(5), 644–664. doi:10.1016/j.technovation.2005.06.016

Belton, V., & Stewart, T. (2002). *Multiple Criteria Decision Analysis: An Integrated Approach.*

Bhattacharyya, A., & Chakraborty, S. (2014). A DEA-TOPSIS-based approach for performance evaluation of Indian technical institutes. *Decision Science Letters, 3*(3), 397–410. doi:10.5267/j.dsl.2014.2.003

Biswas, T., & Saha, P. (2019). Selection of commercially available scooters by new MCDM method. *International Journal of Data and Network Science, 3*, 137–144. doi:10.5267/j.ijdns.2018.12.002

Biswas, T. K., & Das, M. C. (2019). Selection of Commercially Available Electric Vehicle using Fuzzy AHP-MABAC. *Journal of The Institution of Engineers (India): Series C, 100*(3), 531-537. doi:10.1007/s40032-018-0481-3

Bottani, E. (2008). An adapted multi-criteria approach to suppliers and products selection-An application oriented to lead-time reduction. In (pp. 763-781).

Brans, J. P. (1982). L'ingénièrie de la décision; Elaboration d'instruments d'aide à la décision. La méthode PROMETHEE. In R. Nadeau & M. Landry (Eds.), *L'aide à la décision: Nature, Instruments et Perspectives d'Avenir* (pp. 183–213). Presses de l'Université Laval.

Brans, J. P., & Mareschal, B. (2005). Promethee Methods. In *Multiple Criteria Decision Analysis: State of the Art Surveys* (pp. 163–186). Springer New York. doi:10.1007/0-387-23081-5_5

Brans, J. P., & Vincke, P. (1985). A Preference Ranking Organisation Method: (The PROMETHEE Method for Multiple Criteria Decision-Making). *Management Science, 31*(6), 647–656. doi:10.1287/mnsc.31.6.647

Brown, S. M., & Wright, P. K. (1998). A progress report on the manufacturing analysis service, an internet-based reference tool. *Journal of Manufacturing Systems, 17*(5), 389–398. doi:10.1016/S0278-6125(98)80028-9

Cavallo, A., Ghezzi, A., & Balocco, R. (2019). Entrepreneurial ecosystem research: Present debates and future directions. *The International Entrepreneurship and Management Journal, 15*(4), 1291–1321. doi:10.100711365-018-0526-3

Chandrakar, R., & Limje, S. (2018). *A hybrid of QFD and AHP-TOPSIS for Durg dumping waste projects.*

Chen, C.-T., & Hung, W.-Z. (2021). A MCDM Method with Linguistic Variables and Intuitionistic Fuzzy Numbers to Evaluate Product Development Projects. *Int. J. Comput. Intell. Syst., 14*(1), 935–945. doi:10.2991/ijcis.d.210222.003

Coban, A., Ertis, I. F., & Cavdaroglu, N. A. (2018). Municipal solid waste management via multi-criteria decision making methods: A case study in Istanbul, Turkey. *Journal of Cleaner Production, 180*, 159–167. doi:10.1016/j.jclepro.2018.01.130

El-Sawalhi, N. I., & Agha, O. E. (2017). *Multi-Attribute Utility Theory for Selecting an Appropriate Procurement Method in the Construction Projects.*

Fattoruso, G. (2022). Multi-Criteria Decision Making in Production Fields: A Structured Content Analysis and Implications for Practice. *Journal of Risk and Financial Management, 15*(10), 431. doi:10.3390/jrfm15100431

Frazão, T. D. C., Camilo, D. G. G., Cabral, E. L. S., & Souza, R. P. (2018). Multicriteria decision analysis (MCDA) in health care: A systematic review of the main characteristics and methodological steps. *BMC Medical Informatics and Decision Making, 18*(1), 90. doi:10.118612911-018-0663-1 PMID:30382826

Garcia-Garcia, G. (2022). Using Multi-Criteria Decision-Making to optimise solid waste management. *Current Opinion in Green and Sustainable Chemistry, 37*, 100650. doi:10.1016/j.cogsc.2022.100650

Geldermann, J., Spengler, T., & Rentz, O. (2000). Fuzzy outranking for environmental assessment. Case study: Iron and steel making industry. *Fuzzy Sets and Systems, 115*(1), 45–65. doi:10.1016/S0165-0114(99)00021-4

Georgiadis, D. R., Mazzuchi, T. A., & Sarkani, S. (2013). Using multi criteria decision making in analysis of alternatives for selection of enabling technology. *Systems Engineering, 16*(3), 287–303. doi:10.1002ys.21233

Ghaleb, A. M., Kaid, H., Alsamhan, A., Mian, S. H., & Hidri, L. (2020). Assessment and Comparison of Various MCDM Approaches in the Selection of Manufacturing Process. [NA.]. *Advances in Materials Science and Engineering, 2020*, 2020. doi:10.1155/2020/4039253

Hadipour, A., Rajaee, T., & Hadipour, V., & seidirad, s. (. (2015). Multi-criteria decision-making model for wastewater reuse application: A case study from Iran. *Desalination and Water Treatment*. Advance online publication. doi:10.1080/194 43994.2015.1060905

Hajkowicz, S., & Higgins, A. (2008). A comparison of multiple criteria analysis techniques for water resource management. *European Journal of Operational Research, 184*(1), 255–265. doi:10.1016/j.ejor.2006.10.045

Huang, I. B., Keisler, J., & Linkov, I. (2011). Multi-criteria decision analysis in environmental sciences: Ten years of applications and trends. *The Science of the Total Environment*, *409*(19), 3578–3594. doi:10.1016/j.scitotenv.2011.06.022 PMID:21764422

Ishizaka, A., & Siraj, S. (2018). Are multi-criteria decision-making tools useful? An experimental comparative study of three methods. *European Journal of Operational Research*, *264*(2), 462–471. doi:10.1016/j.ejor.2017.05.041

Jacobides, M., MacDuffie, J., & Tae, C. (2015). Agency, Structure, and the Dominance of OEMs: Change and Stability in the Automotive Sector. *Strategic Management Journal*, *37*(9), 1942–1967. Advance online publication. doi:10.1002mj.2426

Kabir, G. (2014). A review of multi-criteria decision-making methods for infrastructure management. In (pp. 1176-1210). doi:10.1080/15732479.2013.795978

Kabir, G., Sadiq, R., & Tesfamariam, S. (2014). A review of multi-criteria decision-making methods for infrastructure management. *Structure and Infrastructure Engineering*, *10*(9), 1176–1210. doi:10.1080/15732479.2013.795978

Kaczyńska, A., Gandotra, N., & Sałabun, W. (2022). A new approach to dealing with interval data in the TOPSIS method. *Procedia Computer Science*, *207*, 4545–4555. doi:10.1016/j.procs.2022.09.518

Kahraman, C., Onar, S. C., ÖZTAYşI, B., ŞEKER, Ş., & KARAşAN, A. (2020). Integration of fuzzy AHP with other fuzzy multicriteria methods: a state of the art survey. *Journal of Multiple-Valued Logic & Soft Computing, 35.*

Khan, F., Ali, Y., & Khan, A. U. (2020). Sustainable hybrid electric vehicle selection in the context of a developing country. *Air Quality, Atmosphere & Health*, *13*(4), 489–499. doi:10.100711869-020-00812-y

Kizielewicz, B., & Dobryakova, L. (2020). How to choose the optimal single-track vehicle to move in the city? Electric scooters study case. *Procedia Computer Science*, *176*, 2243–2253. doi:10.1016/j.procs.2020.09.274

Kowalski, A. F., Hawley, S. L., Hilton, E. J., Becker, A. C., West, A. A., Bochanski, J. J., & Sesar, B. (2009). M Dwarfs in Sloan Digital Sky Survey Stripe 82: Photometric Light Curves and Flare Rate Analysis. *The Astronomical Journal*, *138*(2), 633–648. doi:10.1088/0004-6256/138/2/633

Kubik, A. (2022). Selection of an Electric Scooter for Shared Mobility Services Using Multicriteria Decision Support Methods. *Energies*, *15*(23), 8903. doi:10.3390/en15238903

Kumar, G., & Parimala, N. (2020). A weighted sum method MCDM approach for recommending product using sentiment analysis. *International Journal of Business Information Systems*, *35*(2), 185–203. doi:10.1504/IJBIS.2020.110172

Lammers, R. (2020). *Feeling targeted in a digital era: a study about the influence of online behavioral targeting on consumer attitudes.* University of Twente, Lewandowska,

Majumder, P., Majumder, M., Saha, A. K., Sarkar, K., & Nath, S. (2019). Real time reliability monitoring of hydro-power plant by combined cognitive decision-making technique. *International Journal of Energy Research*, *43*(9), 4912–4939. doi:10.1002/er.4530

Malik, D. A. A., Yusof, Y., & Khalif, K. M. N. K. (2021). A view of MCDM application in education. *Journal of Physics: Conference Series*, *1988*(1), 012063. doi:10.1088/1742-6596/1988/1/012063

Mareschal, B. (1986). Stochastic multicriteria decision-making under uncertainty. *European Journal of Operational Research*, *26*(1), 58–64. doi:10.1016/0377-2217(86)90159-1

Mareschal, B., & Brans, J. P. (1988). Geometrical representations for MCDA. *European Journal of Operational Research*, *34*(1), 69–77. doi:10.1016/0377-2217(88)90456-0

Mareschal, B., & Tsaples, G. (2021). The History and Future of PROMETHEE. In J. Papathanasiou, P. Zaraté, & J. Freire de Sousa (Eds.), EURO Working Group on DSS: A Tour of the DSS Developments Over the Last 30 Years (pp. 259-272). Cham: Springer International Publishing. doi:10.1007/978-3-030-70377-6_14

Mumani, A. A., Magableh, G. M., & Mistarihi, M. Z. (2022). Decision making process in lean assessment and implementation: A review. *Management Review Quarterly*, *72*(4), 1089–1128. doi:10.100711301-021-00222-z

Namin, F. S., Ghadi, A., & Saki, F. (2022). A literature review of Multi Criteria Decision-Making (MCDM) towards mining method selection (MMS). *Resources Policy*, *77*, 102676. doi:10.1016/j.resourpol.2022.102676

Nieto-Morote, A. (2011). A fuzzy ahp multi-criteria decision-making approach applied to combined cooling, heating, and power production systems. In (pp. 497-517). doi:10.1142/S0219622011004427

Palczewski, K., & Sałabun, W. (2019). Identification of the football teams assessment model using the COMET method. *Procedia Computer Science*, *159*, 2491–2501. doi:10.1016/j.procs.2019.09.424

Papathanasiou, J., & Ploskas, N. (2018). *Multiple Criteria Decision Aid: Methods, Examples and Python Implementations*. Springer International Publishing. doi:10.1007/978-3-319-91648-4

Paradowski, B., Bączkiewicz, A., & Watrąbski, J. (2021). Towards proper consumer choices - MCDM based product selection. *Procedia Computer Science*, *192*, 1347–1358. doi:10.1016/j.procs.2021.08.138

Rekik, R., Kallel, I., & Casillas, J. (2016). *Using Multiple Criteria Decision Making Approaches to Assess the Quality of Web Sites*.

Saaty, T. L. (1977). A scaling method for priorities in hierarchical structures. *Journal of Mathematical Psychology*, *15*(3), 234–281. doi:10.1016/0022-2496(77)90033-5

Sałabun, W., & Karczmarczyk, A. (2018). Using the COMET Method in the Sustainable City Transport Problem: An Empirical Study of the Electric Powered Cars. *Procedia Computer Science*, *126*, 2248–2260. doi:10.1016/j.procs.2018.07.224

Sałabun, W., Palczewski, K., & Wątróbski, J. (2019). Multicriteria Approach to Sustainable Transport Evaluation under Incomplete Knowledge: Electric Bikes Case Study. *Sustainability (Basel)*, *11*(12), 3314. doi:10.3390u11123314

Sałabun, W., Shekhovtsov, A., Pamučar, D., Wątróbski, J., Kizielewicz, B., Więckowski, J., Bozanić, D., Urbaniak, K., & Nyczaj, B. (2020). A Fuzzy Inference System for Players Evaluation in Multi-Player Sports: The Football Study Case. *Symmetry*, *12*(12), 2029. doi:10.3390ym12122029

Sandström, R. (1985). An approach to systematic materials selection. *Materials & Design*, *6*(6), 328–338. doi:10.1016/0261-3069(85)90018-4

Shekhovtsov, A., Kozlov, V., Nosov, V., & Sałabun, W. (2020). Efficiency of methods for determining the relevance of criteria in sustainable transport problems: A comparative case study. *Sustainability (Basel)*, *12*(19), 7915. doi:10.3390u12197915

Shekhovtsov, A., & Sałabun, W. (2020). A comparative case study of the VIKOR and TOPSIS rankings similarity. *Procedia Computer Science*, *176*, 3730–3740. doi:10.1016/j.procs.2020.09.014

Stoycheva, S., Marchese, D., Paul, C., Padoan, S., Juhmani, A., & Linkov, I. (2018). Multi-criteria decision analysis framework for sustainable manufacturing in automotive industry. *Journal of Cleaner Production*, *187*, 257–272. doi:10.1016/j.jclepro.2018.03.133

Tjahjadi, J., & Hendijani, R. (2020). Customer's Perception Of Compulsory-View Advertising On Youtube And Its Effect On Their Purchasing Behavior. [IJIRAS]. *International Journal Of Innovative Research And Advanced Studies*, *7*(1), 103–108.

Tranfield, D., Denyer, D., & Smart, P. (2003). Towards a Methodology for Developing Evidence-Informed Management Knowledge by Means of Systematic Review. *British Journal of Management*, *14*(3), 207–222. doi:10.1111/1467-8551.00375

Triantaphyllou, E., Shu, B., Sanchez, S. N., & Ray, T. (1998). Multi-criteria decision making: an operations research approach. Encyclopedia of electrical and electronics engineering, 15(1998), 175-186.

Ulkhaq, M. M., Wijayanti, W. R., Zain, M., Baskara, E., & Leonita, W. (2018). *Combining the AHP and TOPSIS to evaluate car selection.* Paper presented at the HP3C. 10.1145/3195612.3195628

Vaillancourt, K., & Waaub, J.-P. (2004). Equity in international greenhouse gases abatement scenarios: A multicriteria approach. *European Journal of Operational Research*, *153*(2), 489–505. doi:10.1016/S0377-2217(03)00170-X

Vincke, P. (1992). *Multicriteria decision aid*. Wiley.

Wang, Z., Zhang, S., Qiu, L., Gu, Y., & Zhou, H. (2020). A low-carbon-orient product design schemes MCDM method hybridizing interval hesitant fuzzy set entropy theory and coupling network analysis. *Soft Computing*, *24*(7), 5389–5408. doi:10.100700500-019-04296-6

Wątróbski, J., Małecki, K., Iwan, S., Karczmarczyk, A., & Thompson, R. (2017). Multi-Criteria Analysis of Electric Vans for City Logistics. *Sustainability (Basel)*, *9*(8), 1453. doi:10.3390u9081453

Yahya, K., Boussabaine, H., & Alzaed, A. N. (2016). Using life cycle assessment for estimating environmental impacts and eco-costs from the metal waste in the construction industry. *Management of Environmental Quality*, *27*(2), 227–244. doi:10.1108/MEQ-09-2014-0137

Yıldız, H., & Aybar, A. S. (2019). *ReseaRches in economics, econometRics & Finance*. IJOPEC PUBLICATION.

Yuksel, S., Dinçer, H., & Emir, S. (2018). Analysis of service innovation performance in Turkish banking sector using a combining method of fuzzy MCDM and text mining. *MANAS Sosyal Araştırmalar Dergisi, 7*(3).

Zavadskas, E. K., & Turskis, Z. (2011). Multiple criteria decision making (MCDM) methods in economics: An overview. *Technological and Economic Development of Economy, 17*(2), 397–427. doi:10.3846/20294913.2011.593291

Zavadskas, E. K., Turskis, Z., & Kildienė, S. (2014). State of art surveys of overviews on MCDM/MADM methods. *Technological and Economic Development of Economy, 20*(1), 165–179. doi:10.3846/20294913.2014.892037

Zeynali, M., Aghdaie, M., Rezaeiniya, N., & Sarfaraz, H. (2012). A hybrid fuzzy multiple criteria decision making (MCDM) approach to combination of materials selection. *African Journal of Business Management, 6*(45), 11171–11178. doi:10.5897/AJBM11.2022

Zhu, X., Meng, X., & Zhang, M. (2021). Application of multiple criteria decision making methods in construction: a systematic literature review. *Journal of Civil Engineering and Management, 27*(6), 372–403. doi:10.3846/jcem.2021.15260

Ziemba, P. (2020). Multi-Criteria Stochastic Selection of Electric Vehicles for the Sustainable Development of Local Government and State Administration Units in Poland. *Energies, 13*(23), 6299. doi:10.3390/en13236299

Zopounidis, C., Galariotis, E., Doumpos, M., Sarri, S., & Andriosopoulos, K. (2015). Multiple criteria decision aiding for finance: An updated bibliographic survey. *European Journal of Operational Research, 247*(2), 339–348. doi:10.1016/j.ejor.2015.05.032

Chapter 10
Social Media Adoption by the Greek Dairy Industry

Sotiris Karetsos
https://orcid.org/0000-0002-3679-3896
Agricultural University of Athens, Greece

Nikolaos Zafeirakopoulos
Agricultural University of Athens, Greece

Evi Papadopoulou
Agricultural University of Athens, Greece

Constantina Costopoulou
Agricultural University of Athens, Greece

ABSTRACT

Social media have become an important part of modern everyday life and are used for various purposes such as communication and interaction, content sharing, brand awareness, customer engagement, and market research. Numerous businesses employ them as marketing tools, adopting various strategies to achieve their goals. The objective of this chapter is to investigate the social media adoption by the dairy industry in Greece since the last years it has been hit hard by the COVID-19 pandemic and the energy crisis. More specifically, this chapter provides a literature review of social media in dairy industry and examines the digital presence of Greek dairy companies. Next, it analyses data from social media usage of 55 dairy companies in correspondence to their annual turnover for 2022. The results indicate that dairy companies can enhance their business outcomes by leveraging social media more effectively to harness their positive influence.

DOI: 10.4018/978-1-6684-8868-3.ch010

INTRODUCTION

Advances in digital technology have brought new challenges for businesses operating in various business sectors. Companies have adopted contemporary ways of doing business and promoting their activities. According to literature (Lin et. al., 2020; Klos et. al., 2020), modern businesses attempt to reinforce their digital presence to increase the business' credibility and to build their reputation. The term "digital presence" refers to the online business appearance, and regards several channels such as website, social media profiles, e-commerce platforms, mobile apps, email marketing, online advertising, search engine ranking, and user reviews and ratings. Gani and Faroque (2021) state that digital presence is considered among the top businesses' priorities aiming to attract more customers and increase their potential in the rapidly changing and evolving market trends. Social media marketing is a specific aspect of digital presence that focuses on using social media platforms (e.g., Facebook, Instagram, YouTube) to attract and engage customers, promote products, and enhance brand awareness.

Social media platforms have become very popular and have been adopted massively by individuals of all age categories. They could be defined as interactive media technologies that facilitate the creation and sharing of information, ideas, interests, and other forms of expression through virtual communities and networks (Felix et. al., 2017). However, social media is not only a communication tool for individuals but also for businesses that have realized their potential and started adopting them as an important part of their marketing strategies leading to a constant rise in social networking that becomes stronger every day (Dwivedi et. al., 2021). Businesses have increasingly adopted social media for various marketing activities such as branding, market research, customer relationship management, service provision, and sales promotion (Dewnarain et. al., 2018). Moreover, social media are used as a source of information and spread of knowledge changing people's views and opinions. Currently, they belong among the most important business marketing strategies and help to create new business opportunities, develop a stronger market position, or modify consumer's behavior (Smith et. al., 2015). Therefore, social media platforms will need to constantly evolve their strategies to meet the demands of both consumers and marketers.

By leveraging various social media tools, marketers can build relations in real-time, creating a reliable image by implementing a successful social media strategy that has many characteristics. Firstly, it aims to connect with potential customers, it invites them to engage and interact by making interesting and attractive posts. This approach strengthens existing bonds and creates opportunities for new connections. Moreover, consistent engagement with the customers improves the value of the brand and the customer experience. Consistency is another vital aspect of an effective social media strategy. It requires following a regular schedule of postings and giving timely responses to the audience's replies and comments. Unexpected changes in the posting frequency can lead to questions and uncertainty among followers. However, if there is a valid reason for the change, transparent communication can help mitigate any concerns and maintain trust with the audience. Such elements can create a more convincing and effective online presence, attracting and retaining a loyal and enthusiastic customer base (Olson et. al., 2021).

One of the fast-moving consumer goods industries is the dairy industry holding a key position in the food sector. Specifically, statistical data of the Greek dairy industry shows that the first half of 2022, 331,730 tons of cow milk delivered, down from 346,504 tons during the first half of 2021, a 4.26% drop. The number of dairy farmers also keeps steadily decreasing, from 2,160 in 2021 to less than 1,900 since April 2022. Similar reductions are noticed in other types of milk, namely sheep and goat milk. Specifically, deliveries of sheep's milk have fallen to 517,840 tons from 527,784, a 1.88% drop, while goat's milk deliveries slumped 5.62%, from 120,380 tons in the first half of 2021 to 113,606 in 2022. Scarcity and rising costs have boosted producer prices. In June 2022, the producer price for cow's milk was 0.51€ per liter, up from 0.38€, or 34%, from a year earlier; for sheep's milk, prices rose 30%, from 0.93€ per liter to 1.21€; for goat's milk, from 0.58€ to 0.56€, or 30%. Both sheep and goat milk producer prices are at historical highs. As far as it regards the consumers, according to the Greek statistics authority, the price of milk has risen 10.55% since early 2022 and 15.1% year-on-year; cheeses are on average up 15% and 19%, respectively; yogurt is 7% higher than in early 2022 (ELGO, 2023).

The objective of this chapter is to investigate the social media adoption by the dairy industry in Greece. The dairy industry has been studied since in the last three years it has been hit hard by the COVID-19 pandemic restrictions and the energy crisis. The pandemic has heavily affected the dairy industry with disruption and difficulties of moving milk within the supply chains, worker shortages, and lack of operating capital (Wang et. al., 2020). Additionally, the dairy industry faces higher energy and packaging costs, and dairy farmers cope with higher energy and animal feed costs. The remainder of this chapter is structured as follows: Section 2 provides a literature review on social media marketing in dairy industry, revealing an existing gap in the literature from the business side. In this light, Section 3 proposes a methodology used to identify social media adoption by the Greek dairy companies using a social media analytics tool, namely the Fanpage Karma. Finally, Section 5 provides the conclusions along with the limitations of the study.

1. LITERATURE REVIEW

Social media platforms have emerged as powerful marketing tools for companies to connect with consumers, promote their products, and engage in meaningful interactions. In order to acquire a comprehensive overview of the strategies, effectiveness, and challenges faced by dairy companies in their social media marketing efforts, a literature review was conducted. This review is based on the basic principles of the PRISMA guidelines and aims at providing valuable insights into the utilization of social media by the dairy industry (Polanco-Diges and Debasa, 2020; Page et al., 2021). In this light, the research questions addressed through this literature review were:

RQ1: How many publications have been published from 2019 until mid-2023, regarding social media in the dairy industry?
RQ2: How many publications have been published from 2019 until mid-2023, regarding social media data analytics in the dairy industry?

In order to answer the above research question, this review includes the following items: eligibility criteria, information sources and search strategy, study selection, and results. These items are further described, as follows.

Eligibility criteria: The eligibility criteria for this review were established as follows: Inclusion criteria: i) published original research and review articles on social media in dairy industry, ii) articles issued from 2019 until mid-2023; Exclusion criteria: i) manuscripts written in a language other than English, ii) essays and conference proceedings, iii) books or book chapters, and iv) editorial matter.

Information sources and search strategy: The academic research databases Scopus and Web of Science were searched using relevant keywords related to social media and dairy industry, on July 2, 2023. The databases have been searched with appropriate keywords and using operators (i.e., AND, OR) to produce the most accurate results (Table 1).The following search criteria were inputted into both databases: ("social media" OR "data analytics" OR "digital marketing") AND ("dairy products" OR "dairy industry" OR "dairy").For the Scopus database, the search criteria were title, abstract, and keywords. Similarly, for the Web of Science database, the search was conducted using the "topic" option that means searching title, abstract and keywords (defined by the authors and "keywords plus").

Study selection: After the database search stage, a three-step procedure was employed in order to review all identified articles based on the predefined eligibility criteria: This process involved sequentially evaluating: (i) the title, (ii) the

Table 1. Terms used in the databases

Database	Terms used			Filtered by	Fields
Scopus	Social media	AND	Dairy product	Articles	Title
Web of Science	OR data analytics		OR dairy industry	2019-mid 2023	Abstract
	OR digital marketing		OR dairy	English	Keywords

abstract, and (iii) the full text of each article. Two of the authors participated in this three-step procedure reviewing the articles.

Scopus Database Results

According to the established eligibility criteria the results show 83 articles. Then, the results limited to the following research categories: Agricultural and Biological Sciences (35 articles), Business, Management and Accounting (8), Environmental Science (7), Social Sciences (7), Computer Science (0), Engineering (0), Decision Sciences (0), while the following categories were excluded: Medicine, Nursing, Biochemistry, Genetics and Molecular Biology, Veterinary, Psychology, Health Professions, Pharmacology, Toxicology and Pharmaceutics, Immunology and Microbiology, Energy, Neuroscience, Mathematics, Earth and Planetary Sciences, Chemical Engineering, Arts and Humanities. Finally, the total number was 53 articles (it must be noted that four articles fall in more than one category). Next, a more detailed review was carried out in accordance with the three-step procedure. As a result of this procedure, the dataset was reduced to a total of 8 articles (Figure 1). It is noteworthy that searching the Scopus database without time restriction reveals 143 documents, with 100 of them being articles published in journals, and 98 of those articles in the English language. This fact shows the growing interest of the research community in this particular field in recent years.

Web of Science Database Results

Likewise, according to the aforementioned eligibility criteria the results show 58 articles. Then, the results limited to the following research categories: Agriculture (21 articles), Nutrition Dietetics (15), Environmental Sciences Ecology (4), Computer Science (3), Science Technology Other Topics (3), Business Economics (2), Communication (2), Engineering (2), Behavioral Sciences (1). The categories that excluded are: Food Science Technology, Public Environmental Occupational Health,

Figure 1. Results from the Scopus database

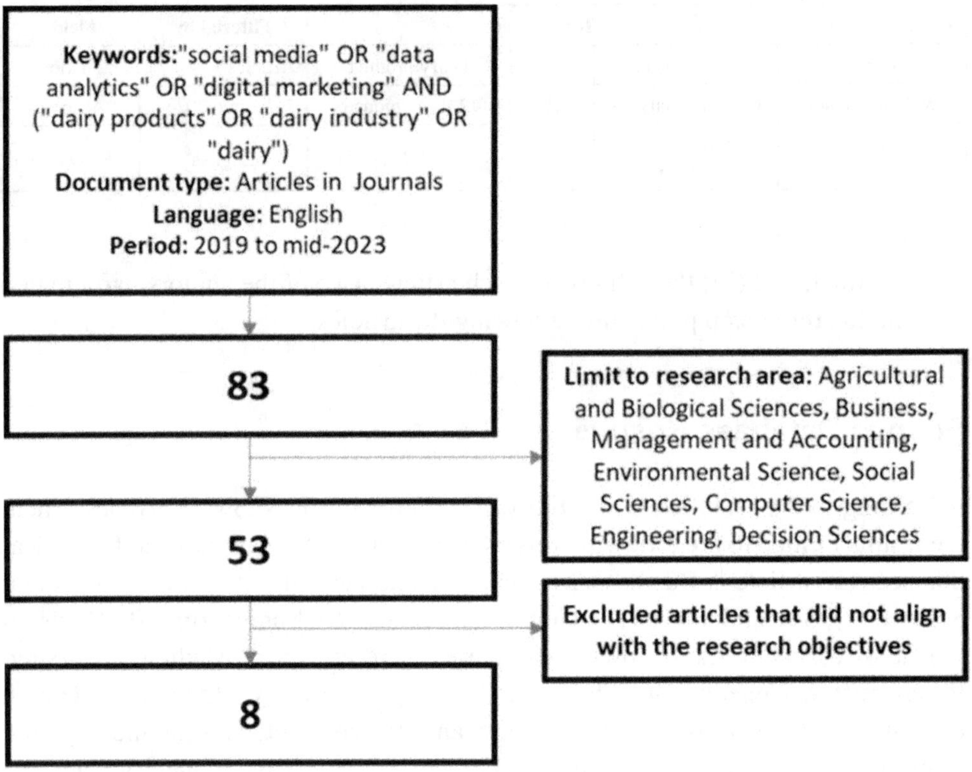

Veterinary Sciences, Pediatrics, Sociology, Biotechnology Applied Microbiology, Energy Fuels, Geology, History Philosophy of Science, Meteorology Atmospheric Sciences, Neurosciences Neurology, Nursing, Obstetrics Gynecology and Water Resources. Finally, the total number was 48 articles (it must be noted that five articles fall in more than one category). Next, a more detailed review was carried out in accordance with the three-step procedure and removing duplicates. As a result of this procedure, the dataset was reduced to a total of 6 articles (Figure 2). Again, it worth noting that searching the Web of Science database without time restriction reveals 86 documents, of which 72 of them were articles in journals and 71 articles in English language. This fact is in line with the results from the Scopus database and underscores that this research field has attracted the interest of the research community in the last years.

In the following, Table 2 illustrates the 14 selected articles retrieved from the two databases. Two of them have been published in 2019, four in 2020, two in 2021, three in 2022 and, three in first half of 2023. According to the affiliation of the first author of the selected articles, three articles come from the USA, two from India,

Figure 2. Results from the Web of Science database

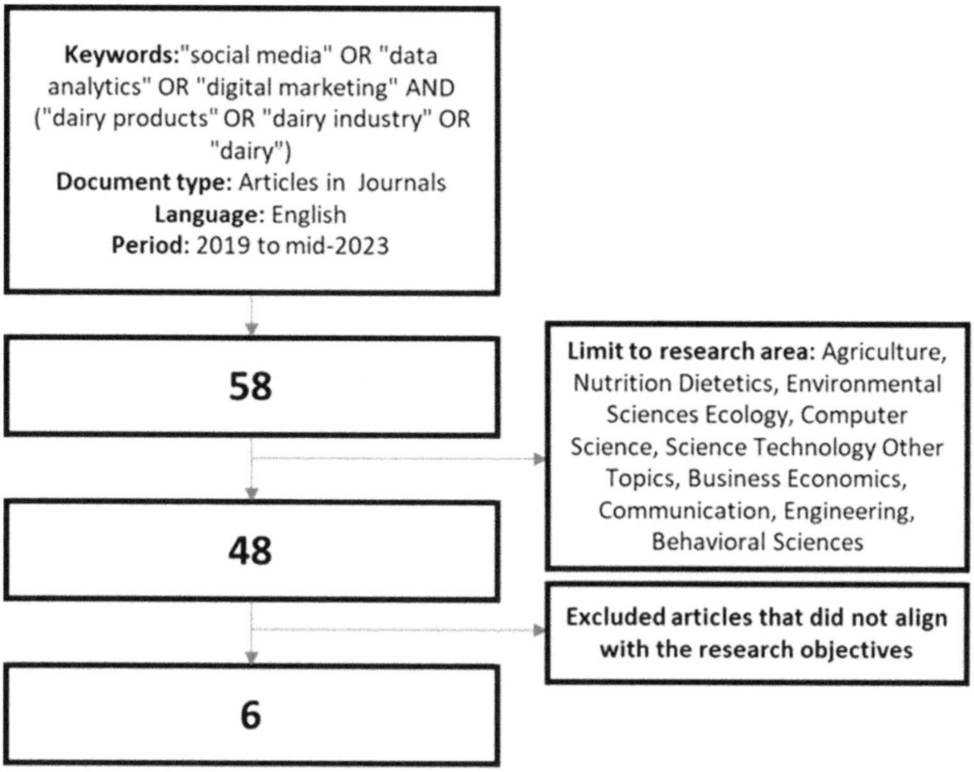

two from Ireland, and one from the following countries: Poland, Slovakia, Canada, Ireland, Australia, the Netherlands, Spain, and Italy. The selected articles cover several topics, including successful marketing strategies for specific dairy products, brand rebuilding after a crisis, the role of social media in agriculture, the impact of technology in the dairy industry, predictive models for detecting lameness in dairy herds. More specifically, in the research of Petrilák, et. al. (2020) it was found that in a sample of 42 small dairy companies in Poland, social media (mainly Facebook and Instagram) are used by a relatively small percentage (33% Facebook, 7% Instagram) for marketing, communication with customers and promotion of their fresh products. Additionally, the usage of social networks such as Facebook by small dairies has a positive impact on the promotion of their brand and generally, on the influence they exert on consumers, while through them the producers themselves build their authenticity (Garner, 2021).Regarding social media analytics tools and their use in surveys in the dairy industry, the findings were minimal to none. Only one study from India utilize social media analytics tools and reveal an increase in demand for organic foods and gluten-free or lactose-free foods, as these are considered healthy.

Table 2. Articles retrieved from the Scopus and Web of Science databases

Author	Title	Journal	Year
Manohar, Sujatha; Rehman, Varisha	Brand resurrection in an emerging economy	Journal of Marketing Communications	2019
Taneja, Mohit; Jalodia, Nikita; Byabazaire, John; Davy, Alan; Olariu, Cristian	Smart Herd management: A microservices-based fog computing–assisted IoT platform towards data-driven smart dairy farming	Software - Practice and Experience	2019
Rodak, Olga	Hashtag hijacking and crowdsourcing transparency: social media affordances and the governance of farm animal protection	Agriculture and Human Values	2020
Petrilák, Marek; Janšto, Erik; Horská, Elena	Communication of local farmers' products through Facebook: The case study of Naše-Vaše	Communication Today	2020
Warner, Daniel; Vasseur, Elsa; Lefebvre, Daniel M.; Lacroix, René	A machine learning based decision aid for lameness in dairy herds using farm-based records	Computers and Electronics in Agriculture	2020
Taneja, Mohit; Byabazaire, John; Jalodia, Nikita; Davy, Alan; Olariu, Cristian; Malone, Paul	Machine learning based fog computing assisted data-driven approach for early lameness detection in dairy cattle	Computers and Electronics in Agriculture	2020
Fanning, Suzanne	We will not stop until the world dreams in cheese: Redefining the Wisconsin cheese brand	Journal of Brand Strategy	2021
Supthanasup, Abhirat; Banwell, Cathy; Kelly, Matthew; Yiengprugsawan, VasoontaraSbirakos	Recipe components and parents' infant and young child feeding concerns: A mixed-methods study of recipe posts shared in thaifacebook groups for parents	Nutrients	2021
Krampe, Caspar; Fridman, Adar	Oatly, a serious 'problem' for the dairy industry? A case study	International Food and Agribusiness Management Review	2022
Alvarez-Mon, Miguel Angel; Fernandez-Lazaro, Cesar I.; Llavero-Valero, Maria; Alvarez-Mon, Melchor; Mora, Samia; Martínez-González, Miguel A.; Bes-Rastrollo, Maira	Mediterranean Diet Social Network Impact along 11 Years in the Major US Media Outlets: Thematic and Quantitative Analysis Using Twitter	International Journal of Environmental Research and Public Health	2022
Garner, Benjamin	Using Social Media to Establish Authenticity: An Analysis of a Small Dairy Farm's Use of Facebook	Journal of Promotion Management	2022
Mishra, Anubhav; Shukla, Anuja	Gyan Fresh: Digital Transformation of Dairy Business with Resilience and Technology Innovation	FIIB Business Review	2023
Borsellino, Valeria; Pecoraro, Nicola; Schimmenti, Emanuele	Promoting dairy products through the web: The case of Pecorino Siciliano PDO during the COVID-19 pandemic	International Journal of Dairy Technology	2023
Erol, Ali E.	Delighted for a dairy queen in Egypt: US foreign policy leadership discourse in the Middle East during Arab Spring	Journal of International and Intercultural Communication	2023

However, its research field differs significantly from the research field of the present study, as it does not exclusively refer to dairy products. At the same time, it mainly concerns the consumer side and it doesn't deal with the social media marketing from business side.

In conclusion, addressing the two research questions raised at the beginning of this section, it is evident that much research has been conducted on the topic of social media in the dairy industry (RQ1). In addition, no articles were identified that specifically refer to social media data analysis by dairy companies (RQ2). These findings show the need for further investigation in this field to better understand the potential implications and opportunities of social media in the dairy industry from the business side perspective.

2. METHODOLOGY

In accordance with, the aforementioned results of the literature review, a methodology is proposed for the evaluation of social media use by the businesses of the Greek dairy industry. It includes three phases, as follows: (i) identification of the sample of dairy companies; (ii) evaluation of the digital presence referring to website elements; and (iii) data collection and analysis of social media profiles, namely Facebook, Instagram, YouTube.

Regarding the first phase, the sample of the Greek dairy businesses is based on the ICAP CRIF registry that contains fifty-five (55) companies. Moreover, these companies according to their annual turnover have been classified into two groups, namely Group A and Group B. Group A includes ten (10) companies that have annual turnover higher than 100 million € and Group B consists of forty-five (45) companies that have annual turnover below 100 million € (Sectoral studies of Dairy and Cheese sector ICAP, 2021). This classification has been used to evaluate dairy companies' performance according to their economic activity.

The second phase aims at evaluating the digital presence (i.e., website and social media platforms) of the dairy companies. The website evaluation includes the following criteria: website existence, date of its official registration recorded through the internet archive (archive.org), supported languages, and social media profiles.

In the third phase, the companies' social media profiles are examined through a social media analytics tool, namely the Fanpage Karma. This tool analyzes and monitors social media platforms and provides valuable information about publication strategies and profile performance in social media such as Facebook, Instagram, and YouTube. It facilitates a relatively accurate determination of the coefficients relating to the number of users' reactions to the shared library content; the number of posts, comments, likes; average number of shared posts per day; the most popular texts, images, videos, links; hashtags used by the librarians. Reports can be exported to spreadsheets, and in this way, the publications themselves can also be analyzed and improved (Calderón-Monge and Ramírez-Hurtado, 2022; Gmiterek, 2021).

3. RESULTS

This section presents the results of the second and third phases of the proposed methodology. In second phase, the Greek dairy businesses were classified according

Figure 3. Geographical distribution of dairy businesses in Greece

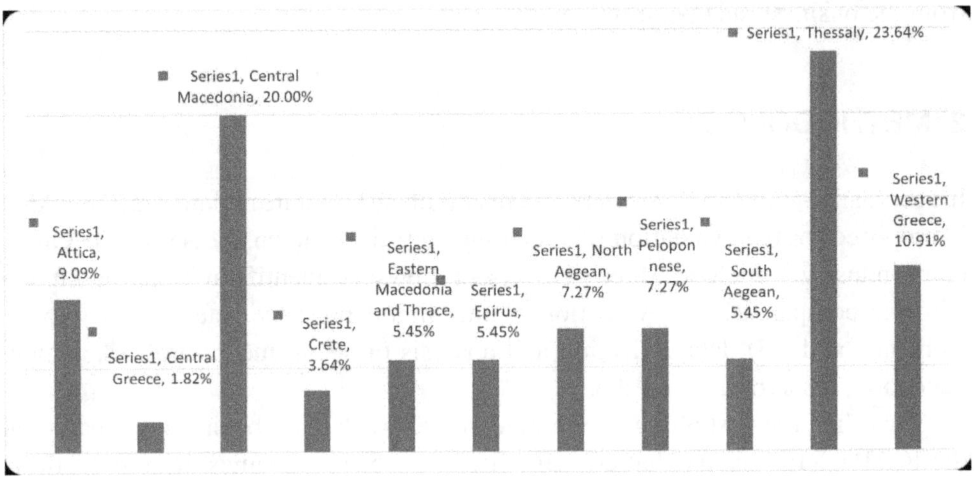

to their geographical location (region), where their headquarters are based. The highest percentage is found in the Region of Thessaly (23.64%)followed by the Region of Central Macedonia (20%), Region of Western Greece (10.91%), Region of Attica (9.09%), Region of Peloponnese (7.27%), Region of North Aegean (7.27%), Region of South Aegean (5.45%), Region of Epirus (5.45%), Region of Eastern Macedonia and Thrace (5.45%).The lowest percentage are found in the Region of Crete and the Region of Central Greece with a percentage of 3.64% and 1.82%, respectively (Figure 3).

According to the corporate websites existence by the Greek dairy companies, the results show that93% of the companies have a website, 5% do not possess a website, and only 2% have a website that is under construction. Then, using the Internet Archive (archive.org) the year that companies' websites were launched has been recorded and classified into seven categories. The results indicate that a significant percentage of companies (46.16%) initiated their website after the year 2010when the economic crisis started in Greece, with the country facing significant financial challenges (Table3). Moreover, the languages supported by each website were recorded. The majority of the websites,98.04%, supports the Greek language and 76.47% also provide support for the English language. Additionally, 21.57% of the websites support German, 11.76% French, 9.80% Italian and 1.96% Russian. In addition, some of them support other languages such as Spanish or Dutch.

As regards the social media evaluation of the companies, the focus has been on five popular social media platforms, namely Facebook, Instagram, Twitter, YouTube, and Pinterest. Each company of the sample has been examined if they maintain an account/profile in these platforms. The results show that 83.64% companies have

Table 3. Launch of the corporate websites

Period	Percentage
1995 - 1998	3,85%
1999 - 2002	19,23%
2003 - 2006	11,54%
2007 - 2010	19,23%
2011 - 2014	17,31%
2015 - 2018	19,23%
2019 - 2022	9,62%

Facebook, 49.09%have Instagram, 45.45%have YouTube, 7.27% have Twitter and, 7.27%have Pinterest. Also, there is a percentage of 14.55%that does not have any presence on social media. It must be noted that each business may maintain profiles on one or more social media.

The findings show that dairy businesses (in Group A and B) use on average1.70 social media platforms. However, the average for Group A is 3.1 platforms, while the average for Group B is about 1.67. The maximum number of platforms for both groups is 4 while the minimum for Group A is 2 and for Group B is none. Then, a statistical analysis showed that there was a statistically significant difference between the two groups (Table 4). More specifically, the t-test of independent samples conducted for the Group A (Mean=3.1, Standard Deviation =0.57) and for the Group B (Mean=1.67, Standard Deviation=1.21) showed a statistically significant difference in the number of social media used ($p<.05$).

Next, the study focused on analyzing data for each social media platform through the Fanpage Karma tool, to determine whether there are statistically significant differences of specific performance indicators for the year 2022 between dairy businesses of Groups A and B. The indicators selected to be studied and analyzed are the following:

Table 4. Number of social media used by dairy companies

	Group A	Group B	pvalue
Mean	3.1 out of 5	1.67 out of 5	.0006
Maximum	4 out of 5	4 out of 5	
Minimum	2 out of 5	0 out of 5	
StandardDeviation	0.57	1.21	
N	10	45	

Number of Posts: Number of posts, that were published in selected period.
Fans: Number of fans/followers on the last day of a selected period.
Engagement: The Engagement shows an average amount of how often a fan interacts with the posts of a page. It is calculated by dividing the daily number of reactions (likes, love, wow, haha etc.), comments and shares by the number of fans. If you are looking at a longer period, it takes the average of the daily Engagement rates.
Total Reactions, Comments, Shares: Number of interactions on page-posts, that were published in selected period.

The data analysis was performed using Stat graphics tool. All tests were put at a significance level of 5% (α=0.05).

Facebook Data Analysis

The total number of companies in Group A maintains a Facebook profile, however, regarding Group B, 33 out of 45 maintain Facebook profiles. Table 5 shows the number of posts for the businesses of the two groups. More specifically, Group A has an average of 102.30 posts, whereas Group B has an average of 57.48 posts. However, based on the values of skewness and kurtosis Group B does not follow the normal distribution (values are outside the range -2 to +2). Figure 4a illustrates the box plots for Groups A and B. For the Group B there is an extreme value (outlier) where the number of posts is 319. This number is quite large compared to the rest of the businesses that affect the distribution with positive symmetry. On the other hand, Group A exhibits a distribution that is almost symmetrical without extreme values. The Mann-Whitney test was chosen, that is a nonparametric test of two independent samples, as it was found that one sample does not follow a normal distribution. Therefore, there are statistically significant differences between the two groups($p<.05$). The median number of posts on Facebook for Group A (Median=97.0) exceeds the median number of posts for Group B (Median=20.0).

In terms of the indicator fans, the average for Group A is 279,919 fans and for Group B is 8,736.73 fans. Based on the values of skewness and kurtosis, the distribution is not normal for both samples (Table 6). Figure 4b shows box plots quite compressed due to the extreme values. In case of Group A there is an extreme value, as the number of Facebook fans is over 2,2 million, which greatly affects the distribution of the sample. In Group B there are 4 outliers, which do not appear clearly due to the box plot compression. Since the distribution is not normal, the nonparametric Mann-Whitney test was applied for both samples. It was found that there are statistically significant differences between the two groups in terms of the

Table 5. Number of posts for Facebook

NumberofPosts	Group A	Group B	p-value
Count	10	33	
Average	102.30	57.48	
Median	97.00	20.00	
Mean Rank	30.30	19.48	
Standard deviation	56.20	69.88	
Coeff. of variation	54.93%	121.57%	.0177
Minimum	29	0	
Maximum	191	319	
Range	162	319	
Stnd. skewness	0.58	4.38	
Stnd. kurtosis	-0.58	5.58	

number of fans (median=59,472 for Group A, and median= 3,094 for Group B) on Facebook (p<.05).

Regarding total reactions, comments, and shares the average is 20,366.20 for Group A and 15,529.50 for Group B. However, based on the values of skewness and kurtosis, the distribution is not normal in Group B (Table 7). Figure 4c presents the

Table 6. Fans for Facebook

Fans	Group A	Group B	p-value
Count	10	33	
Average	27,9919.00	8,736.73	
Median	5,9472.00	3,094.00	
Mean Rank	32,70	18,76	
Standard deviation	69,2747.00	15,178.9	
Coeff. of variation	247,48%	173,737%	.0022
Minimum	907	255	
Maximum	2,245,649	57,594	
Range	2,244,742	57,339	
Stnd. skewness	4.03	6.22	
Stnd. kurtosis	6.34	7.08	

Table 7. Reactions, comments, and shares for Facebook

Total Reactions, Comments, Shares	Group A	Group B	p-value
Count	10	33	.0072
Average	20,366.20	15,529.50	
Median	14,082.00	1,667.00	
Mean Rank	31.40	19.15	
Standard deviation	19,861.80	42,038.90	
Coeff. of variation	97.52%	270.70%	
Minimum	2,385	0	
Maximum	63,377	210,585	
Range	60,992	210,585	
Stnd. skewness	1.68	9.15	
Stnd. kurtosis	0.71	18.66	

box plots for the two groups. In the box plot of Group A, no outliers are observed, but in Group B, three outliers are observed and the distribution shows positive symmetry. Since the distribution is not normal, the nonparametric Mann-Whitney test of two independent samples was applied. It was found that there are statistically significant differences ($p<.05$) between the two groups (Median=14,082 for Group A and Median=1,667 for Group B).

Table 8. Engagement of Facebook

Engagement	Group A	Group B	p-value
Count	10	33	.412
Average	0.0015	0.0016	
Median	0.0009	0.0006	
Mean Rank	24.90	21.12	
Standard deviation	0.0015	0.0027	
Coeff. of variation	99.51%	160.60%	
Minimum	0	0	
Maximum	0.0045	0.0127	
Range	0.0045	0.0127	
Stnd. skewness	1.20	6.20	
Stnd. kurtosis	-0.24	9.81	

Figure 4a. Facebook: Number of posts

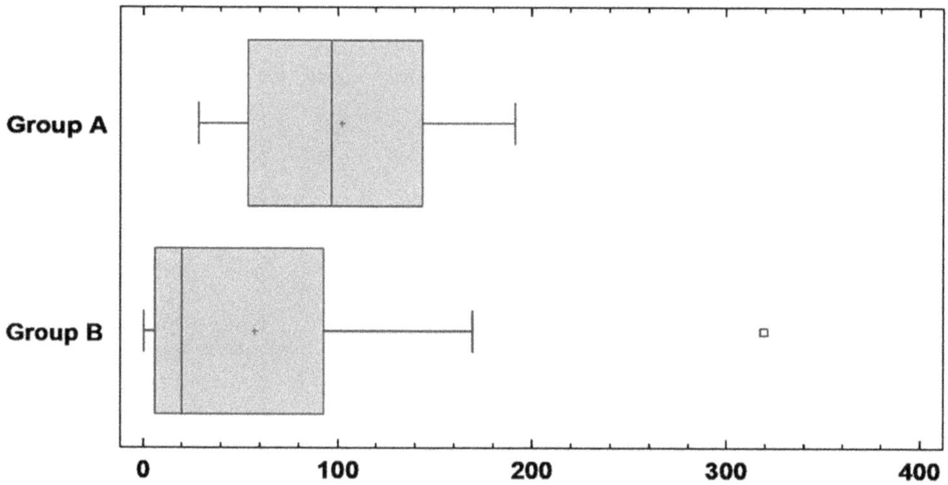

Figure 4b. Facebook: Fans

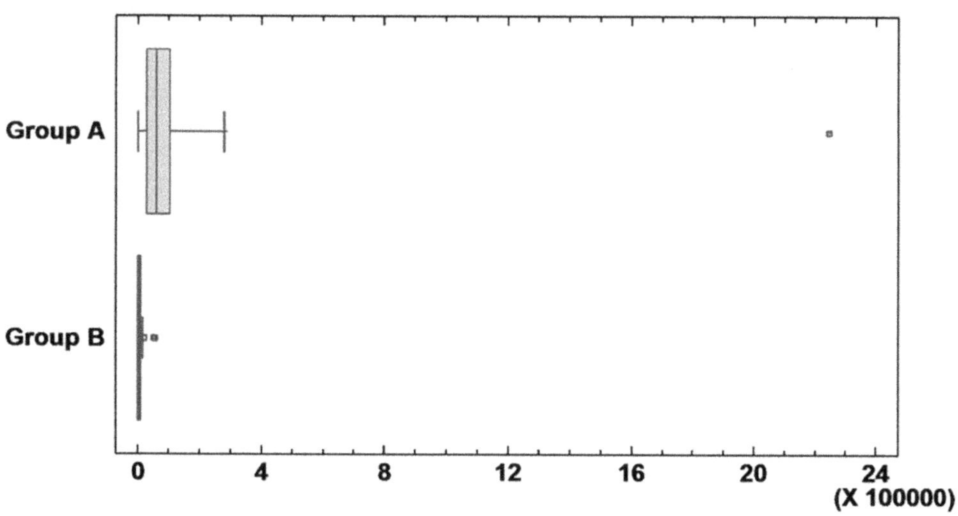

Figure 4c. Facebook: Total reactions, comments, shares

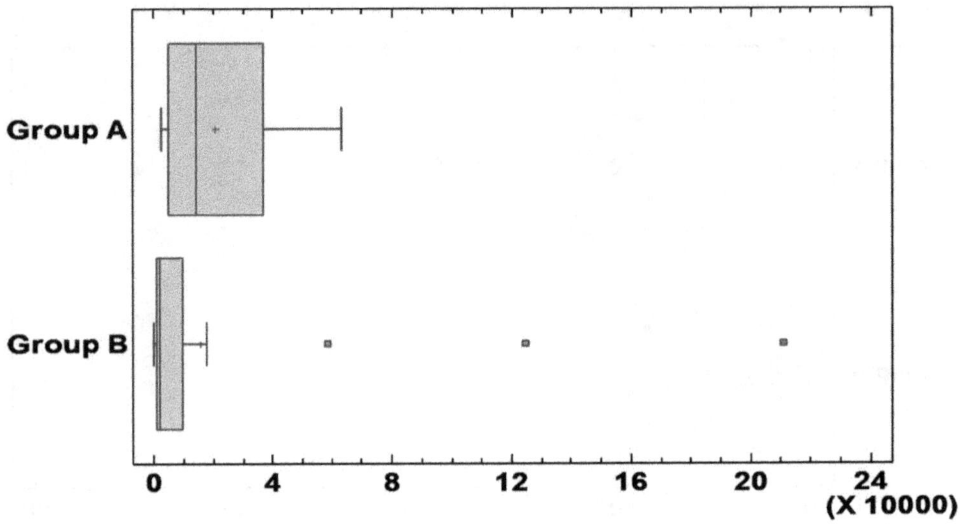

Figure 4d. Facebook: Engagement

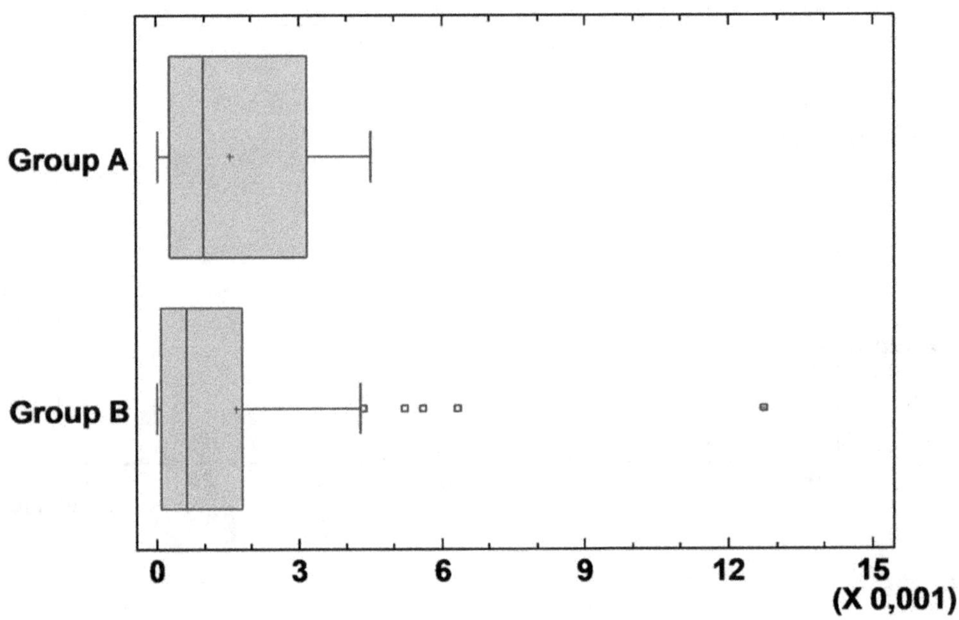

The average engagement, is 0.0015 for Group A, and 0.0016 for Group B. However, based on skewness and kurtosis, the distribution is not normal in Group B (Table 8). Figure 4d presents the box plots for the two groups. Five outliers are shown in Group B that produce positive symmetry. Generally, the engagement is quite low in all companies, which proves that they do not particularly encourage users to interact with their posts. Since the distribution is not normal, the nonparametric Mann-Whitney test of two independent samples was applied. It was found that there are no statistically significant differences between the two groups ($p>.05$). In conclusion, the engagement of Facebook for Group A (Median= 0.00099) and Group B (Median=0.00063) are approximately equal.

Instagram Data Analysis

Nine out of ten companies from Group A and sixteen out of forty-five of Group B maintain Instagram profiles. Table 9 shows the average of total posts for the companies of the two groups. For Group A the average is 91.67 posts, while for Group B is 85.94. In addition, based on the values of skewness and kurtosis the two samples follow a normal distribution (the values are within the range -2 to +2). The box plots of the two groups have a slight positive symmetry without outliers (Figure 5). Since the two groups show normal distribution, the parametric t-test of two independent samples was chosen. It was found that there are no statistically significant differences between the two groups ($p>.05$). In conclusion, the number of posts on Instagram, between Group A are approximately equal.

Table 9. Number of posts for Instagram

Number of Posts	Group A	Group B	p-value
Count	9	16	.833
Average	91.66	85.93	
Median	80.00	79.00	
Standard deviation	58.73	67.61	
Coeff. of variation	64.07%	78.68%	
Minimum	15.00	0	
Maximum	188.00	257.00	
Range	173.00	257.00	
Stnd. skewness	0.43	1.21	
Stnd. kurtosis	-0.63	1.17	

Figure 5. Instagram - Number of posts

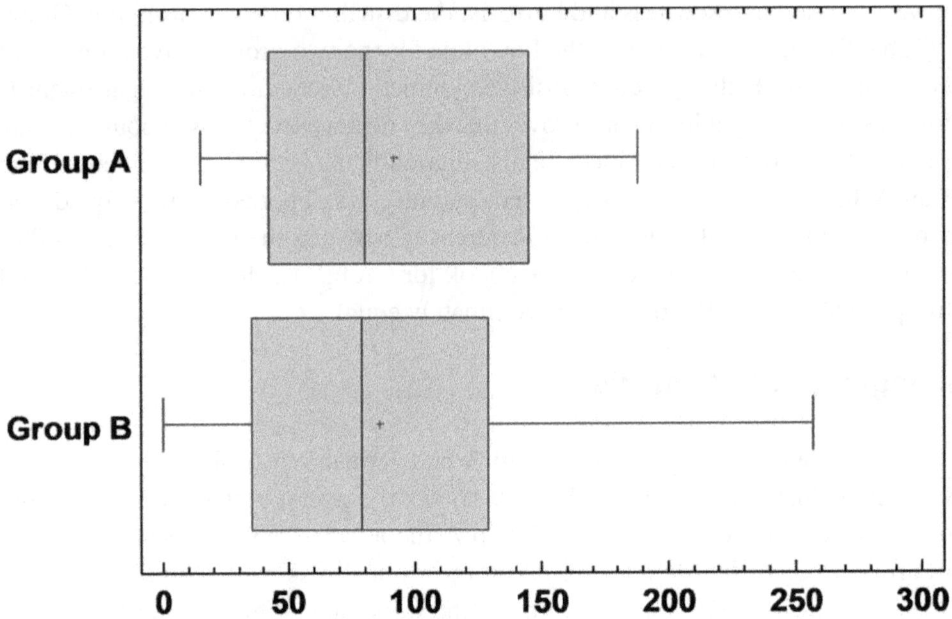

In terms of fans, the average is 13,891.9 for Group A and 2,944.81 for Group B. However, based on the values of skewness and kurtosis, the distribution is not normal in one sample (Table 10). Figure 6 presents the box plots for the two groups. The distribution for the Group A appears symmetrical with one outlier and Group B has positive symmetry and one outlier. Since the distribution is not normal in one of the two samples, the nonparametric Mann-Whitney test of two independent samples was applied. It was found that there are statistically significant differences between the two groups in terms of the number of followers on the Instagram ($p<.05$) and Group A (Median=11,713) has more followers than Group B (Median=971).

In terms of total reactions, comments, and shares on Instagram the average is 16,006.30 for Group A and 5,884.38 for Group B. However, based on values of skewness and kurtosis, the distribution is not normal in one sample (Table 11). Figure 7 presents the box plots for the two groups with the Group Bto have two outliers. Since the distribution is not normal, the nonparametric Mann-Whitney test of two independent samples was applied on one of the two samples. It was found that there are no statistically significant differences between the two groups ($p>.05$). Therefore, it is considered that Group A (Median=10,435.00) and Group B (Median=2,333.50) have no differences.

Regarding the engagement, the average for Group Ais 0.0041 and for Group B is 0.0029 and based on the values of skewness and kurtosis the distribution is normal in

Table 10. Fans for Instagram

Fans	Group A	Group B	p-value
Count	9	16	.0188
Average	13,891,90	2,944.81	
Median	11,713.00	971.00	
Mean Rank	17.67	10.38	
Standard deviation	14,564.00	4,433.58	
Coeff. of variation	104.83%	150.55%	
Minimum	365	22	
Maximum	47,160	17,396	
Range	46,795	17,374	
Stnd. skewness	1.99	4.27	
Stnd. kurtosis	1.95	6.29	

Figure 6. Instagram - Fans

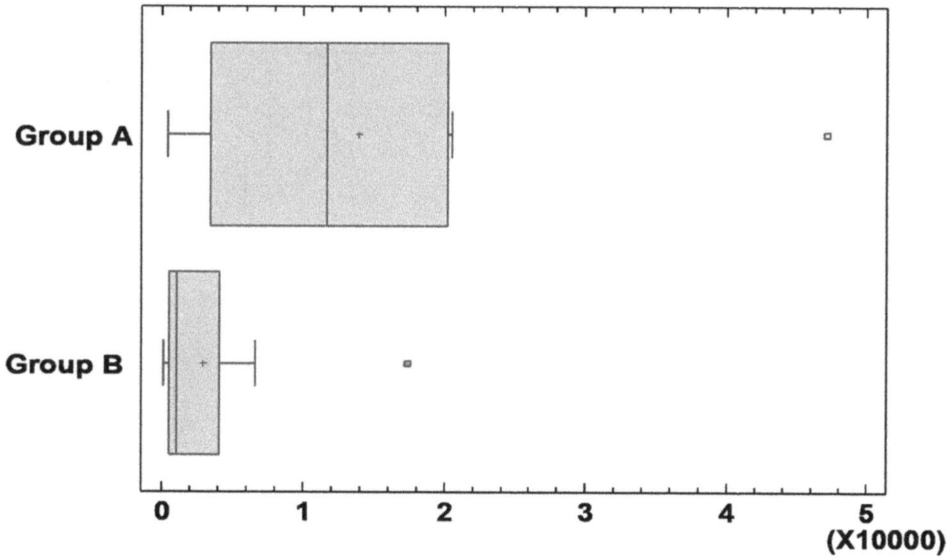

both samples (Table 12). The box plot for Group Ahas a slightly positive symmetry, while for Group B has a negative symmetry (Figure 8). In general, it is observed that the engagement is quite low in all companies, which proves that companies do not

Table 11. Total reactions, comments, shares for Instagram

Total Reactions, Comments, Shares	Group A	Group B	p-value
Count	9	16	.149
Average	16,006.30	5,884.38	
Median	10,435.00	2,333.50	
Mean Rank	15,89	11,38	
Standard deviation	19,691.80	9,848.78	
Coeff. of variation	123,02%	167,372%	
Minimum	1,252	0	
Maximum	60,018	36,286	
Range	58,766	36,286	
Stnd. skewness	1.98	4.08	
Stnd. kurtosis	1.52	5.03	

Figure 7. Instagram – Total reactions, comments, shares

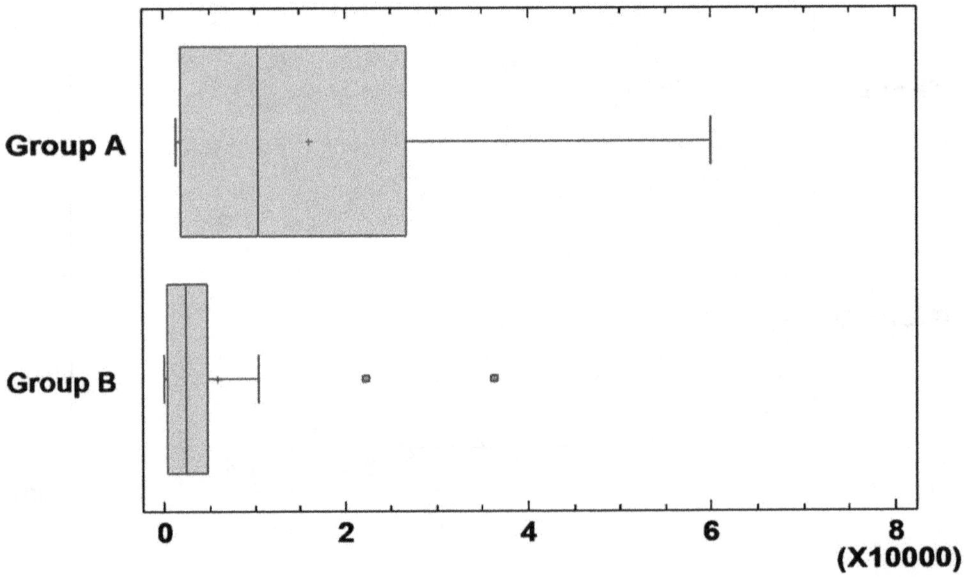

Table 12. Engagement for Instagram

Engagement	Group A	Group B	p-value
Count	9	16	.391
Average	0.0041	0.0029	
Median	0.0036	0.0027	
Standard deviation	0.0033	0.0031	
Coeff. of variation	80.47%	105.78%	
Minimum	0.0004	0	
Maximum	0.0109	0.0094	
Range	0.0105	0.0094	
Stnd. skewness	1.19	1.47	
Stnd. kurtosis	0.63	-0.11	

Figure 8. Instagram - Engagement

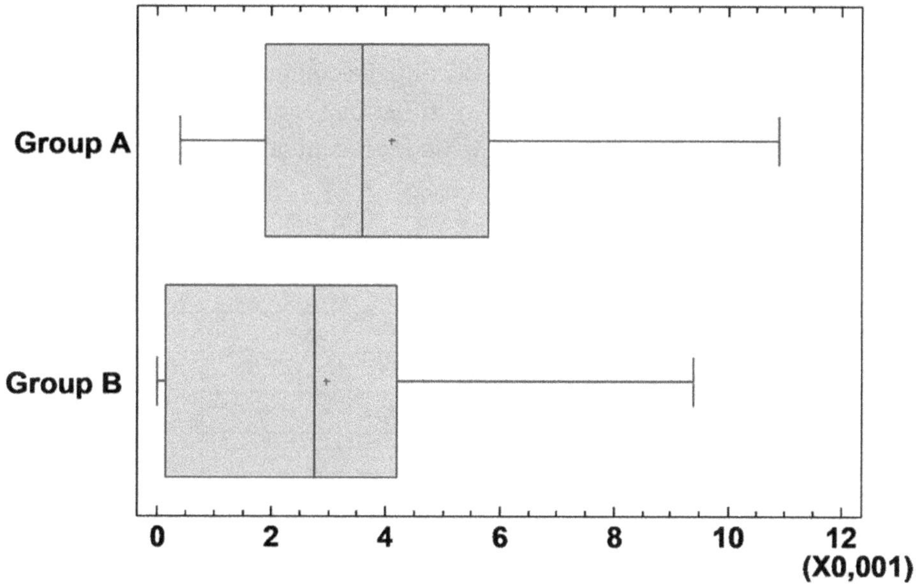

particularly encourage users to interact with their Instagram posts. The parametric t-test of two independent samples was applied (normal distribution for both samples). The results show that there are no statistically significant differences between the two groups. In conclusion, the engagement for both groups is approximately equal.

YouTube Data Analysis

All companies in Group A have a YouTube channel. On the other hand, only 18 out of55 from Group B have a YouTube channel. Table 13presents the average number of posts for businesses for both groups. More specifically, for Group A it is 20.50 posts, while for Group B it is 9.44 posts. Based on the values of skewness and kurtosis one of the two samples does not follow a normal distribution. Figure 9 presents the box plots for both groups. Group A presents positive symmetry without outliers while fourteen companies of Group B have 0 posts in 2022 and only four make use of it. One of them made 159 posts (i.e., videos) that is visible as outlier in the box plot. In conclusion, dairy companies do not make use of the YouTube, even if they have a profile, they do not post any video. Since the distribution is not normal in one of the two samples, a nonparametric Mann-Whitney test of two independent samples was applied. It was found that there are statistically significant differences between the two groups ($p<.05$). Companies in Group A produce a higher number of posts (Median = 10.50) compared to those in Group B, where the Median value is 0.

Regarding fans, the average is 4,569.90 for Group A and 351.50 for Group B. However, based on the values of skewness and kurtosis, in both groups the distribution is not normal (Table 14). Figure 10 presents the box plots for both groups. Group A has an outlier with 22,300 followers (affecting the compression of the box plots) while Group B has two outliers. Since the distribution is not normal in both groups, the nonparametric Mann-Whitney test of two independent samples was performed. It

Table 13. Number of posts for YouTube

Number of Posts	Group A	Group B	p-value
Count	10	18	
Average	20.50	9.44	
Median	10.50	0	
Mean Rank	21.15	10.81	
Standard deviation	22.52	37.37	
Coeff. of variation	109.87%	395.71%	.00059
Minimum	0	0	
Maximum	61	159	
Range	61	159	
Stnd. skewness	1.26	7.31	
Stnd. kurtosis	-0.46	15.49	

Figure 9. YouTube - Number of posts

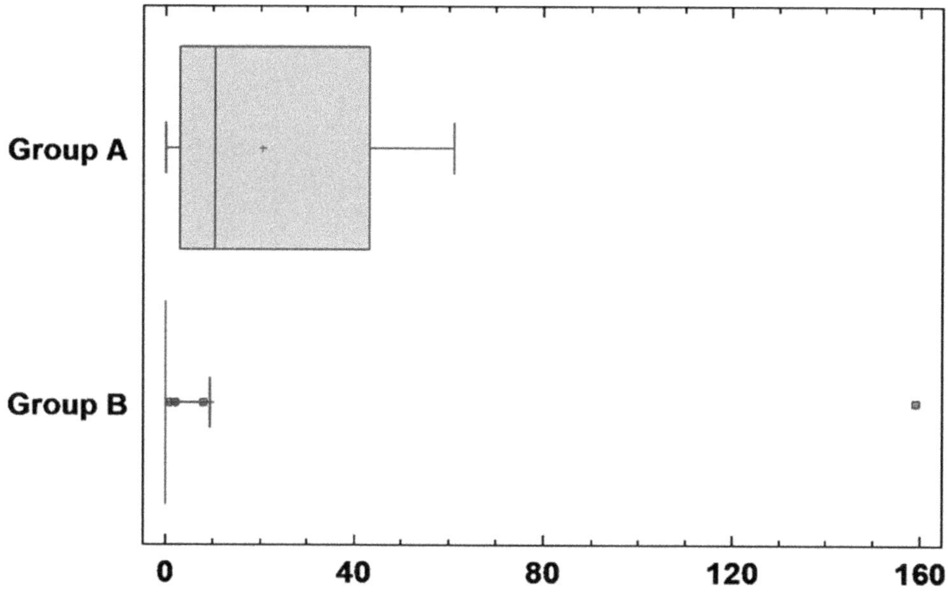

was found that there are statistically significant differences between the two groups (p<.05). Companies in Group A have a higher number of followers (Median=1,960.00) compared to companies in Group B (Median=25.50).

Table 14. Fans for YouTube

Fans	Group A	Group B	p-value
Count	10	18	.0023
Average	4,569.90	351.50	
Median	1,960.00	25.50	
Mean Rank	20.90	10.94	
Standard deviation	6,764.26	604.30	
Coeff. of variation	148.02%	171.94%	
Minimum	41	0	
Maximum	22,300	2,280	
Range	22,259	2,280	
Stnd. skewness	3.05	4.03	
Stnd. kurtosis	3.95	4.98	

Figure 10. YouTube –Fans

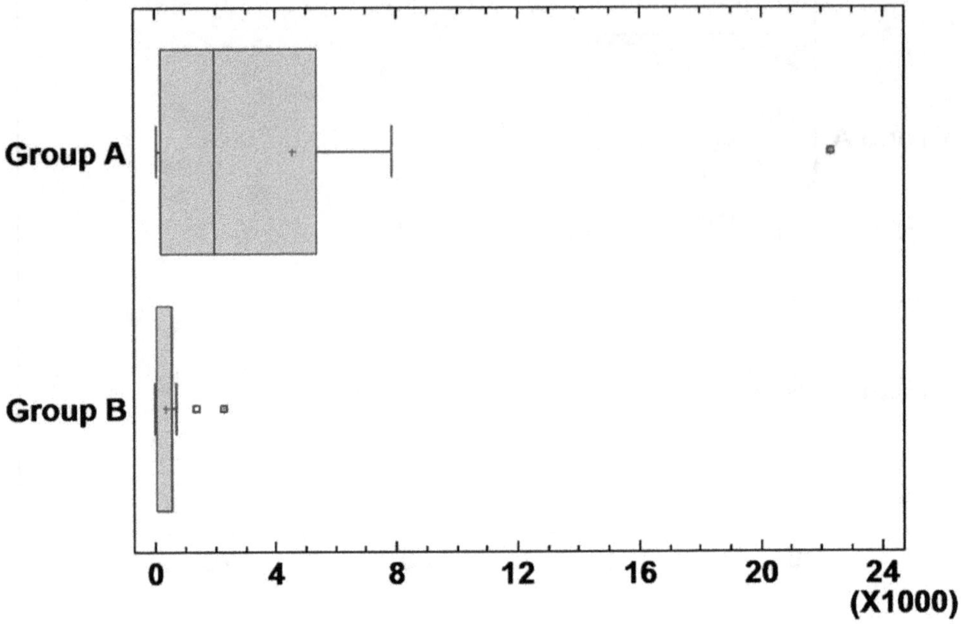

Table 15. Fans of posts for YouTube

Total, Reactions, Comments, Share	Group A	Group B	p-value
Count	10	18	.0005
Average	243.40	42.50	
Median	128.00	0	
Mean Rank	21.20	10.78	
Standard deviation	322.35	164.69	
Coeff. of variation	132.43%	387.51%	
Minimum	0	0	
Maximum	1049	701	
Range	1049	701	
Stnd. skewness	2.58	7.29	
Stnd. kurtosis	2.85	15.42	

Figure 11. YouTube – Total reactions, comments, shares

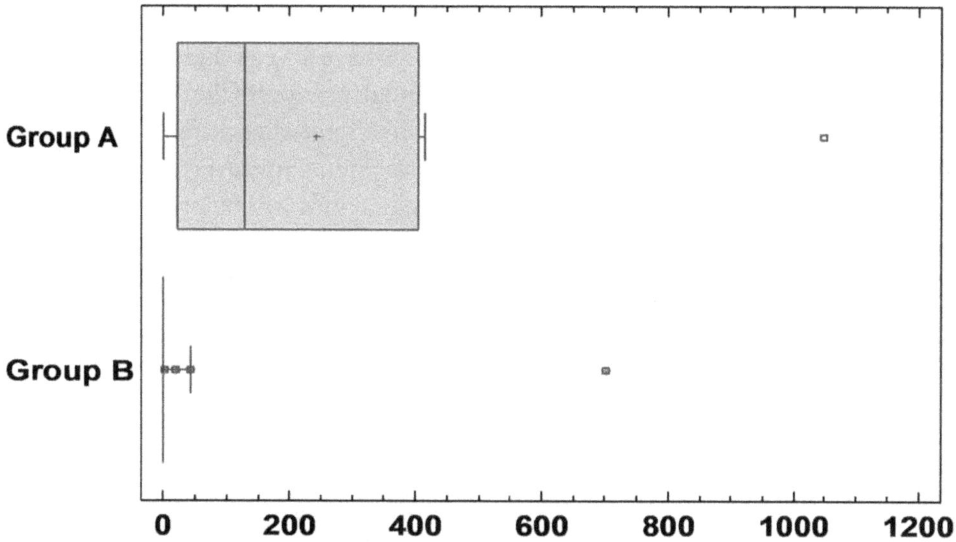

In terms of total reactions, comments, and shares on YouTube the average is 243.40 for Group A and 42.50 for Group B and based on the values of skewness and kurtosis, the distribution is not normal in both samples (Table 15). Figure 11 presents the box plots for both groups that have one outlier each. Since the distribution is not normal in both samples, the nonparametric Mann-Whitney test of two independent samples was applied. It shows that there are statistically significant differences between the two groups ($p<.05$). It is therefore considered that the reactions, comments, and notifications of followers for Group Aare more (Median=128.00) than Group B (Median=0).

In the case of YouTube, it must be noted that it was not possible to retrieve data for the indicator engagement.

4. CONCLUSIONS

Social media can play a significant role in the dairy industry, providing numerous opportunities and advantages for dairy companies. However, based on the results of the literature review, it becomes evident that a research gap exists regarding the utilization of social media by the dairy industry. The review reveals that there has been limited research conducted on the topic of social media in the dairy industry, and no prior studies have analyzed data from social media platforms, such as Facebook, Instagram, and YouTube.

In this context, the present study tried to describe the status of digital presence as well as the social media utilization by the Greek dairy industry for the year 2022. The findings show that the Greek dairy companies have a weak digital presence and poor utilization of social media. However, the annual turnover of the dairy companies plays a significant role and results in statistically significant differences between companies in Group A (i.e., companies that have annual turnover higher than 100 million €) and Group B (companies that have annual turnover below 100 million €) concerning the Fanpage Karma indicators, namely the number of posts, fans, total reactions, comments, and shares. On the other hand, the engagement indicator has been found to be very low for both groups, with no significant differences. This result denotes that both groups have implemented inadequate social media strategies, failing to attract fans' interest and interactions with their posts.

The modern marketing has the digital presence in general and social media in particular at the core of the strategy that is in contrast with the findings of this study that concerns the Greek dairy companies. These results can help key decision-makers of the diary companies to design effective digital marketing strategies. Therefore, it is recommended that they should utilize social media more efficiently to leverage their positive influence on their businesses. On the other hand, social media marketing strategy is not a one-size-fits-all approach, and it may not be suitable. It requires different approaches to ensure the deployment of effective and efficient strategies. In conclusion, Greek dairy companies have the potential to enhance their business outcomes by harnessing the positive influence of social media more effectively.

However, there are limitations to be considered in relation to the interpretation of the results. The Fanpage Karma tool is based on historical data and many metrics for several dairy companies that are not displayed because no one had searched for them, and in that way to start recording data for its indicators. For example, on YouTube, there were no results for the "engagement" indicator, and it was not studied. Regarding future research, it would be necessary to study the differences in performance indicators over a longer period. Moreover, individual companies can be studied and compared to each other, or to the entire industry. Such a study will identify potential disparities in performance indicators or the utilization of social media platforms.

REFERENCES

Alvarez-Mon, M. A., Fernandez-Lazaro, C. I., Llavero-Valero, M., Alvarez-Mon, M., Mora, S., Martínez-González, M. A., & Bes-Rastrollo, M. (2022). Mediterranean Diet Social Network Impact along 11 Years in the Major US Media Outlets: Thematic and Quantitative Analysis Using Twitter. *International Journal of Environmental Research and Public Health*, *19*(2), 784. Advance online publication. doi:10.3390/ijerph19020784 PMID:35055605

Borsellino, V., Pecoraro, N., & Schimmenti, E. (2023). Promoting dairy products through the web: The case of Pecorino Siciliano PDO during the COVID-19 pandemic. *International Journal of Dairy Technology*, *76*(2), 393–407. Advance online publication. doi:10.1111/1471-0307.12933 PMID:36721399

Calderón-Monge, E., & Ramírez-Hurtado, J. M. (2022). Measuring the consumer engagement related to social media: The case of franchising. *Electronic Commerce Research*, *22*(4), 1249–1274. Advance online publication. doi:10.100710660-021-09463-2

Dewnarain, S., Ramkissoon, H., & Mavondo, F. (2019). Social customer relationship management: An integrated conceptual framework. *Journal of Hospitality Marketing & Management*, *28*(2), 172–188. Advance online publication. doi:10.1080/19368623.2018.1516588

Dwivedi, Y. K., Ismagilova, E., Rana, N. P., & Raman, R. (2023). Social Media Adoption, Usage and Impact In Business-To-Business (B2B) Context: A State-Of-The-Art Literature Review. *Information Systems Frontiers*, *25*(3), 971–993. Advance online publication. doi:10.100710796-021-10106-y

Erol, A. E. (2023). Delighted for a dairy queen in Egypt: US foreign policy leadership discourse in the Middle East during Arab Spring. *Journal of International and Intercultural Communication*, *16*(1), 74–89. Advance online publication. doi:10.1080/17513057.2021.1950198

Fanning, S. (2021). We will not stop until the world dreams in cheese: Redefining the wisconsin cheese brand. *Journal of Brand Strategy*, *10*(1).

Felix, R., Rauschnabel, P. A., & Hinsch, C. (2017). Elements of strategic social media marketing: A holistic framework. *Journal of Business Research*, *70*, 118–126. Advance online publication. doi:10.1016/j.jbusres.2016.05.001

Gani, M. O., & Faroque, A. R. (2021). Digital Marketing. In M. Hoque & R. Bashaw (Eds.), *A. Cross-Border E-Commerce Marketing and Management* (pp. 172–202).

Garner, B. (2022). Using Social Media to Establish Authenticity: An Analysis of a Small Dairy Farm's Use of Facebook. *Journal of Promotion Management*, *28*(6), 826–842. Advance online publication. doi:10.1080/10496491.2021.2015514

Gmiterek, G. (2021). Polish university libraries social networking services during the COVID-19 pandemic spring term lockdown. *Journal of Academic Librarianship*, *47*(3), 102331. Advance online publication. doi:10.1016/j.acalib.2021.102331 PMID:36536687

Hellenic Agricultural Organization (ELGO) – DIMITRA, "Management of fresh milk production data", https://www.elgo.gr/index.php?option=com_content&view=article&id=888&Itemid=1267&lang=el (Accessed: 12-02-2023).

Klos, C., Spieth, P., Clauss, T., & Klusmann, C. (2023). Digital Transformation of Incumbent Firms: A Business Model Innovation Perspective. *IEEE Transactions on Engineering Management*, *70*(6), 2017–2033. Advance online publication. doi:10.1109/TEM.2021.3075502

Krampe, C., & Fridman, A. (2022). Oatly, a serious 'problem' for the dairy industry? A case study. *The International Food and Agribusiness Management Review*, *25*(1). Advance online publication. doi:10.22434/IFAMR2021.0058

Manohar, S., & Rehman, V. (2019). Brand resurrection in an emerging economy. *Journal of Marketing Communications*, *25*(7), 783–798. Advance online publication. doi:10.1080/13527266.2018.1455292

Mishra, A., & Shukla, A. (2023). Gyan Fresh: Digital Transformation of Dairy Business with Resilience and Technology Innovation. *FIIB Business Review*, *12*(1), 20–30. Advance online publication. doi:10.1177/23197145221113374

Olson, E. M., Olson, K. M., Czaplewski, A. J., & Key, T. M. (2021). Business strategy and the management of digital marketing. *Business Horizons*, *64*(2), 285–293. Advance online publication. doi:10.1016/j.bushor.2020.12.004

Page, M. J., McKenzie, J. E., Bossuyt, P. M., Boutron, I., Hoffmann, T. C., Mulrow, C. D., Shamseer, L., Tetzlaff, J. M., Akl, E. A., Brennan, S. E., Chou, R., Glanville, J., Grimshaw, J. M., Hróbjartsson, A., Lalu, M. M., Li, T., Loder, E. W., Mayo-Wilson, E., McDonald, S., ... Moher, D. (2021). The PRISMA 2020 statement: An updated guideline for reporting systematic reviews. *BMJ (Clinical Research Ed.)*, *372*. Advance online publication. doi:10.1136/bmj.n71 PMID:33782057

Petrilák, M., Janšto, E., & Horská, E. (2020). Communication of local farmers' products through Facebook: The case study of Naše-Vaše. *Communication Today, 11*(1).

Polanco-Diges, L., & Debasa, F. (2020). The Use of Digital Marketing Strategies in the Sharing Economy: A Literature Review. *Journal of Spatial and Organizational Dynamics, 8*(3).

Rodak, O. (2020). Hashtag hijacking and crowdsourcing transparency: Social media affordances and the governance of farm animal protection. *Agriculture and Human Values, 37*(2), 281–294. Advance online publication. doi:10.100710460-019-09984-5

Smith, K. T., Blazovich, J. L., & Smith, L. M. (2015). Social media adoption by corporations: An examination by platform, industry, size, and financial performance. *Academy of Marketing Studies Journal, 19*(2).

Supthanasup, A., Banwell, C., Kelly, M., & Yiengprugsawan, V. S. (2021). Recipe components and parents' infant and young child feeding concerns: A mixed-methods study of recipe posts shared in thaifacebook groups for parents. *Nutrients, 13*(4), 1186. Advance online publication. doi:10.3390/nu13041186 PMID:33916663

Taneja, M., Byabazaire, J., Jalodia, N., Davy, A., Olariu, C., & Malone, P. (2020). Machine learning based fog computing assisted data-driven approach for early lameness detection in dairy cattle. *Computers and Electronics in Agriculture, 171*, 105286. Advance online publication. doi:10.1016/j.compag.2020.105286

Taneja, M., Jalodia, N., Byabazaire, J., Davy, A., & Olariu, C. (2019). SmartHerd management: A microservices-based fog computing–assisted IoT platform towards data-driven smart dairy farming. *Software, Practice & Experience, 49*(7), 1055–1078. Advance online publication. doi:10.1002pe.2704 PMID:31423028

Wang, Q., Liu, C., Zhao, Y., Kitsos, A., Cannella, M., Wang, S., & Han, L. (2020). Impacts of the COVID-19 pandemic on the dairy industry: Lessons from China and the United States and policy implications. *Journal of Integrative Agriculture, 19*(12), 2903–2915. Advance online publication. doi:10.1016/S2095-3119(20)63443-8

Warner, D., Vasseur, E., Lefebvre, D. M., & Lacroix, R. (2020). A machine learning based decision aid for lameness in dairy herds using farm-based records. *Computers and Electronics in Agriculture, 169*, 105193. Advance online publication. doi:10.1016/j.compag.2019.105193

Compilation of References

Abbott, M., Chiang, K. P., Hwang, Y. S., Paquin, J., & Zwick, D. (2000). The process of on-line store loyalty formation. *Advances in Consumer Research. Association for Consumer Research (U. S.)*, *27*, 145–150.

Abdul, S. B., Soundararajan, V., & Parayitam, S. (2022). The Relationship between Social Media Influence, EWOM, and E-satisfaction of Consumers in India: A Moderated Moderated-mediation Conditional Model. *Global Business Review*, *097215092211301*. Advance online publication. doi:10.1177/09721509221130153

Acar, N., Çizmeci, B., & Turan, A. (2021). A research on consumer perceptions of food and beverage marketing on social media. *OPUS International Journal of Society Researches*, *17*(34), 813–830.

Adjei, M. T., Noble, C. H., & Noble, S. M. (2012). Enhancing Relationships With Customers Through Online Brand Communities. *MIT Sloan Management Review*, *53*(4), 22.

Adunlin, G., Diaby, V., & Xiao, H. (2015). Application of multicriteria decision analysis in health care: A systematic review and bibliometric analysis. *Health Expectations*, *18*(6), 1894–1905. doi:10.1111/hex.12287 PMID:25327341

Afrasiabi, A., Tavana, M., & Di Caprio, D. (2022). An extended hybrid fuzzy multi-criteria decision model for sustainable and resilient supplier selection. *Environmental Science and Pollution Research International*, *29*(25), 37291–37314. doi:10.100711356-021-17851-2 PMID:35050472

Afshari, A., & Khorsand, M. (2020). APPLICATION OF MULTI CRITERIA DECISION MAKING IN. *Health Care*.

Akbarov, S. (2020). The Impact of Social Media Marketing on Consumer - Moderating Role of Gender and Income. Scholedge International Journal of Multidisciplinary & Allied Studies, 7(7), pp. 147-163. https://doi.org/doi:10.19085/sijmas070701

Aktaş, F., Çetiner, H., & Keskin, E. (2022). Gastronomi blogları ve tatma davranışı arasındaki ilişkilerin analizi. *Abant Sosyal Bilimler Dergisi*, *22*(2), 873–886. doi:10.11616/asbi.1102562

Alalwan, A. A., Rana, N. P., Dwivedi, Y. K., & Algharabat, R. (2017). Social Media In Marketing: A Review And Analysis Of The Existing Literature. *Telematics and Informatics*, *34*(7), 1177–1190. doi:10.1016/j.tele.2017.05.008

Alias, M. A., Hashim, S. Z. M., & Samsudin, S. (2008). Multi criteria decision making and its applications: A literature review. *Jurnal Teknologi Maklumat*, *20*(2), 129–152.

Alkış, H., & Karakan, A. (2019). Algılanan sosyal medyanın tüketici davranışı ve satın alma niyetine etkisi üzerine bir araştırma. *Sosyal. Beşeri ve İdari Bilimler Dergisi*, *2*(10), 702–718.

Alvarez-Mon, M. A., Fernandez-Lazaro, C. I., Llavero-Valero, M., Alvarez-Mon, M., Mora, S., Martínez-González, M. A., & Bes-Rastrollo, M. (2022). Mediterranean Diet Social Network Impact along 11 Years in the Major US Media Outlets: Thematic and Quantitative Analysis Using Twitter. *International Journal of Environmental Research and Public Health*, *19*(2), 784. Advance online publication. doi:10.3390/ijerph19020784 PMID:35055605

Ananda, J., Karunasena, G. G., & Pearson, D. (2023). A comparison of online and in-store grocery shopping behaviour and its effects on household food waste. *Technological Forecasting and Social Change*, *194*, 122698. https://doi.org/doi:10.1016/j.techfore.2023.122698

Anderson, M., Sims, J., Price, J., & Brusa, J. (2011). Turning "like" to "buy" social media emerges as a commerce channel. *Booz & Company Inc*, *2*(1), 102–128.

Andreani, F., Gunawan, L., & Haryono, S. (2021). *SOCIAL MEDIA INFLUENCER, BRAND AWARENESS, AND PURCHASE DECISION AMONG GENERATION Z IN SURABAYA*. *Jurnal Manajemen Dan Kewirausahaan*. E-journal., doi:10.9744/jmk.23.1.18-26

Andrews, J. C., Netemeyer, R., Burton, S., & Kees, J. (2021). What consumers actually know: The role of objective nutrition knowledge in processing stop sign and traffic light front-of-pack nutrition labels. *Journal of Business Research*, *128*, 140–155. doi:10.1016/j.jbusres.2021.01.036

An, R., Shi, Y., Shen, J., Bullard, T., Liu, G., Yang, Q., Chen, N., & Cao, L. (2021). Effect of front-of-package nutrition labeling on food purchases: A systematic review. *Public Health*, *191*(February), 59–67. doi:10.1016/j.puhe.2020.06.035 PMID:33517247

Appel, G., Grewal, L., Hadi, R., & Stephen, A. T. (2020). The future of social media in marketing. *Journal of the Academy of Marketing Science*, *48*(1), 79–95. doi:10.100711747-019-00695-1 PMID:32431463

Arora, T., Kumar, A., & Agarwal, B. (2020). Impact of social media advertising on millennials buying behaviour. *International Journal Of Intelligent Enterprise*, *7*(4), 481–500. doi:10.1504/IJIE.2020.110795

Asadabadi, M. R., Chang, E., & Saberi, M. (2019). Are MCDM methods useful? A critical review of Analytic Hierarchy Process (AHP) and Analytic Network Process (ANP). *Cogent Engineering*, *6*(1), 1623153. doi:10.1080/23311916.2019.1623153

Asgari, H., Azimi, G., Titiloye, I., & Jin, X. (2023). Exploring the influences of personal attitudes on the intention of continuing online grocery shopping after the COVID-19 pandemic. *Travel Behaviour & Society*, *33*, 100622. doi:10.1016/j.tbs.2023.100622 PMID:37396502

Aspray, W., Royer, G., & Ocepek, M. G. (2013). *Food in the internet age*. Springer. doi:10.1007/978-3-319-01598-9

Auty, S. (1992). Consumer choice and segmentation in the restaurant industry. *Service Industries Journal*, *12*(3), 324–339. doi:10.1080/02642069200000042

Ayan, B., Can, M., & Gürsoy, U. T. (2019). Sosyal Medya Madenciliği İle Firmaların Twitter Verilerinin İncelenmesi. *Uluslararası İktisadi ve İdari İncelemeler Dergisi*, (23), 237–256.

Aypar, S., & Kazancioğlu, İ. (2020). The Effect Of Food Influencers On Consumers' Intention To Purchase Food Products/Services. *Journal of Gastronomy Hospitality and Travel*, *3*(2), 150–163. doi:10.33083/joghat.2020.40

Ayyildiz, E., Murat, M., Imamoglu, G., & Kose, Y. (2022). A novel hybrid MCDM approach to evaluate universities based on student perspective. *Scientometrics*. Advance online publication. doi:10.100711192-022-04534-z PMID:36339521

Babin, B. J., Darden, W. R., & Griffin, M. (1994). Work and/or fun: Measuring hedonic and utilitarian shopping value. *The Journal of Consumer Research*, *20*(4), 644–656. doi:10.1086/209376

Bączkiewicz, A., & Wątróbski, J. (2022). A Multi-Criteria Approach to Sustainable Energy Management Evaluation Focusing on Renewable Energy Sources. *Procedia Computer Science*, *207*, 4640–4650. doi:10.1016/j.procs.2022.09.528

Bagozzi, R. P., & Yi, Y. (1989). On the use of structural equation models in experimental designs. *JMR, Journal of Marketing Research*, *26*(3), 271–284. doi:10.1177/002224378902600302

Balakrishnan, B. K., Dahnil, M. I., & Yi, W. T. (2014). The Impact of Social Media Marketing Medium toward Purchase Intention and Brand Loyalty among Generation Y. *Procedia: Social and Behavioral Sciences*, *148*, 177–185. doi:10.1016/j.sbspro.2014.07.032

Bandura, A. (1977). *Social learning theory*. Prentice Hall.

Bandura, A. (1986). *Social foundations of thought and action: A social cognitive theory*. Prentice-Hall, Inc.

Bandura, A., Ross, D., & Ross, S. A. (1961). Transmission of aggression through the imitation of aggressive models. *Journal of Abnormal and Social Psychology*, *63*(3), 575–582. doi:10.1037/h0045925 PMID:13864605

Bansal, H. S., & Voyer, P. A. (2000). Word-of-mouth processes within a services purchase decision context. *Journal of Service Research*, *3*(2), 166–177. doi:10.1177/109467050032005

Barber, N., & Scarcelli, J. M. (2010). Enhancing the assessment of tangible service quality through the creation of a cleanliness measurement scale. *Managing Service Quality*, *20*(1), 70–88. doi:10.1108/09604521011011630

Barquera, S., & Rivera, J. A. (2020). Obesity in Mexico: Rapid epidemiological transition and food industry interference in health policies. *Lancet*, *8*(9), 746–747. PMID:32822599

Barr, A. (2013, June 18). From the ashes of Webvan, Amazon builds a grocery business. *Reuters*. https://www.reuters.com/article/ctech-us-amazon-webvan-idCABRE95H1CC20130618

Barsade, S. G. (2002). The ripple effect: Emotional contagion and its influence on group behavior. *Administrative Science Quarterly*, *47*(4), 644–675. doi:10.2307/3094912

Barysevich, A. (2020b). How social media influence 71% consumer buying decisions. Search Engine Watch. https://www.searchenginewatch.com/2020/11/20/how-social-media-influence-71-consumer-buying-decisions/

Basev, S. E. (2022). The impact of social media on children's consumption: Instagram example. *OPUS Journal of Society Research*, *19*(47), 462–476.

Baum, D., Spann, M., Füller, J., & Thürridl, C. (2019). The impact of social media campaigns on the success of new product introductions. *Journal of Retailing and Consumer Services*, *50*, 289–297. doi:10.1016/j.jretconser.2018.07.003

Beatty, S. E., Mayer, M., Coleman, J. E., Reynolds, K. E., & Lee, J. (1996). Customer-sales associate retail relationships. *Journal of Retailing*, *72*(3), 223–247. doi:10.1016/S0022-4359(96)90028-7

Becheikh, N., Landry, R., & Amara, N. (2006). Lessons from innovation empirical studies in the manufacturing sector: A systematic review of the literature from 1993–2003. *Technovation*, *26*(5), 644–664. doi:10.1016/j.technovation.2005.06.016

Bello. (2020). Politicians step up the fight against Mexico's Coca-Cola habit. *The Economist*, October, 29.

Belton, V., & Stewart, T. (2002). *Multiple Criteria Decision Analysis: An Integrated Approach*.

Bentler, P. M. (1990). Comparative fit indexes in structural models. *Psychological Bulletin*, *107*(2), 238–246. doi:10.1037/0033-2909.107.2.238 PMID:2320703

Berry, L. L., Seiders, K., & Grewal, D. (2002). Understanding service convenience. *Journal of Marketing*, *66*(3), 1–17. doi:10.1509/jmkg.66.3.1.18505

Bhattacharyya, A., & Chakraborty, S. (2014). A DEA-TOPSIS-based approach for performance evaluation of Indian technical institutes. *Decision Science Letters*, *3*(3), 397–410. doi:10.5267/j.dsl.2014.2.003

Biswas, T. K., & Das, M. C. (2019). Selection of Commercially Available Electric Vehicle using Fuzzy AHP-MABAC. *Journal of The Institution of Engineers (India): Series C*, *100*(3), 531-537. doi:10.1007/s40032-018-0481-3

Biswas, T., & Saha, P. (2019). Selection of commercially available scooters by new MCDM method. *International Journal of Data and Network Science*, *3*, 137–144. doi:10.5267/j.ijdns.2018.12.002

Bitner, M. J. (1992). Servicescapes: The impact of physical surroundings on customers and employees. *Journal of Marketing*, *56*(2), 57–71. doi:10.1177/002224299205600205

Bleier, A., & Eisenbeiss, M. (2015). Personalized online advertising effectiveness: the interplay of what, when, and where. *Marketing Science*, *34*(5), 669–688. doi:10.1287/mksc.2015.0930

Boerman, S. C., Helberger, N., Van Noort, G., & Hoofnagle, C. J. (2018). Sponsored blog content: what do the regulations say: and what do bloggers say. *Journal Of Intellectual Property, Information Technology And Electronic Commerce Law*, *9*, 146.

Boerman, S. C., Willemsen, L. M., & Van Der Aa, E. P. (2017). "This post is sponsored" effects of sponsorship disclosure on persuasion knowledge and electronic word of mouth in the context of facebook. *Journal of Interactive Marketing*, *38*(1), 82–92. doi:10.1016/j.intmar.2016.12.002

Bolton, R. N., Parasuraman, A., Hoefnagels, A., Migchels, N., Kabadayi, S., Gruber, T., Loureiro, Y. K., & Solnet, D. (2013). Understanding Generation Y and their use of social media: A review and research agenda. *Journal of Service Management*, *24*(3), 245–267. doi:10.1108/09564231311326987

Booms, B. H., & Bitner, M. J. (1982). Marketing services by managing the environment. *The Cornell Hotel and Restaurant Administration Quarterly*, *23*(1), 35–40. doi:10.1177/001088048202300107

Borsellino, V., Pecoraro, N., & Schimmenti, E. (2023). Promoting dairy products through the web: The case of Pecorino Siciliano PDO during the COVID-19 pandemic. *International Journal of Dairy Technology*, *76*(2), 393–407. Advance online publication. doi:10.1111/1471-0307.12933 PMID:36721399

Bottani, E. (2008). An adapted multi-criteria approach to suppliers and products selection-An application oriented to lead-time reduction. In (pp. 763-781).

Bourlier, A., & Gomez, G. (2016). *Strategies for expanding into emerging markets with e-commerce*. Unctad.Org. https://unctad.org/system/files/non-official-document/dtl-eWeek2017c08-euromonitor_en.pdf

Brand, C., Schwanen, T., & Anable, J. (2020). 'Online omnivores' or 'willing but struggling'? Identifying online grocery shopping behavior segments using attitude theory. *Journal of Retailing and Consumer Services*, *57*, 102195. Advance online publication. doi:10.1016/j.jretconser.2020.102195

Brans, J. P. (1982). L'ingénièrie de la décision; Elaboration d'instruments d'aide à la décision. La méthode PROMETHEE. In R. Nadeau & M. Landry (Eds.), *L'aide à la décision: Nature, Instruments et Perspectives d'Avenir* (pp. 183–213). Presses de l'Université Laval.

Brans, J. P., & Mareschal, B. (2005). Promethee Methods. In *Multiple Criteria Decision Analysis: State of the Art Surveys* (pp. 163–186). Springer New York. doi:10.1007/0-387-23081-5_5

Brans, J. P., & Vincke, P. (1985). A Preference Ranking Organisation Method: (The PROMETHEE Method for Multiple Criteria Decision-Making). *Management Science, 31*(6), 647–656. doi:10.1287/mnsc.31.6.647

Brown, S. M., & Wright, P. K. (1998). A progress report on the manufacturing analysis service, an internet-based reference tool. *Journal of Manufacturing Systems, 17*(5), 389–398. doi:10.1016/S0278-6125(98)80028-9

Bryman, A. (2016). Social research methods, 5th ed.; oxford university press: Oxford, UK

Bughin& Jacques. (2015). McKinsey & Company: Brand success in an era of Digital Darwinism. Retrieved March 22, 2021, from https://www.mckinsey.com/ industries/high-tech/our-insights/brand-success-inanera-of-digital-darwinism

Buttle, A. (1998). Word of mouth: Understanding and managing referral marketing. *Journal of Strategic Marketing, 6*(3), 241–254. doi:10.1080/096525498346658

Cairns, G., Angus, K., Hastings, G., & Caraher, M. (2013). Systematic reviews of the evidence on the nature, extent and effects of food marketing to children. A retrospective summary. *Appetite, 62*, 209–215. doi:10.1016/j.appet.2012.04.017 PMID:22561190

Calderón-Monge, E., & Ramírez-Hurtado, J. M. (2022). Measuring the consumer engagement related to social media: The case of franchising. *Electronic Commerce Research, 22*(4), 1249–1274. Advance online publication. doi:10.100710660-021-09463-2

Campo, K., & Breugelmans, E. (2015). Buying Groceries in Brick and Click Stores: Category Allocation Decisions and the Moderating Effect of Online Buying Experience. *Journal of Interactive Marketing, 31*, 63–78. https://doi.org/doi:10.1016/j.intmar.2015.04.001

Cankul, D., Metin, M., & Özvatan, D. (2018). Food and Beverage Business and Social Media Usage. *Journal of Gastronomy Hospitality and Travel, 1*(1), 29–37. doi:10.33083/joghat.2018.4

Carr, C. T., & Hayes, R. A. (2015). Social media: Defining, developing, and divining. *Atlantic Journal of Communication, 23*(1), 46–65. doi:10.1080/15456870.2015.972282

Carsten, P. (2013, October 13). Alibaba to transform China's "e-conomy" with $500 bln marketplace. *Rueters*. https://www.reuters.com/article/alibaba-retail/alibaba-to-transform-chinas-e-conomy-with-500-bln-marketplace-idUSL4N0HY29Y20131013

Cavallo, A., Ghezzi, A., & Balocco, R. (2019). Entrepreneurial ecosystem research: Present debates and future directions. *The International Entrepreneurship and Management Journal, 15*(4), 1291–1321. doi:10.100711365-018-0526-3

Çaycı, A. E. (2019). Sosyal medya'da dijital yemek kültürü. [UKSAD]. *Uluslararası Kültürel ve Sosyal Araştırmalar Dergisi, 5*(1), 120–136.

Chaffey, D. (2023). *2023 Average ad click through rates (CTRS) for paid search, display and social media*. Smart Insights. Retrieved May 17, 2023, From https://www.smartinsights.com/internet-advertising/internet-advertising-analytics/display-advertising-clickthrough-rates/

Chandrakar, R., & Limje, S. (2018). *A hybrid of QFD and AHP-TOPSIS for Durg dumping waste projects.*

Chen, C.-T., & Hung, W.-Z. (2021). A MCDM Method with Linguistic Variables and Intuitionistic Fuzzy Numbers to Evaluate Product Development Projects. *Int. J. Comput. Intell. Syst.*, *14*(1), 935–945. doi:10.2991/ijcis.d.210222.003

Chen, H. (2011). The relationship between comments and recommendation system and online shopper buying behaviour. [). Trans Tech Publications Ltd.]. *Advanced Materials Research*, *204*(210), 197–200. doi:10.4028/www.scientific.net/AMR.204-210.197

Chen, Y., & Xie, J. (2008). Online consumer review: Word-of-mouth as a new element of marketing communication mix. *Management Science*, *54*(3), 477–491. doi:10.1287/mnsc.1070.0810

Cheung, M., & Thadani, R. (2012). The impact of electronic word-of-mouth communication: A literature analysis and integrative model. *Decision Support Systems*, *54*(1), 461–470. doi:10.1016/j.dss.2012.06.008

Chevalier, J. A., & Mayzlin, D. (2006). The effect of word of mouth on sales: Online book reviews. *JMR, Journal of Marketing Research*, *43*(3), 345–354. doi:10.1509/jmkr.43.3.345

Childers, C., & Boatwright, B. (2021). Do digital natives recognize digital influence? Generational differences and understanding of social media influencers. *Journal of Current Issues and Research in Advertising*, *42*(4), 425–442. doi:10.1080/10641734.2020.1830893

Coates, A. E., Hardman, C. A., Halford, J. C. G., Christiansen, P., & Boyland, E. J. (2019). The effect of influencer marketing of food and a "protective" advertising disclosure on children's food intake. *Pediatric Obesity*, *14*(10), e12540. doi:10.1111/ijpo.12540 PMID:31168959

Coates, A. E., Hardman, C. A., Halford, J. C., Christiansen, P., & Boyland, E. J. (2019). Food and beverage cues featured in YouTube videos of social media influencers popular with children: An exploratory study. *Frontiers in Psychology*, *10*, 2142. doi:10.3389/fpsyg.2019.02142 PMID:31616344

Coban, A., Ertis, I. F., & Cavdaroglu, N. A. (2018). Municipal solid waste management via multi-criteria decision making methods: A case study in Istanbul, Turkey. *Journal of Cleaner Production*, *180*, 159–167. doi:10.1016/j.jclepro.2018.01.130

Colchero, M. A., Rivera-Dommarco, J., Popkin, B. M., & Ng, S. W. (2017). In Mexico, evidence of sustained consumer response two years after implementing a sugar-sweetened beverage tax. *Health Affairs*, *36*(3), 564–571. doi:10.1377/hlthaff.2016.1231 PMID:28228484

Collier, J. E., & Barnes, D. C. (2015). Self-service delight: Exploring the hedonic aspects of self-service. *Journal of Business Research*, *68*(5), 986–993. doi:10.1016/j.jbusres.2014.09.036

Comrey, A. L., & Lee, H. B. (2013). A first course in factor analysis. 2nd Edition, Hillsdale: Psychology Press

Court, D., Elzinga, D., Mulder, S., & Vetvik, O. J. (2009). McKinsey & Company. Retrieved January 24, 2021, fromhttps://www.mckinsey.com/business- functions/marketing-andsales/ourinsights/the-consumer-decision-journey

Dabija, D.-C., Bejan, B. M., & Tipi, N. (2018). Generation X versus Millennials communication behavior on social media when purchasing food versus tourist services. *E+M. Ekonomie a Management*, *21*(1), 191–205. doi:10.15240/tul/001/2018-1-013

Davies, A., Dolega, L., & Arribas-Bel, D. (2019). Buy online collect in-store: Exploring grocery click & collect using a national case study. *International Journal of Retail & Distribution Management*, *47*(3), 278–291. doi:10.1108/IJRDM-01-2018-0025

Davis, L., & Hodges, N. (2012). Consumer shopping value: An investigation of shopping trip value, in-store shopping value and retail format. *Journal of Retailing and Consumer Services*, *19*(2), 229–239. doi:10.1016/j.jretconser.2012.01.004

Dedeoğlu, A. Ö., & Kabasakal, E. (2019). Consumer anxiety, well-being and social media use: The Case Of# HealthyNutrition. *Ege Academic Review*, *19*(3), 341–357. doi:10.21121/eab.536840

Dedeoglu, B. B. (2019). Are information quality and source credibility really important for shared content on social media? The moderating role of gender. *International Journal of Contemporary Hospitality Management*, *31*(1), 513–534. doi:10.1108/IJCHM-10-2017-0691

Deighton, J., & Grayson, K. (1995). Marketing and seduction: Building exchange relationships by managing social consensus. *The Journal of Consumer Research*, *21*(4), 660–676. doi:10.1086/209426

Delaney-Klinger, K., Boyer, K. K., & Frohlich, M. (2003). The return of online grocery shopping: A comparative analysis of Webvan and Tesco's operational methods. *The TQM Magazine*, *15*(3), 187–196. doi:10.1108/09544780310469334

Dewnarain, S., Ramkissoon, H., & Mavondo, F. (2019). Social customer relationship management: An integrated conceptual framework. *Journal of Hospitality Marketing & Management*, *28*(2), 172–188. Advance online publication. doi:10.1080/19368623.2018.1516588

Dhanesh, G. S., & Duthler, G. (2019). Relationship management through social media influencers: Effects of followers' awareness of paid endorsement. *Public Relations Review*, *45*(3), 101765. doi:10.1016/j.pubrev.2019.03.002

Diekman, C., Ryan, C. D., & Oliver, T. L. (2022). Misinformation and Disinformation in Food Science and Nutrition: Impact on Practice. *The Journal of Nutrition*. PMID:36913465

Dillman, D. A., Smyth, J. D., & Christian, L. M. (2014). Internet, phone, mail, and mixed-mode surveys: the tailored design method. John wiley & sons.

Donovan, R. J., Rossiter, J. R., Marcoolyn, G., & Nesdale, A. (1994). Store atmosphere and purchasing behavior. *Journal of Retailing*, *70*(3), 283–294. doi:10.1016/0022-4359(94)90037-X

Donthu, N., Kumar, S., Mukherjee, D., Pandey, N., & Lim, W. M. (2021). How to conduct a bibliometric analysis: An overview and guidelines. *Journal of Business Research, 133*, 285–296. doi:10.1016/j.jbusres.2021.04.070

Duan, W., Gu, B., & Whinston, A. B. (2008). The dynamics of online word-of-mouth and product sales—An empirical investigation of the movie industry. *Journal of Retailing, 84*(2), 233–242. doi:10.1016/j.jretai.2008.04.005

Duarte, A., & Dias, P. (2021). TikTok: Usos e motivações entre adolescentes em Portugal. Chasqui. *Chasqui, 1*(147), 81–103. doi:10.16921/chasqui.v1i147.4419

Duecy, E. (2006). NPD: Dinners look for menu variety,'buzz'in full-service eateries. *Nation's Restaurant News, 40*(4), 14.

Dulen, J. (1999). Quality control. *Restaurants & Institutions, 109*(5), 38–44. PMID:10558057

Dwivedi, Y. K., Ismagilova, E., Hughes, D. L., Carlson, J., Filieri, R., Jacobson, J., Jain, V., Karjaluoto, H., Kefi, H., Krishen, A. S., Kumar, V., Rahman, M. M., Raman, R., Rauschnabel, P. A., Rowley, J., Salo, J., Tran, G. A., & Wang, Y. (2021). Setting the future of digital and social media marketing research: Perspectives and research propositions. *International Journal of Information Management, 59*, 102168. doi:10.1016/j.ijinfomgt.2020.102168

Dwivedi, Y. K., Ismagilova, E., Rana, N. P., & Raman, R. (2023). Social Media Adoption, Usage and Impact In Business-To-Business (B2B) Context: A State-Of-The-Art Literature Review. *Information Systems Frontiers, 25*(3), 971–993. Advance online publication. doi:10.100710796-021-10106-y

eBay Inc. (n.d.). *Our history*. Retrieved June 10, 2023, from https://www.ebayinc.com/company/our-history/

El-Sawalhi, N. I., & Agha, O. E. (2017). *Multi-Attribute Utility Theory for Selecting an Appropriate Procurement Method in the Construction Projects.*

Engin, Y., & İbiş, S. (2016). Öğrencilerin Yiyecek Ve İçecek İşletmesi Seçiminde Sosyal Medyanın Rolünün Belirlenmesi Determining The Role of Social Media Use For The Selection of Food and Beverage Enterprise. *Mehmet Akif Ersoy Üniversitesi Sosyal Bilimler Enstitüsü Dergisi, 8*(17), 322–336.

Erdoğmuş, Z. İ., & Karakaya, M. (2022). Engaging with Social Media Influencers on Youtube: A Cluster Analysis. *Istanbul Business Research, 51*(1), 359–373. doi:10.26650/ibr.2022.51.842750

Erkan, I., & Evans, C. (2016). The influence of eWOM in social media on consumers' purchase intentions: An extended approach to information adoption. *Computers in Human Behavior, 61*, 47–55. doi:10.1016/j.chb.2016.03.003

Erol, A. E. (2023). Delighted for a dairy queen in Egypt: US foreign policy leadership discourse in the Middle East during Arab Spring. *Journal of International and Intercultural Communication, 16*(1), 74–89. Advance online publication. doi:10.1080/17513057.2021.1950198

Esfahani, S. (2015). Investigating Information Adoption Tendencies of Restaurants' User-Generated Content Utilizing a Hypothesized Information Adoption Model (Doctoral dissertation, Kent State University).

European Commission. (2023). *Consumer Protection Law*. Retrieved May 17, 2023, from https://commission.europa.eu/law/law-topic/consumer-protection-law_en

European Economic And Social Committee. (2023). *EU consumer and marketing law*. Retrieved May 17, 2023, from https://www.eesc.europa.eu/en/our-work/opinions-information-reports/information-reports/eu-consumer-and-marketing-law

Everett, H. (2019). Digital Marketing for Restaurants: How to Get Found Online. Retrieved March 26, 2020, from: https://upserve.com/restaurantinsider/ digital-marketing- restaurants

Ewing, M. (2019, June 28). 71% More Likely to Purchase Based on Social Media Referrals [Infographic]. *Blog.Hubspot*. https://blog.hubspot.com/blog/tabid/6307/bid/30239/71-More-Likely-to-Purchase-Based-on-Social-Media-Referrals-Infographic.aspx

Fabretti, P. (2012). Community Management. Share This Too: More Social Media Solutions for PR Professionals, 79-87.

Falk, P., & Campbell, C. (Eds.). (1997). *The Shopping Experience*. Routledge. doi:10.4135/9781446216972

Fanning, S. (2021). We will not stop until the world dreams in cheese: Redefining the wisconsin cheese brand. *Journal of Brand Strategy*, *10*(1).

Fattoruso, G. (2022). Multi-Criteria Decision Making in Production Fields: A Structured Content Analysis and Implications for Practice. *Journal of Risk and Financial Management*, *15*(10), 431. doi:10.3390/jrfm15100431

Fehrer, J. A., Woratschek, H., Germelmann, C. C., & Brodie, R. J. (2018). Dynamics and drivers of customer engagement: Within thedyad and beyond. *Journal of Service Management*, *29*(3), 443–467. doi:10.1108/JOSM-08-2016-0236

Felix, R., Rauschnabel, P. A., & Hinsch, C. (2017). Elements of strategic social media marketing: A holistic framework. *Journal of Business Research*, *70*, 118–126. Advance online publication. doi:10.1016/j.jbusres.2016.05.001

Fernandes, R. (2015). A indústria hoteleira e as reclamações online: o caso do TripAdvisor.

Fields, R. (2014). *Restaurant Success by the Numbers: A Money-guy's Guide to Opening the Next New Hot Spot*. Ten Speed Press.

fietkiewicz, k. J., lins, e., baran, k. S., & stock, w. G. (2016, january). Inter-generational comparison of social media use: investigating the online behavior of different generational cohorts. In *2016 49th hawaii international conference on system sciences (hicss)* (pp. 3829-3838). IEEE.

Flatters, P. (2015). Eating Out - Today and Tomorrow Consumer Survey. Retrieved January 25, 2021, from https://trajectorypartnership.com/wpcontent/uploads/2015/07/SaclaReport_v19FINAL.pdf

Florenthal, B., & Shoham, A. (2010). Four-mode channel interactivity concept and channel preferences. *Journal of Services Marketing*, *24*(1), 29–41. doi:10.1108/08876041011017871

Fogel, S. (2010). Issues in Measurement of Word of Mouth in Social Media Marketing. *International Journal of Integrated Marketing Communications*, *2*(2), 54–60.

Food and Agriculture Organization of the United Nations. (2023). Impact assessment of the COVID-19 pandemic in relation to food value chains in the Lori and Tavush regions. *Policy Brief*. Advance online publication. doi:10.4060/cc0477en

Fornell, C., & Larcker, D. F. (1981). Structural equation models with unobservable variables and measurement error: Algebra and statistics. *JMR, Journal of Marketing Research*, *18*(3), 382–388. doi:10.1177/002224378101800313

Franke, N., & Schreier, M. (2008). Product uniqueness as a driver of customer utility in mass customization. *Marketing Letters*, *19*(2), 93–107. doi:10.100711002-007-9029-7

Franses, P. H., & Paap, R. (2001). Quantitative models in marketing research. Cambridge university press.

Frazão, T. D. C., Camilo, D. G. G., Cabral, E. L. S., & Souza, R. P. (2018). Multicriteria decision analysis (MCDA) in health care: A systematic review of the main characteristics and methodological steps. *BMC Medical Informatics and Decision Making*, *18*(1), 90. doi:10.118612911-018-0663-1 PMID:30382826

Freeman, B., Kelly, B., Baur, L., Chapman, K., Chapman, S., Gill, T., & King, L. (2014). Digital junk: Food and beverage marketing on Facebook. *American Journal of Public Health*, *104*(12), e56–e64. doi:10.2105/AJPH.2014.302167 PMID:25322294

Fry, J. N., Shaw, D. C., von Lanzenauer, C. H., & Dipchand, C. R. (1973). Customer loyalty to banks: A longitudinal study. *The Journal of Business*, *46*(4), 517–525. doi:10.1086/295575

Fulberg, P. (2003). Using sonic branding in the retail environment—An easy and effective way to create consumer brand loyalty while enhancing the in-store experience. *Journal of Consumer Behaviour*, *3*(2), 193–198. doi:10.1002/cb.132

Galante, N., García López, E., & Munby, S. (2013, March 1). The future of online grocery in Europe. *McKinsey & Company*. https://www.mckinsey.com/industries/retail/our-insights/the-future-of-online-grocery-in-europe

Galvez, A. (2020). Taking Susto seriously: A critique of behavioral approaches to diabetes. *American Anthropologist*, *122*(3), 647–648. doi:10.1111/aman.13443

Gani, M. O., & Faroque, A. R. (2021). Digital Marketing. In M. Hoque & R. Bashaw (Eds.), *A. Cross-Border E-Commerce Marketing and Management* (pp. 172–202).

Garcia-Garcia, G. (2022). Using Multi-Criteria Decision-Making to optimise solid waste management. *Current Opinion in Green and Sustainable Chemistry*, *37*, 100650. doi:10.1016/j.cogsc.2022.100650

Garner, B. (2022). Using Social Media to Establish Authenticity: An Analysis of a Small Dairy Farm's Use of Facebook. *Journal of Promotion Management*, *28*(6), 826–842. Advance online publication. doi:10.1080/10496491.2021.2015514

Garner, B., & Mady, A. (2023, March 27). · Garner, B., & Mady, A. (2023). Social media branding in the food industry: Comparing B2B and B2C companies' use of sustainability messaging on Twitter. *Journal of Business and Industrial Marketing*. Advance online publication. doi:10.1108/JBIM-09-2022-0418

Gauri, D. K., Jindal, R. P., Ratchford, B., Fox, E., Bhatnagar, A., Pandey, A., Navallo, J. R., Fogarty, J., Carr, S., & Howerton, E. (2021). Evolution of retail formats: Past, present, and future. *Journal of Retailing*, *97*(1), 42–61. doi:10.1016/j.jretai.2020.11.002

Gelbrich, K., & Sattler, B. (2014). Anxiety, crowding, and time pressure in public self-service technology acceptance. *Journal of Services Marketing*, *28*(1), 82–94. doi:10.1108/JSM-02-2012-0051

Geldermann, J., Spengler, T., & Rentz, O. (2000). Fuzzy outranking for environmental assessment. Case study: Iron and steel making industry. *Fuzzy Sets and Systems*, *115*(1), 45–65. doi:10.1016/S0165-0114(99)00021-4

Georgiadis, D. R., Mazzuchi, T. A., & Sarkani, S. (2013). Using multi criteria decision making in analysis of alternatives for selection of enabling technology. *Systems Engineering*, *16*(3), 287–303. doi:10.1002ys.21233

Ghaleb, A. M., Kaid, H., Alsamhan, A., Mian, S. H., & Hidri, L. (2020). Assessment and Comparison of Various MCDM Approaches in the Selection of Manufacturing Process. [NA.]. *Advances in Materials Science and Engineering*, *2020*, 2020. doi:10.1155/2020/4039253

Giumetti, G. W., & Kowalski, R. M. (2022). Cyberbullying via social media and well-being. *Current Opinion in Psychology*, *45*, 101314. doi:10.1016/j.copsyc.2022.101314 PMID:35313180

Gmiterek, G. (2021). Polish university libraries social networking services during the COVID-19 pandemic spring term lockdown. *Journal of Academic Librarianship*, *47*(3), 102331. Advance online publication. doi:10.1016/j.acalib.2021.102331 PMID:36536687

Godes, D., & Mayzlin, D. (2004). Using online conversations to study word-of-mouth communication. *Marketing Science*, *23*(4), 545–560. doi:10.1287/mksc.1040.0071

Gomes, S., & Lopes, J. M. (2022). Evolution of the online grocery shopping experience during the COVID-19 pandemic: Empiric study from Portugal. *Journal of Theoretical and Applied Electronic Commerce Research*, *17*(3), 909–923. doi:10.3390/jtaer17030047

Grau, S. L. (2022). *Celebrity 2.0: The Role of Social Media Influencer Marketing in Building Brands*. Business Expert Press, LLC.

Greene, T., Seet, C., Barrio, A. R., McIntyre, D., Kelly, B., & Bragg, M. A. (2022). Brands with personalities–good for businesses, but bad for public health? A content analysis of how food and beverage brands personify themselves on Twitter. *Public Health Nutrition*, *25*(1), 51–60. doi:10.1017/S1368980021001439 PMID:33820575

Gretzel, U. (2017). Influencer marketing in travel and tourism. In *Advances in social media for travel, tourism, and hospitality* (pp. 147–156). Routledge. doi:10.4324/9781315565736-13

Grewal, D., & Roggeveen, A. L. (2020). Understanding retail experiences and customer journey management. *Journal of Retailing*, *96*(1), 3–8. doi:10.1016/j.jretai.2020.02.002

Griesbach, K., Reich, A., Elliott-Negri, L., & Milkman, R. (2019). Algorithmic control in platform food delivery work. *Socius: Sociological Research for a Dynamic World*, *5*, 1–15. doi:10.1177/2378023119870041

Grover, R., & Vriens, M. (Eds.). (2006). *The handbook of marketing research: Uses, misuses, and future advances*. SAGE Publications, Inc., doi:10.4135/9781412973380

Gružauskas, V., & Burinskienė, A. (2022). The development of sustainable transportation for e-grocery. *Journal of Management*, *38*(1), 69–74. doi:10.38104/vadyba.2022.1.08

Gummesson, E. (1998). Implementation requires a relationship marketing paradigm. *Journal of the Academy of Marketing Science*, *26*(3), 242–249. doi:10.1177/0092070398263006

Günday, G., Kooij, S., Moulton, J., Karabon, M., & Omeñaca, J. (2020, December 2). How European shoppers will buy groceries in the next normal. *McKinsey & Company.* https://www.mckinsey.com/industries/retail/our-insights/how-european-shoppers-will-buy-groceries-in-the-next-normal

GWI. (2023). *Global social media statistics.* Retrieved may 4, 2023, from https://datareportal.com/social-media-users

Hadipour, A., Rajaee, T., & Hadipour, V., & seidirad, s. (. (2015). Multi-criteria decision-making model for wastewater reuse application: A case study from Iran. *Desalination and Water Treatment.* Advance online publication. doi:10.1080/19443994.2015.1060905

Hair, J. F. Jr, Ringle, C. M., & Sarstedt, M. (2011). PLS-SEM: Indeed a silver bullet. *Journal of Marketing Theory and Practice*, *19*(2), 139–151. doi:10.2753/MTP1069-6679190202

Ha, J., & Jang, S. S. (2010). Effects of service quality and food quality: The moderating role of atmospherics in an ethnic restaurant segment. *International Journal of Hospitality Management*, *29*(3), 520–529. doi:10.1016/j.ijhm.2009.12.005

Ha, J., Park, K., & Park, J. (2016). Which restaurant should I choose? Herd behavior in the restaurant industry. *Journal of Foodservice Business Research*, *19*(4), 396–412. doi:10.1080/15378020.2016.1185873

Hajkowicz, S., & Higgins, A. (2008). A comparison of multiple criteria analysis techniques for water resource management. *European Journal of Operational Research*, *184*(1), 255–265. doi:10.1016/j.ejor.2006.10.045

Hamilton, M., Kaltcheva, V. D., & Rohm, A. J. (2016). Social media and value creation: the role of interaction satisfaction and interaction immersion. *Journal of Interactive Marketing*, *36*(1), 121–133. doi:10.1016/j.intmar.2016.07.001

Hamshaw, R. J., Barnett, J., & Lucas, J. S. (2018). Tweeting and eating: The effect of links and likes on food-hypersensitive consumers' perceptions of tweets. *Frontiers in Public Health*, *6*, 118. doi:10.3389/fpubh.2018.00118 PMID:29740573

Hanaysha, J. (2016). The importance of social media advertisements in enhancing brand equity: A study on fast food restaurant industry in Malaysia. *International Journal of Innovation, Management and Technology*, *7*(2), 46–51. doi:10.18178/ijimt.2016.7.2.643

Hartmans, A. (2021, July 2). Jeff Bezos originally wanted to name Amazon 'Cadabra,' and 14 other little-known facts about the early days of the e-commerce giant. *Insider.* https://www.businessinsider.com/jeff-bezos-amazon-history-facts-2017-4

Hede, A. M., & Kellett, P. (2011). Marketing communications for special events: Analysing managerial practice, consumer perceptions and preferences. *European Journal of Marketing*, *45*(6), 987–1004. doi:10.1108/03090561111119930

Heeter, C. (2000). Interactivity in the context of designed experiences. *Journal of Interactive Advertising*, *1*(1), 3–14. doi:10.1080/15252019.2000.10722040

He, H., & Harris, L. (2020). The impact of Covid-19 pandemic on corporate social responsibility and marketing philosophy. *Journal of Business Research*, *116*, 176–182. doi:10.1016/j.jbusres.2020.05.030 PMID:32457556

Hellenic Agricultural Organization (ELGO) – DIMITRA, "Management of fresh milk production data", https://www.elgo.gr/index.php?option=com_content&view=article&id=888&Itemid=1267&lang=el (Accessed: 12-02-2023).

Hennig-Thurau, T., Gwinner, K. P., Walsh, G., & Gremler, D. D. (2004). Electronic Word-of-Mouth via Consumer-Opinion Platforms: What Motivates Consumers to Articulate Themselves on the Internet? *Journal of Interactive Marketing*, *18*(1), 38–52. doi:10.1002/dir.10073

Hirschman, E. C. (1980). Innovativeness, novelty seeking, and consumer creativity. *The Journal of Consumer Research*, *7*(3), 283–295. doi:10.1086/208816

Holbrook, M. B. (1994). The nature of customer value: An axiology of services in the consumption experience. *Service Quality: New Directions in Theory and Practice*, *21*, 21–71. doi:10.4135/9781452229102.n2

Holbrook, M. B. (1999). *Consumer value: A framework for analysis and research.* Routledge.

Holbrook, M. B., & Hirschman, E. C. (1982). The experiential aspects of consumption: Consumer fantasies, feelings, and fun. *The Journal of Consumer Research*, *1*(2), 132–140. doi:10.1086/208906

Hooker, L. (2020). How can retailers thrive in a changing landscape? A review of 2019 and our expectations for 2020. *The Retailer* (winter edition), 28-29.

Hopper, C. (2013). *Selling Eating*. Young &Laramore, Inc.

Hsu, M. H., Yen, C. H., Chiu, C. M., & Chang, C. M. (2006). A longitudinal investigation of continued online shopping behavior: An extension of the theory of planned behavior. *International Journal of Human-Computer Studies*, *64*(9), 889–904. doi:10.1016/j.ijhcs.2006.04.004

Huang, I. B., Keisler, J., & Linkov, I. (2011). Multi-criteria decision analysis in environmental sciences: Ten years of applications and trends. *The Science of the Total Environment*, *409*(19), 3578–3594. doi:10.1016/j.scitotenv.2011.06.022 PMID:21764422

Hu, H., & Jasper, C. R. (2006). Social cues in the store environment and their impact on store image. *International Journal of Retail & Distribution Management*, *34*(1), 25–48. doi:10.1108/09590550610642800

Huizinga, J. (1955). *Homo ludens: A study of the play element inculture*. The Beacon Press. International Data Corporation.

Hurtig, K. (2021, August 6). Time edges out COVID concerns for buying groceries online. *Winsight Grocery Business*. https://www.winsightgrocerybusiness.com/industry-partners/time-edges-out-covid-concerns-buying-groceries-online

Iacobucci, D., Ostrom, A., & Grayson, K. (1995). Distinguishing service quality and customer satisfaction: The voice of the consumer. *Journal of Consumer Psychology*, *4*(3), 277–303. doi:10.120715327663jcp0403_04

Iacopini, I., Petri, G., Barrat, A., & Latora, V. (2019). Simplicial models of social contagion. *Nature Communications*, *10*(1), 1–9. doi:10.103841467-019-10431-6 PMID:31171784

Ishizaka, A., & Siraj, S. (2018). Are multi-criteria decision-making tools useful? An experimental comparative study of three methods. *European Journal of Operational Research*, *264*(2), 462–471. doi:10.1016/j.ejor.2017.05.041

Iyer, G. R., Blut, M., Xiao, S. H., & Grewal, D. (2020). Impulse buying: A meta-analytic review. *Journal of the Academy of Marketing Science*, *48*(3), 384–404. doi:10.100711747-019-00670-w

Jacobides, M., MacDuffie, J., & Tae, C. (2015). Agency, Structure, and the Dominance of OEMs: Change and Stability in the Automotive Sector. *Strategic Management Journal*, *37*(9), 1942–1967. Advance online publication. doi:10.1002mj.2426

Jain, R., & Bagdare, S. (2009). Determinants of customer experience in new format retail stores. *Journal of Marketing Communications*, *5*(2), 34–44.

Jang, S., & Namkung, Y. (2009). Perceived quality, emotions, and behavioral intentions: Application of an extended Mehrabian–Russell model to restaurants. *Journal of Business Research*, *62*(4), 451–460. doi:10.1016/j.jbusres.2008.01.038

Jara, M., Vyt, D., Mevel, O., Morvan, T., & Morvan, N. (2018). Measuring customers benefits of click and collect. *Journal of Services Marketing*, *32*(4), 430–442. doi:10.1108/JSM-05-2017-0158

Jeong, E., & Jang, S. (2011). Restaurant experiences triggering positive electronic word-of-mouth (eWOM) motivations. *International Journal of Hospitality Management*, *30*(2), 356–366. doi:10.1016/j.ijhm.2010.08.005

Jillian, S., Lester, J., & Robert, A. (1992). The Effect of Cues on Service Quality Expectations andService Selection in a Restaurant Setting. *Journal of Services Marketing*, *6*(4).

June, P., & Smith, L. (1987). Service attributes and situational effects on customer preferences for restaurant dining. *Journal of Travel Research*, *26*(2), 20–27. doi:10.1177/004728758702600205

Kabir, G. (2014). A review of multi-criteria decision-making methods for infrastructure management. In (pp. 1176-1210). doi:10.1080/15732479.2013.795978

Kaczyńska, A., Gandotra, N., & Sałabun, W. (2022). A new approach to dealing with interval data in the TOPSIS method. *Procedia Computer Science*, *207*, 4545–4555. doi:10.1016/j.procs.2022.09.518

Kahraman, C., Onar, S. C., ÖZTAYşI, B., ŞEKER, Ş., & KARAşAN, A. (2020). Integration of fuzzy AHP with other fuzzy multicriteria methods: a state of the art survey. *Journal of Multiple-Valued Logic & Soft Computing, 35*.

Kaltcheva, V. D., & Weitz, B. A. (2006). When should a retailer create an exciting store environment? *Journal of Marketing*, *70*(1), 107–118. doi:10.1509/jmkg.70.1.107.qxd

Kamel, M.-A., de Montgolfier, J., Athanassiou, M., & De Mol, A. (2022, March 16). Online grocery strategy: A reality check for disruptors and incumbents. *Bain & Company.* https://www.bain.com/insights/online-grocery-strategy/

Kamenidou, I., Stavrianea, A., & Bara, E. Z. (2020). Generational differences toward organic food behavior: insights from five generational cohorts. *Sustainability (Basel)*, *12*(6), 2299. doi:10.3390u12062299

Kaplan, A. M., & Haenlein, M. (2010). Users of the world, unite! The challenges and opportunities of social media. *Business Horizons*, *53*(1), 59–68. doi:10.1016/j.bushor.2009.09.003

Keller, E. (2007). Unleashing the power of word of mouth: Creating brand advocacy to drive growth. *Journal of Advertising Research*, *47*(4), 448–452. doi:10.2501/S0021849907070468

Kerr, G., & Richards, J. (2021). Redefining advertising in research and practice. *International Journal of Advertising*, *40*(2), 175–198. doi:10.1080/02650487.2020.1769407

Khaleeli, M. (2020). The Effect Of Social Media Advertising And Promotion On Online Purchase Intention. *ResearchGate* https://www.researchgate.net/publication/344337458_THE_EFFECT_OF_SOCIAL_MEDIA_ADVERTISING_AND_PROMOTION_ON_ONLINE_PURCHASE_INTENTION

Khan, F., Ali, Y., & Khan, A. U. (2020). Sustainable hybrid electric vehicle selection in the context of a developing country. *Air Quality, Atmosphere & Health*, *13*(4), 489–499. doi:10.100711869-020-00812-y

Kietzmann, J. H., Hermkens, K., Mccarthy, I. P., & Silvestre, B. S. (2011). Social media? Get serious! Understanding the functional building blocks of social media. *Business Horizons*, *54*(3), 241–251. doi:10.1016/j.bushor.2011.01.005

Kim, H. W., & Kankanhalli, A. (2009). Investigating user resistance to information systems implementation: A status quo bias perspective. *Management Information Systems Quarterly*, *33*(3), 567–582. doi:10.2307/20650309

Kim, S. J., Maslowska, E., & Tamaddoni, A. (2019). The paradox of (dis) trust in sponsorship disclosure: the characteristics and effects of sponsored online consumer reviews. *Decision Support Systems*, *116*, 114–124. doi:10.1016/j.dss.2018.10.014

Kim, W. G., Ng, C. Y. N., & Kim, Y. S. (2009). Influence of institutional DINESERV on customer satisfaction, return intention, and word-of-mouth. *International Journal of Hospitality Management*, *28*(1), 10–17. doi:10.1016/j.ijhm.2008.03.005

Kırcova, İ., Yaman, Y., & Köse, Ş. G. (2021). Instagram, Facebook or Twitter: which engages best? A comparative study of consumer brand engagement and social commerce purchase intention.

Kivela, J., Inbakaran, R., & Reece, J. (1999). Consumer research in the restaurant environment, Part 1: A conceptual model of dining satisfaction and return patronage. *International Journal of Contemporary Hospitality Management*, *11*(5), 205–222. doi:10.1108/09596119910272739

Kizielewicz, B., & Dobryakova, L. (2020). How to choose the optimal single-track vehicle to move in the city? Electric scooters study case. *Procedia Computer Science*, *176*, 2243–2253. doi:10.1016/j.procs.2020.09.274

Klassen, K. M., Borleis, E. S., Brennan, L., Reid, M., McCaffrey, T. A., & Lim, M. S. (2018). What people "like": Analysis of social media strategies used by food industry brands, lifestyle brands, and health promotion organizations on Facebook and Instagram. *Journal of Medical Internet Research*, *20*(6), e10227. doi:10.2196/10227 PMID:29903694

Klos, C., Spieth, P., Clauss, T., & Klusmann, C. (2023). Digital Transformation of Incumbent Firms: A Business Model Innovation Perspective. *IEEE Transactions on Engineering Management*, *70*(6), 2017–2033. Advance online publication. doi:10.1109/TEM.2021.3075502

Knezevic, K., Davidaviciene, D., & Skrobot, S. (2017). Social networks as a communication tool in social supermarkets. *SOTICS 2017 : The Seventh International Conference on Social Media Technologies, Communication, and Informatics*. (pp.5-10).

Kolb, B. (2008). Marketing research: a practical approach. *Sage (Atlanta, Ga.)*.

Kotler, P., Bowen, J. T., Makens, J. &Baloglu, S. (2017). Marketing for hospitality and tourism.

Kowalski, A. F., Hawley, S. L., Hilton, E. J., Becker, A. C., West, A. A., Bochanski, J. J., & Sesar, B. (2009). M Dwarfs in Sloan Digital Sky Survey Stripe 82: Photometric Light Curves and Flare Rate Analysis. *The Astronomical Journal*, *138*(2), 633–648. doi:10.1088/0004-6256/138/2/633

Kozinets, V., De Valck, K., Wojnicki, C., & Wilner, J. (2010). Networked narratives: Understanding word-of-mouth marketing in online communities. *Journal of Marketing*, *74*(2), 71–89. doi:10.1509/jm.74.2.71

Krampe, C., & Fridman, A. (2022). Oatly, a serious 'problem' for the dairy industry? A case study. *The International Food and Agribusiness Management Review*, *25*(1). Advance online publication. doi:10.22434/IFAMR2021.0058

Krupa-Kotara, K., Grajek, M., Rozmiarek, M., Malchrowicz-Mośko, E., Staśkiewicz, W., León-Guereño, P., & Castañeda-Babarro, A. (2023). The Role of Social Media in Internalizing Body Knowledge—A Cross-Sectional Study among Women with Different Food Preferences. *International Journal of Environmental Research and Public Health*, *20*(3), 2069. doi:10.3390/ijerph20032069 PMID:36767433

Kubik, A. (2022). Selection of an Electric Scooter for Shared Mobility Services Using Multicriteria Decision Support Methods. *Energies*, *15*(23), 8903. doi:10.3390/en15238903

Kucharczuk, A. J., Oliver, T. L., & Dowdell, E. B. (2022). Social media's influence on adolescents′ food choices: A mixed studies systematic literature review. *Appetite*, *168*, 105765. doi:10.1016/j.appet.2021.105765 PMID:34687823

Kumar, G., & Parimala, N. (2020). A weighted sum method MCDM approach for recommending product using sentiment analysis. *International Journal of Business Information Systems*, *35*(2), 185–203. doi:10.1504/IJBIS.2020.110172

Labrecque, L. I. (2014). Fostering consumer–brand relationships in social media environments: the role of parasocial interaction. *Journal of Interactive Marketing*, *28*(2), 134–148. doi:10.1016/j.intmar.2013.12.003

Ladhari, R. (2008). Alternative measures of service quality: A review. *Managing Service Quality*, *18*(1), 65–86. doi:10.1108/09604520810842849

Ladhari, R., Brun, I., & Morales, M. (2008). Determinants of dining satisfaction and post-dining behavioral intentions. *International Journal of Hospitality Management*, *27*(4), 563–573. doi:10.1016/j.ijhm.2007.07.025

Lammers, R. (2020). *Feeling targeted in a digital era: a study about the influence of online behavioral targeting on consumer attitudes*. University of Twente, Lewandowska,

Lee, H., Jang, Y., Kim, Y., Choi, H. M., & Ham, S. (2019). Consumers' prestige-seeking behavior in premium food markets: Application of the theory of the leisure class. *International Journal of Hospitality Management*, *77*, 260–269. doi:10.1016/j.ijhm.2018.07.005

Lee, J., & Hong, I. B. (2016). Predicting positive user responses to social media advertising: the roles of emotional appeal, informativeness, and creativity. *International Journal of Information Management*, *36*(3), 360–373. doi:10.1016/j.ijinfomgt.2016.01.001

Leung, L. (2013). Generational differences in content generation in social media: the roles of the gratifications sought and of narcissism. *Computers in Human Behavior*, *29*(3), 997–1006. doi:10.1016/j.chb.2012.12.028

Lewandowska, A., Jankowski, J., Sałabun, W., & Wątróbski, J. (2019). Multicriteria selection of online advertising content for the habituation effect reduction. In Intelligent Information and Database Systems: 11th Asian Conference, ACIIDS 2019, Yogyakarta, Indonesia, April 8–11, 2019 [Springer International Publishing.]. *Proceedings*, *11*(Part II), 499–509.

Lewis, R. (1981). Restaurant advertising: Appeals and consumers' intentions. *Journal of Advertising Research*, *21*(5), 69–74.

Libai, B., Bolton, R., Bügel, M. S., De Ruyter, K., Götz, O., Risselada, H., & Stephen, A. T. (2010). Customer-to-customer interactions: Broadening the scope of word-of-mouth research. *Journal of Service Research*, *13*(3), 267–282. doi:10.1177/1094670510375600

Li, F., Larimo, J., & Leonidou, L. C. (2021). Social media marketing strategy: Definition, conceptualization, taxonomy, validation, and future agenda. *Journal of the Academy of Marketing Science*, *49*(1), 51–70. doi:10.100711747-020-00733-3

Ligas, M., & Chaudhuri, A. (2012). The moderating roles of shopper experience and store type on the relationship between perceived merchandise value and willingness to pay a higher price. *Journal of Retailing and Consumer Services*, *19*(2), 249–258. doi:10.1016/j.jretconser.2012.01.006

Liu, Y. (2006). Word of mouth for movies: Its dynamics and impact on box office revenue. *Journal of Marketing*, *70*(3), 74–89. doi:10.1509/jmkg.70.3.074

Liu, Y., & Jang, S. (2009). Perceptions of Chinese restaurants in the US: What affects customer satisfaction and behavioural intentions? *International Journal of Hospitality Management*, *28*(3), 338–34. doi:10.1016/j.ijhm.2008.10.008

Lunce, S. E., Lunce, L. M., Kawai, Y., & Maniam, B. (2006). Success and failure of pure-play organizations: Webvan versus Peapod, a comparative analysis. *Industrial Management & Data Systems*, *106*(9), 1344–1358. doi:10.1108/02635570610712618

Luo, Q., Forscher, T., Shaheen, S., Deakin, E., & Walker, J. L. (2023). Impact of the COVID-19 pandemic and generational heterogeneity on ecommerce shopping styles – A case study of Sacramento, California. *Communications in Transportation Research*, *3*, 100091. Advance online publication. doi:10.1016/j.commtr.2023.100091

Lütjens, H., Eisenbeiss, M., Fiedler, M., & Bijmolt, T. (2022). Determinants of consumers' attitudes towards digital advertising–a meta-analytic comparison across time and touchpoints. *Journal of Business Research*, *153*, 445–466. doi:10.1016/j.jbusres.2022.07.039

Lu, X., Ba, S., Huang, L., & Feng, Y. (2013). Promotional marketing or word-of-mouth. Evidence from online restaurant reviews. *Information Systems Research*, *24*(3), 596–612. doi:10.1287/isre.1120.0454

Madhavan, M., & Kaliyaperumal, C. (2015). Consumer buying behavior-an overview of theory and models. *St. Theresa journal of humanities and social sciences*, *1*(1), 74–112.

Majumder, P., Majumder, M., Saha, A. K., Sarkar, K., & Nath, S. (2019). Real time reliability monitoring of hydro-power plant by combined cognitive decision-making technique. *International Journal of Energy Research*, *43*(9), 4912–4939. doi:10.1002/er.4530

Ma, L., Ou, W., & Lee, C. S. (2022). Investigating consumers' cognitive, emotional, and behavioral engagement in social media brand pages: a natural language processing approach. *Electronic Commerce Research and Applications*, *54*, 101179. doi:10.1016/j.elerap.2022.101179

Malik, D. A. A., Yusof, Y., & Khalif, K. M. N. K. (2021). A view of MCDM application in education. *Journal of Physics: Conference Series*, *1988*(1), 012063. doi:10.1088/1742-6596/1988/1/012063

Malthouse, E. C., Calder, B. J., Kim, S. J., & Vandenbosch, M. (2016). Evidence that user-generated content that produces engagement increases purchase behaviours. *Journal of Marketing Management*, *32*(5-6), 427–444. doi:10.1080/0267257X.2016.1148066

Manohar, S., & Rehman, V. (2019). Brand resurrection in an emerging economy. *Journal of Marketing Communications*, *25*(7), 783–798. Advance online publication. doi:10.1080/13527266.2018.1455292

Mareschal, B., & Tsaples, G. (2021). The History and Future of PROMETHEE. In J. Papathanasiou, P. Zaraté, & J. Freire de Sousa (Eds.), EURO Working Group on DSS: A Tour of the DSS Developments Over the Last 30 Years (pp. 259-272). Cham: Springer International Publishing. doi:10.1007/978-3-030-70377-6_14

Mareschal, B. (1986). Stochastic multicriteria decision-making under uncertainty. *European Journal of Operational Research*, *26*(1), 58–64. doi:10.1016/0377-2217(86)90159-1

Mareschal, B., & Brans, J. P. (1988). Geometrical representations for MCDA. *European Journal of Operational Research*, *34*(1), 69–77. doi:10.1016/0377-2217(88)90456-0

Martin, R., & Frumkin, P. (2005). Consumer trends: What do they want (and why). *International Journal of Contemporary Hospitality Management*, *39*(21), 58–63.

Mathwick, C., Malhotra, N., & Rigdon, E. (2001). Experiential value: Conceptualization, measurement and application in the catalog and internet shopping environment. *Journal of Retailing*, *77*(1), 39–56. doi:10.1016/S0022-4359(00)00045-2

Mattke, J., Maier, C., Reis, L., & Weitzel, T. (2020). Herd behavior in social media: the role of facebook likes, strength of ties, and expertise. *Information & Management*, *57*(8), 103370. doi:10.1016/j.im.2020.103370

McFadden, L., & Train, E. (1996). Consumers' evaluation of new products: Learning from self and others. *Journal of Political Economy*, *104*(4), 683–703. doi:10.1086/262038

Mcquarrie, E. F., & Phillips, B. J. (2005). Indirect persuasion in advertising: how consumers process metaphors presented in pictures and words. *Journal of Advertising*, *34*(2), 7–20. doi:10.1080/00913367.2005.10639188

Mehrabian, A., & Russell, J. A. (1974). *An approach to environmental psychology*. The Massachusetts Institute of Technology.

Merrilees, B., & Miller, D. (2001). Superstore interactivity: A new self-service paradigm of retail service? *International Journal of Retail & Distribution Management*, *29*(8/9), 379–389. doi:10.1108/09590550110396953

Millan, J., Phakamad, B., Rhodes, S., & Tipon, C. (2022). *Instacart - Accessibility usability evaluation of grocery delivery website for the visually impaired.* https://static1.squarespace.com/static/61b27d1fa32231228c041e6e/t/61b7a9245380f5602fc75808/1639426341268/instacartreport.pdf

Mishra, A., & Shukla, A. (2023). Gyan Fresh: Digital Transformation of Dairy Business with Resilience and Technology Innovation. *FIIB Business Review*, *12*(1), 20–30. Advance online publication. doi:10.1177/23197145221113374

Momin, A. (2023, June 8). Grocery Industry Analysis: What is the Future of Grocery Stores? *PESTLE Analysis*. https://pestleanalysis.com/grocery-industry-analysis/

Moreira, A., Sá, P., & Costa, A. P. (2009). Metodologias de Investigação.

Morgan, B. (2020). Lasting changes to grocery shopping after Covid-19. *Forbes*. https://www.forbes.com/sites/blakemorgan/2020/12/14/3-lasting-changes-to-grocery-shopping-after-covid-19/?sh=3158c55754e7

Moser, C., Schoenebeck, Y., & Reinecke, K. (2016). Technology at the table: Attitudes about mobile phone use at mealtimes. In *Proceedings of the 2016 CHI Conference on Human Factors in Computing Systems*,1881-1892. 10.1145/2858036.2858357

Mumani, A. A., Magableh, G. M., & Mistarihi, M. Z. (2022). Decision making process in lean assessment and implementation: A review. *Management Review Quarterly*, *72*(4), 1089–1128. doi:10.100711301-021-00222-z

Naeem, M. (2021). Do social media platforms develop consumer panic buying during the fear of Covid-19 pandemic. *Journal of Retailing and Consumer Services, 58*, 102226. https://doi.org/doi:10.1016/j.jretconser.2020.102226

Namin, F. S., Ghadi, A., & Saki, F. (2022). A literature review of Multi Criteria Decision-Making (MCDM) towards mining method selection (MMS). *Resources Policy*, *77*, 102676. doi:10.1016/j.resourpol.2022.102676

Nash, J. (2019). Exploring how social media platforms influence fashion consumer decisions in the UK retail sector. *Journal of Fashion Marketing and Management*, *23*(1), 82–103. doi:10.1108/JFMM-01-2018-0012

Nieto-Morote, A. (2011). A fuzzy ahp multi-criteria decision-making approach applied to combined cooling, heating, and power production systems. In (pp. 497-517). doi:10.1142/S0219622011004427

Nunan, D., Malhotra, N. K., & Birks, D. F. (2020). *Marketing research*. Pearson UK.

Olson, E. M., Olson, K. M., Czaplewski, A. J., & Key, T. M. (2021). Business strategy and the management of digital marketing. *Business Horizons*, *64*(2), 285–293. Advance online publication. doi:10.1016/j.bushor.2020.12.004

Oyedele, A., & Simpson, P. M. (2007). An empirical investigation of consumer control factors on intention to use selected self-service technologies. *International Journal of Service Industry Management*, *18*(3), 287–306. doi:10.1108/09564230710751497

Page, M. J., McKenzie, J. E., Bossuyt, P. M., Boutron, I., Hoffmann, T. C., Mulrow, C. D., Shamseer, L., Tetzlaff, J. M., Akl, E. A., Brennan, S. E., Chou, R., Glanville, J., Grimshaw, J. M., Hróbjartsson, A., Lalu, M. M., Li, T., Loder, E. W., Mayo-Wilson, E., McDonald, S., ... Moher, D. (2021). The PRISMA 2020 statement: An updated guideline for reporting systematic reviews. *BMJ (Clinical Research Ed.)*, *372*. Advance online publication. doi:10.1136/bmj.n71 PMID:33782057

Palczewski, K., & Sałabun, W. (2019). Identification of the football teams assessment model using the COMET method. *Procedia Computer Science*, *159*, 2491–2501. doi:10.1016/j.procs.2019.09.424

Pallas, D. (2019). *Mastering Social Media Marketing 2019: How to Dominate Social Media for The Next Decade*. Independently Published.

Pan, B., Maclaurin, T., & Crotts, J. (2007). Travel blogs and the implications for destination marketing. *Journal of Travel Research*, *46*(1), 35–45. doi:10.1177/0047287507302378

Pan, S. L., Cui, M., & Qian, J. (2020). Information resource orchestration during the COVID-19 pandemic: A study of community lockdowns in China. *International Journal of Information Management*, *54*, 102143. Advance online publication. doi:10.1016/j.ijinfomgt.2020.102143 PMID:32394997

Pantano, E., Pizzi, G., Scarpi, D., & Dennis, C. (2020). Competing during a pandemic? Retailers' ups and downs during the COVID-19 outbreak. *Journal of Business Research*, *116*, 209–213. doi:10.1016/j.jbusres.2020.05.036 PMID:32501307

Pantano, E., & Vannucci, V. (2019). Who is innovating? An exploratory research of digital technologies diffusion in retail industry. *Journal of Retailing and Consumer Services*, *49*, 297–304. doi:10.1016/j.jretconser.2019.01.019

Papathanasiou, J., & Ploskas, N. (2018). *Multiple Criteria Decision Aid: Methods, Examples and Python Implementations*. Springer International Publishing. doi:10.1007/978-3-319-91648-4

Paradowski, B., Bączkiewicz, A., & Watrąbski, J. (2021). Towards proper consumer choices - MCDM based product selection. *Procedia Computer Science, 192*, 1347–1358. doi:10.1016/j.procs.2021.08.138

Parasuraman, A., Zeithaml, A., & Berry, L. (1988). Servqual: A multiple- item scale for measuring consumer perc. *Journal of Retailing, 64*(1), 12.

Parikh, A., Behnke, C., Vorvoreanu, M., Almanza, B., & Nelson, D. (2014). Motives for reading and articulating user-generated restaurant reviews on Yelp. com. *Journal of Hospitality and Tourism Technology, 5*(2), 160–176. doi:10.1108/JHTT-04-2013-0011

Patterson, P., Wirtz, J., Walker, R., Pearce, G., & Lovelock, C. (2011). Services marketing.

Pauliene, R., & Sedneva, K. (2019). The Influence of Recommendations in Social Media on Purchase Intentions of Generations Y and Z. *Organizations and Markets in Emerging Economies, 10*(2), 227–256. doi:10.15388/omee.2019.10.12

Peeroo, S., Samy, M., & Jones, B. (2017). Facebook: A blessing or a curse for grocery stores? *International Journal of Retail & Distribution Management, 45*(12), 1242–1259. doi:10.1108/IJRDM-12-2016-0234

Pekerşen, Y., & Kaplan, M. (2020). Tüketicilerin yeme içme alışkanlıkları ve yiyecek-içecek işletmesi tercihlerinde sosyal medya kullanımının rolü: Muğla örneği. *İşletme Araştırmaları Dergisi, 12*(3), 2362-2381.

Petrilák, M., Janšto, E., &Horská, E. (2020). Communication of local farmers' products through Facebook: The case study of Naše-Vaše. *Communication Today, 11*(1).

Philip, L. (2016). Impact of food blogs on the readers. *Journal of Mass Communication and Journalism, 6*(2), 1–3. doi:10.4172/2165-7912.1000300

Phillips, D., & Young, P. (2009). *Online public relations: A practical guide to developing an online strategy in the world of social media*. Kogan Page Publishers.

Pilař, L., Stanislavská, L. K., Kvasnička, R., Hartman, R., & Tichá, I. (2021). Healthy food on instagram social network: Vegan, homemade and clean eating. *Nutrients, 13*(6), 1991. doi:10.3390/nu13061991 PMID:34207910

Polanco-Diges, L., & Debasa, F. (2020). The Use of Digital Marketing Strategies in the Sharing Economy: A Literature Review. *Journal of Spatial and Organizational Dynamics, 8*(3).

Portugal, S. (2016). Os desafios da Restauração Moderna. [Ebook] Lisboa: Sage. Retrieved June 1, 2021, from: https://www.sage.pt/~/media/markets/pt/LP-Software-Restaurantes/EBook-Os-desafios-da restauracaomoderna.pdf

Prasad, S., Garg, A., & Prasad, S. K. (2019). Purchase decision of generation Y in an online environment. *Marketing Intelligence & Planning, 37*(4), 372–385. doi:10.1108/MIP-02-2018-0070

Przyrembel, H. (2004). Food labelling legislation in the EU and consumers information. *Trends in Food Science & Technology*, *15*(7-8), 360–365. doi:10.1016/j.tifs.2003.12.006

Pütter, M. (2017). The Impact of Social Media on Consumer Buying Intention. *Journal of International Business Research and Marketing*, *3*(1), 7–13. doi:10.18775/jibrm.1849-8558.2015.31.3001

Qin, G., & Prybutok, R. (2008). Determinants of customer-perceived service quality in fast-food restaurants and their relationship to customer satisfaction and behavioural intentions. *The Quality Management Journal*, *15*(2), 35–50. doi:10.1080/10686967.2008.11918065

Quesenberry, K. A. (2019). *Social Media Strategy: Marketing, Advertising, and Public Relations in the Consumer Revolution*. Rowman & Littlefield Publishers.

Qutteina, Y., Hallez, L., Raedschelders, M., De Backer, C., & Smits, T. (2022). Food for teens: How social media is associated with adolescent eating outcomes. *Public Health Nutrition*, *25*(2), 290–302. PMID:34325764

Rahımı, Z., & Kırkbir, F. (2022). Sosyal Medya Pazarlama Faaliyetlerinin Yeme-İçme İşletmeleri Müşterilerinin İlhamı Ve Marka Bağlılığı Üzerindeki Etkisi: Karadeniz Teknik Üniversitesi Öğrencileri Üzerinde Bir Çalışma. *Uluslararası İktisadi Ve İdari İncelemeler Dergisi*, (36), 111–130.

Ramanathan, U., Subramanian, N., & Parrott, G. (2017). Role of social media in retail network operations and marketing to enhance customer satisfaction. *International Journal of Operations & Production Management*, *37*(1), 105–123. https://doi.org/doi:10.1108/IJOPM-03-2015-0153

Rasheed, H. S. (2009). Contrasting e-commerce business models: Performance implications for small enterprises. *Journal of Developmental Entrepreneurship*, *14*(1), 89–101. doi:10.1142/S1084946709001168

Ratchford, B., Soysal, G., Zentner, A., & Gauri, D. K. (2022). Online and offline retailing: What we know and directions for future research. *Journal of Retailing*, *98*(1), 152–177. doi:10.1016/j.jretai.2022.02.007

Reardon, T., Belton, B., Liverpool-Tasie, L. S. O., Lu, L., Nuthalapati, C. S. R., Tasie, O., & Zilberman, D. (2021). E-commerce's fast-tracking diffusion and adaptation in developing countries. *Applied Economic Perspectives and Policy*, *43*(4), 1243–1259. doi:10.1002/aepp.13160

Reardon, T., Tomatis, F., & Pedersen, E. (2023). *Evolution of food e-commerce during the COVID-19 pandemic* [Investment brief]. Food and Agricultural Organization of the United States., doi:10.4060/cc3650en

Rekik, R., Kallel, I., & Casillas, J. (2016). *Using Multiple Criteria Decision Making Approaches to Assess the Quality of Web Sites*.

Ribeiro, M. (2019). Zomato em Portugal: A história contada por Miguel Ribeiro. (2019). Retrieved July 20, 2020, from https://medium.com/zomatoblogportugal/zomatoem-portugal-a-hist%C3%B3ria-contada-por-miguel-ribeiro-86925735f3e3

Richards, J., Daugherty, T., & Logan, K. (2009). Advertising History. *Encyclopedia Of Journalism*, 1-15.

Ridgway, N. M., Dawson, S. A., & Bloch, P. H. (1990). Pleasure and arousal in the marketplace: Interpersonal differences in approach-avoidance responses. *Marketing Letters*, *1*(2), 139–147. doi:10.1007/BF00435297

Rigby, D. (2011). The future of shopping. *Harvard Business Review*. https://hbr.org/2011/12/the-future-of-shopping

Rodak, O. (2020). Hashtag hijacking and crowdsourcing transparency: Social media affordances and the governance of farm animal protection. *Agriculture and Human Values*, *37*(2), 281–294. Advance online publication. doi:10.100710460-019-09984-5

Rodgers, S., & Wang, Y. (2011). Electronic word of mouth and consumer generated content: From concept to application. In *Handbook of research on digital media and advertising: User generated content consumption* (pp. 212–231). IGI Global. doi:10.4018/978-1-60566-792-8.ch011

Roggeveen, A. L., & Sethuraman, R. (2020). How the COVID-19 pandemic may change the world of retailing. *Journal of Retailing*, *96*(2), 169–171. doi:10.1016/j.jretai.2020.04.002

Rohm, A., & Kaltcheva, D., VMilne, G.R. (2013). A mixed-method approach to examining brand-consumer interactions driven by social media. *Journal of Research in Interactive Marketing*, *7*(4), 295–311. doi:10.1108/JRIM-01-2013-0009

Rutsaert, P., Regan, Á., Pieniak, Z., McConnon, Á., Moss, A., Wall, P., & Verbeke, W. (2013). The use of social media in food risk and benefit communication. *Trends in Food Science & Technology*, *30*(1), 84–91. doi:10.1016/j.tifs.2012.10.006

Ryu, K., & Jang, S. (2008). DINESCAPE: A scale for customers' perception of dining environments. *Journal of Foodservice Business Research*, *11*(1), 2–22. doi:10.1080/15378020801926551

Saaty, T. L. (1977). A scaling method for priorities in hierarchical structures. *Journal of Mathematical Psychology*, *15*(3), 234–281. doi:10.1016/0022-2496(77)90033-5

Sağtaş, S. (2022). The effect of social media marketing on brand equity and consumer purchasing intention. *Journal of Life Economics*, *9*(1), 21–31. doi:10.15637/jlecon.9.1.02

Sałabun, W., & Karczmarczyk, A. (2018). Using the COMET Method in the Sustainable City Transport Problem: An Empirical Study of the Electric Powered Cars. *Procedia Computer Science*, *126*, 2248–2260. doi:10.1016/j.procs.2018.07.224

Sałabun, W., Palczewski, K., & Wątróbski, J. (2019). Multicriteria Approach to Sustainable Transport Evaluation under Incomplete Knowledge: Electric Bikes Case Study. *Sustainability (Basel)*, *11*(12), 3314. doi:10.3390u11123314

Sałabun, W., Shekhovtsov, A., Pamučar, D., Wątróbski, J., Kizielewicz, B., Więckowski, J., Bozanić, D., Urbaniak, K., & Nyczaj, B. (2020). A Fuzzy Inference System for Players Evaluation in Multi-Player Sports: The Football Study Case. *Symmetry*, *12*(12), 2029. doi:10.3390ym12122029

Sánchez-Fernández, R., & Jiménez-Castillo, D. (2021). How social media influencers affect behavioural intentions towards recommended brands: The role of emotional attachment and information value. *Journal of Marketing Management*, *37*(11-12), 1123–1147. doi:10.1080/0267257X.2020.1866648

Sands, S., Oppewal, H., & Beverland, M. (2015). How in-store educational and entertaining events influence shopper satisfaction. *Journal of Retailing and Consumer Services*, *23*, 9–20. doi:10.1016/j.jretconser.2014.11.004

Sandström, R. (1985). An approach to systematic materials selection. *Materials & Design*, *6*(6), 328–338. doi:10.1016/0261-3069(85)90018-4

Sarsby, A. (2016). *SWOT analysis – A guide to SWOT for business studies students* (1st ed.). Spectaris Ltd.

Sashi, C. (2012). Customer engagement, buyer-seller relationships, and social media. *Management Decision*, *50*(2), 253–272. doi:10.1108/00251741211203551

Seçer, A., & Boğa, M. (2017). Sosyal medyanın tüketicilerin gıda ürünleri satın alma davranışına etkisi. *KSÜ Doğa Bilimleri Dergisi*, *20*(4), 312–319.

Secretaria de Salud. (2013). Estrategia Nacional para Prevencion y Control de Sobrepeso, Obesidad y Diabetes [National Strategy for the Prevention and Control of Overweight, Obesity and Diabetes]. Gobierno de la Republica, Available: https://www.gob.mx/cms/uploads/attachment/file/200355/Estrategia_nacional_para_prevencion_y_control_de_sobrepeso_obesidad_y_diabetes.pdf

Selvi, B. M., & Thomson, J. E. (2016). An exploratory study on the electronic word of mouth communication in promoting brands in the online platforms. *Intelligent Information Management*, *8*(5), 115–141. doi:10.4236/iim.2016.85010

Shah, K. & Brahmbhatt, M. (2017). A Literature Review On Factors Affecting Service Quality In Restaurants

Shekhovtsov, A., Kozlov, V., Nosov, V., & Sałabun, W. (2020). Efficiency of methods for determining the relevance of criteria in sustainable transport problems: A comparative case study. *Sustainability (Basel)*, *12*(19), 7915. doi:10.3390u12197915

Shekhovtsov, A., & Sałabun, W. (2020). A comparative case study of the VIKOR and TOPSIS rankings similarity. *Procedia Computer Science*, *176*, 3730–3740. doi:10.1016/j.procs.2020.09.014

Sheth, J. (2020). Impact of Covid-19 on consumer behavior: Will the old habits return or die? *Journal of Business Research*, *117*, 280–283. doi:10.1016/j.jbusres.2020.05.059 PMID:32536735

Sheth, J. N., Newman, B. I., & Gross, B. L. (1991). Why we buy what we buy: A theory of consumption values. *Journal of Business Research*, *22*(2), 159–170. doi:10.1016/0148-2963(91)90050-8

Shiau, W. L., Dwivedi, Y. K., & Lai, H. H. (2018). Examining the core knowledge on facebook. *International Journal of Information Management*, *43*, 52–63. doi:10.1016/j.ijinfomgt.2018.06.006

Shipman, Z. D. (2020). Factors Affecting Food Choices of Millennials: How they Decide What to Eat? *Journal of Tourismology*, *6*(1), 49–62. doi:10.26650/jot.2020.6.1.0036

Siegrist, M. (2021). Trust and risk perception: A critical review of the literature. *Risk Analysis*, *41*(3), 480–490. doi:10.1111/risa.13325 PMID:31046144

Simeone, M., & Scarpato, D. (2020). Sustainable consumption: How does social media affect food choices? *Journal of Cleaner Production*, *277*, 124036. doi:10.1016/j.jclepro.2020.124036

Smith, K. T., Blazovich, J. L., & Smith, L. M. (2015). Social media adoption by corporations: An examination by platform, industry, size, and financial performance. *Academy of Marketing Studies Journal*, *19*(2).

Sokolova, K., & Kefi, H. (2020). Instagram and YouTube bloggers promote it, why should I buy? How credibility and parasocial interaction influence purchase intentions. *Journal of Retailing and Consumer Services*, *53*, 101742. doi:10.1016/j.jretconser.2019.01.011

Solomon, M. R. (2020). *Consumer Behaviour: Buying, Having and Being* (13th ed.). Pearson Education.

Sparks, B. A., & Browning, V. (2011). The impact of online reviews on hotel booking intentions and perception of trust. *Tourism Management*, *32*(6), 1310–1323. doi:10.1016/j.tourman.2010.12.011

Stanton, J. V. (2019). Changing consumer preferences in emerging markets: Food market challenges in Central Mexico. *Journal of Food Products Marketing*, *25*(4), 378–403. doi:10.1080/10454446.2019.1566807

Stapenhurst, T. (2009). *The benchmarking book*. Routledge. doi:10.4324/9780080943329

Statista (2023). https://www.statista.com/statistics/272014/global-social-networks-ranked-by-number-of-users/

Statista (2023). Number of internet and social media users worldwide as of January 2023. https://www.statista.com/statistics/617136/digital-population-worldwide/

Statista. (2022). Coronavirus (COVID-19) deaths worldwide per one million population as of April 26, 2022, by country. Available: https://www.statista.com/statistics/1104709/coronavirus-deaths-worldwide-per-million-inhabitants/

Statista. (2023A). *Biggest Social Media Platforms 2023*. Retrieved May 3, 2023, from https://www.statista.com/statistics/272014/global-social-networks-ranked-by-number-of-users/

Statista. (2023B). *Global Daily Social Media Usage 2022*. Retrieved May 3, 2023, from https://www.statista.com/statistics/433871/daily-social-media-usage-worldwide/

Statista. (2023C). *Number Of Worldwide Social Network Users 2027*. Retrieved May 3, 2023, from https://www.statista.com/statistics/278414/number-of-worldwide-social-network-users/

Steinfield, C., Ellison, N. B., & Lampe, C. (2008). Social capital, self-esteem, and use of online social network sites: a longitudinal analysis. *Journal of Applied Developmental Psychology*, *29*(6), 434–445. doi:10.1016/j.appdev.2008.07.002

Storms, D. (2014). Social Media Influence on the Restaurant Industry - Social Media. Retrieved December 22, 2020 from, disponível em: https://www.socialmedialink.com/ uncategorized/ social-media-influence-on-therestaurant-industry/

Stoycheva, S., Marchese, D., Paul, C., Padoan, S., Juhmani, A., & Linkov, I. (2018). Multi-criteria decision analysis framework for sustainable manufacturing in automotive industry. *Journal of Cleaner Production*, *187*, 257–272. doi:10.1016/j.jclepro.2018.03.133

Stringam, B. B., & Gerdes, J. Jr. (2010). An analysis of word-of-mouse ratings and guest comments of online hotel distribution sites. *Journal of Hospitality Marketing & Management*, *19*(7), 773–796. doi:10.1080/19368623.2010.508009

Sun, Y., Wang, R., Cao, D., & Lee, R. (2022). Who are social media influencers for luxury fashion consumption of the Chinese Gen Z? Categorisation and empirical examination. *Journal of Fashion Marketing and Management*, *26*(4), 603–621. doi:10.1108/JFMM-07-2020-0132

Supthanasup, A., Banwell, C., Kelly, M., & Yiengprugsawan, V. S. (2021). Recipe components and parents' infant and young child feeding concerns: A mixed-methods study of recipe posts shared in thaifacebook groups for parents. *Nutrients*, *13*(4), 1186. Advance online publication. doi:10.3390/nu13041186 PMID:33916663

Sweeney, J. C., & Soutar, G. N. (2001). Consumer perceived value: The development of a multiple item scale. *Journal of Retailing*, *77*(2), 203–220. doi:10.1016/S0022-4359(01)00041-0

Taillie, L. S., Reyes, M., Colchero, M. A., Popkin, B., & Corvalán, C. (2020). An evaluation of Chile's Law of Food Labeling and Advertising on sugar-sweetened beverage purchases from 2015 to 2017: A before-and-after study. *PLoS Medicine*, *17*(2), 1–22. doi:10.1371/journal.pmed.1003015 PMID:32045424

Taneja, M., Byabazaire, J., Jalodia, N., Davy, A., Olariu, C., & Malone, P. (2020). Machine learning based fog computing assisted data-driven approach for early lameness detection in dairy cattle. *Computers and Electronics in Agriculture*, *171*, 105286. Advance online publication. doi:10.1016/j.compag.2020.105286

Taneja, M., Jalodia, N., Byabazaire, J., Davy, A., & Olariu, C. (2019). SmartHerd management: A microservices-based fog computing–assisted IoT platform towards data-driven smart dairy farming. *Software, Practice & Experience*, *49*(7), 1055–1078. Advance online publication. doi:10.1002pe.2704 PMID:31423028

Tarabasz, A. (2013). The revaluation of communication in customer approach–towards marketing 4.0.

Teerakapibal, S., & Melanthiou, Y. (2020). The new helping the old: Social media as a facilitator for variety seeking in food choices of the grey population. *British Food Journal*, *122*(1), 272–290. doi:10.1108/BFJ-08-2018-0559

The Effect of Promotional Push Notifications from Supermarket Branded Apps on Purchase Behavior - ProQuest. (n.d.). https://search.proquest.com/openview/cf96a2c8a801b6187359f136ca12ed13/1?pq-origsite=gscholar&cbl=2026366&diss=y&casa_token=XXF8MrJyw34AAAAA:WbWQlr48FvV7c-X4S0kJk_Eg0RhcCbrTUGpqr0d9UmoIxAXY7spFrp1HLdVHwnSqPNYex7qHEY8

The next horizon for grocery e-commerce: Beyond the pandemic bump. (2022, April 29). McKinsey & Company. https://www.mckinsey.com/industries/retail/our-insights/the-next-horizon-for-grocery-ecommerce-beyond-the-pandemic-bump#/

Thoumrungroje, A. (2014). The Influence of Social Media Intensity and EWOM on Conspicuous Consumption. *Procedia: Social and Behavioral Sciences*, *148*, 7–15. doi:10.1016/j.sbspro.2014.07.009

Timothy, D. (2019). The influence of social media on consumer buying behavior: a case study of Ho Technical University, Ho. *ResearchGate*. https://www.researchgate.net/publication/333852892_The_influence_of_social_media_on_consumer_buying_behavior_a_case_study_of_Ho_Technical_University_Ho

Titz, K., Lanza-Abbott, A., & Cruz, Y. (2004). The anatomy of restaurant reviews: An exploratory study. *International Journal of Hospitality & Tourism Administration*, *5*(1), 49–65. doi:10.1300/J149v05n01_03

Tjahjadi, J., & Hendijani, R. (2020). Customer's Perception Of Compulsory-View Advertising On Youtube And Its Effect On Their Purchasing Behavior. [IJIRAS]. *International Journal Of Innovative Research And Advanced Studies*, *7*(1), 103–108.

Tranfield, D., Denyer, D., & Smart, P. (2003). Towards a Methodology for Developing Evidence-Informed Management Knowledge by Means of Systematic Review. *British Journal of Management*, *14*(3), 207–222. doi:10.1111/1467-8551.00375

Triantaphyllou, E., Shu, B., Sanchez, S. N., & Ray, T. (1998). Multi-criteria decision making: an operations research approach. Encyclopedia of electrical and electronics engineering, 15(1998), 175-186.

Tsimonis, G., & Dimitriadis, S. (2014). Brand strategies in social media. *Marketing Intelligence & Planning*, *32*(3), 328–344. doi:10.1108/MIP-04-2013-0056

Tsochantaridou, A., Sergentanis, T. N., Grammatikopoulou, M. G., Merakou, K., Vassilakou, T., & Kornarou, E. (2023). Food advertisement and dietary choices in adolescents: an overview of recent studies. *Children (Basel, Switzerland)*, *10*(3), 442. doi:10.3390/children10030442 PMID:36980000

Tucker, K. (2017). *Social media marketing for restaurants* (1st ed.).

Turley, L. W., & Milliman, R. E. (2000). Atmospheric effects on shopping behavior: A review of the experimental evidence. *Journal of Business Research*, *49*(2), 193–211. doi:10.1016/S0148-2963(99)00010-7

Turner, P. (2022). "The Insta-Food Diet". Head of Zeus: London.

Tuten, T. L. (2021). *Social Media Marketing*. Sage Publishing.

Tyrväinen, O., & Karjaluoto, H. (2022). Online grocery shopping before and during the COVID-19 pandemic: A meta-analytical review. *Telematics and Informatics*, *71*, 101839. Advance online publication. doi:10.1016/j.tele.2022.101839 PMID:35607591

Uçan, B. Z., Girgin, G. K., & Karaman, N. (2021). Youtube Yemek Kanallarının Tatma Davranışsal Niyeti Üzerine Etkisi. *Kırklareli Üniversitesi Sosyal Bilimler Dergisi*, *5*(1), 1–28. doi:10.47140/kusbder.887291

Ulkhaq, M. M., Wijayanti, W. R., Zain, M., Baskara, E., & Leonita, W. (2018). *Combining the AHP and TOPSIS to evaluate car selection.* Paper presented at the HP3C. 10.1145/3195612.3195628

Ünal, A. T. (2020). A comparative study of social media addiction among Turkish and Korean university students. *Journal of Economy Culture and Society*, (62), 307–322. doi:10.26650/JECS2020-0064

Unnikrishnan, A., & Figliozzi, M. (2020). *A study of the impact of COVID-19 on home delivery purchases and expenditures* [Working paper]. Portland State University. https://pdxscholar.library.pdx.edu/cengin_fac/557

Vaillancourt, K., & Waaub, J.-P. (2004). Equity in international greenhouse gases abatement scenarios: A multicriteria approach. *European Journal of Operational Research*, *153*(2), 489–505. doi:10.1016/S0377-2217(03)00170-X

Van Rompay, T. J. L., Tanja-Dijkstra, K., Verhoeven, J. W. M., & van Es, A. F. (2012). On store design and consumer motivation: Spatial control and arousal in the retail context. *Environment and Behavior*, *44*(6), 800–820. doi:10.1177/0013916511407309

Vassallo, A., Jones, A., & Freeman, B. (2022). Social media: Frenemy of public health? *Public Health Nutrition*, *25*(1), 61–64. doi:10.1017/S136898002100269X PMID:34165062

Vaterlaus, J. M., Patten, E. V., Roche, C., & Young, J. A. (2015). # Gettinghealthy: The perceived influence of social media on young adult health behaviors. *Computers in Human Behavior*, *45*, 151–157. doi:10.1016/j.chb.2014.12.013

Ventura, V., Cavaliere, A., & Ianno, B. (2021). # Socialfood: Virtuous or vicious? A systematic review. *Trends in Food Science & Technology*, *110*, 674–686. doi:10.1016/j.tifs.2021.02.018

Verdon, J. (2022, March 15). The pandemic changed how we shop for groceries, Adobe report shows. *Forbes*. https://www.forbes.com/sites/joanverdon/2022/03/15/the-pandemic-changed-how-we-shop-for-groceries-adobe-report-shows/?sh=1006da814bb1

Verhoef, C., Lemon, N., Parasuraman, A., Roggeveen, A., Tsiros, M., & Schlesinger, L. A. (2009). Customer experience creation: Determinants, dynamics, and management strategies. *Journal of Retailing*, *85*(1), 31–41. doi:10.1016/j.jretai.2008.11.001

Verma, S., & Yadav, N. (2021). Past, present, and future of electronic word of mouth (EWOM). *Journal of Interactive Marketing*, *53*(1), 111–128. doi:10.1016/j.intmar.2020.07.001

Veryzer, R. W. (1993). Aesthetic response and the influence of design principles on product preferences. In L. McAllister & R. Rothschild (Eds.), *Advances in consumer research* (Vol. 20, pp. 224–231). Association for Consumer Research.

Vieira, V. A., & Vaz Torres, C. (2014). The effect of motivational orientation over arousal-shopping response relationship. *Journal of Retailing and Consumer Services*, *21*(2), 158–167. doi:10.1016/j.jretconser.2013.11.008

Villanueva, J., Yoo, S., & Hanssens, M. (2008). The impact of marketing-induced versus word-of-mouth customer acquisition on customer equity growth. *JMR, Journal of Marketing Research*, *45*(1), 48–59. doi:10.1509/jmkr.45.1.48

Vincke, P. (1992). *Multicriteria decision aid*. Wiley.

Volpe, R., & Boland, M. A. (2022). The economic impacts of Walmart supercenters. *Annual Review of Resource Economics*, *14*(1), 43–62. doi:10.1146/annurev-resource-111820-032827

Walker, R. (2014). *Exploring the Hospitality Industry, 2/e*. Pearson Education India.

Wang, Q., Liu, C., Zhao, Y., Kitsos, A., Cannella, M., Wang, S., & Han, L. (2020). Impacts of the COVID-19 pandemic on the dairy industry: Lessons from China and the United States and policy implications. *Journal of Integrative Agriculture*, *19*(12), 2903–2915. Advance online publication. doi:10.1016/S2095-3119(20)63443-8

Wang, Z., Zhang, S., Qiu, L., Gu, Y., & Zhou, H. (2020). A low-carbon-orient product design schemes MCDM method hybridizing interval hesitant fuzzy set entropy theory and coupling network analysis. *Soft Computing*, *24*(7), 5389–5408. doi:10.100700500-019-04296-6

Warner, D., Vasseur, E., Lefebvre, D. M., & Lacroix, R. (2020). A machine learning based decision aid for lameness in dairy herds using farm-based records. *Computers and Electronics in Agriculture*, *169*, 105193. Advance online publication. doi:10.1016/j.compag.2019.105193

Wątróbski, J., Małecki, K., Iwan, S., Karczmarczyk, A., & Thompson, R. (2017). Multi-Criteria Analysis of Electric Vans for City Logistics. *Sustainability (Basel)*, *9*(8), 1453. doi:10.3390u9081453

Weinberg, B. D., De Ruyter, K., Dellarocas, C., Buck, M., & Keeling, D. I. (2013). Destination social business: exploring an organization's journey with social media, collaborative community and expressive individuality. *Journal of Interactive Marketing*, *27*(4), 299–310. doi:10.1016/j.intmar.2013.09.006

Winzer, E., Naderer, B., Klein, S., Lercher, L., & Wakolbinger, M. (2022). Promotion of Food and Beverages by German-Speaking Influencers Popular with Adolescents on TikTok, YouTube and Instagram. *International Journal of Environmental Research and Public Health, 19*(17), 10911. doi:10.3390/ijerph191710911 PMID:36078625

Wollenburg, J., Hübner, A., Kuhn, H., & Trautrims, A. (2018). From bricks-and-mortar to bricks-and-clicks: Logistics networks in omni-channel grocery retailing. *International Journal of Physical Distribution & Logistics Management, 48*(4), 415–438. doi:10.1108/IJPDLM-10-2016-0290

Woodruff, R. B., Cadotte, E. R., & Jenkins, R. L. (1983). Modeling consumer satisfaction processes using experience-based norms. *JMR, Journal of Marketing Research, 20*(3), 296–304. doi:10.1177/002224378302000308

Wu, F. (2013). In search of negativity bias: An empirical study of perceived helpfulness of online reviews. *Psychology and Marketing, 30*(11), 971–984. doi:10.1002/mar.20660

Xu, J., Shim, S., Lotz, S., & Almeida, D. (2004). Ethnic identity, socialization factors, and culture-specific consumption behavior. *Psychology and Marketing, 21*(2), 93–112. doi:10.1002/mar.10117

Yahya, K., Boussabaine, H., & Alzaed, A. N. (2016). Using life cycle assessment for estimating environmental impacts and eco-costs from the metal waste in the construction industry. *Management of Environmental Quality, 27*(2), 227–244. doi:10.1108/MEQ-09-2014-0137

Yalch, R. F., & Spangenberg, E. R. (2000). The effects of music in a` retail setting on real and perceived shopping times. *Journal of Business Research, 49*(2), 139–147. doi:10.1016/S0148-2963(99)00003-X

Yang, F., Heemsbergen, L., & Fordyce, R. (2021). Comparative analysis of China's Health Code, Australia's COVIDSafe and New Zealand's COVID Tracer Surveillance Apps: A new corona of public health governmentality? *Media International Australia, Incorporating Culture & Policy, 178*(1), 182–197. doi:10.1177/1329878X20968277

Yeh, H., & Choi, M. (2011). MINI-lovers, maxi-mouths: An investigation of antecedents to eWOM intention among brand community members. *Journal of Marketing Communications, 17*(3), 145–162. doi:10.1080/13527260903351119

Yıldız, H., & Aybar, A. S. (2019). *ReseaRches in economics, econometRics & Finance*. IJOPEC PUBLICATION.

Yuksel, S., Dinçer, H., & Emir, S. (2018). Analysis of service innovation performance in Turkish banking sector using a combining method of fuzzy MCDM and text mining. *MANAS Sosyal Araştırmalar Dergisi, 7*(3).

Zahorik, A. J., & Rust, R. T. (1993). Customer satisfaction, customer retention, and market share. *Journal of Retailing, 69*(2), 193–215. doi:10.1016/0022-4359(93)90003-2

Zavadskas, E. K., & Turskis, Z. (2011). Multiple criteria decision making (MCDM) methods in economics: An overview. *Technological and Economic Development of Economy, 17*(2), 397–427. doi:10.3846/20294913.2011.593291

Zavadskas, E. K., Turskis, Z., & Kildienė, S. (2014). State of art surveys of overviews on MCDM/MADM methods. *Technological and Economic Development of Economy*, *20*(1), 165–179. doi:10.3846/20294913.2014.892037

Zehavi, G. (2019, April 16). Online grocery shopping: Past & present. *Medium*. https://gadzehavi.medium.com/online-grocery-shopping-past-present-ace5f21b9598

Zeithaml, A., Bitner, J., & Gremler, D. (2000). *Services Marketing: integrating customer focus across the Firm*. Tata-McGraw-Hall.

Zeithaml, V. A., & Bitner, M. J. (2000). *Services marketing: Integrating customer focus across the firm* (2nd ed.). Irwin/McGraw-Hill.

Zeynali, M., Aghdaie, M., Rezaeiniya, N., & Sarfaraz, H. (2012). A hybrid fuzzy multiple criteria decision making (MCDM) approach to combination of materials selection. *African Journal of Business Management*, *6*(45), 11171–11178. doi:10.5897/AJBM11.2022

Zhang, J., & Du, M. (2020). Utilization and effectiveness of social media message strategy: How B2B brands differ from B2C brands. *Journal of Business and Industrial Marketing*, *35*(4), 721–740. doi:10.1108/JBIM-06-2018-0190

Zhang, T., Omran, B. A., & Cobanoglu, C. (2017). Generation Y's positive and negative eWOM: Use of social media and mobile technology. *International Journal of Contemporary Hospitality Management*, *29*(2), 732–761. doi:10.1108/IJCHM-10-2015-0611

Zhu, F., & Zhang, X. (2010). Impact of online consumer reviews on sales: The moderating role of product and consumer characteristics. Journalof marketing, 74(2), 133-148.

Zhu, X., Meng, X., & Zhang, M. (2021). Application of multiple criteria decision making methods in construction: a systematic literature review. *Journal of Civil Engineering and Management*, *27*(6), 372–403. doi:10.3846/jcem.2021.15260

Ziemba, P. (2020). Multi-Criteria Stochastic Selection of Electric Vehicles for the Sustainable Development of Local Government and State Administration Units in Poland. *Energies*, *13*(23), 6299. doi:10.3390/en13236299

Zolfaghari, A., Thomas-Francois, K., & Somogyi, S. (2022a). Consumer adoption of digital grocery shopping: What is the impact of consumer's prior-to-use knowledge? *British Food Journal*, *125*(4), 1355–1373. doi:10.1108/BFJ-02-2022-0187

Zopounidis, C., Galariotis, E., Doumpos, M., Sarri, S., & Andriosopoulos, K. (2015). Multiple criteria decision aiding for finance: An updated bibliographic survey. *European Journal of Operational Research*, *247*(2), 339–348. doi:10.1016/j.ejor.2015.05.032

Related References

To continue our tradition of advancing information science and technology research, we have compiled a list of recommended IGI Global readings. These references will provide additional information and guidance to further enrich your knowledge and assist you with your own research and future publications.

Abdul Razak, R., & Mansor, N. A. (2021). Instagram Influencers in Social Media-Induced Tourism: Rethinking Tourist Trust Towards Tourism Destination. In M. Dinis, L. Bonixe, S. Lamy, & Z. Breda (Eds.), *Impact of New Media in Tourism* (pp. 135-144). IGI Global. https://doi.org/10.4018/978-1-7998-7095-1.ch009

Abir, T., & Khan, M. Y. (2022). Importance of ICT Advancement and Culture of Adaptation in the Tourism and Hospitality Industry for Developing Countries. In C. Ramos, S. Quinteiro, & A. Gonçalves (Eds.), *ICT as Innovator Between Tourism and Culture* (pp. 30–41). IGI Global. https://doi.org/10.4018/978-1-7998-8165-0.ch003

Abir, T., & Khan, M. Y. (2022). Importance of ICT Advancement and Culture of Adaptation in the Tourism and Hospitality Industry for Developing Countries. In C. Ramos, S. Quinteiro, & A. Gonçalves (Eds.), *ICT as Innovator Between Tourism and Culture* (pp. 30–41). IGI Global. https://doi.org/10.4018/978-1-7998-8165-0.ch003

Abtahi, M. S., Behboudi, L., & Hasanabad, H. M. (2017). Factors Affecting Internet Advertising Adoption in Ad Agencies. *International Journal of Innovation in the Digital Economy*, *8*(4), 18–29. doi:10.4018/IJIDE.2017100102

Afenyo-Agbe, E., & Mensah, I. (2022). Principles, Benefits, and Barriers to Community-Based Tourism: Implications for Management. In I. Mensah & E. Afenyo-Agbe (Eds.), *Prospects and Challenges of Community-Based Tourism and Changing Demographics* (pp. 1–29). IGI Global. doi:10.4018/978-1-7998-7335-8.ch001

Agbo, V. M. (2022). Distributive Justice Issues in Community-Based Tourism. In I. Mensah & E. Afenyo-Agbe (Eds.), *Prospects and Challenges of Community-Based Tourism and Changing Demographics* (pp. 107–129). IGI Global. https://doi.org/10.4018/978-1-7998-7335-8.ch005

Agrawal, S. (2017). The Impact of Emerging Technologies and Social Media on Different Business(es): Marketing and Management. In O. Rishi & A. Sharma (Eds.), *Maximizing Business Performance and Efficiency Through Intelligent Systems* (pp. 37–49). Hershey, PA: IGI Global. doi:10.4018/978-1-5225-2234-8.ch002

Ahmad, A., & Johari, S. (2022). Georgetown as a Gastronomy Tourism Destination: Visitor Awareness Towards Revisit Intention of Nasi Kandar Restaurant. In M. Valeri (Ed.), *New Governance and Management in Touristic Destinations* (pp. 71–83). IGI Global. https://doi.org/10.4018/978-1-6684-3889-3.ch005

Alkhatib, G., & Bayouq, S. T. (2021). A TAM-Based Model of Technological Factors Affecting Use of E-Tourism. *International Journal of Tourism and Hospitality Management in the Digital Age*, *5*(2), 50–67. https://doi.org/10.4018/IJTHMDA.20210701.oa1

Altinay Ozdemir, M. (2021). Virtual Reality (VR) and Augmented Reality (AR) Technologies for Accessibility and Marketing in the Tourism Industry. In C. Eusébio, L. Teixeira, & M. Carneiro (Eds.), *ICT Tools and Applications for Accessible Tourism* (pp. 277-301). IGI Global. https://doi.org/10.4018/978-1-7998-6428-8.ch013

Anantharaman, R. N., Rajeswari, K. S., Angusamy, A., & Kuppusamy, J. (2017). Role of Self-Efficacy and Collective Efficacy as Moderators of Occupational Stress Among Software Development Professionals. *International Journal of Human Capital and Information Technology Professionals*, *8*(2), 45–58. doi:10.4018/IJHCITP.2017040103

Aninze, F., El-Gohary, H., & Hussain, J. (2018). The Role of Microfinance to Empower Women: The Case of Developing Countries. *International Journal of Customer Relationship Marketing and Management*, *9*(1), 54–78. doi:10.4018/IJCRMM.2018010104

Antosova, G., Sabogal-Salamanca, M., & Krizova, E. (2021). Human Capital in Tourism: A Practical Model of Endogenous and Exogenous Territorial Tourism Planning in Bahía Solano, Colombia. In V. Costa, A. Moura, & M. Mira (Eds.), *Handbook of Research on Human Capital and People Management in the Tourism Industry* (pp. 282–302). IGI Global. https://doi.org/10.4018/978-1-7998-4318-4.ch014

Arsenijević, O. M., Orčić, D., & Kastratović, E. (2017). Development of an Optimization Tool for Intangibles in SMEs: A Case Study from Serbia with a Pilot Research in the Prestige by Milka Company. In M. Vemić (Ed.), *Optimal Management Strategies in Small and Medium Enterprises* (pp. 320–347). Hershey, PA: IGI Global. doi:10.4018/978-1-5225-1949-2.ch015

Aryanto, V. D., Wismantoro, Y., & Widyatmoko, K. (2018). Implementing Eco-Innovation by Utilizing the Internet to Enhance Firm's Marketing Performance: Study of Green Batik Small and Medium Enterprises in Indonesia. *International Journal of E-Business Research, 14*(1), 21–36. doi:10.4018/IJEBR.2018010102

Asero, V., & Billi, S. (2022). New Perspective of Networking in the DMO Model. In M. Valeri (Ed.), *New Governance and Management in Touristic Destinations* (pp. 105–118). IGI Global. https://doi.org/10.4018/978-1-6684-3889-3.ch007

Atiku, S. O., & Fields, Z. (2017). Multicultural Orientations for 21st Century Global Leadership. In N. Baporikar (Ed.), *Management Education for Global Leadership* (pp. 28–51). Hershey, PA: IGI Global. doi:10.4018/978-1-5225-1013-0.ch002

Atiku, S. O., & Fields, Z. (2018). Organisational Learning Dimensions and Talent Retention Strategies for the Service Industries. In N. Baporikar (Ed.), *Global Practices in Knowledge Management for Societal and Organizational Development* (pp. 358–381). Hershey, PA: IGI Global. doi:10.4018/978-1-5225-3009-1.ch017

Atsa'am, D. D., & Kuset Bodur, E. (2021). Pattern Mining on How Organizational Tenure Affects the Psychological Capital of Employees Within the Hospitality and Tourism Industry: Linking Employees' Organizational Tenure With PsyCap. *International Journal of Tourism and Hospitality Management in the Digital Age, 5*(2), 17–28. https://doi.org/10.4018/IJTHMDA.2021070102

Ávila, L., & Teixeira, L. (2018). The Main Concepts Behind the Dematerialization of Business Processes. In M. Khosrow-Pour, D.B.A. (Ed.), Encyclopedia of Information Science and Technology, Fourth Edition (pp. 888-898). Hershey, PA: IGI Global. https://doi.org/ doi:10.4018/978-1-5225-2255-3.ch076

Ayorekire, J., Mugizi, F., Obua, J., & Ampaire, G. (2022). Community-Based Tourism and Local People's Perceptions Towards Conservation: The Case of Queen Elizabeth Conservation Area, Uganda. In I. Mensah & E. Afenyo-Agbe (Eds.), *Prospects and Challenges of Community-Based Tourism and Changing Demographics* (pp. 56–82). IGI Global. https://doi.org/10.4018/978-1-7998-7335-8.ch003

Baleiro, R. (2022). Tourist Literature and the Architecture of Travel in Olga Tokarczuk and Patti Smith. In R. Baleiro & R. Pereira (Eds.), *Global Perspectives on Literary Tourism and Film-Induced Tourism* (pp. 202-216). IGI Global. https://doi.org/10.4018/978-1-7998-8262-6.ch011

Barat, S. (2021). Looking at the Future of Medical Tourism in Asia. *International Journal of Tourism and Hospitality Management in the Digital Age*, *5*(1), 19–33. https://doi.org/10.4018/IJTHMDA.2021010102

Barbosa, C. A., Magalhães, M., & Nunes, M. R. (2021). Travel Instagramability: A Way of Choosing a Destination? In M. Dinis, L. Bonixe, S. Lamy, & Z. Breda (Eds.), *Impact of New Media in Tourism* (pp. 173-190). IGI Global. https://doi.org/10.4018/978-1-7998-7095-1.ch011

Bari, M. W., & Khan, Q. (2021). Pakistan as a Destination of Religious Tourism. In E. Alaverdov & M. Bari (Eds.), *Global Development of Religious Tourism* (pp. 1-10). IGI Global. https://doi.org/10.4018/978-1-7998-5792-1.ch001

Bartens, Y., Chunpir, H. I., Schulte, F., & Voß, S. (2017). Business/IT Alignment in Two-Sided Markets: A COBIT 5 Analysis for Media Streaming Business Models. In S. De Haes & W. Van Grembergen (Eds.), *Strategic IT Governance and Alignment in Business Settings* (pp. 82–111). Hershey, PA: IGI Global. doi:10.4018/978-1-5225-0861-8.ch004

Bashayreh, A. M. (2018). Organizational Culture and Organizational Performance. In W. Lee & F. Sabetzadeh (Eds.), *Contemporary Knowledge and Systems Science* (pp. 50–69). Hershey, PA: IGI Global. doi:10.4018/978-1-5225-5655-8.ch003

Bechthold, L., Lude, M., & Prügl, R. (2021). Crisis Favors the Prepared Firm: How Organizational Ambidexterity Relates to Perceptions of Organizational Resilience. In A. Zehrer, G. Glowka, K. Schwaiger, & V. Ranacher-Lackner (Eds.), *Resiliency Models and Addressing Future Risks for Family Firms in the Tourism Industry* (pp. 178–205). IGI Global. https://doi.org/10.4018/978-1-7998-7352-5.ch008

Bedford, D. A. (2018). Sustainable Knowledge Management Strategies: Aligning Business Capabilities and Knowledge Management Goals. In N. Baporikar (Ed.), *Global Practices in Knowledge Management for Societal and Organizational Development* (pp. 46–73). Hershey, PA: IGI Global. doi:10.4018/978-1-5225-3009-1.ch003

Bekjanov, D., & Matyusupov, B. (2021). Influence of Innovative Processes in the Competitiveness of Tourist Destination. In J. Soares (Ed.), *Innovation and Entrepreneurial Opportunities in Community Tourism* (pp. 243–263). IGI Global. https://doi.org/10.4018/978-1-7998-4855-4.ch014

Bharwani, S., & Musunuri, D. (2018). Reflection as a Process From Theory to Practice. In M. Khosrow-Pour, D.B.A. (Ed.), Encyclopedia of Information Science and Technology, Fourth Edition (pp. 1529-1539). Hershey, PA: IGI Global. doi:10.4018/978-1-5225-2255-3.ch132

Bhatt, G. D., Wang, Z., & Rodger, J. A. (2017). Information Systems Capabilities and Their Effects on Competitive Advantages: A Study of Chinese Companies. *Information Resources Management Journal, 30*(3), 41–57. doi:10.4018/IRMJ.2017070103

Bhushan, M., & Yadav, A. (2017). Concept of Cloud Computing in ESB. In R. Bhadoria, N. Chaudhari, G. Tomar, & S. Singh (Eds.), *Exploring Enterprise Service Bus in the Service-Oriented Architecture Paradigm* (pp. 116–127). Hershey, PA: IGI Global. doi:10.4018/978-1-5225-2157-0.ch008

Bhushan, S. (2017). System Dynamics Base-Model of Humanitarian Supply Chain (HSCM) in Disaster Prone Eco-Communities of India: A Discussion on Simulation and Scenario Results. *International Journal of System Dynamics Applications, 6*(3), 20–37. doi:10.4018/IJSDA.2017070102

Binder, D., & Miller, J. W. (2021). A Generations' Perspective on Employer Branding in Tourism. In V. Costa, A. Moura, & M. Mira (Eds.), *Handbook of Research on Human Capital and People Management in the Tourism Industry* (pp. 152–174). IGI Global. https://doi.org/10.4018/978-1-7998-4318-4.ch008

Birch Freeman, A. A., Mensah, I., & Antwi, K. B. (2022). Smiling vs. Frowning Faces: Community Participation for Sustainable Tourism in Ghanaian Communities. In I. Mensah & E. Afenyo-Agbe (Eds.), *Prospects and Challenges of Community-Based Tourism and Changing Demographics* (pp. 83–106). IGI Global. https://doi.org/10.4018/978-1-7998-7335-8.ch004

Biswas, A., & De, A. K. (2017). On Development of a Fuzzy Stochastic Programming Model with Its Application to Business Management. In S. Trivedi, S. Dey, A. Kumar, & T. Panda (Eds.), *Handbook of Research on Advanced Data Mining Techniques and Applications for Business Intelligence* (pp. 353–378). Hershey, PA: IGI Global. doi:10.4018/978-1-5225-2031-3.ch021

Boragnio, A., & Faracce Macia, C. (2021). "Taking Care of Yourself at Home": Use of E-Commerce About Food and Care During the COVID-19 Pandemic in the City of Buenos Aires. In M. Korstanje (Ed.), *Socio-Economic Effects and Recovery Efforts for the Rental Industry: Post-COVID-19 Strategies* (pp. 45–71). IGI Global. https://doi.org/10.4018/978-1-7998-7287-0.ch003

Borges, V. D. (2021). Happiness: The Basis for Public Policy in Tourism. In A. Perinotto, V. Mayer, & J. Soares (Eds.), *Rebuilding and Restructuring the Tourism Industry: Infusion of Happiness and Quality of Life* (pp. 1–25). IGI Global. https://doi.org/10.4018/978-1-7998-7239-9.ch001

Bücker, J., & Ernste, K. (2018). Use of Brand Heroes in Strategic Reputation Management: The Case of Bacardi, Adidas, and Daimler. In A. Erdemir (Ed.), *Reputation Management Techniques in Public Relations* (pp. 126–150). Hershey, PA: IGI Global. doi:10.4018/978-1-5225-3619-2.ch007

Buluk Eşitti, B. (2021). COVID-19 and Alternative Tourism: New Destinations and New Tourism Products. In M. Demir, A. Dalgıç, & F. Ergen (Eds.), *Handbook of Research on the Impacts and Implications of COVID-19 on the Tourism Industry* (pp. 786–805). IGI Global. https://doi.org/10.4018/978-1-7998-8231-2.ch038

Bureš, V. (2018). Industry 4.0 From the Systems Engineering Perspective: Alternative Holistic Framework Development. In R. Brunet-Thornton & F. Martinez (Eds.), *Analyzing the Impacts of Industry 4.0 in Modern Business Environments* (pp. 199–223). Hershey, PA: IGI Global. doi:10.4018/978-1-5225-3468-6.ch011

Buzady, Z. (2017). Resolving the Magic Cube of Effective Case Teaching: Benchmarking Case Teaching Practices in Emerging Markets – Insights from the Central European University Business School, Hungary. In D. Latusek (Ed.), *Case Studies as a Teaching Tool in Management Education* (pp. 79–103). Hershey, PA: IGI Global. doi:10.4018/978-1-5225-0770-3.ch005

Camillo, A. (2021). *Legal Matters, Risk Management, and Risk Prevention: From Forming a Business to Legal Representation*. IGI Global. doi:10.4018/978-1-7998-4342-9.ch004

Căpusneanu, S., & Topor, D. I. (2018). Business Ethics and Cost Management in SMEs: Theories of Business Ethics and Cost Management Ethos. In I. Oncioiu (Ed.), *Ethics and Decision-Making for Sustainable Business Practices* (pp. 109–127). Hershey, PA: IGI Global. doi:10.4018/978-1-5225-3773-1.ch007

Chan, R. L., Mo, P. L., & Moon, K. K. (2018). Strategic and Tactical Measures in Managing Enterprise Risks: A Study of the Textile and Apparel Industry. In K. Strang, M. Korstanje, & N. Vajjhala (Eds.), *Research, Practices, and Innovations in Global Risk and Contingency Management* (pp. 1–19). Hershey, PA: IGI Global. doi:10.4018/978-1-5225-4754-9.ch001

Charlier, S. D., Burke-Smalley, L. A., & Fisher, S. L. (2018). Undergraduate Programs in the U.S: A Contextual and Content-Based Analysis. In J. Mendy (Ed.), *Teaching Human Resources and Organizational Behavior at the College Level* (pp. 26–57). Hershey, PA: IGI Global. doi:10.4018/978-1-5225-2820-3.ch002

Chumillas, J., Güell, M., & Quer, P. (2022). The Use of ICT in Tourist and Educational Literary Routes: The Role of the Guide. In C. Ramos, S. Quinteiro, & A. Gonçalves (Eds.), *ICT as Innovator Between Tourism and Culture* (pp. 15–29). IGI Global. https://doi.org/10.4018/978-1-7998-8165-0.ch002

Dahlberg, T., Kivijärvi, H., & Saarinen, T. (2017). IT Investment Consistency and Other Factors Influencing the Success of IT Performance. In S. De Haes & W. Van Grembergen (Eds.), *Strategic IT Governance and Alignment in Business Settings* (pp. 176–208). Hershey, PA: IGI Global. doi:10.4018/978-1-5225-0861-8.ch007

Damnjanović, A. M. (2017). Knowledge Management Optimization through IT and E-Business Utilization: A Qualitative Study on Serbian SMEs. In M. Vemić (Ed.), *Optimal Management Strategies in Small and Medium Enterprises* (pp. 249–267). Hershey, PA: IGI Global. doi:10.4018/978-1-5225-1949-2.ch012

Daneshpour, H. (2017). Integrating Sustainable Development into Project Portfolio Management through Application of Open Innovation. In M. Vemić (Ed.), *Optimal Management Strategies in Small and Medium Enterprises* (pp. 370–387). Hershey, PA: IGI Global. doi:10.4018/978-1-5225-1949-2.ch017

Daniel, A. D., & Reis de Castro, V. (2018). Entrepreneurship Education: How to Measure the Impact on Nascent Entrepreneurs. In A. Carrizo Moreira, J. Guilherme Leitão Dantas, & F. Manuel Valente (Eds.), *Nascent Entrepreneurship and Successful New Venture Creation* (pp. 85–110). Hershey, PA: IGI Global. doi:10.4018/978-1-5225-2936-1.ch004

David, R., Swami, B. N., & Tangirala, S. (2018). Ethics Impact on Knowledge Management in Organizational Development: A Case Study. In N. Baporikar (Ed.), *Global Practices in Knowledge Management for Societal and Organizational Development* (pp. 19–45). Hershey, PA: IGI Global. doi:10.4018/978-1-5225-3009-1.ch002

De Uña-Álvarez, E., & Villarino-Pérez, M. (2022). Fostering Ecocultural Resources, Identity, and Tourism in Inland Territories (Galicia, NW Spain). In G. Fernandes (Ed.), *Challenges and New Opportunities for Tourism in Inland Territories: Ecocultural Resources and Sustainable Initiatives* (pp. 1-16). IGI Global. https://doi.org/10.4018/978-1-7998-7339-6.ch001

Delias, P., & Lakiotaki, K. (2018). Discovering Process Horizontal Boundaries to Facilitate Process Comprehension. *International Journal of Operations Research and Information Systems*, *9*(2), 1–31. doi:10.4018/IJORIS.2018040101

Denholm, J., & Lee-Davies, L. (2018). Success Factors for Games in Business and Project Management. In *Enhancing Education and Training Initiatives Through Serious Games* (pp. 34–68). Hershey, PA: IGI Global. doi:10.4018/978-1-5225-3689-5.ch002

Deshpande, M. (2017). Best Practices in Management Institutions for Global Leadership: Policy Aspects. In N. Baporikar (Ed.), *Management Education for Global Leadership* (pp. 1–27). Hershey, PA: IGI Global. doi:10.4018/978-1-5225-1013-0.ch001

Deshpande, M. (2018). Policy Perspectives for SMEs Knowledge Management. In N. Baporikar (Ed.), *Knowledge Integration Strategies for Entrepreneurship and Sustainability* (pp. 23–46). Hershey, PA: IGI Global. doi:10.4018/978-1-5225-5115-7.ch002

Dezdar, S. (2017). ERP Implementation Projects in Asian Countries: A Comparative Study on Iran and China. *International Journal of Information Technology Project Management*, *8*(3), 52–68. doi:10.4018/IJITPM.2017070104

Domingos, D., Respício, A., & Martinho, R. (2017). Reliability of IoT-Aware BPMN Healthcare Processes. In C. Reis & M. Maximiano (Eds.), *Internet of Things and Advanced Application in Healthcare* (pp. 214–248). Hershey, PA: IGI Global. doi:10.4018/978-1-5225-1820-4.ch008

Dosumu, O., Hussain, J., & El-Gohary, H. (2017). An Exploratory Study of the Impact of Government Policies on the Development of Small and Medium Enterprises in Developing Countries: The Case of Nigeria. *International Journal of Customer Relationship Marketing and Management*, *8*(4), 51–62. doi:10.4018/IJCRMM.2017100104

Durst, S., Bruns, G., & Edvardsson, I. R. (2017). Retaining Knowledge in Smaller Building and Construction Firms. *International Journal of Knowledge and Systems Science*, *8*(3), 1–12. doi:10.4018/IJKSS.2017070101

Edvardsson, I. R., & Durst, S. (2017). Outsourcing, Knowledge, and Learning: A Critical Review. *International Journal of Knowledge-Based Organizations*, *7*(2), 13–26. doi:10.4018/IJKBO.2017040102

Edwards, J. S. (2018). Integrating Knowledge Management and Business Processes. In M. Khosrow-Pour, D.B.A. (Ed.), Encyclopedia of Information Science and Technology, Fourth Edition (pp. 5046-5055). Hershey, PA: IGI Global. doi:10.4018/978-1-5225-2255-3.ch437

Eichelberger, S., & Peters, M. (2021). Family Firm Management in Turbulent Times: Opportunities for Responsible Tourism. In A. Zehrer, G. Glowka, K. Schwaiger, & V. Ranacher-Lackner (Eds.), *Resiliency Models and Addressing Future Risks for Family Firms in the Tourism Industry* (pp. 103–124). IGI Global. https://doi.org/10.4018/978-1-7998-7352-5.ch005

Eide, D., Hjalager, A., & Hansen, M. (2022). Innovative Certifications in Adventure Tourism: Attributes and Diffusion. In R. Augusto Costa, F. Brandão, Z. Breda, & C. Costa (Eds.), *Planning and Managing the Experience Economy in Tourism* (pp. 161-175). IGI Global. https://doi.org/10.4018/978-1-7998-8775-1.ch009

Ejiogu, A. O. (2018). Economics of Farm Management. In *Agricultural Finance and Opportunities for Investment and Expansion* (pp. 56–72). Hershey, PA: IGI Global. doi:10.4018/978-1-5225-3059-6.ch003

Ekanem, I., & Abiade, G. E. (2018). Factors Influencing the Use of E-Commerce by Small Enterprises in Nigeria. *International Journal of ICT Research in Africa and the Middle East*, *7*(1), 37–53. doi:10.4018/IJICTRAME.2018010103

Ekanem, I., & Alrossais, L. A. (2017). Succession Challenges Facing Family Businesses in Saudi Arabia. In P. Zgheib (Ed.), *Entrepreneurship and Business Innovation in the Middle East* (pp. 122–146). Hershey, PA: IGI Global. doi:10.4018/978-1-5225-2066-5.ch007

El Faquih, L., & Fredj, M. (2017). Ontology-Based Framework for Quality in Configurable Process Models. *Journal of Electronic Commerce in Organizations*, *15*(2), 48–60. doi:10.4018/JECO.2017040104

Faisal, M. N., & Talib, F. (2017). Building Ambidextrous Supply Chains in SMEs: How to Tackle the Barriers? *International Journal of Information Systems and Supply Chain Management*, *10*(4), 80–100. doi:10.4018/IJISSCM.2017100105

Fernandes, T. M., Gomes, J., & Romão, M. (2017). Investments in E-Government: A Benefit Management Case Study. *International Journal of Electronic Government Research*, *13*(3), 1–17. doi:10.4018/IJEGR.2017070101

Figueira, L. M., Honrado, G. R., & Dionísio, M. S. (2021). Human Capital Management in the Tourism Industry in Portugal. In V. Costa, A. Moura, & M. Mira (Eds.), *Handbook of Research on Human Capital and People Management in the Tourism Industry* (pp. 1–19). IGI Global. doi:10.4018/978-1-7998-4318-4.ch001

Gao, S. S., Oreal, S., & Zhang, J. (2018). Contemporary Financial Risk Management Perceptions and Practices of Small-Sized Chinese Businesses. In I. Management Association (Ed.), Global Business Expansion: Concepts, Methodologies, Tools, and Applications (pp. 917-931). Hershey, PA: IGI Global. doi:10.4018/978-1-5225-5481-3.ch041

Garg, R., & Berning, S. C. (2017). Indigenous Chinese Management Philosophies: Key Concepts and Relevance for Modern Chinese Firms. In B. Christiansen & G. Koc (Eds.), *Transcontinental Strategies for Industrial Development and Economic Growth* (pp. 43–57). Hershey, PA: IGI Global. doi:10.4018/978-1-5225-2160-0.ch003

Gencer, Y. G. (2017). Supply Chain Management in Retailing Business. In U. Akkucuk (Ed.), *Ethics and Sustainability in Global Supply Chain Management* (pp. 197–210). Hershey, PA: IGI Global. doi:10.4018/978-1-5225-2036-8.ch011

Gera, R., Arora, S., & Malik, S. (2021). Emotional Labor in the Tourism Industry: Strategies, Antecedents, and Outcomes. In V. Costa, A. Moura, & M. Mira (Eds.), *Handbook of Research on Human Capital and People Management in the Tourism Industry* (pp. 73–91). IGI Global. https://doi.org/10.4018/978-1-7998-4318-4.ch004

Giacosa, E. (2018). The Increasing of the Regional Development Thanks to the Luxury Business Innovation. In L. Carvalho (Ed.), *Handbook of Research on Entrepreneurial Ecosystems and Social Dynamics in a Globalized World* (pp. 260–273). Hershey, PA: IGI Global. doi:10.4018/978-1-5225-3525-6.ch011

Glowka, G., Tusch, M., & Zehrer, A. (2021). The Risk Perception of Family Business Owner-Manager in the Tourism Industry: A Qualitative Comparison of the Intra-Firm Senior and Junior Generation. In A. Zehrer, G. Glowka, K. Schwaiger, & V. Ranacher-Lackner (Eds.), *Resiliency Models and Addressing Future Risks for Family Firms in the Tourism Industry* (pp. 126–153). IGI Global. https://doi.org/10.4018/978-1-7998-7352-5.ch006

Glykas, M., & George, J. (2017). Quality and Process Management Systems in the UAE Maritime Industry. *International Journal of Productivity Management and Assessment Technologies*, *5*(1), 20–39. doi:10.4018/IJPMAT.2017010102

Glykas, M., Valiris, G., Kokkinaki, A., & Koutsoukou, Z. (2018). Banking Business Process Management Implementation. *International Journal of Productivity Management and Assessment Technologies*, *6*(1), 50–69. doi:10.4018/IJPMAT.2018010104

Gomes, J., & Romão, M. (2017). The Balanced Scorecard: Keeping Updated and Aligned with Today's Business Trends. *International Journal of Productivity Management and Assessment Technologies*, *5*(2), 1–15. doi:10.4018/IJPMAT.2017070101

Gomes, J., & Romão, M. (2017). Aligning Information Systems and Technology with Benefit Management and Balanced Scorecard. In S. De Haes & W. Van Grembergen (Eds.), *Strategic IT Governance and Alignment in Business Settings* (pp. 112–131). Hershey, PA: IGI Global. doi:10.4018/978-1-5225-0861-8.ch005

Goyal, A. (2021). Communicating and Building Destination Brands With New Media. In M. Dinis, L. Bonixe, S. Lamy, & Z. Breda (Eds.), *Impact of New Media in Tourism* (pp. 1-20). IGI Global. https://doi.org/10.4018/978-1-7998-7095-1.ch001

Grefen, P., & Turetken, O. (2017). Advanced Business Process Management in Networked E-Business Scenarios. *International Journal of E-Business Research*, *13*(4), 70–104. doi:10.4018/IJEBR.2017100105

Guasca, M., Van Broeck, A. M., & Vanneste, D. (2021). Tourism and the Social Reintegration of Colombian Ex-Combatants. In J. da Silva, Z. Breda, & F. Carbone (Eds.), *Role and Impact of Tourism in Peacebuilding and Conflict Transformation* (pp. 66-86). IGI Global. https://doi.org/10.4018/978-1-7998-5053-3.ch005

Haider, A., & Saetang, S. (2017). Strategic IT Alignment in Service Sector. In S. Rozenes & Y. Cohen (Eds.), *Handbook of Research on Strategic Alliances and Value Co-Creation in the Service Industry* (pp. 231–258). Hershey, PA: IGI Global. doi:10.4018/978-1-5225-2084-9.ch012

Hajilari, A. B., Ghadaksaz, M., & Fasghandis, G. S. (2017). Assessing Organizational Readiness for Implementing ERP System Using Fuzzy Expert System Approach. *International Journal of Enterprise Information Systems*, *13*(1), 67–85. doi:10.4018/IJEIS.2017010105

Haldorai, A., Ramu, A., & Murugan, S. (2018). Social Aware Cognitive Radio Networks: Effectiveness of Social Networks as a Strategic Tool for Organizational Business Management. In H. Bansal, G. Shrivastava, G. Nguyen, & L. Stanciu (Eds.), *Social Network Analytics for Contemporary Business Organizations* (pp. 188–202). Hershey, PA: IGI Global. doi:10.4018/978-1-5225-5097-6.ch010

Hall, O. P. Jr. (2017). Social Media Driven Management Education. *International Journal of Knowledge-Based Organizations*, *7*(2), 43–59. doi:10.4018/IJKBO.2017040104

Hanifah, H., Halim, H. A., Ahmad, N. H., & Vafaei-Zadeh, A. (2017). Innovation Culture as a Mediator Between Specific Human Capital and Innovation Performance Among Bumiputera SMEs in Malaysia. In N. Ahmad, T. Ramayah, H. Halim, & S. Rahman (Eds.), *Handbook of Research on Small and Medium Enterprises in Developing Countries* (pp. 261–279). Hershey, PA: IGI Global. doi:10.4018/978-1-5225-2165-5.ch012

Hartlieb, S., & Silvius, G. (2017). Handling Uncertainty in Project Management and Business Development: Similarities and Differences. In Y. Raydugin (Ed.), *Handbook of Research on Leveraging Risk and Uncertainties for Effective Project Management* (pp. 337–362). Hershey, PA: IGI Global. doi:10.4018/978-1-5225-1790-0.ch016

Hass, K. B. (2017). Living on the Edge: Managing Project Complexity. In Y. Raydugin (Ed.), *Handbook of Research on Leveraging Risk and Uncertainties for Effective Project Management* (pp. 177–201). Hershey, PA: IGI Global. doi:10.4018/978-1-5225-1790-0.ch009

Hawking, P., & Carmine Sellitto, C. (2017). Developing an Effective Strategy for Organizational Business Intelligence. In M. Tavana (Ed.), *Enterprise Information Systems and the Digitalization of Business Functions* (pp. 222–237). Hershey, PA: IGI Global. doi:10.4018/978-1-5225-2382-6.ch010

Hawking, P., & Sellitto, C. (2017). A Fast-Moving Consumer Goods Company and Business Intelligence Strategy Development. *International Journal of Enterprise Information Systems*, *13*(2), 22–33. doi:10.4018/IJEIS.2017040102

Hawking, P., & Sellitto, C. (2017). Business Intelligence Strategy: Two Case Studies. *International Journal of Business Intelligence Research*, *8*(2), 17–30. doi:10.4018/IJBIR.2017070102

Hee, W. J., Jalleh, G., Lai, H., & Lin, C. (2017). E-Commerce and IT Projects: Evaluation and Management Issues in Australian and Taiwanese Hospitals. *International Journal of Public Health Management and Ethics*, *2*(1), 69–90. doi:10.4018/IJPHME.2017010104

Hernandez, A. A. (2018). Exploring the Factors to Green IT Adoption of SMEs in the Philippines. *Journal of Cases on Information Technology*, *20*(2), 49–66. doi:10.4018/JCIT.2018040104

Hollman, A., Bickford, S., & Hollman, T. (2017). Cyber InSecurity: A Post-Mortem Attempt to Assess Cyber Problems from IT and Business Management Perspectives. *Journal of Cases on Information Technology*, *19*(3), 42–70. doi:10.4018/JCIT.2017070104

Ibrahim, F., & Zainin, N. M. (2021). Exploring the Technological Impacts: The Case of Museums in Brunei Darussalam. *International Journal of Tourism and Hospitality Management in the Digital Age*, *5*(1), 1–18. https://doi.org/10.4018/IJTHMDA.2021010101

Igbinakhase, I. (2017). Responsible and Sustainable Management Practices in Developing and Developed Business Environments. In Z. Fields (Ed.), *Collective Creativity for Responsible and Sustainable Business Practice* (pp. 180–207). Hershey, PA: IGI Global. doi:10.4018/978-1-5225-1823-5.ch010

Iwata, J. J., & Hoskins, R. G. (2017). Managing Indigenous Knowledge in Tanzania: A Business Perspective. In P. Jain & N. Mnjama (Eds.), *Managing Knowledge Resources and Records in Modern Organizations* (pp. 198–214). Hershey, PA: IGI Global. doi:10.4018/978-1-5225-1965-2.ch012

Jain, P. (2017). Ethical and Legal Issues in Knowledge Management Life-Cycle in Business. In P. Jain & N. Mnjama (Eds.), *Managing Knowledge Resources and Records in Modern Organizations* (pp. 82–101). Hershey, PA: IGI Global. doi:10.4018/978-1-5225-1965-2.ch006

James, S., & Hauli, E. (2017). Holistic Management Education at Tanzanian Rural Development Planning Institute. In N. Baporikar (Ed.), *Management Education for Global Leadership* (pp. 112–136). Hershey, PA: IGI Global. doi:10.4018/978-1-5225-1013-0.ch006

Janošková, M., Csikósová, A., & Čulková, K. (2018). Measurement of Company Performance as Part of Its Strategic Management. In R. Leon (Ed.), *Managerial Strategies for Business Sustainability During Turbulent Times* (pp. 309–335). Hershey, PA: IGI Global. doi:10.4018/978-1-5225-2716-9.ch017

Jean-Vasile, A., & Alecu, A. (2017). Theoretical and Practical Approaches in Understanding the Influences of Cost-Productivity-Profit Trinomial in Contemporary Enterprises. In A. Jean Vasile & D. Nicolò (Eds.), *Sustainable Entrepreneurship and Investments in the Green Economy* (pp. 28–62). Hershey, PA: IGI Global. doi:10.4018/978-1-5225-2075-7.ch002

Joia, L. A., & Correia, J. C. (2018). CIO Competencies From the IT Professional Perspective: Insights From Brazil. *Journal of Global Information Management*, *26*(2), 74–103. doi:10.4018/JGIM.2018040104

Juma, A., & Mzera, N. (2017). Knowledge Management and Records Management and Competitive Advantage in Business. In P. Jain & N. Mnjama (Eds.), *Managing Knowledge Resources and Records in Modern Organizations* (pp. 15–28). Hershey, PA: IGI Global. doi:10.4018/978-1-5225-1965-2.ch002

K., I., & A, V. (2018). Monitoring and Auditing in the Cloud. In K. Munir (Ed.), *Cloud Computing Technologies for Green Enterprises* (pp. 318-350). Hershey, PA: IGI Global. https://doi.org/ doi:10.4018/978-1-5225-3038-1.ch013

Kabra, G., Ghosh, V., & Ramesh, A. (2018). Enterprise Integrated Business Process Management and Business Intelligence Framework for Business Process Sustainability. In A. Paul, D. Bhattacharyya, & S. Anand (Eds.), *Green Initiatives for Business Sustainability and Value Creation* (pp. 228–238). Hershey, PA: IGI Global. doi:10.4018/978-1-5225-2662-9.ch010

Kaoud, M. (2017). Investigation of Customer Knowledge Management: A Case Study Research. *International Journal of Service Science, Management, Engineering, and Technology*, *8*(2), 12–22. doi:10.4018/IJSSMET.2017040102

Katuu, S. (2018). A Comparative Assessment of Enterprise Content Management Maturity Models. In N. Gwangwava & M. Mutingi (Eds.), *E-Manufacturing and E-Service Strategies in Contemporary Organizations* (pp. 93–118). Hershey, PA: IGI Global. doi:10.4018/978-1-5225-3628-4.ch005

Khan, M. Y., & Abir, T. (2022). The Role of Social Media Marketing in the Tourism and Hospitality Industry: A Conceptual Study on Bangladesh. In C. Ramos, S. Quinteiro, & A. Gonçalves (Eds.), *ICT as Innovator Between Tourism and Culture* (pp. 213–229). IGI Global. https://doi.org/10.4018/978-1-7998-8165-0.ch013

Kinnunen, S., Ylä-Kujala, A., Marttonen-Arola, S., Kärri, T., & Baglee, D. (2018). Internet of Things in Asset Management: Insights from Industrial Professionals and Academia. *International Journal of Service Science, Management, Engineering, and Technology*, *9*(2), 104–119. doi:10.4018/IJSSMET.2018040105

Klein, A. Z., Sabino de Freitas, A., Machado, L., Freitas, J. C. Jr, Graziola, P. G. Jr, & Schlemmer, E. (2017). Virtual Worlds Applications for Management Education. In L. Tomei (Ed.), *Exploring the New Era of Technology-Infused Education* (pp. 279–299). Hershey, PA: IGI Global. doi:10.4018/978-1-5225-1709-2.ch017

Kővári, E., Saleh, M., & Steinbachné Hajmásy, G. (2022). The Impact of Corporate Digital Responsibility (CDR) on Internal Stakeholders' Satisfaction in Hungarian Upscale Hotels. In M. Valeri (Ed.), *New Governance and Management in Touristic Destinations* (pp. 35–51). IGI Global. https://doi.org/10.4018/978-1-6684-3889-3.ch003

Kożuch, B., & Jabłoński, A. (2017). Adopting the Concept of Business Models in Public Management. In M. Lewandowski & B. Kożuch (Eds.), *Public Sector Entrepreneurship and the Integration of Innovative Business Models* (pp. 10–46). Hershey, PA: IGI Global. doi:10.4018/978-1-5225-2215-7.ch002

Kumar, J., Adhikary, A., & Jha, A. (2017). Small Active Investors' Perceptions and Preferences Towards Tax Saving Mutual Fund Schemes in Eastern India: An Empirical Note. *International Journal of Asian Business and Information Management, 8*(2), 35–45. doi:10.4018/IJABIM.2017040103

Latusi, S., & Fissore, M. (2021). Pilgrimage Routes to Happiness: Comparing the Camino de Santiago and Via Francigena. In A. Perinotto, V. Mayer, & J. Soares (Eds.), *Rebuilding and Restructuring the Tourism Industry: Infusion of Happiness and Quality of Life* (pp. 157–182). IGI Global. https://doi.org/10.4018/978-1-7998-7239-9.ch008

Lavassani, K. M., & Movahedi, B. (2017). Applications Driven Information Systems: Beyond Networks toward Business Ecosystems. *International Journal of Innovation in the Digital Economy, 8*(1), 61–75. doi:10.4018/IJIDE.2017010104

Lazzareschi, V. H., & Brito, M. S. (2017). Strategic Information Management: Proposal of Business Project Model. In G. Jamil, A. Soares, & C. Pessoa (Eds.), *Handbook of Research on Information Management for Effective Logistics and Supply Chains* (pp. 59–88). Hershey, PA: IGI Global. doi:10.4018/978-1-5225-0973-8.ch004

Lechuga Sancho, M. P., & Martín Navarro, A. (2022). Evolution of the Literature on Social Responsibility in the Tourism Sector: A Systematic Literature Review. In G. Fernandes (Ed.), *Challenges and New Opportunities for Tourism in Inland Territories: Ecocultural Resources and Sustainable Initiatives* (pp. 169–186). IGI Global. https://doi.org/10.4018/978-1-7998-7339-6.ch010

Lederer, M., Kurz, M., & Lazarov, P. (2017). Usage and Suitability of Methods for Strategic Business Process Initiatives: A Multi Case Study Research. *International Journal of Productivity Management and Assessment Technologies, 5*(1), 40–51. doi:10.4018/IJPMAT.2017010103

Lee, I. (2017). A Social Enterprise Business Model and a Case Study of Pacific Community Ventures (PCV). In V. Potocan, M. Üngan, & Z. Nedelko (Eds.), *Handbook of Research on Managerial Solutions in Non-Profit Organizations* (pp. 182–204). Hershey, PA: IGI Global. doi:10.4018/978-1-5225-0731-4.ch009

Leon, L. A., Seal, K. C., Przasnyski, Z. H., & Wiedenman, I. (2017). Skills and Competencies Required for Jobs in Business Analytics: A Content Analysis of Job Advertisements Using Text Mining. *International Journal of Business Intelligence Research, 8*(1), 1–25. doi:10.4018/IJBIR.2017010101

Levy, C. L., & Elias, N. I. (2017). SOHO Users' Perceptions of Reliability and Continuity of Cloud-Based Services. In M. Moore (Ed.), *Cybersecurity Breaches and Issues Surrounding Online Threat Protection* (pp. 248–287). Hershey, PA: IGI Global. doi:10.4018/978-1-5225-1941-6.ch011

Levy, M. (2018). Change Management Serving Knowledge Management and Organizational Development: Reflections and Review. In N. Baporikar (Ed.), *Global Practices in Knowledge Management for Societal and Organizational Development* (pp. 256–270). Hershey, PA: IGI Global. doi:10.4018/978-1-5225-3009-1.ch012

Lewandowski, M. (2017). Public Organizations and Business Model Innovation: The Role of Public Service Design. In M. Lewandowski & B. Kożuch (Eds.), *Public Sector Entrepreneurship and the Integration of Innovative Business Models* (pp. 47–72). Hershey, PA: IGI Global. doi:10.4018/978-1-5225-2215-7.ch003

Lhannaoui, H., Kabbaj, M. I., & Bakkoury, Z. (2017). A Survey of Risk-Aware Business Process Modelling. *International Journal of Risk and Contingency Management, 6*(3), 14–26. doi:10.4018/IJRCM.2017070102

Li, J., Sun, W., Jiang, W., Yang, H., & Zhang, L. (2017). How the Nature of Exogenous Shocks and Crises Impact Company Performance?: The Effects of Industry Characteristics. *International Journal of Risk and Contingency Management, 6*(4), 40–55. doi:10.4018/IJRCM.2017100103

Lopez-Fernandez, M., Perez-Perez, M., Serrano-Bedia, A., & Cobo-Gonzalez, A. (2021). Small and Medium Tourism Enterprise Survival in Times of Crisis: "El Capricho de Gaudí. In D. Toubes & N. Araújo-Vila (Eds.), *Risk, Crisis, and Disaster Management in Small and Medium-Sized Tourism Enterprises* (pp. 103–129). IGI Global. doi:10.4018/978-1-7998-6996-2.ch005

Mahajan, A., Maidullah, S., & Hossain, M. R. (2022). Experience Toward Smart Tour Guide Apps in Travelling: An Analysis of Users' Reviews on Audio Odigos and Trip My Way. In R. Augusto Costa, F. Brandão, Z. Breda, & C. Costa (Eds.), *Planning and Managing the Experience Economy in Tourism* (pp. 255-273). IGI Global. https://doi.org/10.4018/978-1-7998-8775-1.ch014

Malega, P. (2017). Small and Medium Enterprises in the Slovak Republic: Status and Competitiveness of SMEs in the Global Markets and Possibilities of Optimization. In M. Vemić (Ed.), *Optimal Management Strategies in Small and Medium Enterprises* (pp. 102–124). Hershey, PA: IGI Global. doi:10.4018/978-1-5225-1949-2.ch006

Malewska, K. M. (2017). Intuition in Decision-Making on the Example of a Non-Profit Organization. In V. Potocan, M. Ünğan, & Z. Nedelko (Eds.), *Handbook of Research on Managerial Solutions in Non-Profit Organizations* (pp. 378–399). Hershey, PA: IGI Global. doi:10.4018/978-1-5225-0731-4.ch018

Maroofi, F. (2017). Entrepreneurial Orientation and Organizational Learning Ability Analysis for Innovation and Firm Performance. In N. Baporikar (Ed.), *Innovation and Shifting Perspectives in Management Education* (pp. 144–165). Hershey, PA: IGI Global. doi:10.4018/978-1-5225-1019-2.ch007

Marques, M., Moleiro, D., Brito, T. M., & Marques, T. (2021). Customer Relationship Management as an Important Relationship Marketing Tool: The Case of the Hospitality Industry in Estoril Coast. In M. Dinis, L. Bonixe, S. Lamy, & Z. Breda (Eds.), Impact of New Media in Tourism (pp. 39-56). IGI Global. https://doi.org/doi:10.4018/978-1-7998-7095-1.ch003

Martins, P. V., & Zacarias, M. (2017). A Web-based Tool for Business Process Improvement. *International Journal of Web Portals*, *9*(2), 68–84. doi:10.4018/IJWP.2017070104

Matthies, B., & Coners, A. (2017). Exploring the Conceptual Nature of e-Business Projects. *Journal of Electronic Commerce in Organizations*, *15*(3), 33–63. doi:10.4018/JECO.2017070103

Mayer, V. F., Fraga, C. C., & Silva, L. C. (2021). Contributions of Neurosciences to Studies of Well-Being in Tourism. In A. Perinotto, V. Mayer, & J. Soares (Eds.), *Rebuilding and Restructuring the Tourism Industry: Infusion of Happiness and Quality of Life* (pp. 108–128). IGI Global. https://doi.org/10.4018/978-1-7998-7239-9.ch006

McKee, J. (2018). Architecture as a Tool to Solve Business Planning Problems. In M. Khosrow-Pour, D.B.A. (Ed.), Encyclopedia of Information Science and Technology, Fourth Edition (pp. 573-586). Hershey, PA: IGI Global. doi:10.4018/978-1-5225-2255-3.ch050

McMurray, A. J., Cross, J., & Caponecchia, C. (2018). The Risk Management Profession in Australia: Business Continuity Plan Practices. In N. Bajgoric (Ed.), *Always-On Enterprise Information Systems for Modern Organizations* (pp. 112–129). Hershey, PA: IGI Global. doi:10.4018/978-1-5225-3704-5.ch006

Meddah, I. H., & Belkadi, K. (2018). Mining Patterns Using Business Process Management. In R. Hamou (Ed.), *Handbook of Research on Biomimicry in Information Retrieval and Knowledge Management* (pp. 78–89). Hershey, PA: IGI Global. doi:10.4018/978-1-5225-3004-6.ch005

Melian, A. G., & Camprubí, R. (2021). The Accessibility of Museum Websites: The Case of Barcelona. In C. Eusébio, L. Teixeira, & M. Carneiro (Eds.), *ICT Tools and Applications for Accessible Tourism* (pp. 234–255). IGI Global. https://doi.org/10.4018/978-1-7998-6428-8.ch011

Mendes, L. (2017). TQM and Knowledge Management: An Integrated Approach Towards Tacit Knowledge Management. In D. Jaziri-Bouagina & G. Jamil (Eds.), *Handbook of Research on Tacit Knowledge Management for Organizational Success* (pp. 236–263). Hershey, PA: IGI Global. doi:10.4018/978-1-5225-2394-9.ch009

Menezes, V. D., & Cavagnaro, E. (2021). Communicating Sustainable Initiatives in the Hotel Industry: The Case of the Hotel Jakarta Amsterdam. In F. Brandão, Z. Breda, R. Costa, & C. Costa (Eds.), *Handbook of Research on the Role of Tourism in Achieving Sustainable Development Goals* (pp. 224-234). IGI Global. https://doi.org/10.4018/978-1-7998-5691-7.ch013

Menezes, V. D., & Cavagnaro, E. (2021). Communicating Sustainable Initiatives in the Hotel Industry: The Case of the Hotel Jakarta Amsterdam. In F. Brandão, Z. Breda, R. Costa, & C. Costa (Eds.), *Handbook of Research on the Role of Tourism in Achieving Sustainable Development Goals* (pp. 224-234). IGI Global. https://doi.org/10.4018/978-1-7998-5691-7.ch013

Mitas, O., Bastiaansen, M., & Boode, W. (2022). If You're Happy, I'm Happy: Emotion Contagion at a Tourist Information Center. In R. Augusto Costa, F. Brandão, Z. Breda, & C. Costa (Eds.), *Planning and Managing the Experience Economy in Tourism* (pp. 122-140). IGI Global. https://doi.org/10.4018/978-1-7998-8775-1.ch007

Mnjama, N. M. (2017). Preservation of Recorded Information in Public and Private Sector Organizations. In P. Jain & N. Mnjama (Eds.), *Managing Knowledge Resources and Records in Modern Organizations* (pp. 149–167). Hershey, PA: IGI Global. doi:10.4018/978-1-5225-1965-2.ch009

Mokoqama, M., & Fields, Z. (2017). Principles of Responsible Management Education (PRME): Call for Responsible Management Education. In Z. Fields (Ed.), *Collective Creativity for Responsible and Sustainable Business Practice* (pp. 229–241). Hershey, PA: IGI Global. doi:10.4018/978-1-5225-1823-5.ch012

Monteiro, A., Lopes, S., & Carbone, F. (2021). Academic Mobility: Bridging Tourism and Peace Education. In J. da Silva, Z. Breda, & F. Carbone (Eds.), *Role and Impact of Tourism in Peacebuilding and Conflict Transformation* (pp. 275-301). IGI Global. https://doi.org/10.4018/978-1-7998-5053-3.ch016

Muniapan, B. (2017). Philosophy and Management: The Relevance of Vedanta in Management. In P. Ordóñez de Pablos (Ed.), *Managerial Strategies and Solutions for Business Success in Asia* (pp. 124–139). Hershey, PA: IGI Global. doi:10.4018/978-1-5225-1886-0.ch007

Murad, S. E., & Dowaji, S. (2017). Using Value-Based Approach for Managing Cloud-Based Services. In A. Turuk, B. Sahoo, & S. Addya (Eds.), *Resource Management and Efficiency in Cloud Computing Environments* (pp. 33–60). Hershey, PA: IGI Global. doi:10.4018/978-1-5225-1721-4.ch002

Mutahar, A. M., Daud, N. M., Thurasamy, R., Isaac, O., & Abdulsalam, R. (2018). The Mediating of Perceived Usefulness and Perceived Ease of Use: The Case of Mobile Banking in Yemen. *International Journal of Technology Diffusion*, *9*(2), 21–40. doi:10.4018/IJTD.2018040102

Naidoo, V. (2017). E-Learning and Management Education at African Universities. In N. Baporikar (Ed.), *Management Education for Global Leadership* (pp. 181–201). Hershey, PA: IGI Global. doi:10.4018/978-1-5225-1013-0.ch009

Naidoo, V., & Igbinakhase, I. (2018). Opportunities and Challenges of Knowledge Retention in SMEs. In N. Baporikar (Ed.), *Knowledge Integration Strategies for Entrepreneurship and Sustainability* (pp. 70–94). Hershey, PA: IGI Global. doi:10.4018/978-1-5225-5115-7.ch004

Naumov, N., & Costandachi, G. (2021). Creativity and Entrepreneurship: Gastronomic Tourism in Mexico. In J. Soares (Ed.), *Innovation and Entrepreneurial Opportunities in Community Tourism* (pp. 90–108). IGI Global. https://doi.org/10.4018/978-1-7998-4855-4.ch006

Nayak, S., & Prabhu, N. (2017). Paradigm Shift in Management Education: Need for a Cross Functional Perspective. In N. Baporikar (Ed.), *Management Education for Global Leadership* (pp. 241–255). Hershey, PA: IGI Global. doi:10.4018/978-1-5225-1013-0.ch012

Nedelko, Z., & Potocan, V. (2017). Management Solutions in Non-Profit Organizations: Case of Slovenia. In V. Potocan, M. Üngan, & Z. Nedelko (Eds.), *Handbook of Research on Managerial Solutions in Non-Profit Organizations* (pp. 1–22). Hershey, PA: IGI Global. doi:10.4018/978-1-5225-0731-4.ch001

Nedelko, Z., & Potocan, V. (2017). Priority of Management Tools Utilization among Managers: International Comparison. In V. Wang (Ed.), *Encyclopedia of Strategic Leadership and Management* (pp. 1083–1094). Hershey, PA: IGI Global. doi:10.4018/978-1-5225-1049-9.ch075

Nedelko, Z., Raudeliūnienė, J., & Črešnar, R. (2018). Knowledge Dynamics in Supply Chain Management. In N. Baporikar (Ed.), *Knowledge Integration Strategies for Entrepreneurship and Sustainability* (pp. 150–166). Hershey, PA: IGI Global. doi:10.4018/978-1-5225-5115-7.ch008

Nguyen, H. T., & Hipsher, S. A. (2018). Innovation and Creativity Used by Private Sector Firms in a Resources-Constrained Environment. In S. Hipsher (Ed.), *Examining the Private Sector's Role in Wealth Creation and Poverty Reduction* (pp. 219–238). Hershey, PA: IGI Global. doi:10.4018/978-1-5225-3117-3.ch010

Obicci, P. A. (2017). Risk Sharing in a Partnership. In *Risk Management Strategies in Public-Private Partnerships* (pp. 115–152). Hershey, PA: IGI Global. doi:10.4018/978-1-5225-2503-5.ch004

Obidallah, W. J., & Raahemi, B. (2017). Managing Changes in Service Oriented Virtual Organizations: A Structural and Procedural Framework to Facilitate the Process of Change. *Journal of Electronic Commerce in Organizations*, *15*(1), 59–83. doi:10.4018/JECO.2017010104

Ojo, O. (2017). Impact of Innovation on the Entrepreneurial Success in Selected Business Enterprises in South-West Nigeria. *International Journal of Innovation in the Digital Economy*, *8*(2), 29–38. doi:10.4018/IJIDE.2017040103

Okdinawati, L., Simatupang, T. M., & Sunitiyoso, Y. (2017). Multi-Agent Reinforcement Learning for Value Co-Creation of Collaborative Transportation Management (CTM). *International Journal of Information Systems and Supply Chain Management*, *10*(3), 84–95. doi:10.4018/IJISSCM.2017070105

Olivera, V. A., & Carrillo, I. M. (2021). Organizational Culture: A Key Element for the Development of Mexican Micro and Small Tourist Companies. In J. Soares (Ed.), *Innovation and Entrepreneurial Opportunities in Community Tourism* (pp. 227–242). IGI Global. doi:10.4018/978-1-7998-4855-4.ch013

Ossorio, M. (2022). Corporate Museum Experiences in Enogastronomic Tourism. In R. Augusto Costa, F. Brandão, Z. Breda, & C. Costa (Eds.), Planning and Managing the Experience Economy in Tourism (pp. 107-121). IGI Global. https://doi.org/doi:10.4018/978-1-7998-8775-1.ch006

Ossorio, M. (2022). Enogastronomic Tourism in Times of Pandemic. In G. Fernandes (Ed.), *Challenges and New Opportunities for Tourism in Inland Territories: Ecocultural Resources and Sustainable Initiatives* (pp. 241–255). IGI Global. https://doi.org/10.4018/978-1-7998-7339-6.ch014

Özekici, Y. K. (2022). ICT as an Acculturative Agent and Its Role in the Tourism Context: Introduction, Acculturation Theory, Progress of the Acculturation Theory in Extant Literature. In C. Ramos, S. Quinteiro, & A. Gonçalves (Eds.), *ICT as Innovator Between Tourism and Culture* (pp. 42–66). IGI Global. https://doi.org/10.4018/978-1-7998-8165-0.ch004

Pal, K. (2018). Building High Quality Big Data-Based Applications in Supply Chains. In A. Kumar & S. Saurav (Eds.), *Supply Chain Management Strategies and Risk Assessment in Retail Environments* (pp. 1–24). Hershey, PA: IGI Global. doi:10.4018/978-1-5225-3056-5.ch001

Palos-Sanchez, P. R., & Correia, M. B. (2018). Perspectives of the Adoption of Cloud Computing in the Tourism Sector. In J. Rodrigues, C. Ramos, P. Cardoso, & C. Henriques (Eds.), *Handbook of Research on Technological Developments for Cultural Heritage and eTourism Applications* (pp. 377–400). Hershey, PA: IGI Global. doi:10.4018/978-1-5225-2927-9.ch018

Papadopoulou, G. (2021). Promoting Gender Equality and Women Empowerment in the Tourism Sector. In F. Brandão, Z. Breda, R. Costa, & C. Costa (Eds.), Handbook of Research on the Role of Tourism in Achieving Sustainable Development Goals (pp. 152-174). IGI Global. https://doi.org/ doi:10.4018/978-1-7998-5691-7.ch009

Papp-Váry, Á. F., & Tóth, T. Z. (2022). Analysis of Budapest as a Film Tourism Destination. In R. Baleiro & R. Pereira (Eds.), *Global Perspectives on Literary Tourism and Film-Induced Tourism* (pp. 257-279). IGI Global. https://doi.org/10.4018/978-1-7998-8262-6.ch014

Patiño, B. E. (2017). New Generation Management by Convergence and Individual Identity: A Systemic and Human-Oriented Approach. In N. Baporikar (Ed.), *Innovation and Shifting Perspectives in Management Education* (pp. 119–143). Hershey, PA: IGI Global. doi:10.4018/978-1-5225-1019-2.ch006

Patro, C. S. (2021). Digital Tourism: Influence of E-Marketing Technology. In M. Dinis, L. Bonixe, S. Lamy, & Z. Breda (Eds.), *Impact of New Media in Tourism* (pp. 234-254). IGI Global. https://doi.org/10.4018/978-1-7998-7095-1.ch014

Pawliczek, A., & Rössler, M. (2017). Knowledge of Management Tools and Systems in SMEs: Knowledge Transfer in Management. In A. Bencsik (Ed.), *Knowledge Management Initiatives and Strategies in Small and Medium Enterprises* (pp. 180–203). Hershey, PA: IGI Global. doi:10.4018/978-1-5225-1642-2.ch009

Pejic-Bach, M., Omazic, M. A., Aleksic, A., & Zoroja, J. (2018). Knowledge-Based Decision Making: A Multi-Case Analysis. In R. Leon (Ed.), *Managerial Strategies for Business Sustainability During Turbulent Times* (pp. 160–184). Hershey, PA: IGI Global. doi:10.4018/978-1-5225-2716-9.ch009

Perano, M., Hysa, X., & Calabrese, M. (2018). Strategic Planning, Cultural Context, and Business Continuity Management: Business Cases in the City of Shkoder. In A. Presenza & L. Sheehan (Eds.), *Geopolitics and Strategic Management in the Global Economy* (pp. 57–77). Hershey, PA: IGI Global. doi:10.4018/978-1-5225-2673-5.ch004

Pereira, R., Mira da Silva, M., & Lapão, L. V. (2017). IT Governance Maturity Patterns in Portuguese Healthcare. In S. De Haes & W. Van Grembergen (Eds.), *Strategic IT Governance and Alignment in Business Settings* (pp. 24–52). Hershey, PA: IGI Global. doi:10.4018/978-1-5225-0861-8.ch002

Pérez-Uribe, R. I., Torres, D. A., Jurado, S. P., & Prada, D. M. (2018). Cloud Tools for the Development of Project Management in SMEs. In R. Perez-Uribe, C. Salcedo-Perez, & D. Ocampo-Guzman (Eds.), *Handbook of Research on Intrapreneurship and Organizational Sustainability in SMEs* (pp. 95–120). Hershey, PA: IGI Global. doi:10.4018/978-1-5225-3543-0.ch005

Petrisor, I., & Cozmiuc, D. (2017). Global Supply Chain Management Organization at Siemens in the Advent of Industry 4.0. In L. Saglietto & C. Cezanne (Eds.), *Global Intermediation and Logistics Service Providers* (pp. 123–142). Hershey, PA: IGI Global. doi:10.4018/978-1-5225-2133-4.ch007

Pierce, J. M., Velliaris, D. M., & Edwards, J. (2017). A Living Case Study: A Journey Not a Destination. In N. Silton (Ed.), *Exploring the Benefits of Creativity in Education, Media, and the Arts* (pp. 158–178). Hershey, PA: IGI Global. doi:10.4018/978-1-5225-0504-4.ch008

Pipia, S., & Pipia, S. (2021). Challenges of Religious Tourism in the Conflict Region: An Example of Jerusalem. In E. Alaverdov & M. Bari (Eds.), *Global Development of Religious Tourism* (pp. 135-148). IGI Global. https://doi.org/10.4018/978-1-7998-5792-1.ch009

Poulaki, P., Kritikos, A., Vasilakis, N., & Valeri, M. (2022). The Contribution of Female Creativity to the Development of Gastronomic Tourism in Greece: The Case of the Island of Naxos in the South Aegean Region. In M. Valeri (Ed.), *New Governance and Management in Touristic Destinations* (pp. 246–258). IGI Global. https://doi.org/10.4018/978-1-6684-3889-3.ch015

Radosavljevic, M., & Andjelkovic, A. (2017). Multi-Criteria Decision Making Approach for Choosing Business Process for the Improvement: Upgrading of the Six Sigma Methodology. In J. Stanković, P. Delias, S. Marinković, & S. Rochhia (Eds.), *Tools and Techniques for Economic Decision Analysis* (pp. 225–247). Hershey, PA: IGI Global. doi:10.4018/978-1-5225-0959-2.ch011

Radovic, V. M. (2017). Corporate Sustainability and Responsibility and Disaster Risk Reduction: A Serbian Overview. In M. Camilleri (Ed.), *CSR 2.0 and the New Era of Corporate Citizenship* (pp. 147–164). Hershey, PA: IGI Global. doi:10.4018/978-1-5225-1842-6.ch008

Raghunath, K. M., Devi, S. L., & Patro, C. S. (2018). Impact of Risk Assessment Models on Risk Factors: A Holistic Outlook. In K. Strang, M. Korstanje, & N. Vajjhala (Eds.), *Research, Practices, and Innovations in Global Risk and Contingency Management* (pp. 134–153). Hershey, PA: IGI Global. doi:10.4018/978-1-5225-4754-9.ch008

Raman, A., & Goyal, D. P. (2017). Extending IMPLEMENT Framework for Enterprise Information Systems Implementation to Information System Innovation. In M. Tavana (Ed.), *Enterprise Information Systems and the Digitalization of Business Functions* (pp. 137–177). Hershey, PA: IGI Global. doi:10.4018/978-1-5225-2382-6.ch007

Rao, Y., & Zhang, Y. (2017). The Construction and Development of Academic Library Digital Special Subject Databases. In L. Ruan, Q. Zhu, & Y. Ye (Eds.), *Academic Library Development and Administration in China* (pp. 163–183). Hershey, PA: IGI Global. doi:10.4018/978-1-5225-0550-1.ch010

Ravasan, A. Z., Mohammadi, M. M., & Hamidi, H. (2018). An Investigation Into the Critical Success Factors of Implementing Information Technology Service Management Frameworks. In K. Jakobs (Ed.), *Corporate and Global Standardization Initiatives in Contemporary Society* (pp. 200–218). Hershey, PA: IGI Global. doi:10.4018/978-1-5225-5320-5.ch009

Rezaie, S., Mirabedini, S. J., & Abtahi, A. (2018). Designing a Model for Implementation of Business Intelligence in the Banking Industry. *International Journal of Enterprise Information Systems*, *14*(1), 77–103. doi:10.4018/IJEIS.2018010105

Richards, V., Matthews, N., Williams, O. J., & Khan, Z. (2021). The Challenges of Accessible Tourism Information Systems for Tourists With Vision Impairment: Sensory Communications Beyond the Screen. In C. Eusébio, L. Teixeira, & M. Carneiro (Eds.), *ICT Tools and Applications for Accessible Tourism* (pp. 26–54). IGI Global. https://doi.org/10.4018/978-1-7998-6428-8.ch002

Rodrigues de Souza Neto, V., & Marques, O. (2021). Rural Tourism Fostering Welfare Through Sustainable Development: A Conceptual Approach. In A. Perinotto, V. Mayer, & J. Soares (Eds.), *Rebuilding and Restructuring the Tourism Industry: Infusion of Happiness and Quality of Life* (pp. 38–57). IGI Global. https://doi.org/10.4018/978-1-7998-7239-9.ch003

Romano, L., Grimaldi, R., & Colasuonno, F. S. (2017). Demand Management as a Success Factor in Project Portfolio Management. In L. Romano (Ed.), *Project Portfolio Management Strategies for Effective Organizational Operations* (pp. 202–219). Hershey, PA: IGI Global. doi:10.4018/978-1-5225-2151-8.ch008

Rubio-Escuderos, L., & García-Andreu, H. (2021). Competitiveness Factors of Accessible Tourism E-Travel Agencies. In C. Eusébio, L. Teixeira, & M. Carneiro (Eds.), *ICT Tools and Applications for Accessible Tourism* (pp. 196–217). IGI Global. https://doi.org/10.4018/978-1-7998-6428-8.ch009

Rucci, A. C., Porto, N., Darcy, S., & Becka, L. (2021). Smart and Accessible Cities?: Not Always – The Case for Accessible Tourism Initiatives in Buenos Aries and Sydney. In C. Eusébio, L. Teixeira, & M. Carneiro (Eds.), *ICT Tools and Applications for Accessible Tourism* (pp. 115–145). IGI Global. https://doi.org/10.4018/978-1-7998-6428-8.ch006

Ruhi, U. (2018). Towards an Interdisciplinary Socio-Technical Definition of Virtual Communities. In M. Khosrow-Pour, D.B.A. (Ed.), Encyclopedia of Information Science and Technology, Fourth Edition (pp. 4278-4295). Hershey, PA: IGI Global. doi:10.4018/978-1-5225-2255-3.ch371

Ryan, L., Catena, M., Ros, P., & Stephens, S. (2021). Designing Entrepreneurial Ecosystems to Support Resource Management in the Tourism Industry. In V. Costa, A. Moura, & M. Mira (Eds.), *Handbook of Research on Human Capital and People Management in the Tourism Industry* (pp. 265–281). IGI Global. https://doi.org/10.4018/978-1-7998-4318-4.ch013

Sabuncu, I. (2021). Understanding Tourist Perceptions and Expectations During Pandemic Through Social Media Big Data. In M. Demir, A. Dalgıç, & F. Ergen (Eds.), *Handbook of Research on the Impacts and Implications of COVID-19 on the Tourism Industry* (pp. 330–350). IGI Global. https://doi.org/10.4018/978-1-7998-8231-2.ch016

Safari, M. R., & Jiang, Q. (2018). The Theory and Practice of IT Governance Maturity and Strategies Alignment: Evidence From Banking Industry. *Journal of Global Information Management*, *26*(2), 127–146. doi:10.4018/JGIM.2018040106

Sahoo, J., Pati, B., & Mohanty, B. (2017). Knowledge Management as an Academic Discipline: An Assessment. In B. Gunjal (Ed.), *Managing Knowledge and Scholarly Assets in Academic Libraries* (pp. 99–126). Hershey, PA: IGI Global. doi:10.4018/978-1-5225-1741-2.ch005

Saini, D. (2017). Relevance of Teaching Values and Ethics in Management Education. In N. Baporikar (Ed.), *Management Education for Global Leadership* (pp. 90–111). Hershey, PA: IGI Global. doi:10.4018/978-1-5225-1013-0.ch005

Sambhanthan, A. (2017). Assessing and Benchmarking Sustainability in Organisations: An Integrated Conceptual Model. *International Journal of Systems and Service-Oriented Engineering*, *7*(4), 22–43. doi:10.4018/IJSSOE.2017100102

Sambhanthan, A., & Potdar, V. (2017). A Study of the Parameters Impacting Sustainability in Information Technology Organizations. *International Journal of Knowledge-Based Organizations*, *7*(3), 27–39. doi:10.4018/IJKBO.2017070103

Sánchez-Fernández, M. D., & Manríquez, M. R. (2018). The Entrepreneurial Spirit Based on Social Values: The Digital Generation. In P. Isaias & L. Carvalho (Eds.), *User Innovation and the Entrepreneurship Phenomenon in the Digital Economy* (pp. 173–193). Hershey, PA: IGI Global. doi:10.4018/978-1-5225-2826-5.ch009

Sanchez-Ruiz, L., & Blanco, B. (2017). Process Management for SMEs: Barriers, Enablers, and Benefits. In M. Vemić (Ed.), *Optimal Management Strategies in Small and Medium Enterprises* (pp. 293–319). Hershey, PA: IGI Global. doi:10.4018/978-1-5225-1949-2.ch014

Sanz, L. F., Gómez-Pérez, J., & Castillo-Martinez, A. (2018). Analysis of the European ICT Competence Frameworks. In V. Ahuja & S. Rathore (Eds.), *Multidisciplinary Perspectives on Human Capital and Information Technology Professionals* (pp. 225–245). Hershey, PA: IGI Global. doi:10.4018/978-1-5225-5297-0.ch012

Sarvepalli, A., & Godin, J. (2017). Business Process Management in the Classroom. *Journal of Cases on Information Technology*, *19*(2), 17–28. doi:10.4018/JCIT.2017040102

Saxena, G. G., & Saxena, A. (2021). Host Community Role in Medical Tourism Development. In M. Singh & S. Kumaran (Eds.), *Growth of the Medical Tourism Industry and Its Impact on Society: Emerging Research and Opportunities* (pp. 105–127). IGI Global. https://doi.org/10.4018/978-1-7998-3427-4.ch006

Saygili, E. E., Ozturkoglu, Y., & Kocakulah, M. C. (2017). End Users' Perceptions of Critical Success Factors in ERP Applications. *International Journal of Enterprise Information Systems*, *13*(4), 58–75. doi:10.4018/IJEIS.2017100104

Saygili, E. E., & Saygili, A. T. (2017). Contemporary Issues in Enterprise Information Systems: A Critical Review of CSFs in ERP Implementations. In M. Tavana (Ed.), *Enterprise Information Systems and the Digitalization of Business Functions* (pp. 120–136). Hershey, PA: IGI Global. doi:10.4018/978-1-5225-2382-6.ch006

Schwaiger, K. M., & Zehrer, A. (2021). The COVID-19 Pandemic and Organizational Resilience in Hospitality Family Firms: A Qualitative Approach. In A. Zehrer, G. Glowka, K. Schwaiger, & V. Ranacher-Lackner (Eds.), *Resiliency Models and Addressing Future Risks for Family Firms in the Tourism Industry* (pp. 32–49). IGI Global. https://doi.org/10.4018/978-1-7998-7352-5.ch002

Scott, N., & Campos, A. C. (2022). Cognitive Science of Tourism Experiences. In R. Augusto Costa, F. Brandão, Z. Breda, & C. Costa (Eds.), Planning and Managing the Experience Economy in Tourism (pp. 1-21). IGI Global. https://doi.org/ doi:10.4018/978-1-7998-8775-1.ch001

Seidenstricker, S., & Antonino, A. (2018). Business Model Innovation-Oriented Technology Management for Emergent Technologies. In M. Khosrow-Pour, D.B.A. (Ed.), Encyclopedia of Information Science and Technology, Fourth Edition (pp. 4560-4569). Hershey, PA: IGI Global. doi:10.4018/978-1-5225-2255-3.ch396

Selvi, M. S. (2021). Changes in Tourism Sales and Marketing Post COVID-19. In M. Demir, A. Dalgıç, & F. Ergen (Eds.), *Handbook of Research on the Impacts and Implications of COVID-19 on the Tourism Industry* (pp. 437–460). IGI Global. doi:10.4018/978-1-7998-8231-2.ch021

Senaratne, S., & Gunarathne, A. D. (2017). Excellence Perspective for Management Education from a Global Accountants' Hub in Asia. In N. Baporikar (Ed.), *Management Education for Global Leadership* (pp. 158–180). Hershey, PA: IGI Global. doi:10.4018/978-1-5225-1013-0.ch008

Sensuse, D. I., & Cahyaningsih, E. (2018). Knowledge Management Models: A Summative Review. *International Journal of Information Systems in the Service Sector, 10*(1), 71–100. doi:10.4018/IJISSS.2018010105

Seth, M., Goyal, D., & Kiran, R. (2017). Diminution of Impediments in Implementation of Supply Chain Management Information System for Enhancing its Effectiveness in Indian Automobile Industry. *Journal of Global Information Management, 25*(3), 1–20. doi:10.4018/JGIM.2017070101

Seyal, A. H., & Rahman, M. N. (2017). Investigating Impact of Inter-Organizational Factors in Measuring ERP Systems Success: Bruneian Perspectives. In M. Tavana (Ed.), *Enterprise Information Systems and the Digitalization of Business Functions* (pp. 178–204). Hershey, PA: IGI Global. doi:10.4018/978-1-5225-2382-6.ch008

Shaqrah, A. A. (2018). Analyzing Business Intelligence Systems Based on 7s Model of McKinsey. *International Journal of Business Intelligence Research, 9*(1), 53–63. doi:10.4018/IJBIR.2018010104

Sharma, A. J. (2017). Enhancing Sustainability through Experiential Learning in Management Education. In N. Baporikar (Ed.), *Management Education for Global Leadership* (pp. 256–274). Hershey, PA: IGI Global. doi:10.4018/978-1-5225-1013-0.ch013

Shetty, K. P. (2017). Responsible Global Leadership: Ethical Challenges in Management Education. In N. Baporikar (Ed.), *Innovation and Shifting Perspectives in Management Education* (pp. 194–223). Hershey, PA: IGI Global. doi:10.4018/978-1-5225-1019-2.ch009

Sinthupundaja, J., & Kohda, Y. (2017). Effects of Corporate Social Responsibility and Creating Shared Value on Sustainability. *International Journal of Sustainable Entrepreneurship and Corporate Social Responsibility, 2*(1), 27–38. doi:10.4018/IJSECSR.2017010103

Škarica, I., & Hrgović, A. V. (2018). Implementation of Total Quality Management Principles in Public Health Institutes in the Republic of Croatia. *International Journal of Productivity Management and Assessment Technologies, 6*(1), 1–16. doi:10.4018/IJPMAT.2018010101

Skokic, V. (2021). How Small Hotel Owners Practice Resilience: Longitudinal Study Among Small Family Hotels in Croatia. In A. Zehrer, G. Glowka, K. Schwaiger, & V. Ranacher-Lackner (Eds.), *Resiliency Models and Addressing Future Risks for Family Firms in the Tourism Industry* (pp. 50–73). IGI Global. doi:10.4018/978-1-7998-7352-5.ch003

Smuts, H., Kotzé, P., Van der Merwe, A., & Loock, M. (2017). Framework for Managing Shared Knowledge in an Information Systems Outsourcing Context. *International Journal of Knowledge Management*, *13*(4), 1–30. doi:10.4018/IJKM.2017100101

Sousa, M. J., Cruz, R., Dias, I., & Caracol, C. (2017). Information Management Systems in the Supply Chain. In G. Jamil, A. Soares, & C. Pessoa (Eds.), *Handbook of Research on Information Management for Effective Logistics and Supply Chains* (pp. 469–485). Hershey, PA: IGI Global. doi:10.4018/978-1-5225-0973-8.ch025

Spremic, M., Turulja, L., & Bajgoric, N. (2018). Two Approaches in Assessing Business Continuity Management Attitudes in the Organizational Context. In N. Bajgoric (Ed.), *Always-On Enterprise Information Systems for Modern Organizations* (pp. 159–183). Hershey, PA: IGI Global. doi:10.4018/978-1-5225-3704-5.ch008

Steenkamp, A. L. (2018). Some Insights in Computer Science and Information Technology. In *Examining the Changing Role of Supervision in Doctoral Research Projects: Emerging Research and Opportunities* (pp. 113–133). Hershey, PA: IGI Global. doi:10.4018/978-1-5225-2610-0.ch005

Stipanović, C., Rudan, E., & Zubović, V. (2022). Reaching the New Tourist Through Creativity: Sustainable Development Challenges in Croatian Coastal Towns. In M. Valeri (Ed.), *New Governance and Management in Touristic Destinations* (pp. 231–245). IGI Global. https://doi.org/10.4018/978-1-6684-3889-3.ch014

Tabach, A., & Croteau, A. (2017). Configurations of Information Technology Governance Practices and Business Unit Performance. *International Journal of IT/Business Alignment and Governance*, *8*(2), 1–27. doi:10.4018/IJITBAG.2017070101

Talaue, G. M., & Iqbal, T. (2017). Assessment of e-Business Mode of Selected Private Universities in the Philippines and Pakistan. *International Journal of Online Marketing*, *7*(4), 63–77. doi:10.4018/IJOM.2017100105

Tam, G. C. (2017). Project Manager Sustainability Competence. In *Managerial Strategies and Green Solutions for Project Sustainability* (pp. 178–207). Hershey, PA: IGI Global. doi:10.4018/978-1-5225-2371-0.ch008

Tambo, T. (2018). Fashion Retail Innovation: About Context, Antecedents, and Outcome in Technological Change Projects. In I. Management Association (Ed.), Fashion and Textiles: Breakthroughs in Research and Practice (pp. 233-260). Hershey, PA: IGI Global. https://doi.org/ doi:10.4018/978-1-5225-3432-7.ch010

Tantau, A. D., & Frăţilă, L. C. (2018). Information and Management System for Renewable Energy Business. In *Entrepreneurship and Business Development in the Renewable Energy Sector* (pp. 200–244). Hershey, PA: IGI Global. doi:10.4018/978-1-5225-3625-3.ch006

Teixeira, N., Pardal, P. N., & Rafael, B. G. (2018). Internationalization, Financial Performance, and Organizational Challenges: A Success Case in Portugal. In L. Carvalho (Ed.), *Handbook of Research on Entrepreneurial Ecosystems and Social Dynamics in a Globalized World* (pp. 379–423). Hershey, PA: IGI Global. doi:10.4018/978-1-5225-3525-6.ch017

Teixeira, P., Teixeira, L., Eusébio, C., Silva, S., & Teixeira, A. (2021). The Impact of ICTs on Accessible Tourism: Evidence Based on a Systematic Literature Review. In C. Eusébio, L. Teixeira, & M. Carneiro (Eds.), *ICT Tools and Applications for Accessible Tourism* (pp. 1–25). IGI Global. doi:10.4018/978-1-7998-6428-8.ch001

Trad, A., & Kalpić, D. (2018). The Business Transformation Framework, Agile Project and Change Management. In M. Khosrow-Pour, D.B.A. (Ed.), Encyclopedia of Information Science and Technology, Fourth Edition (pp. 620-635). Hershey, PA: IGI Global. https://doi.org/ doi:10.4018/978-1-5225-2255-3.ch054

Trad, A., & Kalpić, D. (2018). The Business Transformation and Enterprise Architecture Framework: The Financial Engineering E-Risk Management and E-Law Integration. In B. Sergi, F. Fidanoski, M. Ziolo, & V. Naumovski (Eds.), *Regaining Global Stability After the Financial Crisis* (pp. 46–65). Hershey, PA: IGI Global. doi:10.4018/978-1-5225-4026-7.ch003

Trengereid, V. (2022). Conditions of Network Engagement: The Quest for a Common Good. In R. Augusto Costa, F. Brandão, Z. Breda, & C. Costa (Eds.), *Planning and Managing the Experience Economy in Tourism* (pp. 69-84). IGI Global. https://doi.org/10.4018/978-1-7998-8775-1.ch004

Turulja, L., & Bajgoric, N. (2018). Business Continuity and Information Systems: A Systematic Literature Review. In N. Bajgoric (Ed.), *Always-On Enterprise Information Systems for Modern Organizations* (pp. 60–87). Hershey, PA: IGI Global. doi:10.4018/978-1-5225-3704-5.ch004

Vargas-Hernández, J. G. (2017). Professional Integrity in Business Management Education. In N. Baporikar (Ed.), *Management Education for Global Leadership* (pp. 70–89). Hershey, PA: IGI Global. doi:10.4018/978-1-5225-1013-0.ch004

Varnacı Uzun, F. (2021). The Destination Preferences of Foreign Tourists During the COVID-19 Pandemic and Attitudes Towards: Marmaris, Turkey. In M. Demir, A. Dalgıç, & F. Ergen (Eds.), *Handbook of Research on the Impacts and Implications of COVID-19 on the Tourism Industry* (pp. 285–306). IGI Global. https://doi.org/10.4018/978-1-7998-8231-2.ch014

Vasista, T. G., & AlAbdullatif, A. M. (2017). Role of Electronic Customer Relationship Management in Demand Chain Management: A Predictive Analytic Approach. *International Journal of Information Systems and Supply Chain Management, 10*(1), 53–67. doi:10.4018/IJISSCM.2017010104

Vieru, D., & Bourdeau, S. (2017). Survival in the Digital Era: A Digital Competence-Based Multi-Case Study in the Canadian SME Clothing Industry. *International Journal of Social and Organizational Dynamics in IT, 6*(1), 17–34. doi:10.4018/IJSODIT.2017010102

Vijayan, G., & Kamarulzaman, N. H. (2017). An Introduction to Sustainable Supply Chain Management and Business Implications. In M. Khan, M. Hussain, & M. Ajmal (Eds.), *Green Supply Chain Management for Sustainable Business Practice* (pp. 27–50). Hershey, PA: IGI Global. doi:10.4018/978-1-5225-0635-5.ch002

Vlachvei, A., & Notta, O. (2017). Firm Competitiveness: Theories, Evidence, and Measurement. In A. Vlachvei, O. Notta, K. Karantininis, & N. Tsounis (Eds.), *Factors Affecting Firm Competitiveness and Performance in the Modern Business World* (pp. 1–42). Hershey, PA: IGI Global. doi:10.4018/978-1-5225-0843-4.ch001

Wang, C., Schofield, M., Li, X., & Ou, X. (2017). Do Chinese Students in Public and Private Higher Education Institutes Perform at Different Level in One of the Leadership Skills: Critical Thinking?: An Exploratory Comparison. In V. Wang (Ed.), *Encyclopedia of Strategic Leadership and Management* (pp. 160–181). Hershey, PA: IGI Global. doi:10.4018/978-1-5225-1049-9.ch013

Wang, J. (2017). Multi-Agent based Production Management Decision System Modelling for the Textile Enterprise. *Journal of Global Information Management, 25*(4), 1–15. doi:10.4018/JGIM.2017100101

Wiedemann, A., & Gewald, H. (2017). Examining Cross-Domain Alignment: The Correlation of Business Strategy, IT Management, and IT Business Value. *International Journal of IT/Business Alignment and Governance, 8*(1), 17–31. doi:10.4018/IJITBAG.2017010102

Wolf, R., & Thiel, M. (2018). Advancing Global Business Ethics in China: Reducing Poverty Through Human and Social Welfare. In S. Hipsher (Ed.), *Examining the Private Sector's Role in Wealth Creation and Poverty Reduction* (pp. 67–84). Hershey, PA: IGI Global. doi:10.4018/978-1-5225-3117-3.ch004

Yablonsky, S. (2018). Innovation Platforms: Data and Analytics Platforms. In *Multi-Sided Platforms (MSPs) and Sharing Strategies in the Digital Economy: Emerging Research and Opportunities* (pp. 72–95). Hershey, PA: IGI Global. doi:10.4018/978-1-5225-5457-8.ch003

Yaşar, B. (2021). The Impact of COVID-19 on Volatility of Tourism Stocks: Evidence From BIST Tourism Index. In M. Demir, A. Dalgıç, & F. Ergen (Eds.), *Handbook of Research on the Impacts and Implications of COVID-19 on the Tourism Industry* (pp. 23–44). IGI Global. https://doi.org/10.4018/978-1-7998-8231-2.ch002

Yusoff, A., Ahmad, N. H., & Halim, H. A. (2017). Agropreneurship among Gen Y in Malaysia: The Role of Academic Institutions. In N. Ahmad, T. Ramayah, H. Halim, & S. Rahman (Eds.), *Handbook of Research on Small and Medium Enterprises in Developing Countries* (pp. 23–47). Hershey, PA: IGI Global. doi:10.4018/978-1-5225-2165-5.ch002

Zacher, D., & Pechlaner, H. (2021). Resilience as an Opportunity Approach: Challenges and Perspectives for Private Sector Participation on a Community Level. In A. Zehrer, G. Glowka, K. Schwaiger, & V. Ranacher-Lackner (Eds.), *Resiliency Models and Addressing Future Risks for Family Firms in the Tourism Industry* (pp. 75–102). IGI Global. https://doi.org/10.4018/978-1-7998-7352-5.ch004

Zanin, F., Comuzzi, E., & Costantini, A. (2018). The Effect of Business Strategy and Stock Market Listing on the Use of Risk Assessment Tools. In *Management Control Systems in Complex Settings: Emerging Research and Opportunities* (pp. 145–168). Hershey, PA: IGI Global. doi:10.4018/978-1-5225-3987-2.ch007

Zgheib, P. W. (2017). Corporate Innovation and Intrapreneurship in the Middle East. In P. Zgheib (Ed.), *Entrepreneurship and Business Innovation in the Middle East* (pp. 37–56). Hershey, PA: IGI Global. doi:10.4018/978-1-5225-2066-5.ch003

About the Contributors

Theodore Tarnanidis is an Adjunct Lecturer at the International Hellenic University & Researcher in Applications of MCDA in Digital Marketing at the department of Business Administration, University of Macedonia, Greece. He made his post-doc research in the area of sustainable entrepreneurship from the University of Macedonia. He obtained a Ph.D. from the University of London Met., UK. He received his M.B.A from Liverpool University, UK and is a graduate from the University of Macedonia (Business Administration) and Alexander Technological Educational Institute (Marketing). His research focuses on Decision-Making Processes in Sustainable Innovations and Entrepreneurship, Conjoint Models and preference measurement techniques, modelling of purchases and consumer behaviour. His work has been published in various internationally renowned scientific conferences (Academy of Marketing, European Marketing Academy, PROMETHEE Days, Hellenic Operational Research) and in journals (*Journal of Business Ethics*, *World Review of Entrepreneurship, Management and Sustainable Development*, *Journal of Retailing and Consumer Services*, *Current Issues in Tourism*).

Maro Vlachopoulou is a Professor at the Department of Applied Informatics, Dean of the School of Information Sciences, University of Macedonia, Greece. Degree in Business Administration, Aristotle University of Thessaloniki, Greece (1978). Degree in Law, Aristotle University of Thessaloniki, Greece (1989). Postgraduate studies in Marketing, University of Mannheim, Germany (1981), and MBS in Business Administration, Aristotle University of Thessaloniki (1987). PhD in Marketing Information Systems, University of Macedonia, Department of Applied Informatics, Greece (1992). Visiting research professor at the University of Sunderland, UK (1995). Her professional expertise, research and teaching interests include: Digital Marketing, Marketing Information Systems, E-Business/ e-marketing models, emarketplaces, E-Business plan, new technologies and marketing, mobile Business / marketing, SEO & SEM, social media / networks and marketing, ERP (Enterprise Resource Planning), CRM (Customer Relationship Management) systems, Supply Chain Management (SCM) Systems, Knowledge management systems, e-supply chain management / logistics, with particular emphasis on specific applications (agrifood, e-trust, e-health, government, tourism, environment). She has published over 100 papers in scientific journals and organized numerous of conferences.

Jason Papathanasiou is an Assistant Professor at the Department of Business Administration, University of Macedonia, Greece. He holds a PhD in Operational Research and Informatics and a degree in Physics from the Aristotle University of Thessaloniki. He has worked for a number of years at various institutes and has organised and participated in a number of international scientific conferences and workshops. He has published papers in international scientific peer referred journals like the Environmental Monitoring and Assessment, Regional Studies and European Journal of Operational Research and has participated in many research projects in FP6, FP7, Interreg and COST; he is also a member of the TDP Panel of COST.

***

Constantina Costopoulou is the Director of the Informatics Laboratory of the Agricultural Economics & Rural Development Dept. of the Agricultural University of Athens (Greece). She holds a BSc in Mathematics from the National and Kapodistrian University of Athens, an MSc in Software Engineering from Cranfield University (UK) and a PhD from the National Technical University of Athens. Her research interests include Web services, e-commerce, e-government, e-learning, mobile apps, data analytics, digital marketing, blockchain and digital transformation technologies for the agricultural sector. She has published more than 120 papers in scientific journals, edited volumes, and refereed conferences. She has also served as a scientific responsible for several funded European and national projects in the above research areas.

Alexandre Duarte with a PhD in Communication Sciences from University of Minho, a Master degree in Communication & Image and a Bachelor in Marketing & Advertising by IADE, Alexandre is an Assistant Professor in Universidade NOVA de Lisboa, invited Professor in Universidade Católica Portuguesa and researcher of the R&D Unit ICNOVA. Throughout his career, Alexandre had the opportunity to work for several multinational advertising agencies such as TBWA, Saatchi & Saatchi, Ogilvy, W/Portugal, W/Brazil, Lowe&Partners, or BrandiaCentral as a Senior Creative Copywriter. Author of many seminars on communication, regularly participates in different conferences and lectures in both business and academic contexts. Between 2012 and 2014, was the Tutor of the EUROBEST Young Marketers Academy and in the beginning of 2014, was appointed CEO of RESTART, an Institute of Creativity, Arts and New Technologies. In 2018 was invited to teach in the UNIVERSIDADE CATÓLICA PORTUGUESA, where now Coordinates the Post-Graduation Courses in Advertising&Creativity and Service Design and, in 2019 was re-elected member of the Directors Board of EDCOM.

Joana Fernandes with a dual degree in management and marketing, Joana Fernandes recently completed her Master's degree in Communication Sciences from Universidade Católica Portuguesa. She is currently working in the Innovation Department at the insurance company Fidelidade, in a department that drives innovative solutions to contribute to the company's success.

Fuat Fırat is professor of marketing at the University of Texas-Rio Grande Valley. He completed his Ph.D. degree in marketing at Northwestern University. His research interests cover areas such as macro consumer behavior and macromarketing; postmodern culture; brands and branding; transmodern marketing strategies; gender and consumption; marketing and development; and interorganizational relations. His has won the Journal of Macromarketing Charles Slater Award for best article with co-author N. Dholakia, the Journal of Consumer Research best article award with co-author A. Venkatesh, and the Corporate Communications: An International Journal top ranked paper award with co-authors L.T. Christensen and J. Cornelissen. He has published several books including Consuming People: From Political Economy to Theaters of Consumption, co-authored by N. Dholakia, and is the founding editor of Consumption, Markets & Culture.

Edith Galy is an associate professor of International Business in the Robert C. Vackar College of Business and Entrepreneurship at the University of Texas Rio Grande Valley. She received a Ph.D. in International Business from the University of Texas-Pan American in 2003. Her research areas include social media, absorptive capacity, organizational learning, cross-cultural management and innovation management. She has published research articles in academic journals, such as Information & Management, International Journal of Innovation Management, Journal of Global Information Management and Journal of Marketing Development and Competitiveness, among others. She has held various administrative positions at the university including MBA Director and Assessment Coordinator, and has experience building bilingual business education programs.

Emily Goenner Munson received her MA in English Literature and Composition from the University of Nebraska-Lincoln. She is an assistant professor of business communications at St. Cloud State University. She earned the Association of College and University Educators Credential in Effective College Instruction in 2022 and focuses on creating positive and active classroom instruction. She is a regular contributor to online websites and Minnesota Family magazine; her textbook, The Business Communication Workbook: Skills and Strategies for a Working World, will be published in the second edition in August 2023.

Tanu Gupta is a PhD Candidate in Indira Gandhi Delhi Technical University for Women, India. She received a B.Tech degree (2014) in Information Technology and an M.Tech degree (2017) in Computer Science and Engineering from Guru Gobind Singh Indraprastha University, India. She joined Indira Gandhi Delhi Technical University for Women after Post Graduation. Her research interests include Natural Language Processing, Semantic Web and deep learning. She has done research work in healthcare data and also published papers in good journals. She is the member of Computer Society of India and Soft Computing Research Society.

Monica D. Hernandez is currently an Associate Professor of Marketing at Texas Lutheran University. She received a Ph.D. in International Business from the University of Texas-Pan American (2005). She is a Fulbright US Senior Scholar to Spain (2018-19). She has held various administrative positions, including MBA Director and Department Chair. She has published more than 20 articles, 3 book chapters and numerous conference proceedings. Her work has appeared in academic journals, such as European Journal of Marketing, Journal of Business Research and Journal of Consumer Marketing, among others. Her research interest are Digital Marketing, Consumer Psychology, and International Marketing.

Dharshini Karthikeyan completed her Master of Commerce with Banking & Insurance Specialization. She enjoys sharing her skills and contributing her services to society. Dharshini believes in perseverance with progression.

Maria Maria Kalyvaki is an accomplished academic and administrator with an expansive and diverse educational background. Her scholarly journey commenced with a Bachelor's degree in Agricultural Engineering from A.T.E.I. Kalamatas, advancing to an M.B.A. from Southwest Minnesota State University, a Master's degree in Instructional Technology and HR Development from the University of Athens, and culminating in a Ph.D. in Agricultural Communications and Education from Texas Tech University. Her professional career spans across various esteemed institutions, having held both faculty and administrative roles at South Dakota State University, Southwest Minnesota State University, and Texas Tech University. She has also extended her expertise to the United Nations and currently enriches Minnesota State University with her knowledge and experience. Dr. Kalyvaki's research interests are broad, cross-disciplinary, and pioneering, focusing on areas such as the Metaverse, Immersive Learning, Learning Technologies, Higher Education, Marketing, E-commerce, and Agribusiness. Through her expansive career, Dr. Kalyvaki has significantly contributed to the broadening understanding and application of these fields, pushing boundaries and fostering innovation across her areas of research.

Sotirios Karetsos is Assistant Professor at the Informatics Laboratory of the Agricultural University of Athens (AUA). He received his BSc and an integrated Master from the AUA, MSc from the National Technical University of Athens, and PhD from Informatics Laboratory of the AUA. His research interests mainly focus on information systems, electronic and mobile services, electronic and mobile government, electronic and mobile commerce, social media analytics. He has published more than 60 scientific publications in refereed journals, conferences and books. He has also participated in national and European research and development projects.

Pavithra Karthikeyan is a versatile Customer Success Executive with 2.9 years of hands-on experience in handling Enterprise clients in a SAAS industry. Highly competent in Customer Lifecyle Management inclusive of Onboarding, Implementation, Upselling, Product Adoption, Renewal and Collection. MBA graduate with holding certifications from Indian Institute of Management, Lucknow and Scrum Alliance.

George Kartsiotis holds two BSc, two MSc and is now a Phd candidate; he received his first BSc in Mathematics from the Aristotle University, his second BSc in Applied Informatics from the University of Macedonia with honors (1st of his class), his first MSc with honours from the Electrical and Computer Engineering school in Advanced Communication and Intelligent Systems and his second MSc with honors from the Aristotle University of Thessaloniki in Theoretical Computer Science and Control Theory. Currently he is a PhD candidate at the Applied Informatics department at the University of Macedonia and has worked for various computer software and web development companies with extensive experience in vocational education. His main research interests include bio inspired algorithms, optimal path planning, self assembling robots, theoretical computer science and logic related problems.

Şirin Gizem Köse completed Business Administration in English undergraduate program at Marmara University, Production Management and Marketing master's program at Galatasaray University, Business Administration/ Marketing PhD program at Yıldız Technical University. She worked as a research assistant at Yıldız Technical University Business Administration, production management and marketing department between 2014-2021. She works at MEF University Business Administration department as an assistant professor of marketing. Her academic research areas are sustainability, food marketing, and consumer behavior.

Ramya Barathi Manoharan is a graduate student studying Accounting and Finance in Annamalai University. She previously did her undergraduate in Bachelor of Commerce (Hons) in Ethiraj College, Madras University.

Adesegun Oyedele is an Associate Professor of Marketing and International Business at University of Incarnate Word. He received his Phd in marketing from University of Texas Rio Grande Valley. His current research interests is focused on marketing-technology integration, global marketing and entrepreneurship. His research work can be found in the Journal of Services Marketing, Journal of Retailing and Consumer Services (JRCS), Journal of Consumer Behavior, International Marketing Review, Journal of Advertising, Journal of Strategic Marketing, Journal of Business and Industrial Marketing and other Journals relevant to the discipline of marketing and entrepreneurship.

Ece Özer Çizer is a Research Assistant at the Business Administration Department, Faculty of Economics and Administrative Sciences, Yildiz Technical University. Her research interests are marketing, sharing economy, consumer behaviour and digital marketing.

Pallavi Pandey is currently associated with School of Engineering & Technology, K. R. Mangalam University, Gurugram as assistant professor. She has done Ph.D in CSE department, from Indira Gandhi Delhi Technical University for women, Kashmere Gate, New Delhi and did M.Tech. in Computer Science and Engineering, from Jamia Hamdard, Delhi. She has published various international journal with SCI and SCOPUS indexing. She has won premiere research awards in 2021 and 2023 for her publications by IGDTUW, Delhi. Dr. Pallavi Pandey possesses nearly 9 years of teaching experience in B.Tech., BCA and MCA classes. Her research interest includes bio signal processing, AI and machine learning and data mining. She is the member of IEEE.

Efthymia (Evi) Papadopoulou received her BSc in Informatics and Telecommunications from the National and Kapodistrian University of Athens in 2021. She is currently working as an application development analyst in Accenture, Greece, and has participated in a research project of the informatics laboratory of the Agricultural University of Athens. Her research interests focus on applied data analytics and digital marketing.

Cláudia Pernencar Consulting, researching and teaching in digital health. Claudia started as a Product Designer. PhD in Digital Media (NOVA FCSH – UT Austin Portugal Co-lab). She is an invited Professor at ESAD, School of Fine Arts and Design from Polytechnic of Leiria. She is also coordinating the SecLAB3 – Digital Health and Industry 4.0 in the Biopharmaceutical Sector from PICTIS (International Platform for Science, Technology and Innovation and Health). As a ICNOVA researcher, she has been involved with international projects with FIOCRUZ based on practice that aim to develop innovative health interventions. She is Co-founder of the startup UXVolution that connects strategy, design and software engineering through Health User Research.

Yogita Yashveer Raghav is an assistant professor in the computer science department at K R Mangalam University, Gurugram, Haryana is currently pursuing PhD from Banasthali Vidyapith , Rajasthan and has already achieved impressive qualifications, including UGCNET and HTET. With research interests focused on cloud computing and data mining, she has published several articles in national and international journals and conferences, showcasing her expertise in these areas. As a faculty member, she is committed to teaching and mentoring students, sharing her knowledge and passion for computer science with the next generation of professionals. Their dedication to research and publication is a testament to their ongoing commitment to advancing the field and making meaningful contributions to the academic community. She is IEEE member.

Konstantinos Rebholz is a undergraduate student at the International Business department of Perrotis College, American Farm School of Thessaloniki. His academic interests include international business, marketing and social media.

Pradeep Sundar is a highly motivated, passionate and customer-focused CSM with a demonstrated history of 8+ years of customer success and account management experience in SAAS. Confident in my ability to create meaningful relationships with stakeholders, collaborate across matrix teams and drive sustained results. Team-player and an enthusiastic go-getter. Committed to retaining clients for the long term by diligently helping them achieve success.

Nikolaos Sklavounos is an Adjunct Lecturer at the International Hellenic University and at Perrotis College of the American Farm School in Thessaloniki, Greece. He holds a Ph.D. in International Business from the University of Macedonia, Thessaloniki, Greece. His research appears in the European Journal of International Management, Journal of Strategy and Management, Transnational Corporations Review, International Journal of Productivity and Performance Management, Eastern Journal of European Studies, Journal of Business Paradigms, Elsevier Procedia Economics and Finance, Springer Procedia in Business and Economics, East-West Journal of Economics and Business, Scientific Bulletin–Economic Sciences and in the proceedings of several international conferences. His academic interests include international business, international strategic alliances, strategic management, global marketing, exports and human capital.

Nikolaos Zafeirakopoulos holds an integrated master's degree in Agricultural Economy & Rural Development from the Agricultural University of Athens. As part of his academic journey, he completed his internship at "Dimitriaki S.A." (a renown Greek food company), as well as the Greek public organisation "OPEKEPE", which is the Greek Payment Authority of Common Agricultural Policy (C.A.P.) Aid Schemes. His current research interests focus on social media analytics.

Index

B

Bibliometric Analysis 3, 8, 15-16, 19, 23, 205
Brand Promotion 119-120

C

Cashless Payment 129-130, 134, 138
Consumer Attitudes 128-129, 178, 209
Consumer Behavior 3, 11, 16, 31, 33, 47, 58-59, 61, 77-78, 89, 101, 113, 120, 136, 173, 175-177, 190, 194, 204
Consumer Education 111, 113, 115
Consumer Satisfaction 110, 119, 129, 139-140, 142, 144, 149
Content Analysis 19, 113-114, 207
Covid-19 9, 11, 15-16, 30, 32, 49-51, 53, 112, 118-120, 127-130, 134, 137-138, 173-175, 177-179, 186, 188, 192-194, 213, 215, 239-241

D

Delivery 129, 134-135, 139, 150, 173-178, 180, 182-195
Digital Acceptance 47, 52
Digital Presence 213-214, 221, 238
Digital Supermarket 47, 52

E

E-commerce 26, 32, 35, 47, 51, 128, 173, 175-179, 182-192, 194-195, 214, 239
Electronic Word of Mouth 29, 59, 79, 81, 135, 137, 170-171
e-Marketing 134
Engagement 2, 4, 7, 20, 26-27, 30-31, 47, 51, 61-62, 71-72, 74-78, 81, 87-88, 90, 94, 96, 103, 120, 124, 136, 148, 167, 176, 186, 213-214, 224, 226, 228-231, 233, 237-239
Exploratory Study 18, 81, 111, 171

F

Facebook 2-3, 11, 16, 19-21, 26-28, 32, 51, 53, 59, 61-62, 64, 79, 81, 83-84, 120, 124-125, 132, 134, 160, 214, 219, 221, 223-229, 238, 240
Fans 29, 123, 143, 225, 227, 230-231, 234-236, 238
FFV 178-179, 187-188
Food And Grocery 24-25, 30, 34-35, 37, 40, 47-48, 50, 53-54, 119-121, 125, 127-128, 130, 133-134
Food Brand 1, 23, 63, 65, 76-77, 84
Food Brands 3, 15, 56, 62-63, 71, 76, 84, 134
Food Choice 5-6, 9, 11, 14-17, 23
Food Distribution 173, 179
Food Habits 46, 48, 53
Food Industry 3, 7, 9, 11, 15-16, 20, 23, 29, 31, 35, 50, 57, 115, 117, 120-122, 173, 179
Food Marketing 6-7, 9, 16, 18, 57
Food Preference 17
Food Supply Chains 179, 195
Fresh Fruit and Vegetable 173

G

Gen X 24, 35, 39-40, 42, 48
Gen Y 28-29, 40
Gen Z 22, 28-29, 39, 42, 48, 68, 138
Greece 57, 196, 213, 215, 222
Greek Dairy Industry 213, 215, 221, 238
Grocery 8, 24-26, 30, 32-35, 37, 40, 47-55, 86-93, 95-96, 103-105, 119-121, 125, 127-128, 130, 133-134, 173-178, 180-186, 188-195
Grocery Store 86-91, 93, 95-96, 103, 105, 178, 180

I

Income 24, 30-31, 34, 44-46, 48-49, 53
Influencer 1, 7-8, 18-19, 23, 28, 33, 49, 124, 167
Influencer Marketing 1, 8, 18-19, 23, 167
Instagram 2, 8, 17, 20, 22, 27, 40, 51, 53, 55, 59, 61-62, 64, 83-84, 120, 124-125, 132, 134, 214, 219, 221-223, 229-233, 238
Instore Technology 86, 94
Interactivity 86-89, 92-94, 104, 107, 109, 119, 134

L

Labeling System for Food 111-112, 115

M

Marketing Tools 2, 24, 31, 34, 48, 204, 213, 216
MCDA 196, 200, 207, 209
Meta-analysis 174, 195
Mexico 112, 114-115, 117-118

N

Number of Posts 221, 224-225, 227, 229-230, 234-235, 238

O

Online Grocery Shopping 32, 49, 173-178, 180, 188-192, 194-195

P

Perceived Value 30, 86-88, 91-92, 94, 103, 110
PROMETHEE GAIA 196

R

Restaurant Selection Criteria 140
Retailtainment 86-96, 101-103, 105

S

Social Media 1-9, 11, 13-40, 43-44, 46-71, 74, 76-85, 115-117, 119-121, 123-139, 141-142, 148, 167, 169-171, 182, 204, 213, 215-216, 219-223, 237-241
Social Media Channels 1, 8, 23, 27, 127, 134
Social Media Influence 6, 30-31, 44, 48-49, 171
Social Media Marketing 1, 3-7, 9, 16, 19-23, 26-27, 30, 32, 48-49, 61, 119-121, 123-124, 127-130, 133-136, 138-139, 167, 169, 171, 182, 213-216, 220, 238-239
Sponsored Food Advertisement 56, 62, 64-66, 69, 71, 76-77, 84-85
Supply Chain 173, 176-177, 185, 201

T

Technology Acceptance Model (TAM) 174, 195
Theory of Planned Behavior (TPB) 174, 195
Twitter 3, 13, 15, 17, 19-20, 31, 50, 53, 62, 83-84, 111, 113-115, 117, 120, 124, 137, 222-223, 239

U

Unified Theory of Acceptance and Use of

Technology (UTAUT) 174, 195

W

Word-of-Mouth Influence 140-141, 143

Y

YouTube 6-8, 18-19, 22, 27-28, 40, 51, 53, 59, 64, 83-84, 120, 124, 134, 211, 214, 221-223, 234-238

Z

Zomato 40, 53, 140-142, 149-150, 153-156, 158, 160-165, 170, 172

www.ingramcontent.com/pod-product-compliance
Lightning Source LLC
LaVergne TN
LVHW080639011026
849160LV00014B/1266